Short Third Edition

Practical Argument

Laurie G. Kirszner

University of the Sciences, Emeritus

Stephen R. Mandell

Drexel University

bedford/st.martin's
Macmillan Learning
Boston | New York

For Bedford/St. Martin's

Vice President, Editorial, Macmillan Learning Humanities: Edwin Hill
Editorial Director, English: Karen S. Henry
Senior Publisher for Composition, Business and Technical Writing, Developmental
    Writing: Leasa Burton
Executive Editor: John E. Sullivan III
Developmental Editor: Sherry Mooney
Production Editor: Matt Glazer
Media Producer: Sarah O'Connor
Production Supervisor: Lisa McDowell
Marketing Manager: Joy Fisher Williams
Assistant Editor: Jennifer Prince
Copy Editor: Diana Puglisi George
Indexer: Mary White
Photo Editor: Angela Boehler
Photo Researcher: Sheri Blaney
Permissions Editor: Christine Volboril
Senior Art Director: Anna Palchik
Text Design: Jerilyn Bockorick
Cover Design: John Callahan
Cover Photos: (bike) Science Photo Library/Getty Images;
    (backpack) SarapulSar38/Getty Images
Composition: Cenveo Publisher Services
Printing and Binding: King Printing Co., Inc.

Manufactured in the United States of America.

1 0 9 8 7

f e d c

For information, write: Bedford/St. Martin's, 75 Arlington Street, Boston, MA 02116 (617-399-4000)

ISBN 978-1-319-03019-3

Acknowledgments

Text credits and copyrights appear at the back of the book on pages C-1–C-3, which constitute an extension of the copyright page. Art acknowledgments and copyrights appear on the same page as the art selections they cover.

In recent years, many college composition programs have integrated argumentation into their first-year writing sequence, and there are good reasons for this. Argumentation is central to academic and public discourse, so students who are skilled at argumentation are able to participate in the dynamic, ongoing discussions that take place both in their classrooms and in their communities. Clearly, argumentation teaches valuable critical-thinking skills that are necessary for academic success and for survival in today's media-driven society.

What has surprised and troubled us as teachers, however, is that many college argument texts are simply too difficult. Frequently, a divide exists between the pedagogy of these texts and students' ability to understand it. In many cases, technical terminology and excessively abstract discussions lead to confusion instead of clarity. The result is that students' worst fears are realized: instead of feeling that they are part of a discourse community, they see themselves as marginalized outsiders who will never be able to understand, let alone master, the principles of argumentation.

Recognizing that students struggle to master important principles of argumentative thinking and writing, we drew on our years of classroom experience to create an innovative book: *Practical Argument*, Short Third Edition. In this third edition, *Practical Argument* remains a straightforward, accessible, and visually appealing introduction to argumentative writing that explains concepts in understandable, everyday language and illustrates them with examples that actually mean something to students. *Practical Argument*, Short Third Edition, is an alternative for instructors who see currently available argument texts as too big, too complicated, and too intimidating for their students.

In short, our goal in this text is to demystify the study of argument. To this end, we focus on the things that students need to know, omitting the overly technical concepts they often struggle with. For example, *Practical Argument* emphasizes the basic principles of classical argument and downplays the more complex Toulmin logic, treating it as an alternative way of envisioning argument. *Practical Argument* works because its approach is "practical"; it helps students to make connections between what they learn in the classroom and what they experience outside of it. As they do so, they become comfortable with the rhetorical skills that are central to effective argumentation. We believe there's no other book like it.

Organization

Practical Argument, Short Third Edition, includes in one book everything students and instructors need for an argument course.

- **Part 1, Understanding Argument,** discusses the role of argument in everyday life and the value of studying argument, offers definitions of what argument is and is not, explains the means of persuasion (appeals to *logos*, *pathos*, and *ethos*), and defines and illustrates the basic elements of argument (thesis, evidence, refutation, and concluding statement).

- **Part 2, Reading and Responding to Arguments,** explains and illustrates critical thinking and reading; visual argument; writing a rhetorical analysis; logic and logical fallacies; and Rogerian argument, Toulmin logic, and oral arguments.

- **Part 3, Writing an Argumentative Essay,** traces and illustrates the process of planning, drafting, and revising an argumentative essay.

- **Part 4, Using Sources to Support Your Argument,** covers locating and evaluating print and online sources; summarizing, paraphrasing, quoting, and synthesizing sources; documenting sources in MLA style; and using sources reponsibly.

- **Appendixes.** Appendix A provides instruction on writing literary arguments, and Appendix B covers APA documentation style.

Key Features

Concise in a Thoughtful Way

Practical Argument, Short Third Edition, covers everything students need to know about argument but doesn't overwhelm them. It limits technical vocabulary to what students and instructors actually need to understand and discuss key concepts in argument and argumentative writing. In short, *Practical Argument* is argument made accessible.

Argument Step by Step, Supported by Helpful Apparatus

Practical Argument, Short Third Edition, takes students through a step-by-step process of reading and responding to others' arguments and writing, revising, and editing their own arguments. The book uses a classroom-tested, exercise-driven approach that encourages students to participate actively in their own learning process. Chapters progress in a clear, easy-to-understand sequence: students are asked to read arguments, identify their key elements, and develop a response to an issue in the form of a complete, documented argumentative essay based on in-book focused research.

Exercises and writing assignments for each selection provide guidance for students as they work toward creating a finished piece of writing. Throughout the text, checklists, grammar-in-context and summary boxes, and source and gloss notes provide support. In addition, more than a dozen unique templates for paragraph-length arguments—located with the end-of-chapter exercises—provide structures that students can use for guidance as they write definition arguments, cause-and-effect arguments, evaluation arguments, proposal arguments, and ethical arguments. Sentence templates also frequently appear in the questions that follow the readings, providing an opportunity for students to work up to arguments at the paragraph level.

A Thematically Focused Approach with Compelling Chapter Topics

Students learn best when they care about and are engaged in an issue. For this reason, *Practical Argument*, Short Third Edition, uses readings and assignments to help students learn argumentation in the context of one high-interest contemporary issue per chapter. Chapter topics include media violence, free speech, online education, technology and privacy, and how modern technology does, or does not, change the meaning of plagiarism—issues that have real meaning in students' lives.

Readings on Relevant and Interesting Issues

Forty-three accessible professional readings—on issues that students will want to read about and debate—are presented in the text, including selections from journals and blogs. This mix of scholarly and cultural works blends student concerns, such as the cost of higher education, with thought-provoking reflections on more universal questions, such as ethical consumption and the intricacies of free speech. Many visual selections enhance the readings throughout the book, while seventeen sample student essays, more than in any other argument book, provide both realistic models for student writers and additional student voices. Each of these student essays, including complete MLA and APA research papers, is annotated to further assist students in their own writing process.

To help students better understand the context of the sources included in *Practical Argument*, each is marked with an icon that shows how it was originally presented.

Book Magazine or journal National newspaper Speech

Poem Student essay Student newspaper Website

An Open and Inviting Full-Color Design

The fresh, contemporary look of *Practical Argument*, Short Third Edition, will engage students. This open, colorful design eliminates the sea of dense type that is typical of many other argument books. Over a hundred photographs and other visuals—such as graphic novel excerpts, cartoons, advertisements, templates, charts and graphs, Web pages, and fine art—provide appealing and instructive real-world examples. The use of open space and numerous images reinforces the currency of the book's themes and also creates an inviting and visually stimulating format.

Two Versions

Practical Argument, Short Third Edition, is also available in a full-size edition that includes expanded coverage of argumentative strategies and a reader comprising debates and casebooks on current and engaging topics. To order the full-size version of *Practical Argument*, use ISBN **978-1-319-02856-5**.

New to This Edition

Essays, Topics, and Images

The third edition includes twenty-four engaging new professional essays on such timely topics as self-driving cars and free speech on college campuses. These essays have been carefully selected for their high-interest subject matter as well as for their effectiveness as sources and as teaching models for student writing.

More Help with the Writing Process and Academic Writing

In response to instructor requests, we have expanded the templates, making them more useful to students and adding interactivity in the Launch-Pad; included additional annotations in the MLA paper to guide students in the integration of source material; simplified the coverage of Rogerian argument; and provided more background on the rhetorical situation. We have also provided more help with academic writing, including additional material on finding sources as well as expanded examples of MLA and APA documentation. We have substantially expanded our coverage of how to refute opposing arguments, providing students with a firm grasp of how to usefully incorporate conflicting viewpoints into their writing.

Get the Most Out of Your Course with *Practical Argument*

Bedford/St. Martin's offers resources and format choices that help you and your students get even more out of your book and course. To learn more about or to order any of the following products, contact your Macmillan sales representative, email sales support (**sales_support@bfwpub.com**), or look for *Practical Argument*, Short Third Edition, at **macmillanlearning.com**.

LaunchPad for Practical Argument: *Where Students Learn*

LaunchPad provides engaging content and new ways to get the most out of your book. Get an **interactive e-book** combined with **useful, highly relevant materials** in a fully customizable course space; then assign and mix our resources with yours.

- Auto-graded **reading quizzes, comprehension quizzes on argument topics**, and **interactive writing templates** help students to engage actively with the material you assign.

- **Pre-built units**—including readings, videos, quizzes, discussion groups, and more—are **easy to adapt and assign** by adding your own materials and mixing them with our high-quality multimedia content and ready-made assessment options, such as **LearningCurve** adaptive quizzing. The LearningCurve now includes argument modules focusing on topic, purpose, and audience; arguable claims; reasoning and logical fallacies; and persuasive appeals (*logos, pathos,* and *ethos*).

- LaunchPad also provides access to a **Gradebook** that provides a clear window on the performance of your whole class, individual students, and even results of individual assignments.

- A **streamlined interface** helps students focus on what's due, and social commenting tools let them **engage**, make connections, and learn from each other. Use LaunchPad on its own or integrate it with your school's learning management system so that your class is always on the same page.

To get the most out of your book, order LaunchPad for *Practical Argument* packaged with the print book. (LaunchPad for *Practical Argument* can also be purchased on its own.) An activation code is required. To order LaunchPad for *Practical Argument* with the print book, use ISBN **978-1-319-07348-0**.

Choose from Alternative Formats of Practical Argument

Bedford/St. Martin's offers a range of affordable formats, allowing students to choose the one that works best for them. For further details, look for *Practical Argument*, Short Third Edition, at **macmillanlearning.com**.

- *Paperback edition with readings* To order the paperback *Practical Argument: A Text and Anthology*, Third Edition, use **ISBN 978-1-319-02856-5**.

- *Other popular e-book formats* For details, visit **macmillanlearning .com/ebooks**.

Select Value Packages

Add value to your text by packaging one of the following resources with *Practical Argument*, Short Third Edition. To learn more about package options for any of the following products, contact your Bedford/St. Martin's sales representative or visit **macmillanlearning.com**.

Writer's Help 2.0 is a powerful online writing resource that helps students find answers whether they are searching for writing advice on their own or as part of an assignment.

- **Smart search**
  Built on research with more than 1,600 student writers, the smart search in Writer's Help 2.0 provides reliable results even when students use novice terms such as *flow* and *unstuck*.

- **Trusted content from our best-selling handbooks**
  Choose *Writer's Help 2.0, Hacker Version* or *Writer's Help 2.0, Lunsford Version* and ensure that students have clear advice and examples for all of their writing questions.

- **Adaptive exercises that engage students**
  Writer's Help 2.0 includes LearningCurve, game-like online quizzing that adapts to what students already know and helps them focus on what they need to learn.

Student access is packaged with *Practical Argument*, Short Third Edition, at a significant discount. Order ISBN 978-1-319-07350-3 for *Writer's Help 2.0, Hacker Version* or ISBN 978-1-319-07351-0 for *Writer's Help 2.0, Lunsford Version* to ensure your students have easy access to online writing support. Students who rent a book or buy a used book can purchase access to Writer's Help 2.0 at **macmillanhighered.com/writershelp2**.

Instructors may request free access by registering as an instructor at **macmillanhighered.com/writershelp2**.

For technical support, visit **macmillanlearning.com/getsupport**.

Portfolio Keeping, **Third Edition, by Nedra Reynolds and Elizabeth Davis,** provides all the information students need to use the portfolio method successfully in a writing course. *Portfolio Teaching*, a companion guide for instructors, provides the practical information instructors and writing program administrators need to use the portfolio method successfully in a writing course. To order *Portfolio Keeping* packaged with this text, contact your sale representative for a package ISBN.

Instructor Resources

You have a lot to do in your course. Bedford/St. Martin's wants to make it easy for you to find the support you need—and to get it quickly.

Resources for Teaching Practical Argument, Short Third Edition, is available as a PDF that can be downloaded from the Bedford/St. Martin's online catalog. In addition to chapter overviews and teaching tips, the instructor's manual includes sample syllabi, answers to questions that appear within the book, and suggested classroom activities.

Join Our Community! The Macmillan English Community is now Bedford/St. Martin's home for professional resources, featuring Bedford *Bits*, our popular blog site that offers new ideas for the composition classroom and composition teachers. Connect and converse with a growing team of Bedford authors and top scholars who blog on *Bits*: Andrea Lunsford, Nancy Sommers, Steve Bernhardt, Traci Gardner, Barclay Barrios, Jack Solomon, Susan Bernstein, Elizabeth Wardle, Doug Downs, Liz Losh, Jonathan Alexander, and Donna Winchell.

In addition, you'll find an expanding collection of additional resources that support your teaching.

- Sign up for webinars

- Download resources from our professional resources series that support your teaching

- Start a discussion

- Ask a question

- Follow your favorite members

- Review projects in the pipeline

Visit **community.macmillan.com** to join the conversation with your fellow teachers.

Acknowledgments

The following reviewers gave us valuable feedback: Joshua Beach, University of Texas at San Antonio; Jenny Billings Beaver, Rowan Cabarrus Community College; Jade Bittle, Rowan Cabarrus Community College; Shannon Blair, Central Piedmont Community College; Chris Blankenship, Emporia State University; Patricia Colella, Bunker Hill Community College; Jason DePolo, North Carolina A&T State University; Julie Dorris, Arkansas Northeastern College; Sarah Duerden, University of Sheffield; Alan Goldman, Massachusetts Bay Community College; Iris Harvey, Tarrant County Community College; Rebecca Hewett, California State University; Bruce Holmes, Stratford University; Anneliese Homan, State Fair Community College; Ann Hostestler, Goshen College; Elizabeth Hurston, Eastfield College; Ann Johnson, University of Nebraska at Omaha; Virginia Kearney, Baylor University; Audrey Lapointe, Cuyamaca College; Laurie Leach, Hawaii Pacific University; Vicki Martineau-Gilliam, National University; Gwendolyn Miller, University of Wisconsin–Parkside; Deborah Miller-Zournas, Stark State College; James Minor, South Piedmont Community College; Lani Montreal, Malcolm X College; Kathleen Moore, Community College of Vermont–Montpelier; Meltam Oztan, Kent State; Matt Pifer, Husson University; Cory Potter, Bethune-Cookman University; Mandy Reid, Indiana State University; Stuart Rosenberg, Cyprus College; Zahir Small, Santa Fe College; Kymberly Snelling, Metropolitan Community College Ft. Omaha; Rosie Soy, Hudson County Community College; Andrea Spofford, Austin Peay State University; Wes Spratlin, Motlow State Community College; Cheli Turner, Greenville Technical College; Barbara Urban, Central Piedmont Community College–Levine Campus; Sandra Zapp, Paradise Valley Community College.

We thank Jeff Ousborne, Deja Ruddick, Elizabeth Rice, and Michelle McSweeney for their valuable contributions to this text.

At Bedford/St. Martin's, Joan Feinberg, Denise Wydra, Karen Henry, Steve Scipione, Leasa Burton, and John Sullivan were involved and supportive from the start of the project. John, in particular, helped us shape this book and was with us every step of the way. In this third edition, we have had the pleasure of working with Sherry Mooney, our smart, talented, and creative editor. Her addition to our team has made *Practical Argument* a much better book. Matt Glazer patiently and efficiently shepherded the book through the production process. Others on our team included Jennifer Prince, who helped with many details; Joy Fisher Williams and Gillian Daniels, who were instrumental in marketing the book; Sheri Blaney, who found art and obtained permission for it; Christine Volboril, who handled text permissions; and our outstanding copy editor, Diana P. George. We are grateful for their help.

Finally, we would like to thank each other for lunches past—and for many, many lunches to come.

Laurie G. Kirszner
Stephen R. Mandell

BRIEF CONTENTS

CONTENTS

1 The Four Pillars of Argument   23

PART

2 Reading and Responding to Arguments   57

6 Rogerian Argument, Toulmin Logic, and Oral Arguments   191

PART

3   Writing an Argumentative Essay   251

7   Planning, Drafting, and Revising an Argumentative Essay   253

1

Understanding Argument

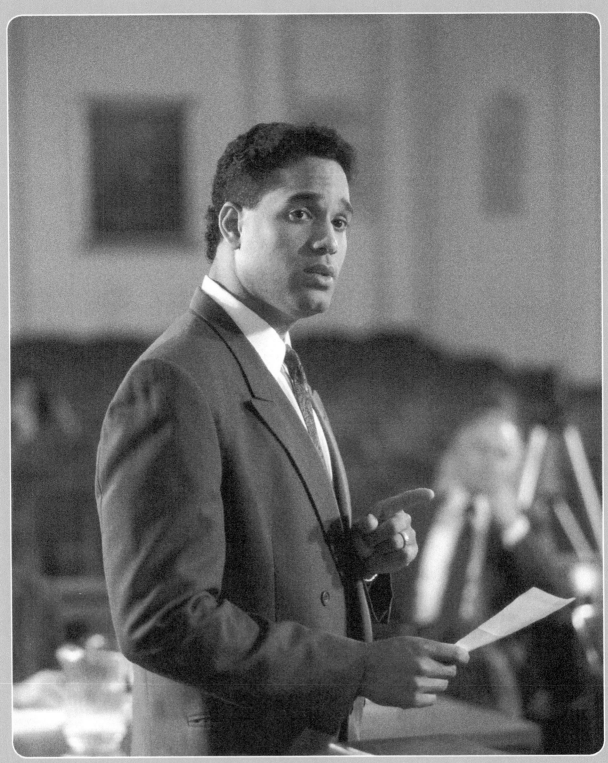

An Introduction to Argument

Recognizing Arguments

Arguments are everywhere. Whenever you turn on the television, read a newspaper or magazine, talk to friends and family, enter an online discussion, or engage in a debate in one of your classes, you encounter arguments. In fact, it is fair to say that much of the interaction that takes place in society involves argument. Consider, for example, a lawyer who tries to persuade a jury that a defendant is innocent, a doctor who wants to convince a patient to undergo a specific form of treatment, a lawmaker who wants to propose a piece of legislation, an executive who wants to institute a particular policy, an activist who wants to pursue a particular social agenda, a parent who wants to convince a child to study harder, a worker who wants to propose a more efficient way of performing a task, an employee who thinks that he or she deserves a raise, or a spokesperson in an infomercial whose goal is to sell something: all these people are engaging in argument.

In college, you encounter arguments on a daily basis; in fact, both class discussions and academic writing often take the form of argument. Consider, for example, the following questions that might be debated (and written about) in a first-year writing class:

- Do the benefits of fracking outweigh its risks?
- How free should free speech be?
- Are helicopter parents ruining their children's lives?
- How far should schools go to keep students safe?
- Do bystanders have an ethical responsibility to help in a crisis?

What these questions have in common is that they all call for argumentation. To answer these questions, students would be expected to state their opinions and support them.

WHY INSTRUCTORS ASSIGN ARGUMENT

Instructors assign argumentative essays for a number of reasons. Here are just a few:

- To encourage students to develop and defend a position

- To help students think critically about their own and other people's ideas

- To give students the tools they need to convince others of the validity of their ideas

- To help students learn to resolve conflicting points of view

Wake Up, America! (1917) James Montgomery Flagg. Published by the Hegeman Print, New York/ Library of Congress Prints and Photographs Division [LC-USZC4-3802].

World War I propaganda poster (1917)

Defining Argument

Now for the obvious question: exactly what is an argument? Perhaps the best way to begin is by explaining what argument is *not*. An argument (at least an academic argument) is not a **quarrel** or an angry exchange. The object of argument is not to attack someone who disagrees with you or to beat an opponent into submission. For this reason, the shouting matches that you routinely see on television or hear on talk radio are not really arguments. Argument is also not **spin**—the positive or biased slant that politicians routinely put on facts—or **propaganda**—information (or misinformation) that is spread to support a particular viewpoint. Finally, argument is not just a contradiction or denial of someone else's position. Even if you establish that an opponent's position is wrong or misguided, you still have to establish that your own position has merit by presenting evidence to support it.

There is a basic difference between **formal arguments**—those that you develop in academic discussion and writing—and **informal arguments**—those that occur in daily life, where people often get into arguments about politics, sports, social issues, and personal relationships. These everyday disputes are often just verbal fights in which one person tries to outshout another. Although they sometimes include facts, they tend to rely primarily on emotion and unsupported opinions. Moreover, such everyday arguments do not have the formal structure of academic arguments: they do not establish a logical link between a particular viewpoint and reliable supporting evidence. There is also no real effort to address opposing arguments. In general, these arguments tend to be disorganized, emotional disputes that have more to do with criticizing an opponent than with advancing and supporting a position on an issue. Although such informal arguments can serve as starting points for helping you think about issues, they do not have the structure or the intellectual rigor of formal arguments.

So exactly what is an argument—or, more precisely, what is an academic argument? An **academic argument** is a type of formal argument that takes a stand, presents evidence, includes documentation, and uses logic to convince an audience to accept (or at least consider) the writer's position. Of course, academic arguments can get heated, but at their core they are civil exchanges. Writers of academic arguments strive to be fair and to show respect for others—especially for those who present opposing arguments.

Keep in mind that arguments take positions with which reasonable people may disagree. For this reason, an argument never actually proves anything. (If it did, there would be no argument.) The best that an argument can do is to convince other people to accept (or at least acknowledge) the validity of its position.

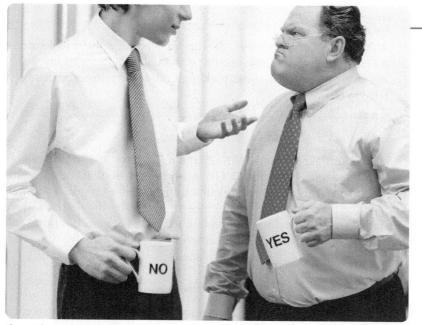

An angry exchange is not an academic argument.

Flying Colours Ltd./Getty Images

WHAT KINDS OF STATEMENTS ARE NOT DEBATABLE?

To be suitable for argument, a statement must be **debatable**: in other words, there must be conflicting opinions or conflicting facts that call the validity of the statement into question. For this reason, the following types of statements are generally *not* suitable for argument:

- **Statements of fact:** A statement of fact can be verified, so it is not debatable. For example, there is no point in arguing that your school makes instructors' lectures available as podcasts. This is a question of fact that can easily be checked. You can, however, argue that making instructors' lectures available as podcasts would (or would not) enhance education at your school. This is a debatable statement that can be supported by facts and examples.

- **Statements of personal preference or taste:** Expressions of personal preference or taste are not suitable for argument. For example, if you say that you don't like the taste of a particular soft drink, no one can legitimately argue that you are wrong. This statement is beyond dispute because it is a matter of personal taste. You could, however, argue that soft drinks should not be sold in school cafeterias because they contribute to obesity. To support this position, you would supply evidence—facts, statistics, and expert opinion.

> **NOTE**
>
> Although personal expressions of religious belief are difficult to debate, the interpretation of religious doctrine is a suitable subject for argument—and so are the political, social, philosophical, and theological effects of religion on society.

It is a mistake to think that all arguments have just two sides—one right side and one wrong side. In fact, many arguments that you encounter in college focus on issues that are quite complex. For example, if you were considering the question of whether the United States should ban torture, you could certainly answer this question with a yes or a no, but this would be an oversimplification. To examine the issue thoroughly, you would have to consider it from a number of angles:

- Should torture be banned in all situations?

- Should torture be used as a last resort to elicit information that could prevent an imminent attack?

- What actually constitutes torture? For example, is sleep deprivation torture? What about a slap on the face? Loud music? A cold cell? Are "enhanced interrogation techniques"—such as waterboarding—torture?

- Who should have the legal right to approve interrogation techniques?

If you were going to write an argument about this issue, you would have to take a position that adequately conveyed its complex nature—for example, "Although torture may be cruel and even inhuman, it is sometimes necessary." To do otherwise might be to commit the **either/or fallacy** (see p. 151)—to offer only two choices when there are actually many others.

Arguments in Real Life

In blogs, social media posts, work-related proposals, letters to the editor, emails to businesses, letters of complaint, and other types of communication, you formulate arguments that are calculated to influence readers. Many everyday situations call for argument:

- A proposal to the manager of the UPS store where you work to suggest a more efficient way of sorting packages

- A letter to your local newspaper in which you argue that creating a walking trail would be good use of your community's tax dollars

- An email to your child's principal asking her to extend after-school hours

- A letter to a credit card company in which you request an adjustment to your bill

- A blog post in which you argue that the federal government could do more to relieve the student loan burden

Because argument is so prevalent, the better your arguing skills, the better able you will be to function—not just in school but also in the wider world. When you have a clear thesis, convincing support, and effective refutation of opposing arguments, you establish your credibility and go a long way toward convincing readers that you are someone worth listening to.

Presenting a good argument does not guarantee that readers will accept your ideas. It does, however, help you to define an issue and to express your position clearly and logically. If you present yourself as a well-informed, reasonable person who is attuned to the needs of your readers—even those who disagree with you—you increase your chances of convincing your audience that your position is worth considering.

Arguments are also central to our democratic form of government. Whether the issue is taxation, health care, border control, the environment, abortion, gun ownership, energy prices, gay marriage, terrorism, or cyber-bullying, political candidates, media pundits, teachers, friends, and family members all try to influence the way we think. So in a real sense, argument is the way that all of us participate in the national (or even global) conversation about ideas that matter. The better you understand the methods of argumentation, the better able you will be to recognize, analyze, and respond to the arguments that you hear. By mastering the techniques of argument, you will become a clearer thinker, a more informed citizen, and a person who is better able to influence those around you.

Black Lives Matter protest

Andrew Burton/Getty Images

Winning and Losing Arguments

People often talk of "winning" and "losing" arguments, and of course, the aim of many arguments is to defeat an opponent. In televised political debates, candidates try to convince viewers that they should be elected. In a courtroom, a defense attorney tries to establish a client's innocence. In a job interview, a potential employee tries to convince an employer that he or she is the best-qualified applicant. However, the goal of an argument is not always to determine a winner and a loser. Sometimes the goal of an argument is to identify a problem and suggest solutions that could satisfy those who hold a number of different positions on an issue.

If, for example, you would like your college bookstore to lower the price of items (such as sweatshirts, coffee mugs, and backpacks) with a school logo, you could simply state your position and then support it with evidence. A more effective way of approaching this problem, however, might be to consider all points of view and find some middle ground. For example, how would lowering these prices affect the bookstore? A short conversation with the manager of the bookstore might reveal that the revenue generated by these products enables the bookstore to discount other items—such as art supplies and computers—as well as to hire student help. Therefore, decreasing the price of products with college logos would negatively affect some students. Even so, the high prices also make it difficult for some students to buy these items.

To address this problem, you could offer a compromise solution: the price of items with college logos could be lowered, but the price of other items—such as magazines and snacks—could be raised to make up the difference.

The Rhetorical Situation

In everyday use, the term *rhetoric* has distinctly negative connotations. When a speech is described as being nothing but *rhetoric*, the meaning is clear: the speech consists of empty words and phrases calculated to confuse and manipulate listeners. When writing instructors use the term *rhetoric*, however, it means something quite different: it refers to the choices someone makes to structure a message—written, oral, or visual.

The **rhetorical situation** refers to the factors that influence the creation of any type of communication—especially its words, images, and structure. Applied to argument, the rhetorical situation refers to five factors you should consider when planning an effective argument. Although every rhetorical situation is different, all rhetorical situations involve the following five elements:

- The writer
- The purpose
- The audience
- The question
- The context

Considering the Writer

Every argument begins with a writer, the person who creates the text. For this reason, it is important to understand how your biases or preconceptions could affect what you produce. For example, if you were home schooled, you might have very definite ideas about education. Likewise, a former Navy Seal might have preconceptions concerning the war in Afghanistan. Strongly held beliefs like these can, and often do, color your arguments. The following factors can affect the tone and content of an argument:

age

education

gender

ethnicity

cultural experiences

political affiliation

religion

sexuality

social standing

Before you plan an argument, ask yourself what preconceived ideas you may have about a particular topic. Do your beliefs prevent you from considering all sides of an issue, reaching a logical and fair conclusion, or acknowledging the validity of opposing arguments? It is important that you present yourself as a fair and open-minded person, one whom readers trust. For this reason, you should maintain a reasonable tone and avoid the use of words or phrases that indicate bias.

Considering the Purpose

A writer's **purpose** is his or her reason for writing. The purpose of an argument is to present a position and to change (or at least influence) people's ideas about an issue. In addition to this general purpose, a writer may have more specific goals. For example, you might want to criticize the actions of others or call into question a particular public policy. You may also want to take a stand on a controversial topic or convince readers that certain arguments are weak. Finally, you may want to propose a solution to a problem or convince readers to adopt a certain course of action.

When you write an argument, you may want to state your purpose directly—usually in your introduction. (Key words in your thesis statement can indicate the direction the argument will take as well as the points that you will discuss.) At other times, especially if you think readers will not readily accept your ideas, you may want to indicate your purpose later in your essay or simply imply it.

Considering the Audience

When you write argumentative essays, you don't write in a vacuum; you write for real people who may or may not agree with you. As you are writing, it is easy to forget this fact and address a general group of readers. However, doing this would be a mistake. Defining your audience and keeping this audience in mind as you write is important because it helps you decide what material to include and how to present it.

One way to define an audience is by its **traits**—the age, gender, interests, values, preconceptions, and level of education of audience members. Each of these traits influences how audience members will react to your ideas, and understanding them helps you determine how to construct your argument. For instance, suppose you were going to write an essay with the following thesis:

Although college is expensive, its high cost is justified.

How you approach this subject would depend on the audience you were addressing. For example, college students, parents, and college administrators would have different ideas about the subject, different perspectives, different preconceptions, and different levels of knowledge. Therefore, the argument you write for each of these audiences would be different from the others in terms of content, organization, and type of appeal.

- **College students** have a local and personal perspective. They know the school and have definite ideas about the value of the education they are getting. Most likely, they come from different backgrounds and have varying financial needs. Depending on their majors, they have different expectations about employment (and salary) when they graduate. Even with these differences, however, these students share certain concerns. Many probably have jobs to help cover their expenses. Many also have student loans that they will need to start paying after graduation.

   An argumentative essay addressing this audience could focus on statistics and expert opinions that establish the worth of a college degree in terms of future employment, job satisfaction, and lifetime earnings.

- **Parents** probably have limited knowledge of the school and the specific classes their children are taking. They have expectations—both realistic and unrealistic—about the value of a college degree. Some parents may be able to help their children financially, and others may be unable to do so. Their own life experiences and backgrounds probably color their ideas about the value of a college education. For example, parents who have gone to college may have different ideas about the value of a degree from those who haven't.

   An argumentative essay addressing this audience could focus on the experience of other parents of college students. It could also include statistics that address students' future economic independence and economic security.

- **College administrators** have detailed knowledge about college and the economic value of a degree. They are responsible for attracting students, scheduling classes, maintaining educational standards, and providing support services. They are familiar with budget requirements, and they understand the financial pressures involved in running a school. They also know how tuition dollars are spent and how much state and federal aid the school needs to stay afloat. Although they are sympathetic to the plight of both students and parents, they have to work with limited resources.

An argumentative essay addressing this audience could focus on the need to make tuition more affordable by cutting costs and providing more student aid.

Another way to define an audience is to determine whether it is *friendly, hostile,* or *neutral.*

- A **friendly audience** is sympathetic to your argument. This audience might already agree with you or have an emotional or intellectual attachment to you or to your position. In this situation, you should emphasize points of agreement and reinforce the emotional bond that exists between you and the audience. Don't assume, however, that because this audience is receptive to your ideas, you do not have to address its concerns or provide support for your points. If readers suspect that you are avoiding important issues or that your evidence is weak, they will be less likely to take your argument seriously—even though they agree with you.

- A **hostile audience** disagrees with your position and does not accept the underlying assumptions of your argument. For this reason, you have to work hard to overcome their preconceived opinions, presenting your points clearly and logically and including a wide range of evidence. To show that you are a reasonable person, you should treat these readers with respect even though they happen to disagree with you. In addition, you should show that you have taken the time to consider their arguments and that you value their concerns. Even with all these efforts, however, the best you may be able to do is get them to admit that you have made some good points in support of your position.

- A **neutral audience** has no preconceived opinions about the issue you are going to discuss. (When you are writing an argument for a college class, you should assume that you are writing for a neutral audience.) For this reason, you need to provide background information about the issue and about the controversy surrounding it. You should also summarize opposing points of view, present them logically, and refute them effectively. This type of audience may not know much about an issue, but it is not necessarily composed of unsophisticated or unintelligent people. Moreover, even though such readers are neutral, you should assume that they are **skeptical**—that is, that they will question your assumptions and require supporting evidence before they accept your conclusions.

> **NOTE**
>
> Some audiences are so diverse that they are difficult to categorize. In this case, it is best to define the audience yourself—for example, *concerned parents, prudent consumers,* or *serious students*—and then address them accordingly.

Keep in mind that identifying a specific audience is not something that you do at the last minute. Because your audience determines the kind of argument you present, you should take the time to make this determination before you begin to write.

Considering the Question

All arguments begin with a question that you are going to answer. To be suitable for argument, this question must have more than one possible answer. If it does not, there is no basis for the argument. For example, there is no point trying to write an argumentative essay on the question of whether head injuries represent a danger for football players. The answer to this question is so obvious that no thoughtful person would argue that they are not. The question of whether the National Football League is doing enough to protect players from head injuries, however, is one on which reasonable people could disagree. Consider the following information:

- In recent years, the NFL has done much to reduce the number of serious head injuries.

- New protocols for the treatment of players who show signs of head trauma, stricter rules against helmet-to-helmet tackles, and the use of safer helmets have reduced the number of concussions.

- Even with these precautions, professional football players experience a high number of head injuries, with one in three players reporting negative effects—some quite serious—from repeated concussions.

Because there are solid arguments on both sides of this issue, you could write an effective argument in which you address this question.

Considering the Context

An argument takes place in a specific **context**—the set of circumstances that surrounds the issue. As you plan your argument, consider the social, historical, and cultural events that define the debate.

Assume that you were going to argue that the public school students in your hometown should be required to purchase iPads. Before you begin your argument, you should give readers the background—the context—they will need to understand the issue. For example, they should know that school officials have been debating the issue for over a year. School administrators say that given the advances in distance learning as well as the high quality of online resources, iPads will enhance the educational experience of students. They also say that it is time to bring the schools' instructional methods into the twenty-first century. Even so, some parents say that requiring the purchase of iPads will put an undue financial burden on them. In addition, teachers point out that a good deal of new material will have to be developed to take advantage of this method of instruction. Finally, not all students will have access at home to the high-speed Internet capacity necessary for this type of instruction.

If it is not too complicated, you can discuss the context of your argument in your introduction; if it requires more explanation, you can discuss it in your first body paragraph. If you do not establish this context early in your essay, however, readers will have a difficult time understanding the issue you are going to discuss and the points you are going to make.

Logos, Pathos, and Ethos

To be effective, your argument has to be persuasive. **Persuasion** is a general term that refers to how a speaker or writer influences an audience to adopt a particular belief or to follow a specific course of action.

In the fifth century BCE, the philosopher Aristotle considered the issue of persuasion. Ancient Greece was primarily an oral culture (as opposed to a written or print culture), so persuasive techniques were most often used in speeches. Public officials had to speak before a citizens' assembly, and people had to make their cases in front of various judicial bodies. The more persuasive the presentation, the better the speaker's chance of success. In *The Art of Rhetoric*, Aristotle examines the three different means of persuasion that a speaker can use to persuade listeners (or writers):

Aristotle, Roman portrait bust. Scala/Ministero per i Beni e le Attività Culturali/Uffizi Gallery, Florence, Italy/Art Resource, NY.

Aristotle

- The appeal to reason (*logos*)
- The appeal to the emotions (*pathos*)
- The appeal to authority (*ethos*)

The Appeal to Reason (Logos)

According to Aristotle, argument is the appeal to reason or logic (***logos***). He assumed that, at their core, human beings are logical and therefore would respond to a well-constructed argument. For Aristotle, appeals to reason focus primarily on the way that an argument is organized, and this organization is determined by formal logic, which uses deductive and inductive reasoning to reach valid conclusions. Aristotle believed that appeals to reason convince an audience that a conclusion is both valid and true (see Chapter 5 for a discussion of deductive and inductive reasoning and logic). Although Aristotle believed that ideally, all arguments should appeal to reason, he knew that given the realities of human nature, reason alone was not always enough. Therefore, when he discusses persuasion, he also discusses the appeals to *ethos* and *pathos*.

Logos *in Action*

Notice how the ad below for the Toyota Prius, a popular hybrid automobile, appeals primarily to reason. It uses facts as well as a logical explanation

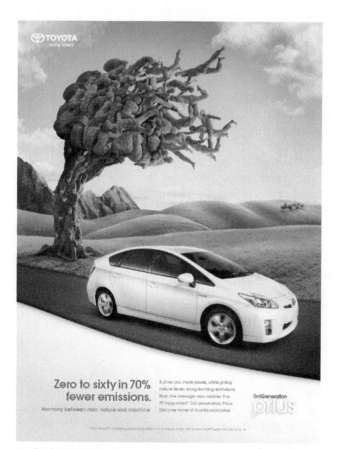

Car shot for Toyota Prius Harmony ad © Trevor Pearson. Background for Toyota Prius Harmony ad © Mark Holthusen Photography. Reproduced with permission of the photographers and Toyota Sales USA.

of how the car works to appeal to reason (as well as to the consumer's desire to help the environment).

You can assess the effectiveness of *logos* (the appeal to reason) in an argument by asking the following questions:

- Does the argument have a clear thesis? In other words, can you identify the main point the writer is trying to make?

- Does the argument include the facts, examples, and expert opinion needed to support the thesis?

- Is the argument well organized? Are the points the argument makes presented in logical order?

- Can you detect any errors in logic (**fallacies**) that undermine the argument's reasoning?

The Appeal to the Emotions (Pathos)

Aristotle knew that an appeal to the emotions (*pathos*) could be very persuasive because it adds a human dimension to an argument. By appealing to an audience's sympathies and by helping them to identify with the subject being discussed, emotional appeals can turn abstract concepts into concrete examples that can compel people to take action. After December 7, 1941, for example, explicit photographs of the Japanese attack on Pearl Harbor helped convince Americans that retaliation was both justified and desirable. Many Americans responded the same way when they saw pictures of planes crashing into the twin towers of the World Trade Center on September 11, 2001.

Although an appeal to the emotions can add to an already strong argument, it does not in itself constitute proof. Moreover, certain kinds of emotional appeals—appeals to fear, hatred, and prejudice, for example—are considered unfair and are not acceptable in college writing. In this sense, the pictures of the attacks on Pearl Harbor and the World Trade Center would be unfair arguments if they were not accompanied by evidence that established that retaliation was indeed necessary.

Pathos *in Action*

The following ad makes good use of the appeal to the emotions. Using a picture of polar bears defaced by graffiti, the ad includes a caption encouraging people to respect the environment. Although the ad contains no supporting evidence, it is effective nonetheless.

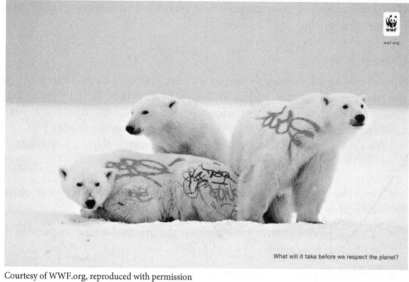

What will it take before we respect the planet?

Courtesy of WWF.org, reproduced with permission

You can assess the effectiveness of *pathos* (the appeal to the emotions) in an argument by asking the following questions:

- Does the argument include words or images designed to move readers?

- Does the argument use emotionally loaded language?

- Does the argument include vivid descriptions or striking examples calculated to appeal to readers' emotions?

- Are the values and beliefs of the writer apparent in the argument?

- Does the tone seem emotional?

The Appeal to Authority (Ethos)

Finally, Aristotle knew that the character and authority of a speaker or writer (**ethos**) could contribute to the persuasiveness of an argument. If the person making the argument is known to be honorable, truthful, knowledgeable, and trustworthy, audiences will likely accept what he or she is saying. If, on the other hand, the person is known to be deceitful, ignorant, dishonest, uninformed, or dishonorable, audiences will probably dismiss his or her argument—no matter how persuasive it might seem. Whenever you analyze an argument, you should try to determine whether the writer is worth listening to—in other words, whether the writer has **credibility**.

(For a discussion of how to establish credibility and demonstrate fairness in your own writing, see Chapter 7.)

Ethos *in Action*

The following ad uses an appeal to authority. It uses an endorsement by the popular tennis star Venus Williams to convince consumers to buy Reebok sneakers. (Recent studies suggest that consumers react positively to ads that feature products endorsed by famous athletes.)

You can assess the effectiveness of *ethos* (the appeal to authority) in an argument by asking the following questions:

- Does the person making the argument demonstrate knowledge of the subject?

- What steps does the person making the argument take to present its position as reasonable?

- Does the argument seem fair?

- If the argument includes sources, do they seem both reliable and credible? Does the argument include proper documentation?

- Does the person making the argument demonstrate respect for opposing viewpoints?

Venus Williams in an ad endorsing Reebok

AP Photo/Kathy Willens

The Rhetorical Triangle

The relationship among the three kinds of appeals in an argument is traditionally represented by a triangle.

LOGOS (reason)
Focuses on the text

ETHOS (authority)
Focuses on the writer

PATHOS (emotions)
Focuses on the audience

In the diagram above—called the **rhetorical triangle**—all sides of the triangle are equal, implying that the three appeals occur in an argument in equal measure. In reality, however, this is seldom true. Depending on the audience, purpose, and situation, an argument may include all three appeals or just one or two. Moreover, one argument might emphasize reason, another might stress the writer's authority (or credibility), and still another might appeal mainly to the emotions. (In each of these cases, one side of the rhetorical triangle would be longer than the others.) In academic writing, for example, the appeal to reason is used most often, and the appeal to the emotions is less common. As Aristotle recognized, however, the three appeals often work together (to varying degrees) to create an effective argument.

Each of the following paragraphs makes an argument against smoking, illustrating how the appeals are used in an argument. Although each paragraph includes all three of the appeals, one appeal outweighs the others. (Keep in mind that each paragraph is aimed at a different audience.)

APPEAL TO REASON (*LOGOS*)

Among young people, the dangers of smoking are clear. According to the World Health Organization, smoking can cause a variety of problems in young people—for example, lung problems and shortness of breath. Smoking also contributes to heart attacks, strokes, and coronary artery disease (72). In addition, teenage smokers have an increased risk of developing lung cancer as they get older (CDC). According to one study, teenage smokers see doctors or other health professionals at higher rates than those who do not smoke (Ardly 112). Finally, teenagers who smoke tend to abuse alcohol and marijuana as well as engage in other risky behaviors (CDC). Clearly, tobacco is a dangerous drug that has serious health risks for teenage smokers. In fact, some studies suggest that smoking takes thirteen to fourteen years off a person's life (American Cancer Society).

APPEAL TO THE EMOTIONS (*PATHOS*)

Every day, almost four thousand young people begin smoking cigarettes, and this number is growing (Family First Aid). Sadly, most of you have no idea what you are getting into. For one thing, smoking yellows your teeth, stains your fingers, and gives you bad breath. The smoke also gets into your hair and clothes and makes you smell. Also, smoking is addictive; once you start, it's hard to stop. After you've been smoking for a few years, you are hooked, and as television commercials for the nicotine patch show, you can have a hard time breaking the habit. Finally, smoking is dangerous. In the United States, one out of every five deaths can be attributed to smoking (Teen Health). If you have ever seen anyone dying of lung cancer, you understand how bad long-term smoking can be. Just look at the pictures on the Internet of diseased, blackened lungs, and it becomes clear that smoking does not make you look cool or sophisticated, no matter what cigarette advertising suggests.

APPEAL TO AUTHORITY (*ETHOS*)

My advice to those who are starting to smoke is to reconsider—before it's too late. I began using tobacco over ten years ago when I was in high school. At first, I started using snuff because I was on the baseball team and wanted to imitate the players in the major leagues. It wasn't long before I had graduated to cigarettes—first a few and then at least a pack a day. I heard the warnings from teachers and the counselors from the D.A.R.E. program, but they didn't do any good. I spent almost all my extra money on cigarettes. Occasionally, I would stop—sometimes for a few days, sometimes for a few weeks—but I always started again. Later, after I graduated, the health plan at my job covered smoking cessation treatment, so I tried everything—the patch, Chantix, therapy, and even hypnosis. Again, nothing worked. At last, after I had been married for four years, my wife sat me down and begged me to quit. Later that night, I threw away my cigarettes and haven't smoked since. Although I've gained some weight, I now breathe easier, and I am able to concentrate better than I could before. Had I known how difficult quitting was going to be, I never would have started in the first place.

When you write an argumentative essay, keep in mind that each type of appeal has its own particular strengths. Your purpose and audience as well as other elements of the rhetorical situation help you determine what strategy to use. Remember, however, that even though most effective arguments use a combination of appeals, one appeal predominates. For example, even though academic arguments may employ appeals to the emotions, they do so sparingly. Most often, they appeal primarily to reason by using facts and statistics—not emotions—to support their points.

 LaunchPad
macmillan learning

For more practice, see the LearningCurve on Persuasive Appeals (*pathos, ethos,* and *logos*) in the LaunchPad for *Practical Argument*.

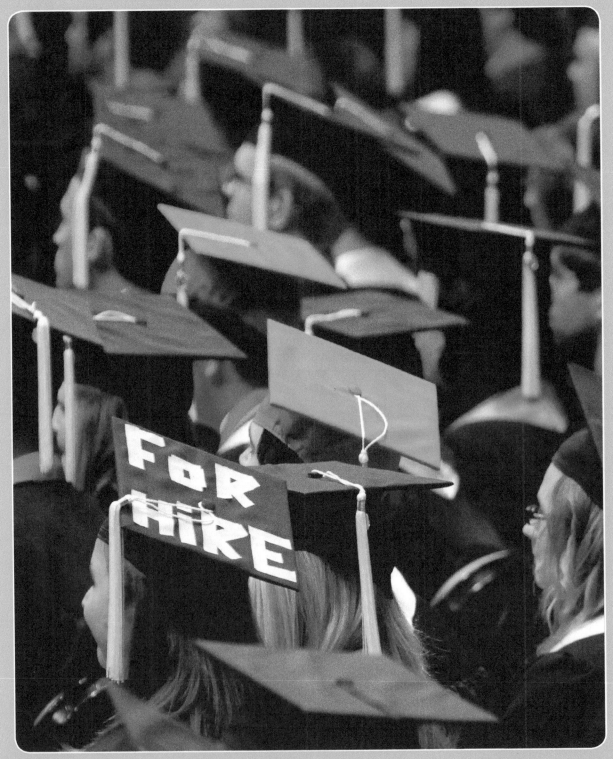

Butch Dill/AP Photos

1

The Four Pillars of Argument

AT ISSUE

Is a College Education Worth the Money?

In recent years, more and more high school graduates have been heading to college, convinced that higher education will enhance their future earning power. At the same time, the cost of a college education has been rising, and so has the amount of student-loan debt carried by college graduates. (During 2014, average tuition and fees at nonprofit private colleges rose 3.7 percent, to $31,231, while tuition for in-state students at four-year public schools went up 2.9 percent to $9,139. On average, 2015 graduates with student-loan debt owed over $35,000.) This situation has led some observers to wonder if the high cost of college actually pays off—not only in dollars but also in future

job satisfaction. Will a college degree protect workers who are threatened by high unemployment, the rise of technology, the declining power of labor unions, and the trend toward outsourcing? Given the high financial cost of college, do the rewards of a college education—emotional and intellectual as well as financial—balance the sacrifices that students make in time and money? These and other questions have no easy answers.

Later in this chapter, you will be introduced to readings that highlight the pros and cons of investing in a college education, and you will be asked to write an argumentative essay in which you take a position on this controversial topic.

In a sense, you already know a lot more than you think you do about how to construct an argumentative essay. After all, an argumentative essay is a variation of the thesis-and-support essays that you have been writing in your college classes: you state a position on a topic, and then you support this position. However, argumentative essays also involve some special concerns in terms of structure, style, and purpose. Throughout this book, we introduce you to the unique features of argument. In this chapter, we focus on structure.

The Elements of Argument

An argumentative essay includes the same three sections—*introduction*, *body*, and *conclusion*—as any other essay. In an argumentative essay, however, the introduction includes an argumentative **thesis statement**, the body includes both the supporting **evidence** and the **refutation** of opposing arguments, and the conclusion includes a strong, convincing **concluding statement** that reinforces the position stated in the thesis.

The following diagram illustrates one way to organize an argumentative essay.

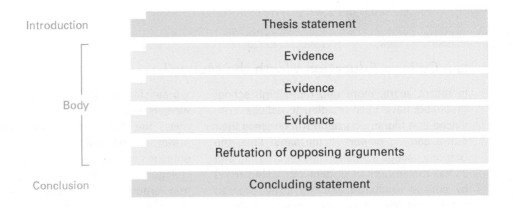

Introduction — Thesis statement

Body — Evidence / Evidence / Evidence / Refutation of opposing arguments

Conclusion — Concluding statement

The elements of an argumentative essay are like the pillars of an ancient Greek temple. Together, the four elements—thesis statement, evidence, refutation of opposing arguments, and concluding statement—help you build a strong argument.

Ancient Greek temple

AP Photo/Alessandro Fucarini

Thesis Statement

A **thesis statement** is a single sentence that states your position on an issue. An argumentative essay must have an **argumentative thesis**—one that takes a firm stand. For example, on the issue of whether colleges should require all students to study a language other than English, your thesis statement could be any of the following (and other positions are also possible):

- Colleges should require all students to study a foreign language.

- Colleges should require all liberal arts majors to study a foreign language.

- Colleges should require all students to take Spanish, Chinese, or Farsi.

- Colleges should not require any students to study a foreign language.

An argumentative thesis must be **debatable**—that is, it must have at least two sides, stating a position with which some reasonable people might disagree. To confirm that your thesis is debatable, you should see if you can formulate an **antithesis**, or opposing argument. For example, the statement, "Our school has a foreign-language requirement" has no antithesis because it is simply a statement of fact; you could not take the opposite position because the facts would not support it. However, the following thesis statement takes a position that *is* debatable (and therefore suitable for an argumentative thesis):

THESIS   Our school should institute a foreign-language requirement.

ANTITHESIS   Our school should not institute a foreign-language requirement.

(For more on thesis statements, see Chapter 7.)

Evidence

Evidence is the material—facts, observations, expert opinion, examples, statistics, and so on—that supports your thesis statement. For example, you could support your position that foreign-language study should be required for all college students by arguing that this requirement will make them more employable, and you could cite employment statistics to support this point. Alternatively, you could use the opinion of an expert on the topic—for example, an experienced college language instructor—to support the opposite position, arguing that students without an interest in language study are wasting their time in such courses.

You will use both *facts* and *opinions* to support the points you make in your arguments. A **fact** is a statement that can be verified (proven to be true). An **opinion** is always open to debate because it is simply a personal judgment. Of course, the more knowledgeable the writer is, the more credible his or her opinion is. Thus, the opinion of a respected expert on language study will carry more weight than the opinion of a student with no particular expertise on the issue. However, if the student's opinion is supported by facts, it will be much more convincing than an unsupported opinion.

FACTS

- Some community colleges have no foreign-language requirements.
- Some selective liberal arts colleges require all students to take two years or more of foreign-language study.
- At some universities, undergraduates must take as many as fourteen foreign-language credits.
- Some schools grant credit for high school language classes, allowing these courses to fulfill the college foreign-language requirement.

UNSUPPORTED OPINIONS

- Foreign-language courses are not as important as math and science courses.
- Foreign-language study should be a top priority on university campuses.
- Engineering majors should not have to take a foreign-language course.
- It is not fair to force all students to study a foreign language.

SUPPORTED OPINIONS

- The university requires all students to take a full year of foreign-language study, but it is not doing enough to support those who need help. For example, it does not provide enough student tutors, and the language labs have no evening hours.
- According to Ruth Fuentes, chair of the Spanish department, nursing and criminal justice majors who take at least two years of Spanish have an easier time finding employment after graduation than students in those majors who do not study Spanish.

Refutation

Because every argument has more than one side, you should not assume that your readers will agree with you. On the contrary, readers usually need to be convinced that your position on an issue has merit.

This means that you need to do more than just provide sufficient evidence in support of your position; you also need to **refute** (disprove or call into question) arguments that challenge your position, possibly acknowledging the strengths of those opposing arguments and then pointing out their shortcomings. For example, if you take a position in favor of requiring foreign-language study for all college students, some readers might argue that college students already have to take too many required courses. After acknowledging the validity of this argument, you could refute it by pointing out that a required foreign-language course would not necessarily be a burden for students because it could replace another, less important required course. (For more on refutation, see Chapter 7.)

Concluding Statement

After you have provided convincing support for your position and refuted opposing arguments, you should end your essay with a strong **concluding statement** that reinforces your position. (The position that you want readers to remember is the one stated in your thesis, not the opposing arguments that you have refuted.) For example, you might conclude an essay in support of a foreign-language requirement by making a specific recommendation or by predicting the possible negative outcome of *not* implementing this requirement.

CHECKLIST

Does Your Argument Stand Up?

When you write an argumentative essay, check to make sure it includes all four of the elements you need to build a strong argument.

☐ Do you have an argumentative **thesis**?

☐ Do you include solid, convincing **evidence** to support your thesis?

☐ Do you include a **refutation** of the most compelling arguments against your position?

☐ Do you include a strong **concluding statement**?

⏺ The following student essay includes all four of the elements that are needed to build a convincing argument.

WHY FOREIGN-LANGUAGE STUDY SHOULD BE REQUIRED

NIA TUCKSON

Introduction

"What do you call someone who speaks three languages? Trilingual. 1
What do you call someone who speaks two languages? Bilingual. What do
you call someone who speaks only one language? American." As this old
joke illustrates, many Americans are unable to communicate in a language
other than English. Given our global economy and American companies'
need to conduct business with other countries, this problem needs to be
addressed. A good first step is to require all college students to study a
foreign language.

Thesis statement

First body paragraph:
Evidence

After graduation, many students will work in fields in which speaking 2
(or reading) another language will be useful or even necessary. For example,
health-care professionals will often be called on to communicate with
patients who do not speak English; in fact, a patient's life may depend on
their ability to do so. Those who work in business and finance may need
to speak Mandarin or Japanese; those who have positions in the military
or in the foreign service may need to speak Persian or Arabic. A working
knowledge of one of these languages can help students succeed in their
future careers, and it can also make them more employable.

Second body paragraph:
Evidence

In addition to strengthening a résumé, foreign-language study can also 3
give students an understanding of another culture's history, art, and literature.
Although such knowledge may never be "useful" in a student's career, it
can certainly enrich the student's life. Too narrow a focus on career can
turn college into a place that trains students rather than educates them.
In contrast, expanding students' horizons to include subjects beyond those
needed for their careers can better equip them to be lifelong learners.

Third body paragraph:
Evidence

When they travel abroad, Americans who can speak a language 4
other than English will find that they are better able to understand
people from other countries. As informal ambassadors for the United
States, tourists have a responsibility to try to understand other
languages and cultures. Too many Americans assume that their own
country's language and culture are superior to all others. This shortsighted

attitude is not likely to strengthen relationships between the United States and other nations. Understanding a country's language can help students to build bridges between themselves and others.

Some students say that learning a language is not easy and that it takes a great deal of time. College students are already overloaded with coursework, jobs, and family responsibilities, and a new academic requirement is certain to create problems. In fact, students may find that adding just six credits of language study will limit their opportunities to take advanced courses in their majors or to enroll in electives that interest them. However, this burden can be eased if other, less important course requirements—such as physical education—are eliminated to make room for the new requirement.

5 Fourth body paragraph: Refutation of opposing argument

Some students may also argue that they, not their school, should be able to decide what courses are most important to them. After all, a student who struggled in high school French and plans to major in computer science might understandably resist a foreign-language requirement. However, challenging college language courses might actually be more rewarding than high school courses were, and the student who struggled in high school French might actually enjoy a college-level French course (or study a different language). Finally, a student who initially plans to major in computer science may actually wind up majoring in something completely different—or taking a job in a country in which English is not spoken.

6 Fifth body paragraph: Refutation of opposing argument

Entering college students sometimes find it hard to envision their personal or professional futures or to imagine where their lives may take them. Still, a well-rounded education, including foreign-language study, can prepare them for many of the challenges that they will face. Colleges can help students keep their options open by requiring at least a year (and preferably two years) of foreign-language study. Instead of focusing narrowly on what interests them today, American college students should take the extra step to become bilingual—or even trilingual—in the future.

7 Conclusion

Concluding statement

⊗ EXERCISE 1.1

The following essay, "Raise the Drinking Age to Twenty-Five," by Andrew Herman, includes all four of the basic elements of argument discussed so far. Read the essay, and then answer the questions that follow it, consulting the diagram on page 24 if necessary.

This commentary appeared on August 22, 2007, on BG Views, a website for Bowling Green State University and the citizens of its community.

RAISE THE DRINKING AGE
TO TWENTY-FIVE

ANDREW HERMAN

As a new school year begins, as dorms fill with new and returning students 1
alike, a single thought frequents the minds of every member of our population:
newfound freedom from a summer of jobs and familial responsibilities.

But our return to school coexists with a possibly lethal counterpart: col- 2
lege drinking.

Nearly everyone is exposed to parties during college, and one would be hard 3
pressed to find a college party without alcohol. Most University students indicate
in countless surveys they have used alcohol in a social setting before age 21.

It is startling just how ineffective current 4
laws have been at curbing underage drinking.

> "It is startling just how ineffective current laws have been."

A dramatic change is needed in the way 5
society addresses drinking and the way we
enforce existing laws, and it can start with a
simple change: making the drinking age 25.

Access and availability are the principal reasons underage drinking has 6
become easy to do. Not through direct availability, but through access to legal-
aged "friends."

In a college setting, it is all but impossible not to know a person who is older 7
than 21 and willing to provide alcohol to younger students. Even if unintentional,
there is no verification that each person who drinks is of the appropriate age.

However, it should be quite easy to ensure underage individuals don't have 8
access to alcohol. In reality, those who abstain from alcohol are in the minority.
Countless people our age consider speeding tickets worse than an arrest for
underage consumption.

Is it truly possible alcohol abuse has become so commonplace, so accept- 9
able, that people forget the facts?

Each year, 1,400 [college students] die from drinking too much. 600,000 10
are victims of alcohol-related physical assault and 17,000 are a result of
drunken driving deaths, many being innocent bystanders.

Perhaps the most disturbing number: 70,000 people, overwhelmingly 11
female, are annually sexually assaulted in alcohol-related situations.

These numbers are difficult to grasp for the sheer prevalence of alcoholic 12
destruction. Yet, we, as college students, are responsible for an overwhelming por-
tion of their incidence. It is difficult to imagine anyone would wish to assume the
role of rapist, murderer, or victim. We all assume these things could never happen
to us, but I am certain victims in these situations thought the same. The simple

truth is that driving under the influence is the leading cause of death for teens. For 10- to 24-year-olds, alcohol is the fourth-leading cause of death, made so by factors ranging from alcohol poisoning to alcohol-related assault and murder.

For the sake of our friends, those we love, our futures, and ourselves, we must take a stand and we must do it now. 13

Advocates of lowering the drinking age assert only four countries worldwide maintain a "21 standard," and a gradual transition to alcohol is useful in reducing the systemic social problems of substance abuse. 14

If those under the age of 21 are misusing alcohol, it makes little sense to grant free rein to those individuals to use it legally. A parent who observes their children abusing the neighbor's dog would be irresponsible to get one of their own without altering such dangerous behavior. 15

Increasing the drinking age will help in the search for solutions to grievous alcoholic problems, making it far more difficult in college environments to find legal-aged providers. 16

By the time we are 25, with careers and possibly families of our own, there is no safety net to allow us to have a "Thirsty Thursday." But increasing the legal age is not all that needs to be done. Drinking to get drunk needs to exist as a social taboo rather than a doorway to popularity. 17

Peer pressure can become a tool to change this. What once was a factor greatly contributing to underage drinking can now become an instrument of good, seeking to end such a dangerous practice as excessive drinking. Laws on drinking ages, as any other law, need to be enforced with the energy and vigor each of us should expect. 18

Alcohol is not an inherently evil poison. It does have its place, as do all things in the great scheme of life. 19

But with alcohol comes the terrible risk of abuse with consequences many do not consider. All too often, these consequences include robbing someone of his life or loved one. All communities in the country, our own included, have been touched by such a tragedy. 20

Because of this, and the hundreds of thousands of victims each year in alcohol-related situations, I ask that you consider the very real possibility of taking the life of another due to irresponsible drinking. 21

If this is not enough, then take time to think, because that life could very well be your own. 22

Identifying the Elements of Argument

1. What is this essay's thesis? Restate it in your own words.

2. List the arguments Herman presents as evidence to support his thesis.

3. Summarize the opposing argument the essay identifies. Then, summarize Herman's refutation of this argument.

4. Restate the essay's concluding statement in your own words.

Is a College Education Worth the Money?

Reread the At Issue box on page 23, which summarizes questions raised on both sides of this issue. As the following sources illustrate, reasonable people may disagree about this controversial topic.

As you review the sources, you will be asked to answer some questions and to complete some simple activities. This work will help you understand both the content and the structure of the sources. When you have finished, you will be ready to write an essay in which you take a position on the topic "Is a College Education Worth the Money?"

Butch Dill/AP Photos

SOURCES

 David Leonhardt, "Is College Worth It? Clearly, New Data Say," p. 33

 Marty Nemko, "We Send Too Many Students to College," p. 37

Jennie Le, "What Does It Mean to Be a College Grad?," p. 41

Dale Stephens, "College Is a Waste of Time," p. 43

 Bridget Terry Long, "College Is Worth It—Some of the Time," p. 45

Mary C. Daly and Leila Bengali, "Is It Still Worth Going to College?," p. 48

This essay appeared in the *New York Times* on May 27, 2014.

IS COLLEGE WORTH IT? CLEARLY, NEW DATA SAY

DAVID LEONHARDT

Rising Value of a College Degree

The pay of people with a four-year college degree has risen compared to that 1 of those with a high school degree but no college credit. The relative pay of people who attended college without earning a four-year degree has stayed flat.

Ratio of average hourly pay, compared with pay of people with a high school degree

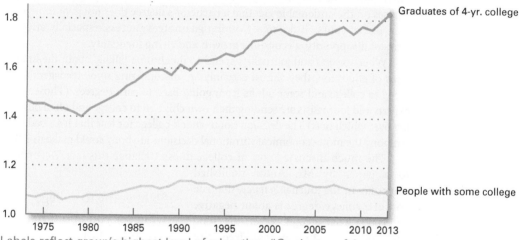

Labels reflect group's highest level of education. "Graduates of 4-year college," for instance, excludes people with graduate degrees.

Data from: *New York Times* analysis of Economic Policy Institute data

Some newly minted college graduates struggle to find work. Others accept jobs 2 for which they feel overqualified. Student debt, meanwhile, has topped $1 trillion.

It's enough to create a wave of questions about whether a college educa- 3 tion is still worth it.

A new set of income statistics answers those questions quite clearly: Yes, col- 4 lege is worth it, and it's not even close. For all the struggles that many young college graduates face, a four-year degree has probably never been more valuable.

The pay gap between college graduates and everyone else reached a record 5 high last year, according to the new data, which is based on an analysis of Labor Department statistics by the Economic Policy Institute in Washington. Americans with four-year college degrees made 98 percent more an hour on average in 2013 than people without a degree. That's up from 89 percent five years earlier, 85 percent a decade earlier, and 64 percent in the early 1980s.

The pay of people with a four-year college degree has risen compared to 6 that of those with a high school degree but no college credit. The relative pay of people who attended college without earning a four-year degree has stayed flat.

There is nothing inevitable about this trend. If there were more college 7 graduates than the economy needed, the pay gap would shrink. The gap's recent growth is especially notable because it has come after a rise in the number of college graduates, partly because many people went back to school during the Great Recession. That the pay gap has nonetheless continued growing means that we're still not producing enough of them.

"We have too few college graduates," says David Autor, an M.I.T. econo- 8 mist, who was not involved in the Economic Policy Institute's analysis. "We also have too few people who are prepared for college."

It's important to emphasize these shortfalls because public discussion 9 today—for which we in the news media deserve some responsibility—often focuses on the undeniable fact that a bachelor's degree does not guarantee success. But of course it doesn't. Nothing guarantees success, especially after 15 years of disappointing economic growth and rising inequality.

When experts and journalists spend so much time talking about the limita- 10 tions of education, they almost certainly are discouraging some teenagers from going to college and some adults from going back to earn degrees. (Those same experts and journalists are sending their own children to college and often obsessing over which one.) The decision not to attend college for fear that it's a bad deal is among the most economically irrational decisions anybody could make in 2014.

The much-discussed cost of college doesn't change this fact. According 11 to a paper by Mr. Autor published Thursday in the journal *Science*, the true cost of a college degree is about negative $500,000. That's right: Over the long run, college is cheaper than free. Not going to college will cost you about half a million dollars.

> "Not going to college will cost you about half a million dollars."

Mr. Autor's paper—building on work by the economists Christopher Avery 12 and Sarah Turner—arrives at that figure first by calculating the very real cost of tuition and fees. This amount is then subtracted from the lifetime gap between the earnings of college graduates and high school graduates. After adjusting for inflation and the time value of money, the net cost of college is negative $500,000, roughly double what it was three decades ago.

This calculation is necessarily imprecise, because it can't control for 13 any pre-existing differences between college graduates and nongraduates— differences that would exist regardless of schooling. Yet other research, comparing otherwise similar people who did and did not graduate from college, has also found that education brings a huge return.

In a similar vein, the new Economic Policy Institute numbers show that 14 the benefits of college don't go just to graduates of elite colleges, who typically go on to earn graduate degrees. The wage gap between people with only a bachelor's degree and people without such a degree has also kept rising.

Tellingly, though, the wage premium for people who have attended col- 15 lege without earning a bachelor's degree—a group that includes community-college graduates—has not been rising. The big economic returns go to people with four-year degrees. Those returns underscore the importance of efforts to reduce the college dropout rate, such as those at the University of Texas, which Paul Tough described in a recent *Times Magazine* article.

But what about all those alarming stories you hear about indebted, jobless 16 college graduates?

The anecdotes may be real, yet the conventional wisdom often exaggerates 17 the problem. Among four-year college graduates who took out loans, average debt is about $25,000, a sum that is a tiny fraction of the economic benefits of college. (My own student debt, as it happens, was almost identical to this figure, in inflation-adjusted terms.) And the unemployment rate in April for people between 25 and 34 years old with a bachelor's degree was a mere 3 percent.

I find the data from the Economic Policy Institute especially telling 18 because the institute—a left-leaning research group—makes a point of arguing that education is not the solution to all of the economy's problems. That is important, too. College graduates, like almost everyone else, are suffering from the economy's weak growth and from the disproportionate share of this growth flowing to the very richest households.

The average hourly wage for college graduates has risen only 1 percent over the 19 last decade, to about $32.60. The pay gap has grown mostly because the average wage for everyone else has fallen—5 percent, to about $16.50. "To me, the picture is people in almost every kind of job not being able to see their wages grow," Lawrence Mishel, the institute's president, told me. "Wage growth essentially stopped in 2002."

From the country's perspective, education can be only part of the solution 20 to our economic problems. We also need to find other means for lifting living standards—not to mention ways to provide good jobs for people without col-lege degrees.

But from almost any individual's perspective, college is a no-brainer. It's 21 the most reliable ticket to the middle class and beyond. Those who question the value of college tend to be those with the luxury of knowing their own chil-dren will be able to attend it.

Not so many decades ago, high school was considered the frontier of educa- 22 tion. Some people even argued that it was a waste to encourage Americans from humble backgrounds to spend four years of life attending high school. Today, obvi-ously, the notion that everyone should attend 13 years of school is indisputable.

But there is nothing magical about 13 years of education. As the economy 23 becomes more technologically complex, the amount of education that people need will rise. At some point, 15 years or 17 years of education will make more sense as a universal goal.

That point, in fact, has already arrived. 24

⊙ AT ISSUE: SOURCES FOR STRUCTURING AN ARGUMENT

1. Paraphrase this essay's thesis statement by filling in the following template.
   Because _____,
   a four-year college degree is now more important than ever.

2. To support his position, Leonhardt relies largely on statistics. Where does he include other kinds of supporting evidence?

3. Look at the graph that follows paragraph 1, and read its caption. What does this image add to the essay? Would Leonhardt's argument have been as convincing without the graph? Why or why not?

4. In paragraph 8, Leonhardt quotes economist David Autor. How do you suppose Marty Nemko (p. 37) would respond to Autor's statements?

5. In paragraph 16, Leonhardt asks a question to introduce an argument opposed to his position. What is this argument? Does he refute it effectively in the discussion that follows?

6. In paragraph 22, Leonhardt begins his conclusion with an **analogy**. What two things is he comparing? What point is he making? Do you think this concluding strategy is effective? Why or why not? How else could he have ended his essay?

This undated essay is from MartyNemko.com.

WE SEND TOO MANY STUDENTS TO COLLEGE

MARTY NEMKO

Among my saddest moments as a career counselor is when I hear a story like 1 this: "I wasn't a good student in high school, but I wanted to prove to myself that I can get a college diploma—I'd be the first one in my family to do it. But it's been six years and I still have 45 units to go."

I have a hard time telling such people the killer statistic: According to the 2 U.S. Department of Education, if you graduated in the bottom 40 percent of your high school class and went to college, 76 of 100 won't earn a diploma, even if given 8½ years. Yet colleges admit and take the money from hundreds of thousands of such students each year!

Even worse, most of those college dropouts leave college having learned 3 little of practical value (see below) and with devastated self-esteem and a mountain of debt. Perhaps worst of all, those people rarely leave with a career path likely to lead to more than McWages. So it's not surprising that when you hop into a cab or walk into a restaurant, you're likely to meet workers who spent years and their family's life savings on college, only to end up with a job they could have done as a high school dropout.

Perhaps yet more surprising, even the high school students who are fully 4 qualified to attend college are increasingly unlikely to derive enough benefit to justify the often six-figure cost and four to eight years it takes to graduate—and only 40 percent of freshmen graduate in four years; 45 percent never graduate at all. Colleges love to trumpet the statistic that, over their lifetimes, college graduates earn more than nongraduates. But that's terribly misleading because you could lock the college-bound in a closet for four years and they'd earn more than the pool of non-college-bound—they're brighter, more motivated, and have better family connections. Too, the past advantage of college graduates in the job market is eroding: ever more students are going to college at the same time as ever more employers are offshoring ever more professional jobs. So college graduates are forced to take some very nonprofessional jobs. For example, Jill Plesnarski holds a bachelor's degree in biology from the private ($160,000 published total cost for four years) Moravian College. She had hoped to land a job as a medical research lab tech, but those positions paid so little that she opted for a job at a New Jersey sewage treatment plant. Today, although she's since been promoted, she must still occasionally wash down the tower that holds raw sewage.

Or take Brian Morris. After completing his bachelor's degree in liberal 5 arts from the University of California, Berkeley, he was unable to find a decent-paying job, so he went yet deeper into debt to get a master's degree from the private Mills College. Despite those degrees, the best job he could land was teaching a three-month-long course for $3,000. At that point, Brian was married and had a baby, so to support them, he reluctantly took a job as a truck driver. Now Brian says, "I just *have* to get out of trucking."

Colleges are quick to argue that a college education is more about enlightenment than employment. That may be the biggest deception of all. There is a Grand Canyon of difference between what the colleges tout in their brochures and websites and the reality. 6

Colleges are businesses, and students are a cost item while research is a profit center. So colleges tend to educate students in the cheapest way possible: large lecture classes, with small classes staffed by rock-bottom-cost graduate students and, in some cases, even by undergraduate students. Professors who bring in big research dollars are almost always rewarded, while even a fine teacher who doesn't bring in the research bucks is often fired or relegated to the lowest rung: lecturer. 7

> "Colleges are businesses, and students are a cost item."

So, no surprise, in the definitive *Your First College Year* nationwide survey conducted by UCLA researchers (data collected in 2005, reported in 2007), only 16.4 percent of students were very satisfied with the overall quality of instruction they received and 28.2 percent were neutral, dissatisfied, or very dissatisfied. A follow-up survey of seniors found that 37 percent reported being "frequently bored in class," up from 27.5 percent as freshmen. 8

College students may be dissatisfied with instruction, but despite that, do they learn? A 2006 study funded by the Pew Charitable Trusts found that 50 percent of college *seniors* failed a test that required them to do such basic tasks as interpret a table about exercise and blood pressure, understand the arguments of newspaper editorials, or compare credit card offers. Almost 20 percent of seniors had only basic quantitative skills. For example, the students could not estimate if their car had enough gas to get to the gas station. 9

What to do? Colleges, which receive billions of tax dollars with minimum oversight, should be held at least as accountable as companies are. For example, when some Firestone tires were defective, the government nearly forced it out of business. Yet year after year, colleges turn out millions of defective products: students who drop out or graduate with far too little benefit for the time and money spent. Yet not only do the colleges escape punishment; they're rewarded with ever greater taxpayer-funded student grants and loans, which allow colleges to raise their tuitions yet higher. 10

What should parents and guardians do? 11

1. If your student's high school grades and SAT or ACT are in the bottom half of his high school class, resist colleges' attempts to woo him. Their marketing to your child does *not* indicate that the colleges believe he will succeed there. Colleges make money whether or not a student learns, whether or not she graduates, and whether or not he finds good employment. If a physician recommended a treatment that cost a fortune and 12

required years of effort without disclosing the poor chances of it working, she'd be sued and lose in any court in the land. But colleges—one of America's most sacred cows—somehow seem immune.

So let the buyer beware. Consider nondegree options: 13

- Apprenticeship programs (a great portal to apprenticeship websites: www.khake.com/page58.html)

- Short career-preparation programs at community colleges

- The military

- On-the-job training, especially at the elbow of a successful small business owner

2. Let's say your student *is* in the top half of his high school class and is moti- 14 vated to attend college by more than the parties, being able to say she went to college, and the piece of paper. Then have her apply to perhaps a dozen colleges. Colleges vary less than you might think, yet financial aid awards can vary wildly. It's often wise to choose the college that requires you to pay the least cash and take on the smallest loan. College is among the few products where you don't get what you pay for—price does not indicate quality.

3. If your child is one of the rare breed who, on graduating high school, knows 15 what he wants to do and isn't unduly attracted to college academics or the *Animal House* environment that college dorms often are, then take solace in the fact that in deciding to forgo college, he is preceded by scores of others who have successfully taken that noncollege road less traveled. Examples: the three most successful entrepreneurs in the computer industry, Bill Gates, Michael Dell, and Apple cofounder Steve Wozniak, all do not have a college degree. Here are some others: Malcolm X, Rush Limbaugh, Barbra Streisand, PBS *NewsHour's* Nina Totenberg, Tom Hanks, Maya Angelou, Ted Turner, Ellen DeGeneres, former governor Jesse Ventura, IBM founder Thomas Watson, architect Frank Lloyd Wright, former Israeli president David Ben-Gurion, Woody Allen, Warren Beatty, Domino's pizza chain founder Tom Monaghan, folksinger Joan Baez, director Quentin Tarantino, ABC-TV's Peter Jennings, Wendy's founder Dave Thomas, Thomas Edison, Blockbuster Video founder and owner of the Miami Dolphins Wayne Huizenga, William Faulkner, Jane Austen, McDonald's founder Ray Kroc, Oracle founder Larry Ellison, Henry Ford, cosmetics magnate Helena Rubinstein, Benjamin Franklin, Alexander Graham Bell, Coco Chanel, Walter Cronkite, Walt Disney, Bob Dylan, Leonardo DiCaprio, cookie maker Debbi Fields, Sally Field, Jane Fonda, Buckminster Fuller, DreamWorks cofounder David Geffen, *Roots* author Alex Haley, Ernest Hemingway, Dustin Hoffman, famed anthropologist Richard Leakey, airplane inventors Wilbur and Orville Wright, Madonna, satirist H. L. Mencken, Martina Navratilova, Rosie O'Donnell, Nathan Pritikin (Pritikin diet), chef Wolfgang Puck, Robert

Redford, oil billionaire John D. Rockefeller, Eleanor Roosevelt, NBC mogul David Sarnoff, and seven U.S. presidents from Washington to Truman.

4. College is like a chain saw. Only in certain situations is it the right tool. 16 Encourage your child to choose the right tool for her post–high school experience.

⊙ AT ISSUE: SOURCES FOR STRUCTURING AN ARGUMENT

1. Which of the following statements best summarizes Nemko's position? Why?

   ■ "We Send Too Many Students to College" (title)

   ■ "There is a Grand Canyon of difference between what the colleges tout in their brochures and websites and the reality" (para. 6).

   ■ "Colleges, which receive billions of tax dollars with minimum oversight, should be held at least as accountable as companies are" (10).

   ■ "College is like a chain saw. Only in certain situations is it the right tool" (16).

2. Where does Nemko support his thesis with appeals to logic? Where does he appeal to the emotions? Where does he use an appeal to authority? Which of these three kinds of appeals do you find the most convincing? Why?

3. List the arguments Nemko uses to support his thesis in paragraphs 2–4.

4. In paragraph 4, Nemko says, "Colleges love to trumpet the statistic that, over their lifetimes, college graduates earn more than nongraduates." In paragraph 6, he says, "Colleges are quick to argue that a college education is more about enlightenment than employment." How does he refute these two opposing arguments? Are his refutations effective?

5. Nemko draws an analogy between colleges and businesses, identifying students as a "cost item" (7). Does this analogy—including his characterization of weak students as "defective products" (10)—work for you? Why or why not?

6. What specific solutions does Nemko propose for the problem he identifies? To whom does he address these suggestions—and, in fact, his entire argument?

7. Reread paragraph 15. Do you think the list of successful people who do not hold college degrees is effective support for Nemko's position? What kind of appeal does this paragraph make? How might you refute its argument?

This personal essay is from talk.onevietnam.org, where it appeared on May 9, 2011.

WHAT DOES IT MEAN TO BE A COLLEGE GRAD?

JENNIE LE

After May 14th, I will be a college graduate. By fall, there will be no more a cappella rehearsals, no more papers or exams, no more sleepless nights, no more weekday drinking, no more 1 AM milk tea runs, no more San Francisco Bay Area exploring. I won't be with the people I now see daily. I won't have the same job with the same awesome boss. I won't be singing under Sproul every Monday. I won't be booked with weekly gigs that take me all over California. I won't be lighting another VSA Culture Show.

I will also have new commitments: weekly dinner dates with my mom, brother/sister time with my other two brothers, job hunting and career building, car purchasing and maintenance. In essence, my life will be—or at least feel—completely different. From what college alumni have told me, I will soon miss my college days after they are gone.

But in the bigger picture, outside of the daily tasks, what does it mean to hold a college degree? My fellow graduating coworker and I discussed the importance (or lack thereof) of our college degrees: while I considered hanging up my two diplomas, she believed that having a bachelor's was so standard and insubstantial,

> "Nowadays, holding a college degree (or two) seems like the norm."

only a professional degree is worth hanging up and showing off. Nowadays, holding a college degree (or two) seems like the norm; it's not a very outstanding feat.

However, I'd like to defend the power of earning a college degree. Although holding a degree isn't as powerful as it was in previous decades, stats still show that those who earn bachelor's degrees are likely to earn twice as much as those who don't. Also, only 27 percent of Americans can say they have a bachelor's degree or higher. Realistically, having a college degree will likely mean a comfortable living and the opportunity to move up at work and in life.

Personally, my degrees validate my mother's choice to leave Vietnam. She moved here for opportunity. She wasn't able to attend college here or in Vietnam or choose her occupation. But her hard work has allowed her children to become the first generation of Americans in the family to earn college degrees: she gave us the ability to make choices she wasn't privileged to make. Being the fourth and final kid to earn my degree in my family, my mom can now boast about having educated children who are making a name for themselves (a son who is a computer-superstar, a second son and future dentist studying at UCSF, another son who is earning his MBA and manages at Mattel, and a daughter who is thankful to have three brothers to mooch off of).

For me, this degree symbolizes my family being able to make and take the ⁶ opportunities that we've been given in America, despite growing up with gang members down my street and a drug dealer across from my house. This degree will also mean that my children will have more opportunities because of my education, insight, knowledge, and support.

Even though a college degree isn't worth as much as it was in the past, ⁷ it still shows that I—along with my fellow graduates and the 27 percent of Americans with a bachelor's or higher—will have opportunities unheard of a generation before us, showing everyone how important education is for our lives and our futures.

⊘AT ISSUE: SOURCES FOR STRUCTURING AN ARGUMENT

1. What purpose do the first two paragraphs of this essay serve? Do you think they are necessary? Do you think they are interesting? How else could Le have opened her essay?

2. Where does Le state her thesis? Do you think she should have stated it more forcefully? Can you suggest a more effectively worded thesis statement for this essay?

3. In paragraph 3, Le summarizes an opposing argument. Paraphrase this argument. How does she refute it? Can you think of other arguments against her position that she should have addressed?

4. In paragraphs 5–6, Le includes an appeal to the emotions. Does she offer any other kind of supporting evidence? If so, where? What other kinds of evidence do you think she should include? Why?

5. Echoing a point she made in paragraph 4, Le begins her conclusion with "Even though a college degree isn't worth as much as it was in the past, . . ." Does this concluding statement undercut her argument, or is the information presented in paragraph 4 enough to address this potential problem?

This essay appeared on CNN.com on June 3, 2011.

COLLEGE IS A WASTE OF TIME

DALE STEPHENS

I have been awarded a golden ticket to the heart of Silicon Valley: the Thiel 1
Fellowship. The catch? For two years, I cannot be enrolled as a full-time student at an academic institution. For me, that's not an issue; I believe higher
education is broken.

I left college two months ago because it rewards conformity rather than 2
independence, competition rather than collaboration, regurgitation rather
than learning, and theory rather than application. Our creativity, innovation,
and curiosity are schooled out of us.

Failure is punished instead of seen as a learning opportunity. We think of 3
college as a stepping-stone to success rather than a means to gain knowledge.
College fails to empower us with the skills necessary to become productive
members of today's global entrepreneurial economy.

College is expensive. The College Board Policy Center found that the cost of 4
public university tuition is about 3.6 times higher today than it was 30 years ago,
adjusted for inflation. In the book *Academically Adrift*, sociology professors
Richard Arum and Josipa Roksa say that 36 percent of college graduates showed
no improvement in critical thinking, complex reasoning, or writing after four
years of college. Student loan debt in the United States, unforgivable in the case
of bankruptcy, outpaced credit card debt in 2010 and will top $1 trillion in 2011.

Fortunately, there are 5
productive alternatives to
college. Becoming the next
Mark Zuckerberg or mastering the phrase "Would you
like fries with that?" are not the only options.

> "Fortunately, there are productive alternatives to college."

The success of people who never completed or attended college makes us 6
question whether what we need to learn is taught in school. Learning by doing—in
life, not classrooms—is the best way to turn constant iteration into true innovation. We can be productive members of society without submitting to academic or
corporate institutions. We are the disruptive generation creating the "free agent
economy" built by entrepreneurs, creatives, consultants, and small businesses
envisioned by Daniel Pink in his book, *A Whole New Mind: Why Right Brainers
Will Rule the Future.*

We must encourage young people to consider paths outside college. 7
That's why I'm leading UnCollege: a social movement empowering individuals to take their education beyond the classroom. Imagine if millions of my
peers copying their professors' words verbatim started problem-solving in the
real world. Imagine if we started our own companies, our own projects, and

our own organizations. Imagine if we went back to learning as practiced in French salons, gathering to discuss, challenge, and support each other in improving the human condition.

A major function of college is to signal to potential employers that one is 8 qualified to work. The Internet is replacing this signaling function. Employers are recruiting on LinkedIn, Facebook, StackOverflow, and Behance. People are hiring on Twitter, selling their skills on Google, and creating personal portfolios to showcase their talent. Because we can document our accomplishments and have them socially validated with tools such as LinkedIn Recommendations, we can turn experiences into opportunity. As more and more people graduate from college, employers are unable to discriminate among job seekers based on a college degree and can instead hire employees based on their talents.

Of course, some people want a formal education. I do not think everyone 9 should leave college, but I challenge my peers to consider the opportunity cost of going to class. If you want to be a doctor, going to medical school is a wise choice. I do not recommend keeping cadavers in your garage. On the other hand, what else could you do during your next 50-minute class? How many e-mails could you answer? How many lines of code could you write?

Some might argue that college dropouts will sit in their parents' base- 10 ments playing *Halo 2*, doing Jell-O shots, and smoking pot. These are valid but irrelevant concerns, for the people who indulge in drugs and alcohol do so before, during, and after college. It's not a question of authorities; it's a question of priorities. We who take our education outside and beyond the classroom understand how actions build a better world. We will change the world regardless of the letters after our names.

⊙ AT ISSUE: SOURCES FOR STRUCTURING AN ARGUMENT

1. In paragraph 1, Stephens says, "I believe higher education is broken." Is this statement his essay's thesis? Explain.

2. List Stephens's criticisms of college education.

3. Why does Stephens begin by introducing himself as a winner of a Thiel Fellowship? Is this introductory strategy an appeal to *logos*, *ethos*, or *pathos*? Explain.

4. List the evidence that Stephens uses to support his position. Do you think this essay needs more supporting evidence? If so, what kind of support would you suggest Stephens add?

5. In paragraphs 9 and 10, Stephens considers possible arguments against his thesis. What are these opposing arguments? Does he refute them effectively?

6. Throughout this essay, Stephens uses the pronoun *we* (as well as the pronoun *I*). Do these first-person pronouns refer to college students in general? To certain kinds of students? To Thiel fellows? Explain.

This article first appeared in the online publication "Examining the Value of a College Degree," produced by PayScale.

COLLEGE IS WORTH IT—SOME OF THE TIME

BRIDGET TERRY LONG

Is it still worthwhile to attend college? This has been a constant question, and as an economist and higher education researcher, I can wholeheartedly say yes. The data are clear: individuals with at least some college education make more money than those with only a high school degree. And let us not forget about the non-monetary returns, such as better working conditions, lower rates of disability, and increased civic engagement. 1

However, the conversation has become more complicated as research has pointed to another important fact: yes, college is worth it, but not always. We no longer think that all educations are financially good investments—the specifics matter. The answer for any student depends upon three important factors: the college attended, the field of study, and the cost or debt taken. 2

> "We no longer think that all educations are financially good investments—the specifics matter."

First, the college a student attends makes a difference, as we can see from the Payscale data. But these recent data underscore a longer-term trend. In a 1999 study, a co-author and I documented increasing inequality among college-educated workers.[1] While those near the top of the income distribution (i.e., the 90th percentile) experienced larger returns to their educations over time, after accounting for inflation, those near the bottom of the distribution (i.e., the 10th percentile) earned less in 1995 than 1972. Our examination of the reasons behind these changes highlights the important role of increasing segregation in higher education, where the top students have become more and more concentrated at institutions with much greater resources. The colleges rated "most competitive" often spend more than three times per student than "less competitive" colleges. 3

However, selectivity rating alone does not necessarily predict which schools have the highest rates of student success. A 2009 study documents the fact that graduation rates differ not only by college selectivity but also within a selectivity group. For example, among colleges rated as "very competitive," six-year graduation rates averaged from 30 percent for the bottom 10 schools to 82 percent for the top 10 schools.[2] Selectivity does not necessarily guarantee high levels of degree completion. 4

---

[1]Hoxby, Caroline and Bridget Terry Long. (1999) "Explaining Rising Inequality among the College-Educated." National Bureau of Economic Research (NBER) Working Paper No. 6873.
[2]Hess, Frederick M., Mark Schneider, Kevin Carey, and Andrew P. Kelly. (2009) *Diplomas and Dropouts: Which Colleges Actually Graduate Their Students (and Which Don't)*. American Enterprise Institute.

A large part of the problem to understanding which colleges are good 5 investments is the lack of good measures of college quality. Most existing measures rely heavily on the academic achievements of students before they even step foot on the college campus. Meanwhile, there are few measures of the quality of the postsecondary learning experience or the value-added to the student. Hence, we rely on indicators such as earnings and loan default rates. While it is helpful to have this information to establish minimum thresholds of what might be a financially worthwhile education, they are not sufficient to help students compare possible colleges and make the decision about where they, as individuals, might maximize their benefits.

The second thing that increasingly matters in college investments is the 6 field of study. While many students do not work in the field of their college major, typically, students majoring in engineering and the sciences reap the largest benefits. However, income is not the only thing that varies by major: as emphasized by the Great Recession, unemployment rates also differ by field of study. Interestingly, although education majors may not make the most money, they have among the lowest unemployment rates.

The first two factors, the chosen college and major, focus on potential benefits, 7 but those benefits must be compared to costs to determine whether a college education is worthwhile. We focus most of our attention on price and debt load as a measure of the burden of college costs. Debt is a reality of higher education today, and some debt is fine if it makes possible a beneficial educational investment. However, the level of debt that is reasonable depends greatly on the school attended and major. One might judge $10,000 of total debt for an engineering degree to be fine, while the opposite would be true for a six-week certificate program.

Unfortunately, students typically have such poor counseling on how much 8 debt is appropriate given their plans, and with large levels of unmet financial need, many turn to multiple sources of debt, such as credit cards and private loans, without fully understanding how this will affect them over the longer term. Moreover, recent graduates (or dropouts) fresh out of school have little appreciation for how their investments may pay off 10 years from now when their current reality is living at home with their parents. In other words, it's difficult to internalize long-term benefits when the costs are so heavily weighed up front.

Ultimately, knowing whether college is a good investment depends on 9 which college, which major, at what price (or debt). Looking at the averages is no longer as meaningful, given the importance of match for an individual student with specific interests, talents, and resources. And while I would underscore the fact that for the vast majority of students, most combinations of college/major/debt they would choose are worthwhile investments, we have reached a time when the benefits of college may not far exceed the costs for increasing numbers of students.

Even if only a small percentage of investments are "bad"—ones in which 10 the college attended has low levels of success and gives credentials with little value while making students take out large amounts of debt—we have reached an enrollment level in which a small percentage translates into thousands and thousands of students each year. And that is a problem that cannot be ignored.

⊘ AT ISSUE: SOURCES FOR STRUCTURING AN ARGUMENT

1. In paragraph 1, Long introduces herself as "an economist and higher education researcher." Why do you think she does this? Is she appealing here to *logos*, *ethos*, or *pathos*?

2. Long begins her essay with a question. What attitude toward college tuition does she assume her readers have? How can you tell? How else might she have opened her discussion?

3. According to Long, in what sense has "the conversation [about whether college is a worthwhile investment] become more complicated" (para. 2)? What "three important factors" does she consider?

4. Outline the structure of this essay, filling in the template below with Long's thesis statement and key points.

   Thesis statement:

   Support

   ■ *First important factor:* _____

   ■ *Second important factor:* _____

   ■ *Third important factor:* _____

5. In paragraphs 9 and 10, what does Long conclude about the value of a college education? What reservations does she have? How does the discussion in these paragraphs answer the question she asks in paragraph 1?

6. Could Long's entire essay be seen as a refutation of the position she takes in the essay's first paragraph? Explain.

7. If Long were making recommendations about how to solve the "problem that cannot be ignored" (10), what do you think she might recommend?

This economic letter was originally posted by the Federal Reserve Bank of San Francisco at www.frbsf.org, where it appeared on May 5, 2014.

IS IT STILL WORTH GOING TO COLLEGE?

MARY C. DALY AND LEILA BENGALI

Media accounts documenting the rising cost of a college education and rela- 1 tively bleak job prospects for new college graduates have raised questions about whether a four-year college degree is still the right path for the average American. In this *Economic Letter*, we examine whether going to college remains a worthwhile investment. Using U.S. survey data, we compare annual labor earnings of college graduates with those of individuals with only a high school diploma. The data show college graduates outearn their high school counterparts as much as in past decades. Comparing the earnings benefits of college with the costs of attending a four-year program, we find that college is still worth it. This means that, for the average student, tuition costs for the majority of college education opportunities in the United States can be recouped by age 40, after which college graduates continue to earn a return on their investment in the form of higher lifetime wages.

Earnings Outcomes by Educational Attainment

A common way to track the value of going to college is to estimate a college 2 earnings premium, which is the amount college graduates earn relative to high school graduates. We measure earnings for each year as the annual labor income for the prior year, adjusted for inflation using the consumer price index (CPI-U), reported in 2011 dollars. The earnings premium refers to the difference between average annual labor income for high school and college graduates. We use data on household heads and partners from the Panel Study of Income Dynamics (PSID). The PSID is a longitudinal study that follows individuals living in the United States over a long time span. The survey began in 1968 and now has more than 40 years of data including educational attainment and labor market income. To focus on the value of a college degree relative to less education, we exclude people with more than a four-year degree.

Figure 1 shows the earnings premium relative to high school graduates 3 for individuals with a four-year college degree and for those with some college but no four-year degree. The payoff from a degree is apparent. Although the premium has fluctuated over time, at its lowest in 1980 it was about $15,750, meaning that individuals with a four-year college degree earned about 43 percent more on average than those with only a high school degree. In 2011, the latest data available in our sample, college graduates earned on average about $20,050 (61 percent) more per year than high school graduates.

Over the entire sample period the college earnings premium has averaged about $20,300 (57 percent) per year. The premium is much smaller, although not zero, for workers with some college but no four-year degree.

Figure 1: Earnings Premium over High School Education

2011 $ (000)

Data from: PSID and authors' calculations. Premium defined as difference in mean annual labor income. Blue bars denote NBER recession dates.

A potential shortcoming of the results in Figure 1 is that they combine the   4
earnings outcomes for all college graduates, regardless of when they earned a degree. This can be misleading if the value from a college education has varied across groups from different graduation decades, called "cohorts." To examine whether the college earnings premium has changed from one generation to the next, we take advantage of the fact that the PSID follows people over a long period of time, which allows us to track college graduation dates and subsequent earnings.

Using these data we compute the college earnings premium for three col-   5
lege graduate cohorts, namely those graduating in the 1950s–60s, the 1970s–80s, and the 1990s–2000s. The premium measures the difference between the average annual earnings of college graduates and high school graduates over their work lives. To account for the fact that high school graduates gain work experience during the four years they are not in college, we compare earnings of college graduates in each year since graduation to earnings of high school graduates in years since graduation plus four. We also adjust the estimates for any large annual fluctuations by using a three-year centered moving average, which plots a specific year as the average of earnings from that year, the year before, and the year after.

Figure 2 shows that the college earnings premium has risen consistently 6 across cohorts. Focusing on the most recent college graduates (1990s–2000s) there is little evidence that the value of a college degree has declined over time, and it has even risen somewhat for graduates five to ten years out of school.

Figure 2: College Earnings Premium by Graduation Decades

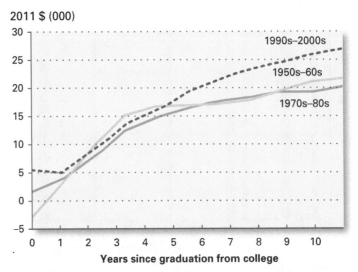

Data from: PSID and authors' calculations. Premium defined as difference in mean annual labor income of college graduates in each year since graduation and earnings of high school graduates in years since graduation plus four. Values are three-year centered moving averages of annual premiums.

The figure also shows that the gap in earnings between college and high 7 school graduates rises over the course of a worker's life. Comparing the earnings gap upon graduation with the earnings gap 10 years out of school illustrates this. For the 1990s–2000s cohort the initial gap was about $5,400, and in 10 years this gap had risen to about $26,800. Other analysis confirms that college graduates start with higher annual earnings, indicated by an initial earnings gap, and experience more rapid growth in earnings than members of their age cohort with only a high school degree. This evidence tells us that the value of a college education rises over a worker's life.

Of course, some of the variation in earnings between those with and with- 8 out a college degree could reflect other differences. Still, these simple estimates are consistent with a large and rigorous literature documenting the substantial premium earned by college graduates (Barrow and Rouse 2005, Card 2001, Goldin and Katz 2008, and Cunha, Karahan, and Soares 2011). The main message from these and similar calculations is that on average the value of college is high and not declining over time.

Finally, it is worth noting that the benefits of college over high school also depend on employment, where college graduates also have an advantage. High school graduates consistently face unemployment rates about twice as high as those for college graduates, according to Bureau of Labor Statistics data. When the labor market takes a turn for the worse, as during recessions, workers with lower levels of education are especially hard-hit (Hoynes, Miller, and Schaller 2012). Thus, in good times and in bad, those with only a high school education face a lower probability of employment, on top of lower average earnings once employed.

The Cost of College

Although the value of college is apparent, deciding whether it is worthwhile means weighing the value against the costs of attending. Indeed, much of the debate about the value of college stems not from the lack of demonstrated benefit but from the overwhelming cost. A simple way to measure the costs against the benefits is to find the breakeven amount of annual tuition that would make the average student indifferent between going to college versus going directly to the workforce after high school.

> "Although the value of college is apparent, deciding whether it is worthwhile means weighing the value against the costs of attending."

To simplify the analysis, we assume that college lasts four years, students enter college directly from high school, annual tuition is the same all four years, and attendees have no earnings while in school. To focus on more recent experiences yet still have enough data to measure earnings since graduation, we use the last two decades of graduates (1990s and 2000s) and again smooth our estimates by using three-year centered moving averages.

We calculate the cost of college as four years of tuition plus the earnings missed from choosing not to enter the workforce. To estimate what students would have received had they worked, we use the average annual earnings of a high school graduate zero, one, two, and three years since graduation.

To determine the benefit of going to college, we use the difference between the average annual earnings of a college graduate with zero, one, two, three, and so on, years of experience and the average annual earnings of a high school graduate with four, five, six, seven, and so on years of experience. Because the costs of college are paid today but the benefits accrue over many future years when a dollar earned will be worth less, we discount future earnings by 6.67 percent, which is the average rate on an AAA bond from 1990 to 2011.

With these pieces in place, we can calculate the breakeven amount of tuition for the average college graduate for any number of years; allowing more time to regain the costs will increase our calculated tuition ceiling.

If we assume that accumulated earnings between college graduates and non-graduates will equalize 20 years after graduating from high school (at age 38), the resulting estimate for breakeven annual tuition would be about $21,200. This amount may seem low compared to the astronomical costs for a year at some prestigious institutions; however, about 90 percent of students at public four-year colleges and about 20 percent of students at private nonprofit four-year colleges faced lower annual inflation-adjusted published tuition and fees in 2013–14 (College Board 2013). Although some colleges cost more, there is no definitive evidence that they produce far superior results for all students (Dale and Krueger 2011).

Table 1 shows more examples of maximum tuitions and the corresponding 16 percent of students who pay less for different combinations of breakeven years and discount rates. Note that the tuition estimates are those that make the costs and benefits of college equal. So, tuition amounts lower than our estimates make going to college strictly better in terms of earnings than not going to college.

Table 1: Maximum Tuitions by Breakeven Age and Discount Rates

	Breakeven age	
	33 (15 yrs after HS)	38 (20 yrs after HS)
Accumulated earnings with constant annual premium	$880,134	$830,816
Discount rate	Maximum tuition (% students paying less)	
5%	$14,385 (53–62%)	$29,111 (82–85%)
6.67%*	$9,869 (37–53%)	$21,217 (69–73%)
9%	$4,712 (0–6%)	$12,653 (53–62%)

*Average AAA bond rate 1990–2011 (rounded; Moody's).

Data from: PSID, College Board, and authors' calculations. Premia held constant 15 or 20 years after high school (HS) graduation. Percent range gives lower and upper bounds of the percent of full-time undergraduates at four-year institutions who faced lower annual inflation-adjusted published tuition and fees in 2013–14.

Although other individual factors might affect the net value of a college 17 education, earning a degree clearly remains a good investment for most young people. Moreover, once that investment is paid off, the extra income from the college earnings premium continues as a net gain to workers with a college degree. If we conservatively assume that the annual premium stays around $28,650, which is the premium 20 years after high school graduation for graduates in the 1990s–2000s, and accrues until the Social Security normal retirement age of 67, the college graduate would have made about $830,800 more than the high school graduate. These extra earnings can be spent, saved, or reinvested to pay for the college tuition of the graduate's children.

Conclusion

Although there are stories of people who skipped college and achieved finan- 18 cial success, for most Americans the path to higher future earnings involves a four-year college degree. We show that the value of a college degree remains high, and the average college graduate can recover the costs of attending in less than 20 years. Once the investment is paid for, it continues to pay dividends through the rest of the worker's life, leaving college graduates with substantially higher lifetime earnings than their peers with a high school degree. These findings suggest that redoubling the efforts to make college more accessible would be time and money well spent.

References

Barrow, L., and Rouse, C.E. (2005). "Does college still pay?" *The Economist's Voice* 2(4), pp. 1–8.

Card, D. (2001). "Estimating the return to schooling: progress on some persistent econometric problems." *Econometrica* 69(5), pp. 1127–1160.

College Board. (2013). "Trends in College Pricing 2013."

Cunha, F., Karahan, F., and Soares, I. (2011). "Returns to Skills and the College Premium." *Journal of Money, Credit, and Banking* 43(5), pp. 39–86.

Dale, S., and Krueger, A. (2011). "Estimating the Return to College Selectivity over the Career Using Administrative Earnings Data." *NBER Working Paper* 17159.

Goldin, C., and Katz, L. (2008). *The Race between Education and Technology.* Cambridge and London: The Belknap Press of Harvard University Press.

Hoynes, H., Miller, D., and Schaller, J. (2012). "Who Suffers During Recessions?" *Journal of Economic Perspectives* 26(3), pp. 27–48.

⊖ AT ISSUE: SOURCES FOR STRUCTURING AN ARGUMENT

1. Why does the title of this essay include the word "still"? What does *still* imply in this context?

2. This essay is an "economic letter" from the Federal Reserve Bank of San Francisco, and its language is more technical, and more math- and business-oriented, than that of the other readings in this chapter. In addition, this reading selection *looks* somewhat different from the others. What specific format features set this reading apart from others in the chapter?

3. What kind of supporting evidence do the writers use? Do you think they should have included any other kinds of support—for example, expert opinion? Why or why not?

4. In paragraph 10, the writers make a distinction between the "value of college" and the question of whether a college education is "worth-while." Explain the distinction they make here.

5. For the most part, this report appeals to *logos* by presenting factual information. Does it also include appeals to *pathos* or *ethos*? If so, where? If not, should it have included these appeals?

TEMPLATE FOR STRUCTURING AN ARGUMENT

Write a one-paragraph argument in which you take a position on the topic of whether a college education is a good investment. Follow the template below, filling in the lines to create your argument.

Whether or not a college education is worth the money is a controversial topic. Some people believe that _____

_____

_____. Others challenge this position, claiming that _____

_____.

However, _____

_____. Although both sides of this issue have merit, it seems clear that a college education (is/is not) a worthwhile investment because _____

_____.

 EXERCISE 1.2

Interview two classmates on the topic of whether a college education is a worthwhile investment. Revise the one-paragraph argument that you drafted above so that it includes your classmates' views on the issue.

 EXERCISE 1.3

Write an essay on the topic "Is a College Education Worth the Money?" Cite the readings on pages 33–54, and be sure to document your sources and to include a works-cited page. (See Chapter 10 for information on documenting sources.)

 EXERCISE 1.4

Review the four-point checklist on page 27, and apply each question to your essay. Does your essay include all four elements of an argumentative essay? Add any missing elements. Then, label your essay's thesis statement, evidence, refutation of opposing arguments, and concluding statement.

 EXERCISE 1.5

Read the short essay that follows. What, if anything, do you think should be added to the writer's discussion to make it more convincing? Should anything be deleted or changed? Incorporating what you have learned about the structure and content of an effective argument, write a one-paragraph response to the essay.

This essay appeared on Businessweek.com in March 2011.

PRACTICAL EXPERIENCE TRUMPS FANCY DEGREES

TONY BRUMMEL

So you got great grades and earned your bachelor's degree? Congratulations. 1
You may have been better off failing college and then starting a venture and
figuring out why you didn't pass your classroom tests.

Being successful in business is absolutely not contingent on having a bach- 2
elor's degree—or any other type of degree, for that matter. A do-or-die work
ethic, passion, unwavering persistence, and vision mean more than anything
that can be taught in a classroom. How many college professors who teach
business have actually started a business?

I am the sole owner of the top independent rock   "I have blazed   3
record label (according to Nielsen-published market
share). Historically, the music industry is thought of   my own trail."
as residing in New York City, Los Angeles, and
Nashville. But I have blazed my own trail, segregating my business in its own
petri dish here in Chicago. I started the business as a part-time venture in 1989
with $800 in seed capital. In 2009, Victory Records grossed $20 million. We've
released more than 500 albums, including platinum-selling records for the
groups Taking Back Sunday and Hawthorne Heights.

Because I never went to college and didn't automatically have industry 4
contacts, I had to learn all of the business fundamentals through trial and error
when I started my own company. The skills I learned on my own have carried
me through 20 years of business. Making mistakes forces one to learn.

If you have a brand that people care about and loyal, hard-working 5
employees coupled with a robust network of smart financial advisers, fellow
entrepreneurs, and good legal backup, you will excel. There are plenty of people with degrees and MBAs who could read the books and earn their diplomas
but cannot apply what they learned to building a successful enterprise.

⊙ EXERCISE 1.6

Study the image that opens this chapter. What argument could it suggest
about the issue of whether a college education is worth the money?

Reading and Responding to Arguments

2

Thinking and Reading Critically

AT ISSUE

Do Violent Media Images Trigger Violent Behavior?

In recent years, the popular media seem to have become increasingly violent. This is particularly true of visuals in video games and on some Internet sites, but graphically violent images also appear regularly in films, on TV, in comic books, and even in newspapers. Some research has suggested that these violent images can have a negative effect on those who view them, particularly on adolescents and young children. In fact, some media critics believe that these violent images have helped to create an increasingly violent culture, which in turn has inspired young people to commit violent crimes (including school shootings) such as the massacres at Virginia Tech in 2007 and Newtown, Connecticut, in 2012. The shooter who killed 12 people

and injured 58 others at the premiere of *The Dark Knight Rises* in Aurora, Colorado, on July 20, 2012, was a devotee of violent role-playing video games, and some news reports emphasized that fact. Other observers, however, argue that violent media images are not to blame for such events—and that, in fact, these images may provide a safe outlet for aggression.

In this chapter and in the chapter that follows, you will be asked to read essays and study images that shed light on the relationship between media violence and violent behavior. In the process, you will learn critical-thinking and active reading strategies that will help you learn to examine and interpret texts and images.

Now that you understand the structure of an argumentative essay, you can turn your attention to reading arguments more closely. These arguments may be the subject of class discussion, or they may be source material for the essays you write. In any case, you will need to know how to get the most out of reading them.

Thinking Critically

When you **think critically**, you do not simply accept ideas at face value. Instead, you question these ideas, analyzing them in order to understand them better. You also challenge their underlying assumptions and form your own judgments about them. Throughout this book, discussions and readings encourage you to think critically. The box below shows you where in this text to find material that will help you develop your critical-thinking skills.

USING CRITICAL-THINKING SKILLS

Reading (see Chapter 2): When you read a text, you use critical-thinking skills to help you understand what the text says and what it suggests. You ask questions and look for answers, challenging the ideas you read and probing for information. *Previewing, highlighting,* and *annotating* are active reading strategies that require you to use critical-thinking skills.

Analyzing Visual Texts (see Chapter 3): When you examine an image, you use critical-thinking skills to help you understand what you are seeing, using previewing, highlighting, and annotating to help you analyze the image and interpret its persuasive message.

Writing a Rhetorical Analysis (see Chapter 4): When you write a rhetorical analysis of a text, you use critical-thinking skills to analyze its elements and to help you understand how the writer uses various appeals and rhetorical strategies to influence readers. Critical-thinking skills can also help you to understand the argument's context. Finally, you use critical-thinking skills to evaluate the overall effectiveness of the argument.

Analyzing an Argument's Logic (see Chapter 5): When you analyze an argument's logic, you use critical-thinking skills to help you understand the relationships among ideas and the form the argument takes as well as to determine whether its conclusions are both valid and true. You also use critical-thinking skills to identify any **logical fallacies** that may undermine the argument.

Writing an Essay (see Chapter 7): When you plan an essay, you use critical-thinking skills to probe a topic, to consider what you already know and what you need to find out, to identify your essay's main idea, and to decide how to support it—that is, which ideas to include and how to arrange them. As you draft and revise, you use critical-thinking skills to evaluate your supporting evidence, to make sure your arguments are reasonable and fair, and to decide whether ideas are arranged effectively within paragraphs and in the essay as a whole. *Freewriting, brainstorming, clustering,* and *outlining* are activities that require you to use critical-thinking skills.

Refuting Opposing Arguments (see Chapter 7): When you refute opposing arguments, you use critical-thinking skills to identify and evaluate arguments against your position—and to challenge or possibly argue against them.

Evaluating Sources (see Chapter 8): When you evaluate sources, you use critical-thinking skills to assess your sources in terms of their *accuracy, credibility, objectivity,* and *comprehensiveness* and to determine whether a source is trustworthy and appropriate for your purpose and audience.

Summarizing (see Chapter 9): When you summarize a passage, you use critical-thinking skills to identify the writer's main idea.

Paraphrasing (see Chapter 9): When you paraphrase a passage, you use critical-thinking skills to identify the writer's main idea, the most important supporting details and examples, and the ways in which key ideas are related.

Synthesizing (see Chapter 9): When you synthesize, you use critical-thinking skills to analyze sources and integrate them with your own ideas.

Reading Critically

When you read an argument, you should approach it with a critical eye. Contrary to what you may think, **reading critically** does not mean arguing with every idea you encounter. What it does mean is commenting on, questioning, and evaluating these ideas.

As a critical reader, you do not simply accept that what you are reading is true. Instead, you assess the accuracy of the facts in your sources, and you consider whether opinions are convincingly supported by evidence. You try to judge the appropriateness and reliability of a writer's sources, and you evaluate the scope and depth of the evidence and the relevance of that evidence to the topic. You also consider opposing arguments carefully, weighing them against the arguments developed in your sources. Finally, you watch out for possible **bias** in your sources—and you work hard to keep your own biases in check.

GUIDELINES FOR READING CRITICALLY

As a critical reader, you need to read carefully, keeping the following guidelines in mind:

- Assess the accuracy of a source's information.
- Be sure opinions are supported convincingly.
- Evaluate the supporting evidence.
- Consider opposing arguments.
- Be on the lookout for bias—in your sources and in yourself.

 LaunchPad macmillan learning   For more practice, see the LearningCurve on Reading Critically in the LaunchPad for *Practical Argument.*

Becoming an Active Reader

Reading critically means being an active rather than a passive reader. Being an **active reader** means participating in the reading process by taking the time to preview a source and then to read it carefully, highlighting and annotating it. This process will prepare you to discuss the source with others and to respond in writing to what you have read.

Previewing

When you approach an argument for the first time, you **preview** it, skimming the argument to help you form a general impression of the writer's position on the issue, the argument's key supporting points, and the context for the writer's remarks.

Begin by looking at the title, the first paragraph (which often contains a thesis statement or overview), and the last paragraph (which often includes a concluding statement or a summary of the writer's key points). Also look at the topic sentences of the essay's body paragraphs. In addition, note any headings, words set in boldface or italic type, and bulleted or numbered lists in the body of the argument. If the argument includes visuals—charts, tables, graphs, photos, and so on—look at them as well. Finally, if an argument includes a headnote or background on the author or on the text, be sure to read this material. It can help you to understand the context in which the author is writing.

When you have finished previewing the argument, you should have a good general sense of what the writer wants to communicate.

Close Reading

Now, you are ready to read through the argument more carefully. As you read, look for words and phrases that help to shape the structure of the argument and signal the arrangement of the writer's ideas. These words and phrases will help you understand the flow of ideas as well as the content and emphasis of the argument.

COMPREHENSION CLUES

- Phrases that signal emphasis (the *primary* reason, the *most important* problem)

- Repeated words and phrases

- Words and phrases that signal addition (*also, in addition, furthermore*)

- Words and phrases that signal time sequence (*first, after that, next, then, finally*)

- Words and phrases that identify causes and effects (*because, as a result, for this reason*)

- Words and phrases that introduce examples (*for example, for instance*)

- Words and phrases that signal comparison (*likewise, similarly, in the same way*)

- Words and phrases that signal contrast (*although, in contrast, on the other hand*)

- Words and phrases that signal contradiction (*however, on the contrary*)

- Words and phrases that signal a move from general to specific (*in fact, specifically, in other words*)

- Words and phrases that introduce summaries or conclusions (*to sum up, in conclusion*)

⊖ EXERCISE 2.1

"Violent Media Is Good for Kids" is an essay by Gerard Jones, a comic book writer and author of several books about popular media. In this essay, which begins on the following page, Jones argues that violent comic books and video games serve a useful function for young people.

In preparation for class discussion and other activities that will be assigned later in this chapter, preview the essay. Then, read it carefully, and answer the questions that follow it.

This article appeared in *Mother Jones* on June 28, 2000.

VIOLENT MEDIA IS GOOD FOR KIDS

GERARD JONES

At 13 I was alone and afraid. Taught by my well-meaning, progressive, English-teacher parents that violence was wrong, that rage was something to be overcome and cooperation was always better than conflict, I suffocated my deepest fears and desires under a nice-boy persona. Placed in a small, experimental school that was wrong for me, afraid to join my peers in their bumptious rush into adolescent boyhood, I withdrew into passivity and loneliness. My parents, not trusting the violent world of the late 1960s, built a wall between me and the crudest elements of American pop culture.

A scene from Gerard Jones and Will Jacobs's comic book *Monsters from Outer Space.*
© Gerard Jones, Gene Ha, Will Jacobs.

1

2

Then the Incredible Hulk smashed through it.

One of my mother's students con-vinced her that Marvel Comics, despite their apparent juvenility and violence, were in fact devoted to lofty messages of pacifism and tolerance. My mother borrowed some, thinking they'd be good for me. And so they were. But not because they preached lofty messages of benevolence. They were good for me because they were juvenile. And violent.

3

The character who caught me, and freed me, was the Hulk: overgendered and undersocialized, half-naked and half-witted, raging against a frightened world that misunderstood and persecuted him. Suddenly I had a fantasy self to carry my stifled rage and buried desire for power. I had a fantasy self who was a self: unafraid of his desires and the world's disapproval, unhesitating and effective in action. "Puny boy follow Hulk!" roared my fantasy self, and I followed.

4

I followed him to new friends—other sensitive geeks chasing their own inner brutes—and I followed him to the arrogant, self-exposing, self-assertive, superheroic decision to become a writer. Eventually, I left him behind, followed more sophisticated heroes, and finally my own lead along a twisting path to a career and an identity. In my 30s, I found myself writing action movies and

5

comic books. I wrote some Hulk stories, and met the geek-geniuses who created him. I saw my own creations turned into action figures, cartoons, and computer games. I talked to the kids who read my stories. Across generations, genders, and ethnicities I kept seeing the same story: people pulling themselves out of emotional traps by immersing themselves in violent stories. People integrating the scariest, most fervently denied fragments of their psyches into fuller senses of selfhood through fantasies of superhuman combat and destruction.

I have watched my son living the same story—transforming himself into a 6 bloodthirsty dinosaur to embolden himself for the plunge into preschool, a Power Ranger to muscle through a social competition in kindergarten. In the first grade, his friends started climbing a tree at school. But he was afraid: of falling, of the centipedes crawling on the trunk, of sharp branches, of his friends' derision. I took my cue from his own fantasies and read him old Tarzan comics, rich in combat and bright with flashing knives. For two weeks he lived in them. Then he put them aside. And he climbed the tree.

A scene from Gerard Jones and Gene Ha's comic book *Oktane*. © Gerard Jones, Gene Ha, Will Jacobs.

But all the while, especially in the wake of 7 the recent burst of school shootings, I heard pop psychologists insisting that violent stories are harmful to kids, heard teachers begging parents to keep their kids away from "junk culture," heard a guilt-stricken friend with a son who loved Pokémon lament, "I've turned into the bad mom who lets her kid eat sugary cereal and watch cartoons!"

That's when I started the research. 8

"Fear, greed, power-hunger, rage: these 9 are aspects of our selves that we try not to experience in our lives but often want, even need, to experience vicariously through stories of others," writes Melanie Moore, Ph.D., a psychologist who works with urban teens. "Children need violent entertainment in order to explore the inescapable feelings that they've been taught to deny, and to reintegrate those feelings into a more whole, more complex, more resilient selfhood."

Moore consults to public schools and local 10 governments, and is also raising a daughter. For the past three years she and I have been studying the ways in which children use violent stories to meet their emotional and developmental needs—and the ways in which adults can help them use those stories healthily. With her help I developed *Power Play*, a program for helping young people improve their self-knowledge and sense of potency through heroic, combative storytelling.

We've found that every aspect of even the trashiest pop-culture story can 11 have its own developmental function. Pretending to have superhuman powers helps children conquer the feelings of powerlessness that inevitably come with being so young and small. The dual-identity concept at the heart of many superhero stories helps kids negotiate the conflicts between the inner self and the public self as they work through the early stages of socialization. Identification with a rebellious, even destructive, hero helps children learn to push back against a modern culture that cultivates fear and teaches dependency.

At its most fundamental level, what we call "creative violence"—head-   12
bonking cartoons, bloody video games, playground karate, toy guns—gives children a tool to master their rage. Children will feel rage. Even the sweetest and most civilized of them, even those whose parents read the better class of literary magazines, will feel rage. The world is uncontrollable and incomprehensible; mastering it is a terrifying, enraging task. Rage can be an energizing emotion, a shot of courage to push us to resist greater threats, take more control, than we ever thought we could. But rage is also the emotion our culture distrusts the most. Most of us are taught early on to fear our own. Through immersion in imaginary combat and identification with a violent protagonist, children engage the rage they've stifled, come to fear it less, and become more capable of utilizing it against life's challenges.

> "Rage can be an energizing emotion."

I knew one little girl who went around exploding with fantasies so violent   13
that other moms would draw her mother aside to whisper, "I think you should know something about Emily. . . ." Her parents were separating, and she was small, an only child, a tomboy at an age when her classmates were dividing sharply along gender lines. On the playground she acted out *Sailor Moon°* fights, and in the classroom she wrote stories about people being stabbed with knives. The more adults tried to control her stories, the more she acted out the roles of her angry heroes: breaking rules, testing limits, roaring threats.

A Japanese cartoon series about magical girls

Then her mother and I started helping her tell her stories. She wrote them,   14
performed them, drew them like comics: sometimes bloody, sometimes tender, always blending the images of pop culture with her own most private fantasies. She came out of it just as fiery and strong, but more self-controlled and socially competent: a leader among her peers, the one student in her class who could truly pull boys and girls together.

The title character of *Oktane* gets nasty.
© Gerard Jones, Gene Ha, Will Jacobs.

I worked with an older girl, a   15
middle-class "nice girl," who held herself together through a chaotic family situation and a tumultuous adolescence with gangsta rap. In the mythologized street violence of Ice T, the rage and strutting of his music and lyrics, she found a theater of the mind in which she could

be powerful, ruthless, invulnerable. She avoided the heavy drug use that sank many of her peers, and flowered in college as a writer and political activist.

I'm not going to argue that violent entertainment is harmless. I think it   16
has helped inspire some people to real-life violence. I am going to argue that it's helped hundreds of people for every one it's hurt, and that it can help far more if we learn to use it well. I am going to argue that our fear of "youth violence" isn't well-founded on reality, and that the fear can do more harm than the reality. We act as though our highest priority is to prevent our children from growing up into murderous thugs—but modern kids are far more likely to grow up too passive, too distrustful of themselves, too easily manipulated.

We send the message to our children in a hundred ways that their craving   17
for imaginary gun battles and symbolic killings is wrong, or at least dangerous. Even when we don't call for censorship or forbid *Mortal Kombat*, we moan to other parents within our kids' earshot about the "awful violence" in the entertainment they love. We tell our kids that it isn't nice to play-fight, or we steer them from some monstrous action figure to a pro-social doll. Even in the most progressive households, where we make such a point of letting children feel what they feel, we rush to substitute an enlightened discussion for the raw material of rageful fantasy. In the process, we risk confusing them about their natural aggression in the same way the Victorians° confused their children about their sexuality. When we try to protect our children from their own feelings and fantasies, we shelter them not against violence but against power and selfhood.

The people who lived during the reign of Victoria (1819–1901), queen of Great Britain and Ireland, who are often associated with prudish behavior.

Identifying the Elements of Argument

1. What is Jones's thesis? Restate it in your own words.

2. What arguments does Jones present as evidence in support of his thesis?

3. What arguments against his position does Jones identify? How does he refute them?

4. Paraphrase Jones's concluding statement.

Highlighting

After you read an argument, read through it again, this time highlighting as you read. When you **highlight**, you use underlining and symbols to identify the essay's most important points. (Note that the word *highlighting* does not necessarily refer to the underlining done with a yellow highlighter pen.) This active reading strategy will help you to understand the writer's ideas and to see connections among those ideas when you reread.

How do you know what to highlight? As a general rule, you look for the same signals that you looked for when you read the essay the first time—for example, the essay's thesis and topic sentences and the words and phrases that identify the writer's intent and emphasis. This time, however, you physically mark these elements and use various symbols to indicate your reactions to them.

> ## SUGGESTIONS FOR HIGHLIGHTING
>
> - Underline key ideas—for example, ideas stated in topic sentences.
>
> - Box or circle words or phrases you want to remember.
>
> - Place a check mark or a star next to an important idea.
>
> - Place a double check mark or double star next to an especially significant idea.
>
> - Draw lines or arrows to connect related ideas.
>
> - Write a question mark near an unfamiliar reference or a word you need to look up.
>
> - Number the writer's key supporting points or examples.

⚙ Here is how a student, Katherine Choi, highlighted the essay "When Life Imitates Video" by John Leo, which appears below. Choi was preparing to write an essay about the effects of media violence on children and adolescents. She began her highlighting by underlining and starring the thesis statement (para. 2). She then circled references to Leo's two key examples, "Colorado massacre" (1) and "Paducah, Ky." (7) and placed question marks beside them to remind herself to find out more about them. In addition, she underlined and starred some particularly important points (2, 8, 9) as well as what she identified as the essay's concluding statement (11).

This essay first appeared in *U.S. News & World Report* on May 3, 1999.

WHEN LIFE IMITATES VIDEO

JOHN LEO

Marching through a large building using various bombs and guns to pick off   1
? victims is a conventional video-game scenario. In the (Colorado massacre,) Dylan Klebold and Eric Harris used pistol-grip shotguns, as in some video-arcade games. The pools of blood, screams of agony, and pleas for mercy must have been familiar—they are featured in some of the newer and more realistic kill-for-kicks games. "With each kill," the *Los Angeles Times* reported, "the

teens cackled and shouted as though playing one of the morbid video games they loved." And they ended their spree by shooting themselves in the head, the final act in the game *Postal*, and, in fact, the only way to end it.

Did the sensibilities created by the modern, video kill games play a role in the Littleton massacre? Apparently so. Note the cool and casual cruelty, the outlandish arsenal of weapons, the cheering and laughing while hunting down victims one by one. All of this seems to reflect the style and feel of the video killing games they played so often.

No, there isn't any direct connection between most murderous games and most murders. And yes, the primary responsibility for protecting children from dangerous games lies with their parents, many of whom like to blame the entertainment industry for their own failings.

But there is a cultural problem here: We are now a society in which the chief form of play for millions of youngsters is making large numbers of people die. Hurting and maiming others is the central fun activity in video games played so addictively by the young. A widely cited survey of 900 fourth-through eighth-grade students found that almost half of the children said their favorite electronic games involve violence. Can it be that all this constant training in make-believe killing has no social effects?

Dress rehearsal. The conventional argument is that this is a harmless activity among children who know the difference between fantasy and reality. But the games are often played by unstable youngsters unsure about the difference. Many of these have been maltreated or rejected and left alone most of the time (a precondition for playing the games obsessively). Adolescent feelings of resentment, powerlessness, and revenge pour into the killing games. In these children, the games can become a dress rehearsal for the real thing.

Psychologist David Grossman of Arkansas State University, a retired Army officer, thinks "point and shoot" video games have the same effect as military strategies used to break down a soldier's aversion to killing. During World War II, only 15 to 20 percent of all American soldiers fired their weapon in battle. Shooting games in which the target is a man-shaped outline, the Army found, made recruits more willing to "make killing a reflex action."

Video games are much more powerful versions of the military's primitive discovery about overcoming the reluctance to shoot. Grossman says Michael Carneal, the schoolboy shooter in Paducah, Ky, showed the effects of video-game lessons in killing. Carneal coolly shot nine times, hitting eight people, five of them in the head or neck. Head shots pay a bonus in many video games. Now the Marine Corps is adapting a version of *Doom*, the hyperviolent game played by one of the Littleton killers, for its own training purposes.

More realistic touches in video games help blur the boundary between fantasy and reality—guns carefully modeled on real ones, accurate-looking wounds, screams, and other sound effects, even the recoil of a heavy rifle. Some newer games seem intent on erasing children's empathy and concern for others. Once the intended victims of video slaughter were mostly gangsters or aliens. Now some games invite players to blow away ordinary people who have done nothing wrong—pedestrians, marching bands, an elderly woman with a walker. In these games, the shooter is not a hero, just a violent sociopath. One ad for a Sony game says: "Get in touch with your gun-toting, testosterone-pumping, cold-blooded murdering side."

These killings are supposed to be taken as harmless over-the-top jokes. 9 But the bottom line is that the young are being invited to enjoy the killing of vulnerable people picked at random. This looks like the final lesson in a course to eliminate any lingering resistance to killing.

SWAT teams and cops now turn up as the intended victims of some 10 video-game killings. This has the effect of exploiting resentments toward law enforcement and making real-life shooting of cops more likely. This sensibility turns up in the hit movie *Matrix*: world-saving hero Keanu Reeves, in a mandatory Goth-style, long black coat packed with countless heavy-duty guns, is forced to blow away huge numbers of uniformed law-enforcement people.

"We have to start worrying about what we are putting into the minds of 11 our young," says Grossman. "Pilots train on flight simulators, drivers on driving simulators, and now we have our children on murder simulators." If we want to avoid more Littleton-style massacres, we will begin taking the social effects of the killing games more seriously.

⊙ EXERCISE 2.2

Look carefully at Katherine Choi's highlighting of John Leo's essay on pages 68–70. How would your own highlighting of this essay be similar to or different from hers?

⊙ EXERCISE 2.3

Reread "Violent Media Is Good for Kids" (pp. 64–67). As you read, highlight the essay by underlining and starring important points, boxing or circling key words, writing question marks beside references that need further explanation, or drawing lines and arrows to connect related ideas.

Annotating

As you highlight, you should also annotate what you are reading. **Annotating** means making notes—of your questions, reactions, and ideas for discussion or writing—in the margins or between the lines. Keeping this kind of informal record of ideas as they occur to you will prepare you for class discussion and provide a useful source of material when you write.

As you read an argument and think critically about what you are reading, use the questions in the following checklist to help you make useful annotations.

CHECKLIST

Questions for Annotating

☐ What issue is the writer focusing on?

☐ Does the writer take a clear stand on this issue?

☐ What is the writer's thesis?

☐ What is the writer's purpose (his or her reason for writing)?

☐ What kind of audience is the writer addressing?

☐ Does the argument appear in a popular periodical or in a scholarly journal?

☐ Does the writer seem to assume readers will agree with the essay's position?

☐ What evidence does the writer use to support the essay's thesis? Does the writer include enough evidence?

☐ Does the writer consider (and refute) opposing arguments?

☐ Do you understand the writer's vocabulary?

☐ Do you understand the writer's references?

☐ Do you agree with the points the writer makes?

☐ Do the views the writer expresses agree or disagree with the views presented in other essays you have read?

⟳ The following pages, which reproduce Katherine Choi's highlighting of John Leo's essay on pages 68–70, also include her marginal annotations. In these annotations, Choi put Leo's thesis and some of his key points into her own words and recorded a few questions that she intended to explore further. She also added notes to clarify his references to two iconic school shootings. Finally, she identified arguments against Leo's position and his refutation of these arguments.

This essay first appeared in *U.S. News & World Report* on May 3, 1999.

WHEN LIFE IMITATES VIDEO

JOHN LEO

Marching through a large building using various bombs and guns to pick off 1 victims is a conventional video-game scenario. In the (Colorado massacre) Dylan Klebold and Eric Harris used pistol-grip shotguns, as in some video-arcade games. The pools of blood, screams of agony, and pleas for mercy must have been familiar—they are featured in some of the newer and more realistic kill-for-kicks games. "With each kill," the *Los Angeles Times* reported, "the teens cackled and shouted as though playing one of the morbid video games they loved." And they ended their spree by shooting themselves in the head, the final act in the game *Postal*, and, in fact, the only way to end it.

Columbine H.S., 1999

Did the sensibilities created by the modern, video kill games play a role 2 in the Littleton massacre? Apparently so. Note the cool and casual cruelty, the outlandish arsenal of weapons, the cheering and laughing while hunting down victims one by one. All of this seems to reflect the style and feel of the video killing games they played so often.

No, there isn't any direct connection between most murderous games and 3 most murders. And yes, the primary responsibility for protecting children from dangerous games lies with their parents, many of whom like to blame the entertainment industry for their own failings.

But there is a cultural problem here: We are now a society in which the 4 chief form of play for millions of youngsters is making large numbers of people die. Hurting and maiming others is the central fun activity in video games played so addictively by the young. A widely cited survey of 900 fourth-through eighth-grade students found that almost half of the children said their favorite electronic games involve violence. Can it be that all this constant training in make-believe killing has no social effects?

Dress rehearsal. The conventional argument is that this is a harmless 5 activity among children who know the difference between fantasy and reality. But the games are often played by unstable youngsters unsure about the difference. Many of these have been maltreated or rejected and left alone most of the time (a precondition for playing the games obsessively). Adolescent feelings of resentment, powerlessness, and revenge pour into the killing games. In these children, the games can become a dress rehearsal for the real thing.

Psychologist David Grossman of Arkansas State University, a retired 6 Army officer, thinks "point and shoot" video games have the same effect as military strategies used to break down a soldier's aversion to killing. During World War II, only 15 to 20 percent of all American soldiers fired their weapon in battle. Shooting games in which the target is a man-shaped outline, the Army found, made recruits more willing to "make killing a reflex action."

Video games are much more powerful versions of the military's primitive 7 discovery about overcoming the reluctance to shoot. Grossman says Michael Carneal, the schoolboy shooter in Paducah, Ky, showed the effects of video-game lessons in killing. Carneal coolly shot nine times, hitting eight people, five of them in the head or neck. Head shots pay a bonus in many video games. Now the Marine Corps is adapting a version of *Doom*, the hyperviolent game played by one of the Littleton killers, for its own training purposes.

More realistic touches in video games help blur the boundary between 8 fantasy and reality—guns carefully modeled on real ones, accurate-looking wounds, screams, and other sound effects, even the recoil of a heavy rifle. Some newer games seem intent on erasing children's empathy and concern for others. Once the intended victims of video slaughter were mostly gangsters or aliens. Now some games invite players to blow away ordinary people who have done nothing wrong—pedestrians, marching bands, an elderly woman with a walker. In these games, the shooter is not a hero, just a violent sociopath.

One ad for a Sony game says: "Get in touch with your gun-toting, testosterone-pumping, cold-blooded murdering side."

These killings are supposed to be taken as harmless over-the-top jokes. But the bottom line is that the young are being invited to enjoy the killing of vulnerable people picked at random. This looks like the final lesson in a course to eliminate any lingering resistance to killing.   9   ✳

SWAT teams and cops now turn up as the intended victims of some video-game killings. This has the effect of exploiting resentments toward law enforcement and making real-life shooting of cops more likely. This sensibility turns up in the hit movie *Matrix*: world-saving hero Keanu Reeves, in a mandatory Goth-style, long black coat packed with countless heavy-duty guns, is forced to blow away huge numbers of uniformed law-enforcement people.   10

"We have to start worrying about what we are putting into the minds of our young," says Grossman. "Pilots train on flight simulators, drivers on driving simulators, and now we have our children on murder simulators." If we want to avoid more Littleton-style massacres, we will begin taking the social effects of the killing games more seriously.   11   *Recommendation for action*

✳

⊃ EXERCISE 2.4

Reread Gerard Jones's "Violent Media Is Good for Kids" (pp. 64–67). As you read, refer to the "Questions for Annotating" checklist (p. 71), and use them as a guide as you write your own reactions and questions in the margins of Jones's essay. In your annotations, note where you agree or disagree with Jones, and briefly explain why. Quickly summarize any points that you think are particularly important. Look up any unfamiliar words or references you have identified, and write down brief definitions or explanations. Think about these annotations as you prepare to discuss the Jones essay in class (and, eventually, to write about it).

⊃ EXERCISE 2.5

Exchange books with another student, and read his or her highlighting and annotating. How are your written responses similar to the other student's? How are they different? Do your classmate's responses help you to see anything new about Jones's essay?

⊃ EXERCISE 2.6

The following letter to the editor of a college newspaper takes a position on the issue of how violent media—in this case, video games—influence young people. Read the letter, highlighting and annotating it.

Now, consider how this letter is similar to and different from Gerard Jones's essay (pp. 64–67). First, identify the writer's thesis, and restate it in your own words. Then, consider the benefits of the violent video games the writer identifies. Are these benefits the same as those Jones identifies?

In paragraph 4, the writer summarizes arguments against her position. Does Jones address any of these same arguments? If so, does he refute them in the same way this writer does? Finally, read the letter's last paragraph. How is this writer's purpose for writing different from Jones's?

This letter to the editor was published on October 22, 2003, in *Ka Leo o Hawai'i*, the student newspaper of the University of Hawaii at Manoa.

DON'T WITHHOLD VIOLENT GAMES

JESSICA ROBBINS

Entertainment and technology have changed. Video games today are more 1 graphic and violent than they were a few years ago. There is a concern about children being influenced by the content of some of these video games. Some states have already passed laws which ban minors from the viewing or purchasing of these video games without an accompanying adult. I believe this law should not exist.

Today's technology has truly enriched our entertainment experience. 2 Today's computer and game consoles are able to simulate shooting, killing, mutilation, and blood through video games. It was such a problem that in 1993 Congress passed a law prohibiting the sale or rental of adult video games to minors. A rating system on games, similar to that placed on movies, was put into place, which I support. This helps to identify the level of violence that a game might have. However, I do not believe that this rating should restrict people of any age from purchasing a game.

Currently there is no significant evidence that supports the argument that 3 violent video games are a major contributing factor in criminal and violent behavior. Recognized universities such as MIT and UCLA described the law as misguided, citing that "most studies and experiments on video games containing violent content have not found adverse effects." In addition, there actually are benefits from playing video games. They provide a safe outlet for aggression and frustration, increased attention performance, along with spatial and coordination skills.

> "[T]here actually are benefits from playing video games."

Some argue that there is research that shows real-life video game play is 4
related to antisocial behavior and delinquency, and that there is need for a law
to prevent children from acting out these violent behaviors. This may be true,
but researchers have failed to indicate that this antisocial and aggressive
behavior is not mostly short-term. We should give children the benefit of the
doubt. Today's average child is competent and intelligent enough to recognize
the difference between the digital representation of a gun and a real 28-inch
military bazooka rocket launcher. They are also aware of the consequences of
using such weapons on real civilians.

Major software companies who create video games should write 5
Congress and protest this law on the basis of a nonexistent correlation
between violence and video games. If the law is modified to not restrict
these games to a particular age group, then these products will not be
unfairly singled out.

⊙ EXERCISE 2.7

The following document, a statement on media violence released by the
American Psychological Association (APA) in 2015, includes a list of
specific recommendations. What position does this document take? Draft
a thesis statement that summarizes this position. Then, consider how
Gerard Jones (pp. 64–67) would respond to this thesis—and to the APA's
specific recommendations.

This document was posted to APA.org to replace the outdated 1985 resolution on violence
on television.

VIOLENCE IN MASS MEDIA
AMERICAN PSYCHOLOGICAL ASSOCIATION

On the recommendation of the Board of Directors and the Board for the 1
Advancement of Psychology in the Public Interest, Council voted to adopt the
following resolution, as amended, as APA policy, replacing the 1985 resolution on television violence:

Whereas the consequences of aggressive and violent behavior have 2
brought human suffering, lost lives, and economic hardship to our society as
well as an atmosphere of anxiety, fear, and mistrust;

Whereas in recent years the level of violence in American society and 3
the level of violence portrayed in television, film, and video have escalated
markedly;

Whereas the great majority of research studies have found a relation 4
between viewing mass media violence and behaving aggressively;

Whereas the conclusion drawn on the basis of over 30 years of research 5
and a sizeable number of experimental and field investigations (Huston, et al.,
1992; NIMH, 1982; Surgeon General, 1972) is that viewing mass media violence leads to increases in aggressive attitudes, values, and behavior, particularly in children, and has a long-lasting effect on behavior and personality,
including criminal behavior;

Whereas viewing violence desensitizes the viewer to violence, resulting in 6
calloused attitudes regarding violence toward others and a decreased likeli-
hood to take action on behalf of a victim when violence occurs;

Whereas viewing violence increases viewers' tendencies for becoming 7
involved with or exposing themselves to violence;

Whereas viewing violence increases fear of becoming a victim of violence, 8
with a resultant increase in self-protective behaviors and mistrust of others;

Whereas many children's television programs and films contain some 9
form of violence, and children's access to adult-oriented media violence is
increasing as a result of new technological advances;

Therefore be it resolved that the American Psychological Association: 10

1. urges psychologists to inform the television and film industry personnel who
    are responsible for violent programming, their commercial advertisers, legisla-
    tors, and the general public that viewing violence in the media produces
    aggressive and violent behavior in children who are susceptible to such effects;

2. encourages parents and other child care providers to monitor and super-
    vise television, video, and film viewing by children;

3. supports the inclusion of clear and easy-to-use warning labels for violent
    material in television, video, and film programs to enable viewers to make
    informed choices;

4. supports the development of technologies that empower viewers to pre-
    vent the broadcast of violent material in their homes;

5. supports the development, implementation, and evaluation of school-
    based programs to educate children and youth regarding means for criti-
    cally viewing, processing, and evaluating video and film portrayals of
    both aggressive and prosocial behaviors;

6. requests the television and film industry to reduce direct violence in "real
    life" fictional children's programming or violent incidents in cartoons
    and other television or film productions, and to provide more program-
    ming designed to mitigate possible effects of television and film violence,
    consistent with the guarantees of the First Amendment;

7. urges the television and film industry to foster programming that models
    prosocial behaviors and seeks to resolve the problem of violence in society;

8. offers to the television and film industry assistance in developing programs that illustrate psychological methods to control aggressive and violent behavior, and alternative strategies for dealing with conflict and anger;

9. supports revision of the Film Rating System to take into account violence content that is harmful to children and youth;

10. urges industry, government, and private foundations to develop and implement programs to enhance the critical viewing skills of teachers, parents, and children regarding media violence and how to prevent its negative effects;

11. recommends that the Federal Communications Commission (FCC) review, as a condition for license renewal, the programming and outreach efforts and accomplishments of television stations in helping to solve the problem of youth violence;

12. urges industry, government, and private foundations to support research activities aimed at the amelioration of the effects of high levels of mass media violence on children's attitudes and behavior (DeLeon, 1995).

Writing a Critical Response

Sometimes you will be asked to write a **critical response**—a paragraph or more in which you analyze ideas presented in an argument and express your reactions to them.

Before you can respond in writing to an argument, you need to be sure that you understand the writer's position and that you have a sense of how supporting ideas are arranged—and why. You also need to consider how convincingly the writer conveys his or her position.

If you have read the argument carefully, highlighting and annotating it according to the guidelines outlined in this chapter, you should have a good idea what the writer wants to communicate to readers as well as how successfully the argument makes its point.

Before you begin to write a critical response to an argument, you should consider the questions in the checklist on page 78.

Begin your critical response by identifying your source and its author; then, write a clear, concise summary of the writer's position. Next, analyze the argument's supporting points one by one, considering the strength of the evidence that is presented. Also consider whether the writer addresses all significant opposing arguments and whether those arguments are refuted convincingly. Quote, summarize, and paraphrase the writer's key points as you go along, being careful to quote accurately and not to misrepresent the writer's ideas or distort them by quoting out of context. (For information

Questions for Critical Reading

☐ What is the writer's general subject?

☐ What purpose does the writer have for presenting this argument?

☐ What is the writer's position?

☐ Does the writer support ideas mainly with facts or with opinion?

☐ What evidence does the writer present to support this position?

☐ Is the evidence convincing? Is there enough evidence?

☐ Does the writer present opposing ideas and refute them effectively?

☐ What kind of audience does the writer seem to be addressing?

☐ Does the writer see the audience as hostile, friendly, or neutral?

☐ Does the writer establish himself or herself as well informed? As a fair and reasonable person?

☐ Does the writer seem to exhibit bias? If so, how does this bias affect the argument?

on summarizing, paraphrasing, quoting, and synthesizing sources, see Chapter 9.) As you write, identify arguments you find unconvincing, poorly supported, or irrelevant. At the end of your critical response, sum up your assessment of the argument in a strong concluding statement.

⏺ Katherine Choi, the student who highlighted and annotated "When Life Imitates Video" by John Leo (pp. 71–73), used those notes to help her develop the following critical response to Leo's article.

RESPONSE TO "WHEN LIFE IMITATES VIDEO"

KATHERINE CHOI

Article's source and author identified

Summary of writer's position

Analysis of supporting evidence

In "When Life Imitates Video," John Leo takes the position that "video kill games" (para. 2) can actually lead to violent behavior. In fact, he suggests a cause-and-effect connection between such games and the notorious 1999 murder spree at Colorado's Columbine High School, which occurred shortly before Leo wrote his essay.   1

Although Leo acknowledges in paragraph 3 that there is no "direct connection" between video games and this crime and agrees that parents   2 bear the "primary responsibility" for keeping violent games out of the hands of their children, he insists that our culture is also responsible. He is very critical of our society's dependence on violent video games, which he considers "training in make-believe killing" (para 4). This argument is convincing, up to a point. The problem is that Leo's primary support for this argument is a reference to an unnamed "widely cited survey" (para. 4), for which he provides no date. In addition, his use of a weak rhetorical question at the end of paragraph 4 instead of a strong statement of his position does little to help to support his argument.

Leo cites an opposing argument at the beginning of paragraph 5— the "conventional argument" that video games are harmless because children can tell the difference between fantasy and reality. He refutes this argument with unsupported generalizations rather than with specifics, pointing out the possibility that the games will often be played by "unstable youngsters" who channel their "adolescent feelings of resentment, powerlessness, and revenge" into the games.

3 Analysis of Leo's discussion of an opposing argument

The key piece of supporting evidence for Leo's claim that video games are dangerous comes in paragraph 6 with the expert opinion of a psychology professor who is also a retired army officer. The professor, David Grossman, draws an analogy between adolescents' video games and military training games designed to encourage soldiers to shoot their enemies. Although this analogy is interesting, it is not necessarily valid. For one thing, the army training Grossman refers to took place during World War II; for another, the soldiers were aware that the games were preparing them for actual combat.

4 Analysis of supporting evidence

In paragraph 7, Leo goes on to cite Grossman's comments about the young shooter in a 1997 attack in Paducah, Kentucky, and the Marines' use of *Doom* to train soldiers. Again, both discussions are interesting, and both are relevant to the connection between video games and violence. The problem is that neither discussion establishes a cause-and-effect relationship between violent video games and violent acts.

5 Analysis of supporting evidence

It may be true, as Leo observes, that video games are becoming more and more violent and that the victims in these games are increasingly likely to be police officers. Still, Leo fails to make his point because he never establishes that real-life violence is also increasing; therefore, he is not able to demonstrate a causal connection. His concluding

6

Concecluding statement

statement—"If we want to avoid more Littleton-style massacres, we will begin taking the social effects of the killing games more seriously"—combines a frightening prediction and a strong recommendation for action. Unfortunately, although Leo's essay will frighten many readers, it does not convincingly establish the need for the action he recommends.

Work Cited

Leo, John. "When Life Imitates Video." *Practical Argument*, 3rd ed., edited by Laurie G. Kirszner and Stephen R. Mandell. Bedford/St. Martin's, 2017, pp. 68–70.

TEMPLATE FOR WRITING A CRITICAL RESPONSE

Write a one-paragraph critical response to Gerard Jones's essay on pages 64–67. Use the following template to shape your paragraph.

According to Gerard Jones, violent media can actually have positive effects on young people because _____

_____

_____. Jones also believes that violent media are a positive influence on children because _____

_____.

Jones makes some good points. For example, he says that _____

_____

_____. However, _____

_____. All in

all, _____

_____.

⊝ EXERCISE 2.8

Expand the one-paragraph critical response that you wrote above into a more fully developed critical response to Gerard Jones's essay on pages 64–67. Refer to the highlighting and annotations that you did for Exercises 2.3 and 2.4. (If you like, you can expand your response with references to recent news events involving violent acts.)

Decoding Visual Arguments

Do Violent Media Images Trigger Violent Behavior? (continued)

In Chapter 2, you read essays focusing on whether violence on TV and in other popular media can be blamed (at least in part) for the violence in our society. Now, you will be introduced to a variety of visual texts that offer additional insights into this issue. At the same time, you will learn how to use the critical-reading strategies that you practiced in Chapter 2 to help you to **decode**, or interpret, visual texts and to use visuals as springboards for discussion and writing or as sources in your essays.

A **visual argument** can be an advertisement, a chart or graph or table, an infographic, a diagram, a Web page, a photograph, a drawing, or a painting. Like an argumentative essay, a visual argument can take a position. Unlike an argumentative essay, however, a visual argument communicates its position (and offers evidence to support that position) largely through images rather than words.

Thinking Critically about Visual Arguments

When you approach a visual argument—particularly one that will be the subject of class discussion or writing—you should do so with a critical eye. Your primary goal is to understand the point that the creator of the visual is trying to make, but you also need to understand how the message is conveyed. In addition, you need to evaluate whether the methods used to persuade the audience are both logical and convincing.

VISUALS VERSUS VISUAL ARGUMENTS

Not every visual is an argument; many simply present information. For example, a diagram of a hunting rifle, with its principal parts labeled, tells viewers what the weapon looks like and how it works. However, a photo of two toddlers playing with a hunting rifle could make a powerful argument about the need for gun safety. Conversely, a photo of a family hunting trip featuring a teenager proudly holding up a rifle while his parents look on approvingly might make a positive argument for access to guns.

Using Active Reading Strategies with Visual Arguments

As you learned in Chapter 2, being a critical reader involves responding actively to the text of an argument. The active reading strategies that you practiced in Chapter 2—*previewing, close reading, highlighting,* and *annotating*—can also be applied to visual arguments.

When you approach a visual argument, you should look for clues to its main idea, or message. Some visuals, particularly advertising images, include words (sometimes called *body copy*) as well, and this written text often conveys the main ideas of the argument. Apart from words, however, the images themselves can help you understand the visual's purpose, its intended audience, and the argument that it is making.

COMPREHENSION CLUES

- The individual images

- The relative distance between images (close together or far apart)

- The relative size of the images

- The relationship between images and background

- The use of empty space

- The use of color and shading (for example, contrast between light and dark)

- If people are pictured, their activities, gestures, facial expressions, positions, body language, dress, and so on

APPEALS: *LOGOS, PATHOS,* AND *ETHOS*

As you study a visual argument, you should consider the appeal (or appeals) that the visual uses to convince its audience.

- An ad produced by Mothers Against Drunk Drivers (MADD) that includes statistics about alcohol-related auto fatalities might appeal to logic (*logos*).

- Another MADD ad could appeal to the emotions (*pathos*) by showing photographs of an accident scene.

- Still another ad could appeal to authority (*ethos*) by featuring a well-known sports figure warning of the dangers of drunk driving.

(For more on these appeals, see pp. 14–21.)

The following illustration makes a strong visual argument, using the image of a young child holding a mutilated teddy bear to make an emotional appeal to those concerned about children's exposure to television violence.

This illustration by Todd Davidson first appeared in the *Age* newspaper, Melbourne, Australia, on March 22, 1998.

© Todd Davidson/Illustration Source

The visual on the previous page includes three dominant images: the child, the teddy bear, and a giant TV screen projecting an image of a hand holding a knife. The placement of the child in the center of the visual, with the teddy bear on one side and the knife on the other, suggests that the child (and, by extension, all children) is caught between the innocence of childhood and the violence depicted in the media. The hand holding the knife on the television screen is an extension of the child's actual arm, suggesting that the innocent world of the child is being taken over by the violent world of the media.

To emphasize this conflict between innocence and violence, the teddy bear is set against a dark background, while the TV, with its disturbing image, is paradoxically set against a light background. (The image of the child is split, with half against each background, suggesting the split between the two worlds the child is exposed to.) The child's gaze is directed at his mutilated teddy bear, apparently the victim of his own violent act. The expression on the child's face makes it clear that he does not understand the violence he is caught up in.

Because it treats subject matter that is familiar to most people—TV violence and children's vulnerability to it—this visual is easy to understand. Its powerful images are not difficult to interpret, and its message is straightforward: TV violence is, at least in part, responsible for real-world violence. The visual's accessibility suggests that it is aimed at a wide general audience (rather than, for example, child psychologists or media analysts).

The visual's purpose is somewhat more complex. It could be to criticize the media, to warn parents and others about the threat posed by media violence, or to encourage the audience to take action.

Now, turn your attention to the two graphs on the facing page. These graphs, which appeared in the 2012 *Washington Post* article "Ten-Country Comparison Suggests There's Little or No Link between Video Games and Gun Murders," by Max Fisher, appeal to logic by providing statistics as evidence to support the article's position. Thus, the graphs present a strong visual argument about the relationship between violent video games and crime—an argument that is more powerful than the argument the article alone would present.

The graphs use a simple, open design and a minimum of words to make their information accessible to most people who will look at them. The main idea, or message, they convey is summarized by the article's thesis statement, supporting the idea that contrary to expectations, the data suggest "a slight downward shift in violence as video game consumption increases."

This idea is likely to come as a surprise to most people, who might assume a causal relationship between violent video games and violent crime. However, as the graphs show, this is not the case. Thus, the graphs serve as a clear **refutation** of a commonly held assumption. Because the two graphs (and the article in which they appeared) present information that is intended to contradict the audience's probable assumptions, their purpose seems to be to convince people to change the way they look at video games.

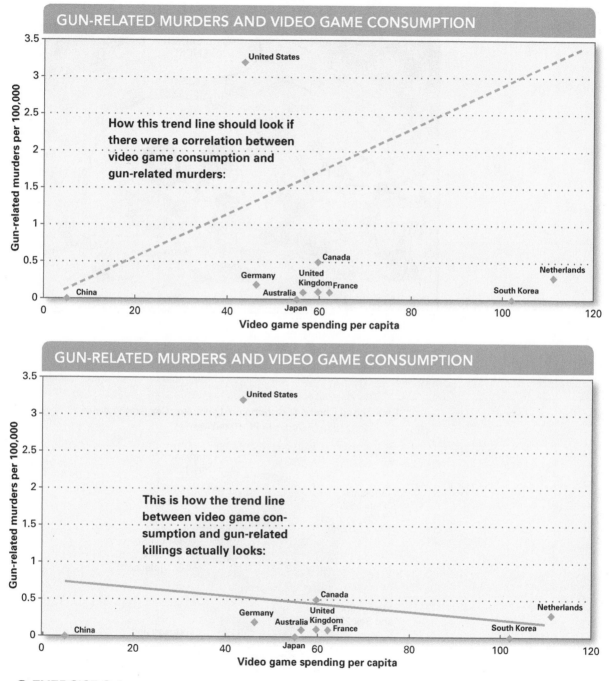

→ EXERCISE 3.1

Look at the visuals on the pages that follow, and then answer the
questions on page 91.

Bob Engelhart, Violent Video Games

Bob Englehart. Courtesy of Cagle Cartoons.

Parenthood Library, Distribution of Language, Sex, and Violence Codes in PG-Rated Movies

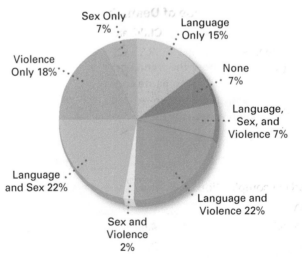

From Amy I. Nathanson & Joanne Cantor (1998), Protecting Children from Harmful Television: TV Ratings and the V-Chip. From Parenthood in America, University of Wisconsin–Madison General Library System.

Boy Playing Violent Video Game

Jochen Tack/imageBROKER/Agefotostock

Ways to Die in Children's Cartoons

A study in the *British Medical Journal* indicated that two thirds of cartoon movies included the deaths of characters, compared with half in adult films. Parents are five times as likely to die in cartoon films compared with adult dramas.

Type of Death, by Percentage of Films

Type of death	Children's animated films	Comparison films
No on-screen deaths	33.3	50.0
Animal attacks	11.1	0
Falling	11.1	33.3
Other murder	8.9	4.4
Drowning	6.7	1.1
Gunshot	6.7	14.4
Magic	6.7	0
Illness/medical complications	4.4	8.9
Other injury	4.4	2.2
Stabbing/impaling	4.4	2.2
Motor vehicle crash	2.2	8.9
Killed in combat	0	3.3
Suicide	0	1.1

Lauren Dazzara, Why Gaming Is a Positive Element in Life

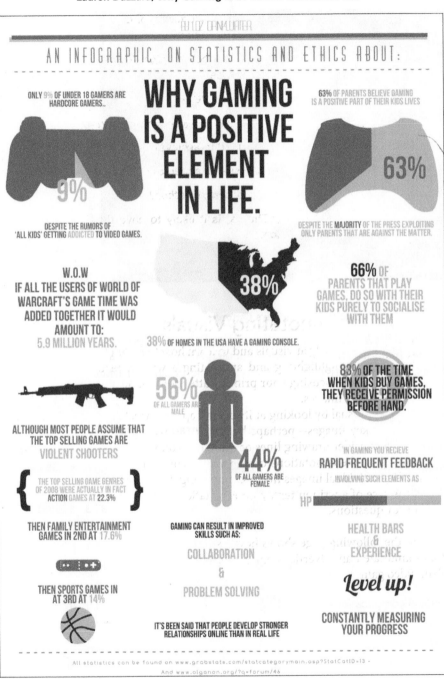

© Loz Dizarra

Identifying the Elements of a Visual Argument

1. Do you see all of the visuals on pages 87–90 as arguments, or do you think some were created solely to present information?

2. What main idea, or message, does each visual communicate? State the main idea of each visual in a single sentence.

3. What elements in each visual support this main idea?

4. If the visual includes words as well as images, are the words necessary?

5. What purpose does each visual seem designed to achieve?

6. What kind of audience do you think each visual is aimed at?

7. Does the visual appeal primarily to *logos, pathos,* or *ethos*?

8. Do you think the visual is effective? That is, is it likely to have the desired effect on its intended audience?

Highlighting and Annotating Visuals

Now, it is time to look more closely at visuals and to learn how to *highlight* and *annotate* them. Unlike highlighting and annotating a written text, marking a visual text involves focusing your primary attention not on any words that appear but on the images.

After previewing the visual by looking at its overall appearance, begin highlighting to identify key images—perhaps by starring, boxing, or circling them—and then consider drawing lines or arrows to connect related images. Next, go on to make annotations on the visual, commenting on the effectiveness of its individual images in communicating the message of the whole. As in the case of a written text, your annotations can be in the form of comments or questions.

The visual on the following page shows how a student, Jason Savona, highlighted and annotated an advertisement for *Grand Theft Auto IV,* a popular violent video game.

Rockstar North, Advertisement for *Grand Theft Auto IV*

Top of gun = taller than tallest building

Huge lone figure looking down on city

"Liberty City" skyline (looks like NY)

Hazy yellow sky

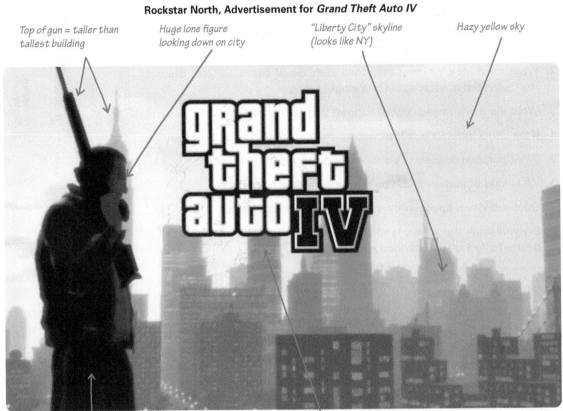

The Advertising Archives

Dark image stands out against lighter background

Name of game centered; large type in contrasting black and white for emphasis

⊙ EXERCISE 3.2

Look at the visual on the following page, and then highlight and annotate it to identify its most important images and their relationship to one another. When you have finished, think about how the images work together to communicate a central message to the audience. What argument does this visual make?

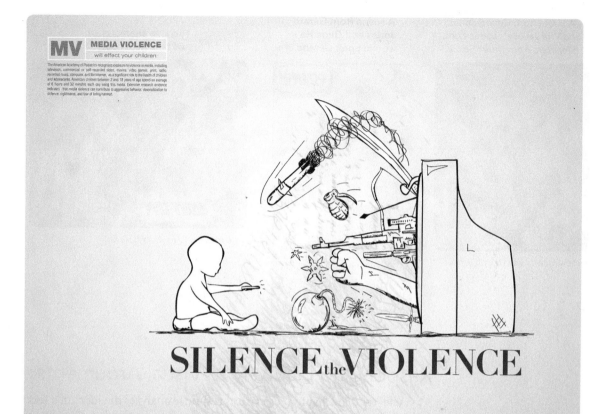

© Nate Londa

⤷ EXERCISE 3.3

Interview a classmate about his or her experiences with video games—or with actual violence. Does your classmate see any links between the kinds of videos that are watched by friends and family members and the violence (or lack of violence) that occurs in his or her community? Write a paragraph summarizing your interview.

⤷ EXERCISE 3.4

Study the following three visuals (and their captions), all of which appear in Gerard Jones's essay, "Violent Media Is Good for Kids" (pp. 64–67). Look at each visual with a critical eye, and then consider how effectively each one supports the central argument that Jones makes in his essay.

A scene from Gerard Jones and Will Jacobs's comic book *Monsters from Outer Space*.

© Gerard Jones, Gene Ha, Will Jacobs.

A scene from Gerard Jones and Gene Ha's comic book *Oktane*.

© Gerard Jones, Gene Ha, Will Jacobs.

The title character of *Oktane* gets nasty.

© Gerard Jones, Gene Ha, Will Jacobs.

Responding Critically to Visual Arguments

As you learned in Chapter 2, a **critical response** analyzes the ideas in a text and expresses your reactions to them. When you respond in writing to a visual argument, you rely on your highlighting and annotations to help you understand the writer's ideas and see how the words and images work together to make a particular point.

As you prepare to write a critical response to a visual argument, keep in mind the questions in the following checklist.

CHECKLIST

Questions for Responding to Visual Arguments

☐ In what source did the visual appear? What is the target audience for this source?

☐ For what kind of audience was the visual created? Hostile? Friendly? Neutral?

☐ For what purpose was the visual created?

☐ Who (or what organization) created the visual? What do you know about the background and goals of this person or group?

(*continued*)

☐ What issue is the visual addressing?

☐ What position does the visual take on this issue? How can you tell? Do you agree with this position?

☐ Does the visual include words? If so, are they necessary? What points do they make? Does the visual need more—or different— written text?

☐ Does the visual seem to be a *refutation*—that is, an argument against a particular position?

☐ Is the visual effective? Attractive? Interesting? Clear? Convincing?

When you write a critical response, begin by identifying the source and purpose of the visual. Then, state your reaction to the visual, and examine its elements one at a time, considering how effective each is and how well the various elements work together to create a convincing visual argument. End with a strong concluding statement that summarizes your reaction.

⬇ The critical response that follows was written by the student who highlighted and annotated the advertisement for *Grand Theft Auto IV* on page 92.

RESPONSE TO *GRAND THEFT AUTO IV*

JASON SAVONA

The advertisement for *Grand Theft Auto IV* presents a disturbing preview of the game. Rather than highlighting the game's features and challenges, this ad promotes the game's violence. As a result, it appeals more to those who are looking for video games that depict murder and other crimes than to those who choose a video game on the basis of the skill it requires.

The "hero" of this game is Niko Bellic, a war veteran from Eastern Europe who has left his country to build a new life in the fictional Liberty City. Instead of finding peace, he has found a new kind of war. Now,

1 Identification of visual's source

Reaction to visual

2 Analysis of visual's elements

trapped in the corrupt world of organized crime, Bellic is willing to do whatever it takes to fight his way out. His idea of justice is vigilante justice: he makes his own rules. The ad conveys this sense of Bellic as a loner and an outsider by showing him as a larger-than-life figure standing tall and alone against a background of the Liberty City skyline.

In the ad, Niko Bellic holds a powerful weapon in his huge hands, 3 and the weapon extends higher than the tallest building behind it, dominating the picture. Clearly, Bellic means business. As viewers look at the picture, the dark image of the gun and the man who holds it comes to the foreground, and everything else—the light brown buildings, the city lights, the yellow sky—fades into the background. In the center, the name of the game is set in large black-and-white type that contrasts with the ad's hazy background, showing the importance of the product's name.

This image, clearly aimed at young players of violent video games, 4 would certainly be appealing to those who want to have a feeling of

Concluding statement   power. What it says is, "A weapon makes a person powerful." This is a very dangerous message.

TEMPLATE FOR RESPONDING TO VISUAL ARGUMENTS

Write a one-paragraph critical response to the visual you highlighted and annotated in Exercise 3.2 on pages 92–93. Use the following template to shape your paragraph.

The visual created by Nate Londa shows _____

_____.

This visual makes a powerful statement about _____.

_____ The central image shows _____

_____.

_____ The background enhances the central image because

_____

_____.

_____ The visual includes words as well as images.

These words suggest _____

_____

The goal of the organization that posted the visual seems to be to _____

_____.

_____ The visual (is / is not) effective because _____

_____

◗ EXERCISE 3.5

Consulting the one-paragraph critical response that you wrote above, write a more fully developed critical response to the visual on page 93. Refer to the highlighting and annotating that you did for Exercise 3.2.

AP Photo/Sakchai Lalit

Writing a Rhetorical Analysis

Is It Ethical to Buy Counterfeit Designer Merchandise?

The demand for counterfeit designer merchandise—handbags, shoes, and jewelry—has always been great. Wishing to avoid the high prices of genuine designer goods, American consumers spend hundreds of millions of dollars per year buying cheap imitations that are made primarily in factories in China (and in other countries as well). According to United States Customs and Border Protection statistics, the counterfeit goods seized in 2013 had a retail value of over $1.7 billion. In 2014, that figure went down to $1.2 billion, but much more counterfeit merchandise gets into the United States than is seized. However hard they try, law enforcement officials cannot seem to stem the tide of counterfeit merchandise that is sold in stores, in flea markets, and by street vendors as well as through the Internet. As long as people want these illegal goods, there will be a market for them.

Purchasing counterfeit designer goods is not a victimless crime, however. Buyers are stealing the intellectual property of legitimate businesses that, unlike the manufacturers of fakes, pay their employees fair wages and provide good working conditions. In addition, because counterfeit goods are of low quality, they do not last as long as the genuine articles. This is not a serious problem when people are buying fake watches and handbags, but it can be life threatening when the counterfeit products include pharmaceuticals, tools, baby food, or automobile parts.

Later in this chapter, you will read a rhetorical analysis of an essay that takes a position on this issue, and you will be asked to write a rhetorical analysis of your own about another essay on this topic.

What Is a Rhetorical Analysis?

When you write a **rhetorical analysis,** you systematically examine the strategies a writer employs to achieve his or her purpose. In the process, you explain how these strategies work together to create an effective (or ineffective) argument. To carry out this task, you consider the argument's **rhetorical situation**, the writer's **means of persuasion**, and the **rhetorical strategies** that the writer uses.

OVERVIEW: "LETTER FROM BIRMINGHAM JAIL" BY MARTIN LUTHER KING JR.

Here and throughout the rest of this chapter, we will be analyzing "Letter from Birmingham Jail" by Martin Luther King Jr., which can be found online.

In 1963, civil rights leader Martin Luther King Jr. organized a series of nonviolent demonstrations to protest the climate of segregation that existed in Birmingham, Alabama. He and his followers met opposition not only from white moderates but also from some African-American clergymen who thought that King was a troublemaker. During the demonstrations, King was arrested and jailed for eight days. He wrote his "Letter from Birmingham Jail" on April 16, 1963, from the city jail in response to a public statement by eight white Alabama clergymen titled "A Call for Unity." This statement asked for an end to the demonstrations, which the clergymen called "untimely," "unwise," and "extreme." (Their letter was addressed to the "white and Negro" population of Birmingham, not to King, whom they considered an "outsider.")

King knew that the world was watching and that his response to the white clergymen would have both national and international significance. As a result, he used a variety of rhetorical strategies to convince readers that his demands were both valid and understandable and that contrary to the opinions of some, his actions were well within the mainstream of American social and political thought. Today, King's "Letter from Birmingham Jail" stands as a model of clear and highly effective argumentation.

© Bettmann/Corbis

Martin Luther King Jr.
in Birmingham Jail
(April 1963)

Considering the Rhetorical Situation

Arguments do not take place in isolation. They are written by real people in response to a particular set of circumstances called the **rhetorical situation** (see pp. 9–14). The rhetorical situation consists of the following five elements:

- The writer
- The writer's purpose
- The writer's audience
- The question
- The context

By analyzing the rhetorical situation, you are able to determine why the writer made the choices he or she did and how these choices affect the argument.

ANALYZING THE RHETORICAL SITUATION

To help you analyze the rhetorical situation of an argument, look for information about the essay and its author.

1. **Look at the essay's headnote.** If the essay you are reading has a headnote, it can contain useful information about the writer, the issue being discussed, and the structure of the essay. For this reason, it is a good idea to read headnotes carefully.

2. **Look for clues within the essay.** The writer's use of particular words and phrases can sometimes provide information about his or her preconceptions as well as about the cultural context of the argument. Historical or cultural references can indicate what ideas or information the writer expects readers to have.

3. **Search the Web.** Often, just a few minutes online can give you a lot of useful information—such as the background of a particular debate or the biography of the writer. By looking at titles of the other books or essays the writer has written, you may also be able to get an idea of his or her biases or point of view.

The Writer

Begin by trying to determine whether anything in the writer's background (for example, the writer's education, experience, race, gender, political beliefs, religion, age, and experiences) has influenced the content of the argument. Also consider whether the writer seems to have any preconceptions about the subject.

ANALYZING THE WRITER

- What is the writer's background?
- How does the writer's background affect the content of the argument?
- What preconceptions about the subject does the writer seem to have?

If you were analyzing "Letter from Birmingham Jail," it would help to know that Martin Luther King Jr. was pastor of the Dexter Avenue Baptist Church in Montgomery, Alabama. In 1956, he organized a bus boycott that led to a United States Supreme Court decision that outlawed segregation on Alabama's buses. In addition, King was a leader of the Southern Christian Leadership Conference and strongly believed in nonviolent protest. His books include *Stride towards Freedom* (1958) and *Why We Can't Wait* (1964). His "I Have a Dream" speech, which he delivered on the steps of the Lincoln Memorial on August 28, 1963, is considered by scholars to be one of the most influential speeches of the twentieth century. In 1964, King won the Nobel Prize for peace.

In "Letter from Birmingham Jail," King addresses the injustices that he sees in America—especially in the South—and makes a strong case

"I Have a Dream" speech, Washington, D.C. (August 1963)

Hulton-Deutsch Collection/Corbis

for civil rights for all races. Throughout his argument, King includes numerous references to the Bible, to philosophers, and to political and religious thinkers. By doing so, he makes it clear to readers that he is aware of the social, cultural, religious, and political implications of his actions. Because he is a clergyman, King suggests that by battling injustice, he, like the apostle Paul, is doing God's work. This point is made clear in the following passage (para. 3):

> But more basically, I am in Birmingham because injustice is here. Just as the prophets of the eighth century B.C. left their villages and carried their "thus saith the Lord" far beyond the boundaries of their home towns, and just as the Apostle Paul left his village of Tarsus and carried the gospel of Jesus Christ to the far corners of the Greco-Roman world, so am I compelled to carry the gospel of freedom beyond my own home town. Like Paul, I must constantly respond to the Macedonian call for aid.

The Writer's Purpose

Next, consider what the writer hopes to achieve with his or her argument. In other words, ask yourself if the writer is trying to challenge people's ideas, persuade them to accept new points of view, or influence their behavior.

ANALYZING THE WRITER'S PURPOSE

- Does the writer state his or her purpose directly, or is the purpose implied?

- Is the writer's purpose simply to convince or to encourage action?

- Does the writer rely primarily on logic or on emotion?

- Does the writer have a hidden agenda?

It is clear that Martin Luther King Jr. wrote "Letter from Birmingham Jail" to convince readers that even though he had been arrested, his actions were both honorable and just. To get readers to understand that, like Henry David Thoreau, he is protesting laws that he considers wrong, he draws a distinction between just and unjust laws. For him, a law is just if it "squares with the moral law or the law of God" (16). A law is unjust if it "is out of harmony with the moral law" (16). As a clergyman and a civil rights leader, King believed that he had an obligation both to point out the immorality of unjust laws and to protest them—even if it meant going to jail.

The Writer's Audience

To analyze the writer's audience, begin by considering whether the writer seems to see readers as friendly, hostile, or neutral. (For a discussion of types of audiences, see pp. 10–13). Also, determine how much knowledge the writer assumes that readers have. Then, consider how the writer takes into account factors like the audience's race, religion, gender, education, age, and ethnicity. Next, decide what preconceptions the writer thinks readers have about the subject. Finally, see if the writer shares any common ground with readers.

ANALYZING THE WRITER'S AUDIENCE

- Who is the writer's intended audience?

- Does the writer see the audience as informed or uninformed?

- Does the writer see the audience as hostile, friendly, or neutral?

- What values does the writer think the audience holds?

- What does the writer seem to assume about the audience's background?

- On what points do the writer and the audience agree? On what points do they disagree?

In "Letter from Birmingham Jail," King aims his argument at more than one audience. First, he speaks directly to eight clergymen from Birmingham, who are at worst a hostile audience and at best a skeptical one. They consider King to be an outsider whose actions are "unwise and untimely" (1). Before addressing their concerns, King tries to establish common ground, referring to his readers as "fellow clergymen" and "my Christian and Jewish brothers." He then goes on to say that he wishes that the clergymen had supported his actions instead of criticizing them. King ends his letter on a conciliatory note by asking his readers to forgive him if he has overstated his case or been unduly harsh.

In addition to addressing clergymen, King also speaks to white moderates, who he assumes are sympathetic to his cause but concerned about his methods. He knows that he has to influence this segment of his audience if he is to gain wide support for his cause. For this reason, King uses a restrained tone and emphasizes the universality of his message, ending his letter with a plea that is calculated to console and inspire those people who need reassurance (50):

Let us all hope that the dark clouds of racial prejudice will soon pass away and the deep fog of misunderstanding will be lifted from our fear-drenched communities, and in some not too distant tomorrow the radiant stars of love and brotherhood will shine over our great nation with all their scintillating beauty.

The Question

Try to determine what question the writer is trying to answer. Is the question suitable for argument? Decide if there are good arguments on both sides of the issue. For example, what issue (or issues) is the writer confronting? Does he or she address them adequately?

ANALYZING THE QUESTION

- What is the central question of the argument?

- Are there solid arguments on both sides of the issue?

- Has the writer answered the question fully enough?

The question King attempts to answer in "Letter from Birmingham Jail" is why he has decided to come to Birmingham to lead protests. Because the answer to this question is complicated, King addresses a number of issues. Although his main concern is with racial segregation in Alabama, he also is troubled by the indifference of white moderates who have urged him to call off his protests. In addition, he feels that he needs to explain his actions (for example, engaging in nonviolent protests) and address those who doubt his motives. King answers his critics (as well as his central question) by saying that because the people of the United States are interconnected, the injustices in one state will eventually affect the entire country.

The Context

The **context** is the situation that creates the need for the argument. As you analyze an argument, try to determine the social, historical, economic, political, and cultural events that set the stage for the argument and the part that these events play in the argument itself.

ANALYZING THE CONTEXT

- What situation (or situations) set the stage for the argument?

- What social, economic, political, and cultural events triggered the argument?

- What historical references situate this argument in a particular place or time?

The immediate context of "Letter to Birmingham Jail" is well known: Martin Luther King Jr. wrote an open letter to eight white clergymen in which he defended his protests against racial segregation. However, the wider social and political context of the letter is less well known.

In 1896, the U.S. Supreme Court ruled in *Plessy v. Ferguson* that "separate but equal" accommodations on railroad cars gave African Americans the equal protection guaranteed by the Fourteenth Amendment of the U.S. Constitution. Well into the twentieth century, this decision was used to justify separate public facilities—including restrooms, water fountains, and even schools and hospitals—for blacks and whites.

In the mid-1950s, state support for segregation of the races and discrimination against African Americans had begun to be challenged. For example, Supreme Court decisions in 1954 and 1955 found that segregation in the public schools and other publicly financed locations was unconstitutional. At the same time, whites and blacks alike were calling for an end to racial discrimination. Their actions took the form of marches, boycotts, and sit-ins (organized nonviolent protests whose participants refused to move from a public area). Many whites, however, particularly in the South, strongly resisted any sudden changes in race relations.

King's demonstrations in Birmingham, Alabama, took place within this larger social and political context. His campaign was a continuation of the push for equal rights that had been gaining momentum in the United States for decades. King, along with the Southern Christian Leadership

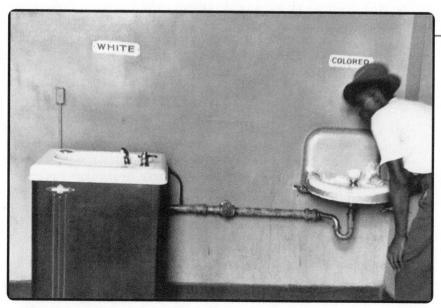

Segregated water fountains in North Carolina (1950)

© Elliott Erwitt/Magnum

Conference, had dispatched hundreds of people to Birmingham to engage in nonviolent demonstrations against those who were determined to keep African Americans from gaining their full rights as citizens.

Considering the Means of Persuasion: *Logos, Pathos, Ethos*

In the introduction to this book, you learned how writers of argument use three means of persuasion—*logos, pathos,* and *ethos*—to appeal to readers. You also saw how the **rhetorical triangle** represents the way these three appeals come into play within an argument. (See p. 19 for more information about the rhetorical triangle.) Of course, the degree to which a writer uses each of these appeals depends on the rhetorical situation. Moreover, a single argument can use more than one appeal—for example, an important research source would involve both the logic of the argument (*logos*) and the credibility of the writer (*ethos*). In "Letter from Birmingham Jail," King uses all three appeals.

The Appeal to Reason (Logos)

In "Letter from Birmingham Jail," King attempts to demonstrate the logic of his position. In paragraph 15, for example, he says that there are two types of laws—just and unjust. He then points out that he has both a legal and a moral responsibility to "disobey unjust laws." In paragraph 16, King supports his position with references to various philosophers and theologians—for example, St. Thomas Aquinas, Martin Buber, and Paul Tillich. He also develops the logical argument that even though all Americans should obey the law, they are responsible to a higher moral authority—God.

The Appeal to the Emotions (Pathos)

Throughout "Letter from Birmingham Jail," King attempts to create sympathy for his cause. In paragraph 14, for example, he catalogues the injustices of life in the United States for African Americans. He makes a particularly emotional appeal by quoting a hypothetical five-year-old boy who might ask, "Daddy, why do white people treat colored people so mean?" In addition, he includes vivid images of racial injustice to provoke anger against those who deny African Americans equal rights. In this way, King creates sympathy (and possibly empathy) in readers.

The Appeal to Authority (Ethos)

To be persuasive, King has to establish his credibility. In paragraph 2, for example, he reminds readers that he is the president of the Southern Christian Leadership Conference, "an organization operating in every

southern state." In paragraph 3, he compares himself to the apostle
Paul, who carried the gospel "to the far corners of the Greco-Roman
world." In addition, King attempts to show readers that what he is doing
is well within the mainstream of American political and social thought.
By alluding to Thomas Jefferson, Henry David Thoreau, and the 1954
U.S. Supreme Court decision that outlawed segregation in public
schools, he tries to demonstrate that he is not the wild-eyed radical that
some believe him to be. Thus, King establishes himself in both secular
and religious terms as a leader who has the stature and the authority to
present his case.

Considering the Writer's Rhetorical Strategies

Writers use various **rhetorical strategies** to present their ideas and opinions.
Here are a few of the elements that you should examine when analyzing and
evaluating an argument.

Thesis

The **thesis**—the main idea or claim that the argument supports—is of
primary importance in every argument. When you analyze an argument, you should always ask, "What is the essay's thesis, and why does
the writer state it as he or she does?" You should also consider at what
point in the argument the thesis is stated and what the effect of this
placement is.

In "Letter from Birmingham Jail," Martin Luther King Jr. begins by
telling readers that he is "confined here in the Birmingham city jail" and
that he is writing his letter to answer clergymen who have called his demonstrations "unwise and untimely." King clearly (and unapologetically)
states his thesis ("But more basically, I am in Birmingham because injustice
is here") at the beginning of the third paragraph, right after he explains his
purpose, so that readers will have no doubt what his position is as they
read the rest of his argument.

Organization

The **organization** of an argument—how a writer arranges ideas—is also
important. For example, after stating his thesis, King tells readers why he
is in Birmingham and what he hopes to accomplish: he wants unjust laws
to be abolished and the 1954 Supreme Court ruling to be enforced. King
then **refutes**—disproves or calls into question—the specific charges that
were leveled at him by the white clergymen who want him to stop his
protests.

The structure of "Letter from Birmingham Jail" enables King to make his points clearly, logically, and convincingly:

- King begins his argument by addressing the charge that his actions are untimely. If anything, says King, his actions are not timely enough: after all, African Americans have waited more than 340 years for their "constitutional and God-given rights" (14).

- He then addresses the issue of his willingness to break laws and makes the distinction between just and unjust laws.

- After chiding white moderates for not supporting his cause, he addresses their claim that he is extreme. According to King, this charge is false: if he had not embraced a philosophy of nonviolent protest, the streets of the South would "be flowing with blood" (29).

- King then makes the point that the contemporary church must recapture the "sacrificial spirit of the early church" (42). He does this by linking his struggle for freedom with the "sacred heritage of our nation and the eternal will of God" (44).

- King ends his argument by asserting both his humility and his unity with the white clergy.

Evidence

To convince an audience, a writer must support the thesis with **evidence**—facts, observations, expert opinion, and so on. King presents a great deal of evidence to support his arguments. For instance, he uses numerous examples (both historical and personal) as well as many references to philosophers, political thinkers, and theologians (such as Jesus, St. Paul, St. Augustine, Amos, Martin Luther, and Abraham Lincoln). According to King, these figures, who were once considered "extremists," were not afraid of "making waves" when the need arose. Now, however, they are well within the mainstream of social, political, and religious thought. King also presents reasons, facts, and quotations to support his points.

Stylistic Techniques

Writers also use stylistic techniques to make their arguments more memorable and more convincing. For example, in "Letter from Birmingham Jail," King uses figurative devices such as *similes*, *metaphors*, and *allusions* to enhance his argument.

Simile A **simile** is a figure of speech that compares two unlike things using the word *like* or *as*.

Like a boil that can never be cured so long as it is covered up but must be opened with all its ugliness to the natural medicines of air and light, injustice must be exposed, . . . before it can be cured. (24)

Isn't this like condemning a robbed man because his possession of money precipitated the evil act of robbery? (25)

Metaphor A **metaphor** is a comparison in which two dissimilar things are compared without the word *like* or *as*. A metaphor suggests that two things that are very different share a quality.

Frankly, I have yet to engage in a direct-action campaign that was "well timed" in the view of those who have not suffered unduly from the disease of segregation. (13)

[W]hen you see the vast majority of your twenty million Negro brothers smothering in an airtight cage of poverty . . . (14)

Allusion An **allusion** is a reference within a work to a person, literary or biblical text, or historical event in order to enlarge the context of the situation being written about. The writer expects readers to recognize the allusion and to make the connection to the text they are reading.

I would agree with St. Augustine that "an unjust law is no law at all." (15)

Of course, there is nothing new about this kind of civil disobedience. It was evidenced sublimely in the refusal of Shadrach, Meshach, and Abednego to obey the laws of Nebuchadnezzar, on the ground that a higher moral law was at stake. (21) [King expects his audience of clergymen to recognize this reference to the Book of Daniel in the Old Testament.]

In addition to those figurative devices, King uses stylistic techniques such as *parallelism*, *repetition*, and *rhetorical questions* to further his argument.

Parallelism **Parallelism**, the use of similar grammatical structures to emphasize related ideas, makes a passage easier to follow.

In any nonviolent campaign there are four basic steps: collection of the facts to determine whether injustices exist; negotiation; self-purification; and direct action. (6)

Shallow understanding from people of good will is more frustrating than absolute misunderstanding from people of ill will. Lukewarm acceptance is much more bewildering than outright rejection. (23)

I wish you had commended the Negro sit-inners and demonstrators of Birmingham for their sublime courage, their willingness to suffer, and their amazing discipline in the midst of great provocation. (47)

Repetition   Intentional **repetition** involves repeating a word or phrase for emphasis, clarity, or emotional impact.

> "Are you able to accept blows without retaliating?" "Are you able to endure the ordeal of jail?" (8)

> If I have said anything in this letter that overstates the truth and indicates an unreasonable impatience, I beg you to forgive me. If I have said anything that understates the truth and indicates my having patience that allows me to settle for anything less than brotherhood, I beg God to forgive me. (49)

Rhetorical questions   A **rhetorical question** is a question that is asked to encourage readers to reflect on an issue, not to elicit a reply.

> One may well ask: "How can you advocate breaking some laws and obeying others?" (15)

> Will we be extremists for hate or for love? (31)

Assessing the Argument

No rhetorical analysis of an argument would be complete without an assessment of its effectiveness—whether the rhetorical strategies the writer uses create a clear and persuasive argument or whether they fall short. When you write a rhetorical analysis, you can begin with an assessment of the argument as a whole and go on to support it, or you can begin with a discussion of the various rhetorical strategies that the writer uses and then end with your assessment of the argument.

After analyzing "Letter from Birmingham Jail," you could reasonably conclude that King has written a highly effective argument that is likely to convince his readers that his presence in Birmingham is both justified and necessary. Using *logos*, *pathos*, and *ethos*, he constructs a multifaceted argument that is calculated to appeal to the various segments of his audience—Southern clergymen, white moderates, and African Americans. In addition, King uses similes, metaphors, and allusions to enrich his argument and to make it more memorable, and he uses parallelism, repetition, and rhetorical questions to emphasize ideas and to reinforce his points. Because it is so clear and powerful, King's argument—in particular, the distinction between just and unjust laws—addresses not only the injustices that were present in 1963 when it was written but also the injustices and inequalities that exist today. In this sense, King has written an argument that has broad significance beyond the audiences for which it was originally intended.

CHECKLIST

Preparing to Write a Rhetorical Analysis

As you read, ask the following questions:

- [ ] Who is the writer? Is there anything in the writer's background that might influence what is (or is not) included in the argument?

- [ ] What is the writer's purpose? What does the writer hope to achieve?

- [ ] What question has the writer decided to address? How broad is the question?

- [ ] What situation created the need for the argument?

- [ ] At what points in the argument does the writer appeal to logic? To the emotions? How does the writer try to establish his or her credibility?

- [ ] What is the argument's thesis? Where is it stated? Why?

- [ ] How does the writer organize the argument? How effective is this arrangement of ideas?

- [ ] What evidence does the writer use to support the argument? Does the writer use enough evidence?

- [ ] Does the writer use similes, metaphors, and allusions?

- [ ] Does the writer use parallelism, repetition, and rhetorical questions?

- [ ] Given your analysis, what is your overall assessment of the argument?

Sample Rhetorical Analysis

In preparation for a research paper, Deniz Bilgutay, a student in a writing class, read the following essay, "Terror's Purse Strings" by Dana Thomas, which makes an argument against buying counterfeit designer goods. Deniz then wrote the rhetorical analysis that appears on pages 115–117. (Deniz Bilgutay's research paper, "The High Cost of Cheap Counterfeit Goods," uses "Terror's Purse Strings" as a source. See Appendix B.)

This essay appeared in the *New York Times* on August 30, 2007.

TERROR'S PURSE STRINGS

DANA THOMAS

Luxury fashion designers are busily putting final touches on the handbags   1
they will present during the spring-summer 2008 women's wear shows, which
begin next week in New York City's Bryant Park. To understand the importance of the handbag in fashion today consider this: According to consumer
surveys conducted by Coach, the average American woman was buying two
new handbags a year in 2000; by 2004, it was more than four. And the average
luxury bag retails for 10 to 12 times its production cost.

"There is a kind of an obsession with bags," the designer Miuccia Prada   2
told me. "It's so easy to make money."

Counterfeiters agree. As soon as a handbag hits big, counterfeiters around the   3
globe churn out fake versions by the thousands. And they have no trouble selling
them. Shoppers descend on Canal Street in New York, Santee Alley in Los Angeles, and flea markets and purse parties around the country to pick up knockoffs
for one-tenth the legitimate bag's retail cost, then pass them off as real.

"Judges, prosecutors, defense attorneys shop here," a private investigator   4
told me as we toured the counterfeit section of Santee Alley. "Affluent people
from Newport Beach." According to a study by the British law firm Davenport
Lyons, two-thirds of British consumers are "proud to tell their family and
friends" that they bought fake luxury fashion items.

At least 11 percent of the world's clothing is fake, according to 2000 figures   5
from the Global Anti-Counterfeiting Group in Paris. Fashion is easy to copy:
counterfeiters buy the real items, take them apart, scan the pieces to make patterns, and produce almost-perfect fakes.

Most people think that buying an imitation handbag or wallet is harmless, a victimless
crime. But the counterfeiting rackets are run by
crime syndicates that also deal in narcotics,
weapons, child prostitution, human trafficking,

> "At least 11 percent   6
> of the world's
> clothing is fake . . ."

*An international criminal
police organization*

and terrorism. Ronald K. Noble, the secretary general of Interpol,° told the
House of Representatives Committee on International Relations that profits
from the sale of counterfeit goods have gone to groups associated with Hezbollah, the Shiite terrorist group, paramilitary organizations in Northern Ireland,
and FARC, the Revolutionary Armed Forces of Colombia.

Sales of counterfeit T-shirts may have helped finance the 1993 World   7
Trade Center bombing, according to the International AntiCounterfeiting
Coalition. "Profits from counterfeiting are one of the three main sources of
income supporting international terrorism," said Magnus Ranstorp, a terrorism
expert at the University of St. Andrews, in Scotland.

Most fakes today are produced in China, a good many of them by children.   8
Children are sometimes sold or sent off by their families to work in clandestine factories that produce counterfeit luxury goods. Many in the West consider this an urban myth. But I have seen it myself.

On a warm winter afternoon in Guangzhou, I accompanied Chinese police   9
officers on a factory raid in a decrepit tenement. Inside, we found two dozen
children, ages 8 to 13, gluing and sewing together fake luxury-brand handbags.
The police confiscated everything, arrested the owner, and sent the children out.
Some punched their timecards, hoping to still get paid. (The average Chinese
factory worker earns about $120 a month; the counterfeit factory worker earns
half that or less.) As we made our way back to the police vans, the children threw
bottles and cans at us. They were now jobless and, because the factory owner
housed them, homeless. It was *Oliver Twist* in the 21st century.

What can we do to stop this? Much like the war on drugs, the effort to   10
protect luxury brands must go after the source: the counterfeit manufacturers.

The company that took me on the Chinese raid is one of the only luxury-goods makers that works directly with Chinese authorities to shut down factories, and it has one of the lowest rates of counterfeiting.

Luxury brands also need to teach consumers that the traffic in fake 11 goods has many victims. But most companies refuse to speak publicly about counterfeiting—some won't even authenticate questionable items for concerned customers—believing, like Victorians,° that acknowledging despicable actions tarnishes their sterling reputations.

So it comes down to us. If we stop knowingly buying fakes, the supply 12 chain will dry up and counterfeiters will go out of business. The crime syndicates will have far less money to finance their illicit activities and their terrorist plots. And the children? They can go home.

The people who lived during the reign of Victoria (1819–1901), queen of Great Britain and Ireland, who are often associated with prudish behavior

A POWERFUL CALL TO ACTION
DENIZ BILGUTAY

In her *New York Times* essay, "Terror's Purse Strings," writer Dana Thomas uses the opening of New York's fashion shows as an opportunity to expose a darker side of fashion—the impact of imitation designer goods. Thomas explains to her readers why buying counterfeit luxury items, like fake handbags, is a serious problem. Her first goal is to raise awareness of the dangerous ties between counterfeiters who sell fake luxury merchandise and international criminal organizations that support terrorism and child labor. Her second goal is to explain how people can be a part of the solution by refusing to buy the counterfeit goods that finance these criminal activities. By establishing her credibility, building her case slowly, and appealing to both logic and emotions, Thomas succeeds in writing an interesting and informative argument.

1 Context

Topic

Analysis of writer's purpose

Thesis statement: Assessment of essay

For Thomas's argument to work, she has to earn her readers' trust. She does so first by anticipating a sympathetic, well-intentioned, educated audience and then by establishing her own credibility. To avoid sounding accusatory, Thomas assumes that her readers are unaware of the problem posed by counterfeit goods. She demonstrates this by presenting basic factual information and by acknowledging what "most people think" or what "many in the West consider": that buying counterfeit goods is harmless. She also acknowledges her readers' high level of education by

2 Analysis of writer's audience

Writer's use of similes, metaphors, allusions

drawing comparisons with history and literature—specifically, the Victorians and *Oliver Twist*. To further earn the audience's trust, she uses her knowledge and position to gain credibility. As the Paris correspondent for *Newsweek* and as the author of a book on luxury goods, Thomas has credibility. Showing her familiarity with the world of fashion by referring to a conversation with renowned designer Miuccia Prada, she further establishes this credibility. Later in the article, she shares her experience of witnessing the abuse that accompanies the production of fake designer handbags. This anecdote allows her to say, "I've seen it myself," confirming her knowledge not just of the fashion world but also of the world of counterfeiting. Despite her authority, she does not distance herself from readers. In fact, she goes out of her way to identify with them, using informal style and first person, noting "it comes down to us" and asking what "we" can do.

In Thomas's argument, both the organization and the use of evidence   3 are effective. Thomas begins her article with statements that are easy to accept, and as she proceeds, she addresses more serious issues. In the first paragraph, she simply asks readers to "understand the importance of the handbag in fashion today." She demonstrates the wide-ranging influence and appeal of counterfeit designer goods, pointing out that "at least 11 percent of the world's clothing is fake." Thomas then makes the point that the act of purchasing these seemingly frivolous goods can actually have serious consequences. For example, crime syndicates and possibly even terrorist organizations actually run "the counterfeiting rackets" that produce these popular items. To support this point, she relies on two kinds of evidence—quotations from terrorism experts (specifically, the leader of a respected international police organization as well as a scholar in the field) and her own personal experience at a Chinese factory. Both kinds of evidence appeal to our emotions. Discussions of terrorism, especially those that recall the terrorist attacks on the United States, create fear. Descriptions of child labor in China encourage readers to feel sympathy.

Thomas waits until the end of her argument to present her thesis   4 because she assumes that her readers know little about the problem she is discussing. The one flaw in her argument is her failure to provide the evidence needed to establish connections between some causes and their effects. For example in paragraph 7, Thomas says that the sale of counterfeit T-shirts "may have helped finance the 1993 Word Trade Center bomb-

Writer's use of ethos

Analysis of the writer

Analysis of essay's organization

Writer's use of logos

Writer's use of evidence

Writer's use of pathos

Analysis of the essay's weakness

ing." By using the word *may*, she qualifies her claim and weakens her argument. The same is true when Thomas says that profits from the sale of counterfeit goods "have gone to groups associated with Hezbollah, the Shiite terrorist group." Readers are left to wonder what specific groups are "associated with Hezbollah" and whether these groups are in fact terrorist organizations. Without this information, her assertion remains unsupported. In spite of these shortcomings, Thomas's argument is clear and well organized. More definite links between causes and effects, however, would have made it more convincing than it is.

⊘ EXERCISE 4.1

Read the following essay, "Sweatshop Oppression," by Rajeev Ravisankar. Then, write a one-paragraph rhetorical analysis of the essay. Follow the template on page 119, filling in the blanks to create your analysis.

This opinion essay was published in the *Lantern*, the student newspaper of the Ohio State University, on April 19, 2006.

SWEATSHOP OPPRESSION

RAJEEV RAVISANKAR

Being the "poor" college students that we all are, many of us undoubtedly 1 place an emphasis on finding the lowest prices. Some take this to the extreme and camp out in front of a massive retail store in the wee hours of the morning on Black Friday,° waiting for the opportunity to buy as much as we can for as little as possible.

The Friday after Thanksgiving, traditionally the biggest shopping day of the year

What often gets lost in this rampant, low-cost driven consumerism is the 2 high human cost it takes to achieve lower and lower prices. Specifically, this means the extensive use of sweatshop labor.

Many of us are familiar with the term sweatshop,° but have difficulty 3 really understanding how abhorrent the hours, wages, and conditions are. Many of these workers are forced to work 70–80 hours per week making pennies per hour. Workers are discouraged or intimidated from forming unions.

A work environment with long hours, low wages, and difficult or dangerous conditions

They must fulfill certain quotas for the day and stay extra hours (with no 4 pay) if these are not fulfilled. Some are forced to sit in front of a machine for hours as they are not permitted to take breaks unless the manager allows them to do so. Unsanitary bathrooms, poor ventilation, and extreme heat, upward of 90 degrees, are also prevalent. Child labor is utilized in some factories as well.

Facing mounting pressure from labor rights activists, trade unions, student protests, and human-rights groups, companies claimed that they would make improvements. Many of the aforementioned conditions, however, persist. In many cases, even a few pennies more could make a substantial difference in the lives of these workers. Of course, multinational corporations are not interested in giving charity; they are interested in doing anything to increase profits. Also, many consumers in the West refuse to pay a little bit more even if it would improve the lives of sweatshop workers.

> "[Corporations] are interested in doing anything to increase profits."

Free-market economic fundamentalists have argued that claims made by those who oppose sweatshops actually have a negative impact on the plight of the poor in the developing world. They suggest that by criticizing labor and human-rights conditions, anti-sweatshop activists have forced companies to pull out of some locations, resulting in workers losing their jobs. To shift the blame in this manner is to neglect a simple fact: Companies, not the anti-sweatshop protestors, make the decision to shift to locations where they can find cheaper labor and weaker labor restrictions.

Simply put, the onus should always be on companies such as Nike, Reebok, Adidas, Champion, Gap, Wal-Mart, etc. They are to blame for perpetuating a system of exploitation which seeks to get as much out of each worker for the least possible price.

By continuing to strive for lower wages and lower input costs, they are taking part in a phenomenon which has been described as "the race to the bottom." The continual decline of wages and working conditions will be accompanied by a lower standard of living. This hardly seems like the best way to bring the developing world out of the pits of poverty.

So what can we do about it? Currently, the total disregard for human well-being through sweatshop oppression is being addressed by a number of organizations, including University Students against Sweatshops. USAS seeks to make universities source their apparel in factories that respect workers' rights, especially the right to freely form unions.

According to an article in *The Nation*, universities purchase nearly "$3 billion in T-shirts, sweatshirts, caps, sneakers and sports uniforms adorned with their institutions' names and logos." Because brands do not want to risk losing this money, it puts pressure on them to provide living wages and reasonable conditions for workers. Campaigns such as this are necessary if we are to stop the long race to the bottom.

TEMPLATE FOR WRITING A RHETORICAL ANALYSIS

Ravisankar begins his essay by _____
_____
_____. The problem he identifies is _____
_____
_____. Ravisankar assumes his readers are _____
_____
_____. His purpose in this essay is to _____
_____
In order to accomplish this purpose, he appeals mainly to _____
_____
_____. He also appeals to _____
_____
In his essay, Ravisankar addresses the main argument against his thesis, the idea that _____
_____
_____
He refutes this argument by saying _____
_____
_____
Finally, he concludes by making the point that _____
_____
Overall, the argument Ravisankar makes is effective [or ineffective] because _____
_____
_____
_____

⤷ EXERCISE 4.2

Read the following essay, "Where Sweatshops Are a Dream," by Nicholas D. Kristof. Then, write a rhetorical analysis of Kristof's essay. Be sure to consider the rhetorical situation, the means of persuasion, and the writer's rhetorical strategies. End your rhetorical analysis with an assessment of the strengths and weaknesses of Kristof's argument.

This opinion column was published in the *New York Times* on January 15, 2009.

WHERE SWEATSHOPS ARE A DREAM

NICHOLAS D. KRISTOF

Before Barack Obama and his team act on their talk about "labor standards," I'd like to offer them a tour of the vast garbage dump here in Phnom Penh. 1

This is a Dante-like vision of hell. It's a mountain of festering refuse, a half-hour hike across, emitting clouds of smoke from subterranean fires. 2

The miasma of toxic stink leaves you gasping, breezes batter you with filth, and even the rats look forlorn. Then the smoke parts and you come across a child ambling barefoot, searching for old plastic cups that recyclers will buy for five cents a pound. Many families actually live in shacks on this smoking garbage. 3

Mr. Obama and the Democrats who favor labor standards in trade agreements mean well, for they intend to fight back at oppressive sweatshops abroad. But while it shocks Americans to hear it, the central challenge in the poorest countries is not that sweatshops exploit too many people, but that they don't exploit enough. 4

Talk to these families in the dump, and a job in a sweatshop is a cherished dream, an escalator out of poverty, the kind of gauzy if probably unrealistic ambition that parents everywhere often have for their children. 5

"I'd love to get a job in a factory," said Pim Srey Rath, a 19-year-old woman scavenging for plastic. "At least that work is in the shade. Here is where it's hot." 6

Another woman, Vath Sam Oeun, hopes her 10-year-old boy, scavenging beside her, grows up to get a factory job, partly because she has seen other children run over by garbage trucks. Her boy has never been to a doctor or a dentist and last bathed when he was 2, so a sweatshop job by comparison would be far more pleasant and less dangerous. 7

I'm glad that many Americans are repulsed by the idea of importing products made by barely paid, barely legal workers in dangerous factories. Yet sweatshops are only a symptom of poverty, not a cause, and banning them closes off one route out of poverty. At a time of tremendous economic distress and protectionist pressures, there's a special danger that tighter labor standards will be used as an excuse to curb trade. 8

> "[S]weatshops are only a symptom of poverty, not a cause."

When I defend sweatshops, people always ask me: But would you want to work in a sweatshop? No, of course not. But I would want even less to pull a 9 rickshaw. In the hierarchy of jobs in poor countries, sweltering at a sewing machine isn't the bottom.

My views on sweatshops are shaped by years living in East Asia, watching   10
as living standards soared—including those in my wife's ancestral village in southern China—because of sweatshop jobs.

Manufacturing is one sector that can provide millions of jobs. Yet sweat-   11
shops usually go not to the poorest nations but to better-off countries with more reliable electricity and ports.

I often hear the argument: Labor standards can improve wages and work-   12
ing conditions, without greatly affecting the eventual retail cost of goods. That's true. But labor standards and "living wages" have a larger impact on production costs that companies are always trying to pare. The result is to push companies to operate more capital-intensive factories in better-off nations like Malaysia, rather than labor-intensive factories in poorer countries like Ghana or Cambodia.

Cambodia has, in fact, pursued an interesting experiment by working   13
with factories to establish decent labor standards and wages. It's a worthwhile idea, but one result of paying above-market wages is that those in charge of hiring often demand bribes—sometimes a month's salary—in exchange for a job. In addition, these standards add to production costs, so some factories have closed because of the global economic crisis and the difficulty of compet-ing internationally.

The best way to help people in the poorest countries isn't to campaign   14
against sweatshops but to promote manufacturing there. One of the best things America could do for Africa would be to strengthen our program to encourage African imports, called AGOA, and nudge Europe to match it.

Among people who work in development, many strongly believe (but few   15
dare say very loudly) that one of the best hopes for the poorest countries would be to build their manufacturing industries. But global campaigns against sweatshops make that less likely.

Look, I know that Americans have a hard time accepting that sweatshops   16
can help people. But take it from 13-year-old Neuo Chanthou, who earns a bit less than $1 a day scavenging in the dump. She's wearing a "Playboy" shirt and hat that she found amid the filth, and she worries about her sister, who lost part of her hand when a garbage truck ran over her.

"It's dirty, hot, and smelly here," she said wistfully. "A factory is better."   17

SAVE FREEDOM OF SPEECH

BUY WAR BONDS

5

Understanding Logic and Recognizing Logical Fallacies

(AT ISSUE)

How Free Should Free Speech Be?

Ask almost anyone what makes a society free and one of the answers will be free speech. The free expression of ideas is integral to freedom itself, and protecting that freedom is part of a democratic government's job: in a sense, this means that most people see free speech as one of the cornerstones of equality. Everyone's opinion can, and indeed must, be heard.

But what happens when those opinions are offensive, or even dangerous? If free speech has limits, is it still free? When we consider the question abstractly, it's very easy to say no. How can it be free if there are limits to how free it is, and who gets to decide those limits? It's dangerous to give anyone that kind of authority. After all, there is no shortage of historical evidence linking censorship with tyranny. When we think of limiting free speech, we think of totalitarian regimes, like Nazi Germany.

But what happens when the people arguing for the right to be heard are Nazis themselves? In places like Israel and France, where the legacy of Nazi Germany is still all too real, there are some

things you simply cannot say. Anti-Semitic language is considered "hate speech," and those who perpetuate it face stiff fines, if not imprisonment. It might seem outrageous to those of us who live in the United States. If you live in Israel, however, chances are that the legacy of the Holocaust is not that far away. And there are people in France who can still remember the day Nazi troops marched into Paris. Should they have to listen to what neo-Nazis have to say?

On American college campuses, free speech is often considered fundamental to a liberal education, and in many ways, encountering ideas that make you feel uncomfortable is a necessary part of a college education. But the question of free speech is easy to answer when it's theoretical: when the issue is made tangible by racist language or by a discussion of a traumatic experience, it becomes much more difficult to navigate. For example, should African-American students have to listen to "the n-word" in a discussion of *Huckleberry Finn*? Should a nineteen-year-old rape survivor have to sit through a

(continued)

(*continued*)

discussion of rape in American literature? Advocates of unlimited free speech respond to these objections by pointing out that censorship is a slippery slope: once you can penalize a person for saying something hateful, there will be no end to the subjects that will be off-limits.

Later in this chapter, you will be asked to think more about this issue. You will be given several sources to consider and asked to write a logical argument that takes a position on how free free speech should be.

The word *logic* comes from the Greek word *logos*, roughly translated as "word," "thought," "principle," or "reason." **Logic** is concerned with the principles of correct reasoning. By studying logic, you learn the rules that determine the validity of arguments. In other words, logic enables you to tell whether a conclusion correctly follows from a set of statements or assumptions.

Why should you study logic? One answer is that logic enables you to make valid points and draw sound conclusions. An understanding of logic also enables you to evaluate the arguments of others. When you understand the basic principles of logic, you know how to tell the difference between a strong argument and a weak argument—between one that is well reasoned and one that is not. This ability can help you cut through the tangle of jumbled thought that characterizes many of the arguments you encounter daily—on television, radio, and the Internet; in the press; and from friends. Finally, logic enables you to communicate clearly and forcefully. Understanding the characteristics of good arguments helps you to present your own ideas in a coherent and even compelling way.

Kobe Bryant, who played for the Los Angeles Lakers, arguing with a referee

Mark Ralston/Getty

Specific rules determine the criteria you use to develop (and to evaluate) arguments logically. For this reason, you should become familiar with the basic principles of *deductive* and *inductive reasoning*—two important ways information is organized in argumentative essays. (Keep in mind that a single argumentative essay might contain both deductive reasoning and inductive reasoning. For the sake of clarity, however, we will discuss them separately.)

What Is Deductive Reasoning?

Most of us use deductive reasoning every day—at home, in school, on the job, and in our communities—usually without even realizing it.

Deductive reasoning begins with **premises**—statements or assumptions on which an argument is based or from which conclusions are drawn. Deductive reasoning moves from general statements, or premises, to specific conclusions. The process of deduction has traditionally been illustrated with a **syllogism**, which consists of a *major premise*, a *minor premise*, and a *conclusion*:

Thomas Jefferson

© RMN-Grand Palais/Art Resource, NY

MAJOR PREMISE	All Americans are guaranteed freedom of speech by the Constitution.
MINOR PREMISE	Sarah is an American.
CONCLUSION	Therefore, Sarah is guaranteed freedom of speech.

A syllogism begins with a **major premise**—a general statement that relates two terms. It then moves to a **minor premise**—an example of the statement that was made in the major premise. If these two premises are linked correctly, a **conclusion** that is supported by the two premises logically follows. (Notice that the conclusion in the syllogism above contains no terms that do not appear in the major and minor premises.) The strength of deductive reasoning is that if readers accept the major and minor premises, the conclusion must necessarily follow.

Thomas Jefferson used deductive reasoning in the Declaration of Independence. When, in 1776, the Continental Congress asked him to draft this document, Jefferson knew that he had to write a powerful argument that would convince the world that the American colonies were justified in breaking away from England. He knew how compelling a deductive argument could be, and so he organized the Declaration of Independence to reflect the traditional structure of deductive logic. It contains a major premise, a minor premise (supported by evidence), and a conclusion. Expressed as a syllogism, here is the argument that Jefferson used:

MAJOR PREMISE	When a government oppresses people, the people have a right to rebel against that government.
MINOR PREMISE	The government of England oppresses the American people.
CONCLUSION	Therefore, the American people have the right to rebel against the government of England.

In practice, deductive arguments are more complicated than the simple three-part syllogism suggests. Still, it is important to understand the basic structure of a syllogism because a syllogism enables you to map out your argument, to test it, and to see if it makes sense.

Constructing Sound Syllogisms

A syllogism is **valid** when its conclusion follows logically from its premises. A syllogism is **true** when the premises are consistent with the facts. To be **sound**, a syllogism must be *both* valid and true.

Consider the following valid syllogism:

MAJOR PREMISE	All state universities must accommodate disabled students.
MINOR PREMISE	UCLA is a state university.
CONCLUSION	Therefore, UCLA must accommodate disabled students.

In the valid syllogism above, both the major premise and the minor premise are factual statements. If both these premises are true, then the conclusion must also be true. Because the syllogism is both valid and true, it is also sound.

However, a syllogism can be valid without being true. For example, look at the following syllogism:

MAJOR PREMISE	All recipients of support services are wealthy.
MINOR PREMISE	Dillon is a recipient of support services.
CONCLUSION	Therefore, Dillon is wealthy.

As illogical as it may seem, this syllogism is valid: its conclusion follows logically from its premises. The major premise states that *recipients of support services*—all such *recipients*—are wealthy. However, this premise is clearly false: some recipients of support services may be wealthy, but more are probably not. For this reason, even though the syllogism is valid, it is not true.

Keep in mind that validity is a test of an argument's structure, not of its soundness. Even if a syllogism's major and minor premises are true, its conclusion may not necessarily be valid.

Consider the following examples of invalid syllogisms.

Syllogism with an Illogical Middle Term

A syllogism with an illogical middle term cannot be valid. The **middle term** of a syllogism is the term that occurs in both the major and minor premises but not in the conclusion. (It links the major term and the minor term together in the syllogism.) A middle term of a valid syllogism must refer to *all* members of the designated class or group—for example, *all* dogs, *all* people, *all* men, or *all* women.

Consider the following invalid syllogism:

MAJOR PREMISE   All dogs are mammals.

MINOR PREMISE   Some mammals are porpoises.

CONCLUSION   Therefore, some porpoises are dogs.

Cartoonstock.com

Even though the statements in the major and minor premises are true, the syllogism is not valid. *Mammals* is the middle term because it appears in both the major and minor premises. However, because the middle term *mammal* does not refer to *all mammals*, it cannot logically lead to a valid conclusion.

In the syllogism that follows, the middle term *does* refer to all members of the designated group, so the syllogism is valid:

MAJOR PREMISE	All dogs are mammals.
MINOR PREMISE	Ralph is a dog.
CONCLUSION	Therefore, Ralph is a mammal.

Syllogism with a Key Term Whose Meaning Shifts

A syllogism that contains a key term whose meaning shifts cannot be valid. For this reason, the meaning of a key term must remain consistent throughout the syllogism.

Consider the following invalid syllogism:

MAJOR PREMISE	Only man is capable of analytical reasoning.
MINOR PREMISE	Anna is not a man.
CONCLUSION	Therefore, Anna is not capable of analytical reasoning.

In the major premise, *man* refers to mankind—that is, to all human beings. In the minor premise, however, *man* refers to males. In the following valid syllogism, the key terms remain consistent:

MAJOR PREMISE	All educated human beings are capable of analytical reasoning.
MINOR PREMISE	Anna is an educated human being.
CONCLUSION	Therefore, Anna is capable of analytical reasoning.

Syllogism with Negative Premise

If *either* premise in a syllogism is negative, then the conclusion must also be negative.

The following syllogism is not valid:

MAJOR PREMISE	Only senators can vote on legislation.
MINOR PREMISE	No students are senators.
CONCLUSION	Therefore, students can vote on legislation.

Because one of the premises of the syllogism above is negative ("No students are senators"), the only possible valid conclusion must also be negative ("Therefore, no students can vote on legislation").

If *both* premises are negative, however, the syllogism cannot have a valid conclusion:

MAJOR PREMISE Disabled students may not be denied special help.

MINOR PREMISE Jen is not a disabled student.

CONCLUSION Therefore, Jen may not be denied special help.

In the syllogism above, both premises are negative. For this reason, the syllogism cannot have a valid conclusion. (How can Jen deserve special help if she is not a disabled student?) To have a valid conclusion, this syllogism must have only one negative premise:

MAJOR PREMISE Disabled students may not be denied special help.

MINOR PREMISE Jen is a disabled student.

CONCLUSION Therefore, Jen may not be denied special help.

Recognizing Enthymemes

An **enthymeme** is a syllogism with one or two parts of its argument—usually, the major premise—missing. In everyday life, we often leave out parts of arguments—most of the time because we think they are so obvious (or clearly implied) that they don't need to be stated. We assume that the people hearing or reading the arguments will easily be able to fill in the missing parts.

Many enthymemes are presented as a conclusion plus a reason. Consider the following enthymeme:

Robert has lied, so he cannot be trusted.

In the statement above, the minor premise and the conclusion are stated, but the major premise is only implied. Once the missing term has been supplied, the logical structure of the enthymeme becomes clear:

MAJOR PREMISE People who lie cannot be trusted.

MINOR PREMISE Robert has lied.

CONCLUSION Therefore, Robert cannot be trusted.

It is important to identify enthymemes in arguments you read because some writers, knowing that readers often accept enthymemes uncritically, use them intentionally to unfairly influence readers.

Consider this enthymeme:

Because Liz receives a tuition grant, she should work.

Although some readers might challenge this statement, others will accept it uncritically. When you supply the missing premise, however, the underlying assumptions of the enthymeme become clear—and open to question:

MAJOR PREMISE	All students who receive tuition grants should work.
MINOR PREMISE	Liz receives a tuition grant.
CONCLUSION	Therefore, Liz should work.

Perhaps some people who receive tuition grants should work, but should everyone? What about those who are ill or who have disabilities? What about those who participate in varsity sports or have unpaid internships? The enthymeme oversimplifies the issue and should not be accepted at face value.

At first glance, the following enthymeme might seem to make sense:

North Korea is ruled by a dictator, so it should be invaded.

However, consider the same enthymeme with the missing term supplied:

MAJOR PREMISE	All countries governed by dictators should be invaded.
MINOR PREMISE	North Korea is a country governed by a dictator.
CONCLUSION	Therefore, North Korea should be invaded.

Once the missing major premise has been supplied, the flaws in the argument become clear. Should *all* nations governed by dictators be invaded? Who should do the invading? Who would make this decision? What would be the consequences of such a policy? As this enthymeme illustrates, if the major premise of a deductive argument is questionable, then the rest of the argument will also be flawed.

BUMPER-STICKER THINKING

Bumper stickers often take the form of enthymemes:

- Self-control beats birth control.

- Peace is patriotic.

- A woman's place is in the House . . . and in the Senate.

- Ban cruel traps.

- Evolution is a theory—kind of like gravity.

- I work and pay taxes so wealthy people don't have to.

- The Bible says it, I believe it, that settles it.

- No one needs a mink coat except a mink.

- Celebrate diversity.

Most often, bumper stickers state just the conclusion of an argument and omit both the major and minor premises. Careful readers, however, will supply the missing premises and thus determine whether the argument is sound.

Bumper stickers on a car. © Dave G. Houser/Corbis.

⊕ EXERCISE 5.1

Read the following paragraph. Then, restate its main argument as a syllogism.

Drunk Driving Should Be Legalized

In ordering states to enforce tougher drunk driving standards by making it a crime to drive with a blood-alcohol concentration of .08 percent or higher, government has been permitted to criminalize the content of drivers' blood instead of their actions. The assumption that a driver who has been drinking automatically presents a danger to society even when no harm has been caused is a blatant violation of civil liberties. Government should not be concerned with the probability and propensity of a drinking driver to cause an accident; rather, laws should deal only with actions that damage person or property. Until they actually commit a crime, drunk drivers should be liberated from the force of the law. (From "Legalize Drunk Driving," by Llewellyn H. Rockwell Jr., WorldNetDaily.com)

⊘ EXERCISE 5.2

Read the following paragraphs. Then, answer the questions that follow.

Animals Are Equal to Humans

According to the United Nations, a person may not be killed, exploited, cruelly treated, intimidated, or imprisoned for no good reason. Put another way, people should be able to live in peace, according to their own needs and preferences.

Who should have these rights? Do they apply to people of all races? Children? People who are brain damaged or senile? The declaration makes it clear that basic rights apply to everyone. To make a slave of someone who is intellectually handicapped or of a different race is no more justifiable than to make a slave of anyone else.

The reason why these rights apply to everyone is simple: regardless of our differences, we all experience a life with its mosaic of thoughts and feelings. This applies equally to the princess and the hobo, the brain surgeon and the dunce. Our value as individuals arises from this capacity to experience life, not because of any intelligence or usefulness to others. Every person has an inherent value, and deserves to be treated with respect in order to make the most of their unique life experience. (Excerpted from "Human and Animal Rights," by Animal Liberation.org)

1. What unstated assumptions about the subject does the writer make? Does the writer expect readers to accept these assumptions? How can you tell?

2. What kind of supporting evidence does the writer provide?

3. What is the major premise of this argument?

4. Express the argument that is presented in these paragraphs as a syllogism.

5. Evaluate the syllogism you constructed. Is it true? Is it valid? Is it sound?

⊘ EXERCISE 5.3

Read the following five arguments, and determine whether each is sound. (To help you evaluate the arguments, you may want to try arranging them as syllogisms.)

1. All humans are mortal. Max is human. Therefore, Max is mortal.

2. Alison should order eggs or oatmeal for breakfast. She won't order eggs, so she should order oatmeal.

3. The cafeteria does not serve meat loaf on Friday. Today is not Friday. Therefore, the cafeteria will not serve meat loaf.

4. All reptiles are cold-blooded. Geckos are reptiles. Therefore, geckos are cold-blooded.

5. All triangles have three equal sides. The figure on the board is a triangle. Therefore, it must have three equal sides.

⊗ EXERCISE 5.4

Read the following ten enthymemes, which come from bumper stickers. Supply the missing premises, and then evaluate the logic of each argument.

1. If you love your pet, don't eat meat.
2. War is terrorism.
3. Real men don't ask for directions.
4. Immigration is the sincerest form of flattery.
5. I eat local because I can.
6. Don't blame me; I voted for the other guy.
7. I read banned books.
8. Love is the only solution.
9. It's a child, not a choice.
10. Think. It's patriotic.

Writing Deductive Arguments

Deductive arguments begin with a general principle and reach a specific conclusion. They develop that principle with logical arguments that are supported by evidence—facts, observations, the opinions of experts, and so on. Keep in mind that no single structure is suitable for all deductive (or inductive) arguments. Different issues and different audiences will determine how you arrange your ideas.

In general, deductive essays can be structured in the following way:

INTRODUCTION	Presents an overview of the issue States the thesis
BODY	Presents evidence: point 1 in support of the thesis Presents evidence: point 2 in support of the thesis Presents evidence: point 3 in support of the thesis Refutes the arguments against the thesis
CONCLUSION	Brings argument to a close Concluding statement reinforces the thesis

⊖ EXERCISE 5.5

The following student essay, "College Should Be for Everyone," includes all the elements of a deductive argument. The student who wrote this essay was responding to the question, "Should everyone be encouraged to go to college?" After you read the essay, answer the questions on pages 136–137, consulting the outline on page 133 if necessary.

COLLEGE SHOULD BE FOR EVERYONE

CRYSTAL SANCHEZ

Overview of issue

Thesis statement

Until the middle of the twentieth century, college was largely for the   1
rich. The G.I. Bill, which paid for the education of veterans returning from World War II, helped to change this situation. By 1956, nearly half of those who had served in World War II, almost 7.8 million people, had taken advantage of this benefit (U.S. Department of Veterans Affairs). Even today, however, college graduates are still a minority of the population. According to the U.S. Census Bureau, only 27.5 percent of Americans age twenty-five or older have a bachelor's degree. In many ways, this situation is not good for the country. Why should college be just for the privileged few? Because a college education provides important benefits, such as increased wages for our citizens and a stronger democracy for our nation, every U.S. citizen should have the opportunity to attend college.

Evidence: Point 1

One reason everyone should have the opportunity to go to college is   2
that a college education gives people a chance to discover what they are good at. It is hard for people to know if they are interested in statistics or public policy or marketing unless they have the chance to explore these subjects. College—and only college—can give them this opportunity. Where else can a person be exposed to a large number of courses taught by experts in a variety of disciplines? Such exposure can open new areas of interest and lead to a much wider set of career options—and thus to a better life (Stout). Without college, most people have limited options and never realize their true potential. Although life and work experiences can teach a person a lot of things, the best education is the broad kind that college offers.

Evidence: Point 2 .

Another reason everyone should have the opportunity to go to   3
college is that more and more jobs are being phased out or moved overseas. Americans should go to college to develop the skills that they will

need to get the best jobs that will remain in the United States. Over the last few decades, midlevel jobs have been steadily disappearing. If this trend continues, the American workforce will be divided in two. One part will consist of low-wage, low-skill service jobs, such as those in food preparation and retail sales, and the other part will be high-skill, high-wage jobs, such as those in management and professional fields like business and engineering. According to a recent report, to compete in the future job market, Americans will need the skills that colleges teach. Future workers will need to be problem solvers who can think both critically and creatively and who can adapt to unpredictable situations. They will also need a global awareness, knowledge of many cultures and disciplines, and the ability to communicate in different forms of media. To master these skills, Americans have to be college educated ("Ten Skills for the Future Workforce").

Perhaps the best reason everyone should have the opportunity to go to college is that education is an essential component of a democratic society. Those without the ability to understand and analyze news reports are not capable of contributing to the social, political, and economic growth of the country. Democracy requires informed citizens who will be able to analyze complicated issues in areas such as finance, education, and public health; weigh competing claims of those running for public office; and assess the job performance of elected officials. By providing students with the opportunity to study subjects such as history, philosophy, English, and political science, colleges and universities help them to acquire the critical-thinking skills that they will need to participate fully in American democracy.

4　Evidence: Point 3

Some people oppose the idea that everyone should have the opportunity to attend college. One objection is that educational resources are limited. Some say that if students enter colleges in great numbers they will overwhelm the higher-education system (Stout). This argument exaggerates the problem. As with any other product, if demand rises, supply will rise to meet that demand. In addition, with today's extensive distance-learning options and the availability of open educational resources—free, high-quality, digital materials—it will be possible to educate large numbers of students at a reasonable cost ("Open Educational Resources"). Another objection to encouraging everyone to attend college is that underprepared students will require so much help that they will take time and attention away from better students. This argument is actually a red herring.° Most schools already provide resources, such as tutoring and

5　Refutation of opposing arguments

An irrelevant side issue used as a diversion

writing centers, for students who need them. With some additional funding, these schools could expand the services they already provide. This
course of action will be expensive, but it is a lot less expensive than leaving millions of young people unprepared for jobs of the future.

A college education gave the returning veterans of World War II   6
many opportunities and increased their value to the nation. Today, a college education could do the same for many citizens. This country has an
obligation to offer all students access to an affordable and useful education. Not only will the students benefit personally, but the nation will also.
Concluding statement   If we do not adequately prepare students for the future, then we will all
suffer the consequences.

Works Cited

"Open Educational Resources." *Center for American Progress*, 7 Feb.
    2012, www.americanprogress.org/issues/labor/news/2012
    /02/07/11114/open-educational-resources/.

Stout, Chris. "Top Five Reasons Why You Should Choose to Go to Col-
    lege." *Ezine Articles*, 2008, ezinearticles.com/?Top-Five-Reasons-
    Why-You-Should-Choose-To-Go-To-College&id=384395.

"Ten Skills for the Future Workforce." *The Atlantic,* 22 June 2011,
    www.theatlantic.com/education/archive/2011/06/ten-skills-for-future
    -work/473484/.

United States, Census Bureau. "Bachelor's Degree Attainment Tops 30
    Percent for the First Time, Census Bureau Reports." *US Census
    Bureau Newsroom*, 23 Feb. 2012, www.census.gov/newsroom
    /releases/archives/education/cb12-33.html.

---, Department of Veterans Affairs. "Born of Controversy: The GI Bill of
    Rights." *GI Bill History*, 20 Oct. 2008, www.va.gov/opa/publications
    /celebrate/gi-bill.pdf.

Identifying the Elements of a Deductive Argument

1. Paraphrase this essay's thesis.

2. What arguments does the writer present as evidence to support her
   thesis? Which do you think is the strongest argument? Which is the
   weakest?

3. What opposing arguments does the writer address? What other
   opposing arguments could she have addressed?

4. What points does the conclusion emphasize? Do you think that any other points should be emphasized?

5. Construct a syllogism that expresses the essay's argument. Then, check your syllogism to make sure it is sound.

What Is Inductive Reasoning?

Inductive reasoning begins with specific observations (or evidence) and goes on to draw a general conclusion. You can see how induction works by looking at the following list of observations:

- Nearly 80 percent of ocean pollution comes from runoff.

- Runoff pollution can make ocean water unsafe for fish and people.

- In some areas, runoff pollution has forced beaches to be closed.

- Drinking water can be contaminated by runoff.

- More than one third of shellfish growing in waters in the United States are contaminated by runoff.

- Each year, millions of dollars are spent to restore polluted areas.

- There is a causal relationship between agricultural runoff and water-borne organisms that damage fish.

After studying these observations, you can use inductive reasoning to reach the conclusion that runoff pollution (rainwater that becomes polluted after

| Sign warning of contaminated water

© Krista Kennella/ZUMA PRESS

it comes in contact with earth-bound pollutants such as fertilizer, pet waste, sewage, and pesticides) is a problem that must be addressed.

Children learn about the world by using inductive reasoning. For example, very young children see that if they push a light switch up, the lights in a room go on. If they repeat this action over and over, they reach the conclusion that every time they push a switch, the lights will go on. Of course, this conclusion does not always follow. For example, the light bulb may be burned out or the switch may be damaged. Even so, their conclusion usually holds true. Children also use induction to generalize about what is safe and what is dangerous. If every time they meet a dog, the encounter is pleasant, they begin to think that all dogs are friendly. If at some point, however, a dog snaps at them, they question the strength of their conclusion and modify their behavior accordingly.

Scientists also use induction. In 1620, Sir Francis Bacon first proposed the **scientific method**—a way of using induction to find answers to questions. When using the scientific method, a researcher proposes a hypothe-

REACHING INDUCTIVE CONCLUSIONS

Here are some of the ways you can use inductive reasoning to reach conclusions:

- **Particular to general:** This form of induction occurs when you reach a general conclusion based on particular pieces of evidence. For example, suppose you walk into a bathroom and see that the mirrors are fogged. You also notice that the bathtub has drops of water on its sides and that the bathroom floor is wet. In addition, you see a damp towel draped over the sink. Putting all these observations together, you conclude that someone has recently taken a bath. (Detectives use induction when gathering clues to solve a crime.)

- **General to general:** This form of induction occurs when you draw a conclusion based on the consistency of your observations. For example, if you determine that Apple Inc. has made good products for a long time, you conclude it will continue to make good products.

- **General to particular:** This form of induction occurs when you draw a conclusion based on what you generally know to be true. For example, if you believe that cars made by the Ford Motor Company are reliable, then you conclude that a Ford Focus will be a reliable car.

- **Particular to particular:** This form of induction occurs when you assume that because something works in one situation, it will also work in another similar situation. For example, if Krazy Glue fixed the broken handle of one cup, then you conclude it will probably fix the broken handle of another cup.

sis and then makes a series of observations to test this hypothesis. Based on these observations, the researcher arrives at a conclusion that confirms, modifies, or disproves the hypothesis.

Making Inferences

Unlike deduction, which reaches a conclusion based on information provided by the major and minor premises, induction uses what you know to make a statement about something that you don't know. While deductive arguments can be judged in absolute terms (they are either **valid** or **invalid**), inductive arguments are judged in relative terms (they are either **strong** or **weak**).

You reach an inductive conclusion by making an **inference**—a statement about what is unknown based on what is known. (In other words, you look at the evidence and try to figure out what is going on.) For this reason, there is always a gap between your observations and your conclusion. To bridge this gap, you have to make an **inductive leap**—a stretch of the imagination that enables you to draw an acceptable conclusion. Therefore, inductive conclusions are never certain (as deductive conclusions are) but only probable. The more evidence you provide, the stronger and more probable your conclusions (and your argument) are.

Public-opinion polls illustrate how inferences are used to reach inductive conclusions. Politicians and news organizations routinely use public-opinion polls to assess support (or lack of support) for a particular policy, proposal, or political candidate. After surveying a sample population—registered voters, for example—pollsters reach conclusions based on their responses. In other words, by asking questions and studying the responses of a sample group of people, pollsters make inferences about the larger group—for example, which political candidate is ahead and by how much. How solid these inferences are depends to a great extent on the sample populations the pollsters survey. In an election, for example, a poll of randomly chosen individuals will be less accurate than a poll of registered voters or likely voters. In addition, other factors (such as the size of the sample and the way questions are worded) can determine the relative strength of the inductive conclusion.

As with all inferences, a gap exists between a poll's data—the responses to the questions—and the conclusion. The larger and more representative the sample, the smaller the inductive leap necessary to reach a conclusion and the more accurate the poll. If the gap between the data and the conclusion is too big, however, the pollsters will be accused of making a **hasty generalization** (see p. 150). Remember, no matter how much support you present, an inductive conclusion is only probable, never certain. The best you can do is present a convincing case and hope that your audience will accept it.

Constructing Strong Inductive Arguments

When you use inductive reasoning, your conclusion is only as strong as the **evidence**—the facts, details, or examples—that you use to support it. For this reason, you should be on the lookout for the following problems that can occur when you try to reach an inductive conclusion.

Generalization Too Broad

The conclusion you state cannot go beyond the scope of your evidence. Your evidence must support your generalization. For instance, you cannot survey just three international students in your school and conclude that the school does not go far enough to accommodate international students. To reach such a conclusion, you would have to consider a large number of international students.

Insufficient Evidence

The evidence on which you base an inductive conclusion must be **representative**, not atypical or biased. For example, you cannot conclude that students are satisfied with the course offerings at your school by sampling just first-year students. To be valid, your conclusion should be based on responses from a cross section of students from all years.

Irrelevant Evidence

Your evidence has to support your conclusion. If it does not, it is **irrelevant**. For example, if you assert that many adjunct faculty members make substantial contributions to your school, your supporting examples must be adjunct faculty, not tenured or junior faculty.

Exceptions to the Rule

There is always a chance that you will overlook an exception that may affect the strength of your conclusion. For example, not everyone who has a disability needs special accommodations, and not everyone who requires special accommodations needs the same services. For this reason, you should avoid using words like *every*, *all*, and *always* and instead use words like *most*, *many*, and *usually*.

⊙ EXERCISE 5.6

Read the following arguments, and decide whether each is a deductive argument or an inductive argument and write "D" or "I" on the lines below.

1. Freedom of speech is a central principle of our form of government. For this reason, students should be allowed to wear T-shirts that call for the legalization of marijuana. _____

2. The Chevy Cruze Eco gets twenty-seven miles a gallon in the city and forty-six miles a gallon on the highway. The Honda Accord gets twenty-seven miles a gallon in the city and thirty-six miles a gallon on the highway. Therefore, it makes more sense for me to buy the Chevy Cruze Eco. _____

3. In Edgar Allan Poe's short story "The Cask of Amontillado," Montresor flatters Fortunato. He lures him to his vaults where he stores wine. Montresor then gets Fortunato drunk and chains him to the wall of a crypt. Finally, Montresor uncovers a pile of building material and walls up the entrance to the crypt. Clearly, Montresor has carefully planned to murder Fortunato for a very long time. _____

4. All people should have the right to die with dignity. Garrett is a terminally ill patient, so he should have access to doctor-assisted suicide. _____

5. Last week, we found unacceptably high levels of pollution in the ocean. On Monday, we also found high levels of pollution. Today, we found even higher levels of pollution. We should close the ocean beaches to swimmers until we can find the source of this problem. _____

⊘ EXERCISE 5.7

Read the following arguments. Then, decide whether they are deductive or inductive. If they are inductive arguments, evaluate their strength. If they are deductive arguments, evaluate their soundness.

1. *The Farmer's Almanac* says that this winter will be very cold. The National Weather Service also predicts that this winter will be very cold. So, this should be a cold winter.

2. Many walled towns in Europe do not let people drive cars into their centers. San Gimignano is a walled town in Europe. It is likely that we will not be able to drive our car into its center.

3. The window at the back of the house is broken. There is a baseball on the floor. A few minutes ago, I saw two boys playing catch in a neighbor's yard. They must have thrown the ball through the window.

4. Every time I go to the beach I get sunburned. I guess I should stop going to the beach.

5. All my instructors have advanced degrees. George Martin is one of my instructors. Therefore, George Martin has an advanced degree.

6. My last two boyfriends cheated on me. All men are terrible.

7. I read a study published by a pharmaceutical company that said that Accutane was safe. Maybe the government was too quick to pull this drug off the market.

8. Chase is not very good-looking, and he dresses badly. I don't know how he can be a good architect.

9. No fictional character has ever had a fan club. Harry Potter does, but he is the exception.

10. Two weeks ago, my instructor refused to accept a late paper. She did the same thing last week. Yesterday, she also told someone that because his paper was late, she wouldn't accept it. I'd better get my paper in on time.

⊙ EXERCISE 5.8

Read the inductive paragraph below, written by student Pooja Vaidya, and answer the questions that follow it.

Years ago, when my friend took me to a game between the Philadelphia Eagles and the Dallas Cowboys in Philadelphia, I learned a little bit about American football and a lot about the behavior of football fans. Many of the Philadelphia fans were dressed in green and white football jerseys, each with a player's name and number on the back. One fan had his face painted green and wore a green cape with a large white *E* on it. He ran up and down the aisles in his section and led cheers. When the team was ahead, everyone joined in. When the team fell behind, this fan literally fell on his knees, cried, and begged the people in the stands to support the Eagles. (After the game, several people asked him for his autograph.) A group of six fans sat without shirts. They wore green wigs, and each had one letter of the team's name painted on his bare chest. Even though the temperature was below freezing, none of these fans ever put on his shirt. Before the game, many fans had been drinking at tailgate parties in the parking lot, and as the game progressed, they continued to drink beer in the stadium. By the beginning of the second half, fights were breaking out all over the stadium. Guards grabbed the people who were fighting and escorted them to a holding area under the stadium where a judge held "Eagles Court." At one point, a fan wearing a Dallas jersey tried to sit down in the row behind me. Some of the Eagles fans were so threatening that the police had to escort the Dallas fan out of the stands for his own protection. When the game ended in an Eagles victory, the fans sang the team's fight song as they left the stadium. I concluded that for many

Eagles fans, a day at the stadium is an opportunity to engage in behavior that in any other context would be unacceptable and even abnormal.

1. Which of the following statements could you *not* conclude from this paragraph?

    a. All Eagles fans act in outrageous ways at games.

    b. At football games, the fans in the stands can be as violent as the players on the field.

    c. The atmosphere at the stadium causes otherwise normal people to act abnormally.

    d. Spectator sports encourage fans to act in abnormal ways.

    e. Some people get so caught up in the excitement of a game that they act in uncharacteristic ways.

2. Paraphrase the writer's conclusion. What evidence is provided to support this conclusion?

3. What additional evidence could the writer have provided? Is this additional evidence necessary, or does the conclusion stand without it?

4. The writer makes an inductive leap to reach the paragraph's conclusion. Do you think this leap is too great?

5. Does this paragraph make a strong inductive argument? Why or why not?

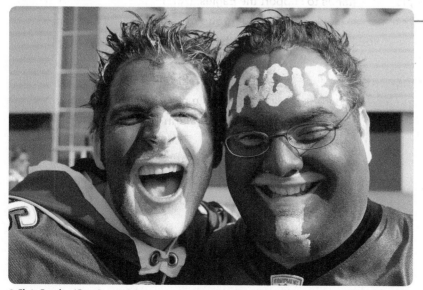

Philadelphia Eagles fans

© Chris Graythen/Getty Images Sports

Writing Inductive Arguments

Inductive arguments begin with evidence (specific facts, observations, expert opinion, and so on), draw inferences from the evidence, and reach a conclusion by making an inductive leap. Keep in mind that inductive arguments are only as strong as the link between the evidence and the conclusion, so the stronger this link is, the stronger the argument will be.

Inductive essays frequently have the following structure:

INTRODUCTION	Presents the issue
	States the thesis
BODY	Presents evidence: facts, observations, expert opinion, and so on
	Draws inferences from the evidence
	Refutes the arguments against the thesis
CONCLUSION	Brings argument to a close
	Concluding statement reinforces the thesis

⊙ EXERCISE 5.9

The following essay includes all the elements of an inductive argument. After you read the essay, answer the questions on page 146, consulting the outline above if necessary.

This essay appeared in *Slate* on September 2, 2006.

PLEASE DO NOT FEED THE HUMANS

WILLIAM SALETAN

Dug

In 1894, Congress established Labor Day to honor those who "from rude 1 nature have delved° and carved all the grandeur we behold." In the century since, the grandeur of human achievement has multiplied. Over the past four decades, global population has doubled, but food output, driven by increases in productivity, has outpaced it. Poverty, infant mortality, and hunger are receding. For the first time in our planet's history, a species no longer lives at the mercy of scarcity. We have learned to feed ourselves.

We've learned so well, in fact, that we're getting fat. Not just the United 2 States or Europe, but the whole world. Egyptian, Mexican, and South African women are now as fat as Americans. Far more Filipino adults are now overweight than underweight. In China, one in five adults is too heavy, and the rate of overweight children is 28 times higher than it was two decades ago. In Thailand, Kuwait, and Tunisia, obesity, diabetes, and heart disease are soaring.

Hunger is far from conquered. But since 1990, the global rate of malnutri- 3
tion has declined an average of 1.7 percent a year. Based on data from the
World Health Organization and the U.N. Food and Agriculture Organization,
for every two people who are malnourished, three are now overweight or
obese. Among women, even in most African countries, overweight has sur-
passed underweight. The balance of peril is shifting.

Fat is no longer a rich man's disease. For middle- and high-income Amer- 4
icans, the obesity rate is 29 percent. For low-income Americans, it's 35 percent.
Among middle- and high-income kids aged 15 to 17, the rate of overweight is
14 percent. Among low-income kids in the same age bracket, it's
23 percent. Globally, weight has tended to rise with income. But a study in
Vancouver, Canada, published three months ago, found that preschoolers in
"food-insecure" households were twice as likely as other kids to be overweight
or obese. In Brazilian cities, the poor have become fatter than the rich.

Technologically, this is a triumph. In the early days of our species, even the 5
rich starved. Barry Popkin, a nutritional epidemiologist at the University of
North Carolina, divides history into several epochs. In the hunter-gatherer era,
if we didn't find food, we died. In the agricultural era, if our crops perished, we
died. In the industrial era, famine receded, but infectious diseases killed us.
Now we've achieved such control over nature that we're dying not of starvation
or infection, but of abundance. Nature isn't killing us. We're killing ourselves.

You don't have to go hungry anymore; we can fill you with fats and carbs 6
more cheaply than ever. You don't have to chase your food; we can bring it to
you. You don't have to cook it; we can deliver it ready-to-eat. You don't have
to eat it before it spoils; we can pump it full of preservatives so it lasts forever.
You don't even have to stop when you're full. We've got so much food to sell,
we want you to keep eating.

What happened in America is happening everywhere, only faster. Fewer 7
farmers' markets, more processed food. Fewer whole grains, more refined
ones. More sweeteners, salt, and trans fats. Cheaper meat, more animal fat.
Less cooking, more eating out. Bigger portions, more snacks.

Kentucky Fried Chicken and Pizza Hut are spreading across the planet. 8
Coca-Cola is in more than 200 countries. Half of McDonald's business is
overseas. In China, animal-fat intake has tripled in 20 years. By 2020, meat
consumption in developing countries will grow by 106 million metric tons,
outstripping growth in developed countries by a factor of more than five.
Forty years ago, to afford a high-fat diet, your country needed a gross national
product per capita of nearly $1,500. Now the price is half that. You no longer
have to be rich to die a rich man's death.

Soon, it'll be a poor man's death. The rich have Whole Foods, gyms, and per- 9
sonal trainers. The poor have 7-Eleven, Popeye's, and streets unsafe for walking.
When money's tight, you feed your kids at Wendy's and stock up on macaroni and
cheese. At a lunch buffet, you do what your ancestors did: store all the fat you can.

That's the punch line: Technology has changed everything but us. We 10
evolved to survive scarcity. We crave fat. We're quick to gain weight and slow

to lose it. Double what you serve us, and we'll double what we eat. Thanks to technology, the deprivation that made these traits useful is gone. So is the link between flavors and nutrients. The modern food industry can sell you sweetness without fruit, salt without protein, creaminess without milk. We can fatten you and starve you at the same time.

> "We evolved to survive scarcity."

And that's just the diet side of the equation. Before technology, adult men had 11 to expend about 3,000 calories a day. Now they expend about 2,000. Look at the new Segway scooter. The original model relieved you of the need to walk, pedal, or balance. With the new one, you don't even have to turn the handlebars or start it manually. In theory, Segway is replacing the car. In practice, it's replacing the body.

In country after country, service jobs are replacing hard labor. The folks 12 who field your customer service calls in Bangalore are sitting at desks. Nearly everyone in China has a television set. Remember when Chinese rode bikes? In the past six years, the number of cars there has grown from six million to 20 million. More than one in seven Chinese has a motorized vehicle, and households with such vehicles have an obesity rate 80 percent higher than their peers.

The answer to these trends is simple. We have to exercise more and 13 change the food we eat, donate, and subsidize. Next year, for example, the U.S. Women, Infants, and Children program, which subsidizes groceries for impoverished youngsters, will begin to pay for fruits and vegetables. For 32 years, the program has fed toddlers eggs and cheese but not one vegetable. And we wonder why poor kids are fat.

The hard part is changing our mentality. We have a distorted body image. 14 We're so used to not having enough, as a species, that we can't believe the problem is too much. From China to Africa to Latin America, people are trying to fatten their kids. I just got back from a vacation with my Jewish mother and Jewish mother-in-law. They told me I need to eat more.

The other thing blinding us is liberal guilt. We're so caught up in the idea 15 of giving that we can't see the importance of changing behavior rather than filling bellies. We know better than to feed buttered popcorn to zoo animals, yet we send it to a food bank and call ourselves humanitarians. Maybe we should ask what our fellow humans actually need.

Identifying the Elements of an Inductive Argument

1. What is this essay's thesis? Restate it in your own words.

2. Why do you think Saletan places the thesis where he does?

3. What evidence does Saletan use to support his conclusion?

4. What inductive leap does Saletan make to reach his conclusion? Do you think he should have included more evidence?

5. Overall, do you think Saletan's inductive argument is relatively strong or weak? Explain.

Recognizing Logical Fallacies

When you write arguments in college, you follow certain rules that ensure fairness. Not everyone who writes arguments is fair or thorough, however. Sometimes you will encounter arguments in which writers attack the opposition's intelligence or patriotism and base their arguments on questionable (or even false) assumptions. As convincing as these arguments can sometimes seem, they are not valid because they contain **fallacies**—errors in reasoning that undermine the logic of an argument. Familiarizing yourself with the most common logical fallacies can help you to evaluate the arguments of others and to construct better, more effective arguments of your own.

The following pages define and illustrate some logical fallacies that you should learn to recognize and avoid.

Begging the Question

The fallacy of **begging the question** assumes that a statement is self-evident (or true) when it actually requires proof. A conclusion based on such assumptions cannot be valid. For example, someone who is very religious could structure an argument the following way:

MAJOR PREMISE	Everything in the Bible is true.
MINOR PREMISE	The Bible says that Noah built an ark.
CONCLUSION	Therefore, Noah's Ark really existed.

A person can accept the conclusion of this syllogism only if he or she also accepts the major premise, which has not been proven true. Some people might find this line of reasoning convincing, but others would not—even if they were religious.

Begging the question occurs any time someone presents a debatable statement as if it were true. For example, look at the following statement:

> You have unfairly limited my right of free speech by refusing to print my editorial in the college newspaper.

This statement begs the question because it assumes what it should be proving—that refusing to print an editorial violates a person's right to free speech.

Circular Reasoning

Closely related to begging the question, **circular reasoning** occurs when someone supports a statement by restating it in different terms. Consider the following statement:

> Stealing is wrong because it is illegal.

Waterfall, by M. C. Escher. The artwork creates the illusion of water flowing uphill and in a circle. Circular reasoning occurs when the conclusion of an argument is the same as one of the premises.

The conclusion of the statement on the previous page is essentially the same as its beginning: stealing (which is illegal) is against the law. In other words, the argument goes in a circle.

Here are some other examples of circular reasoning:

- Lincoln was a great president because he is the best president we ever had.

- I am for equal rights for women because I am a feminist.

- Illegal immigrants should be deported because they are breaking the law.

All of the statements above have one thing in common: they attempt to support a statement by simply repeating the statement in different words.

Weak Analogy

An **analogy** is a comparison between two items (or concepts)—one familiar and one unfamiliar. When you make an analogy, you explain the unfamiliar item by comparing it to the familiar item.

Although analogies can be effective in arguments, they have limitations. For example, a senator who opposed a government bailout of the financial industry in 2008 made the following argument:

> This bailout is doomed from the start. It's like pouring milk into a leaking bucket. As long as you keep pouring milk, the bucket stays full. But when you stop, the milk runs out the hole in the bottom of the bucket. What we're doing is throwing money into a big bucket and not fixing the hole. We have to find the underlying problems that have caused this part of our economy to get in trouble and pass legislation to solve them.

The problem with using analogies such as this one is that analogies are never perfect. There is always a difference between the two things being compared. The larger this difference, the weaker the analogy—and the weaker the argument that it supports. For example, someone could point out to the senator that the financial industry—and by extension, the whole economy—is much more complex and multifaceted than a leaking bucket. To analyze the economy, the senator would have to expand his discussion beyond this single analogy (which cannot carry the weight of the entire argument) as well as supply the evidence to support his contention that the bailout was a mistake from the start.

Ad Hominem Fallacy (Personal Attack)

The **ad hominem fallacy** occurs when someone attacks the character or the motives of a person instead of focusing on the issues. This line of reasoning is illogical because it focuses attention on the person making the argument, sidestepping the argument itself.

Consider the following statement:

> Dr. Thomson, I'm not sure why we should believe anything you have to say about this community health center. Last year, you left your husband for another man.

The above attack on Dr. Thomson's character is irrelevant; it has nothing to do with her ideas about the community health center. Sometimes, however, a person's character may have a direct relation to the issue. For example, if Dr. Thomson had invested in a company that supplied medical equipment to the health center, this fact would have been relevant to the issue at hand.

The ad hominem fallacy also occurs when you attempt to undermine an argument by associating it with individuals who are easily attacked. For example, consider this statement:

> I think your plan to provide universal heath care is interesting. I'm sure Marx and Lenin would agree with you.

Instead of focusing on the specific provisions of the health-care plan, the opposition unfairly associates it with the ideas of Karl Marx and Vladimir Lenin, two well-known Communists.

The Granger Collection

Ad hominem attack against Charles Darwin, originator of the theory of evolution by natural selection

Creating a Straw Man

This fallacy most likely got its name from the use of straw dummies in military and boxing training. When writers create a **straw man**, they present a weak argument that can easily be refuted. Instead of attacking the real issue, they focus on a weaker issue and give the impression that they have effectively refuted an opponent's argument. Frequently, the straw man is an extreme or oversimplified version of the opponent's actual position. For example, during a debate about raising the minimum wage, a senator made the following comment:

> Those who oppose raising the minimum wage are heartless. They obviously don't care if children starve.

© SOTK2011/Alamy

Instead of focusing on the minimum wage, the senator misrepresents the opposing position so that it appears cruel. As this example shows, the straw man fallacy is dishonest because it intentionally distorts an opponent's position to mislead readers.

Hasty or Sweeping Generalization (Jumping to a Conclusion)

A **hasty or sweeping generalization** (also called **jumping to a conclusion**) occurs when someone reaches a conclusion that is based on too little evidence. Many people commit this fallacy without realizing it. For example, when Richard Nixon was elected president in 1972, film critic Pauline Kael is supposed to have remarked, "How can that be? No one I know voted for Nixon!" The general idea behind this statement is that if Kael's acquaintances didn't vote for Nixon, then neither did most other people. This assumption is flawed because it is based on a small sample.

Sometimes people make hasty generalizations because they strongly favor one point of view over another. At other times, a hasty generalization is simply the result of sloppy thinking. For example, it is easier for a student to simply say that an instructor is an unusually hard grader than to survey the instructor's classes to see if this conclusion is warranted (or to consider other reasons for his or her poor performance in a course).

Either/Or Fallacy (False Dilemma)

The **either/or fallacy** (also called a **false dilemma**) occurs when a person says that there are just two choices when there are actually more. In many cases, the person committing this fallacy tries to force a conclusion by presenting just two choices, one of which is clearly more desirable than the other. (Parents do this with young children all the time: "Eat your carrots, or go to bed.")

Politicians frequently engage in this fallacy. For example, according to some politicians, you are either pro-life or pro-choice, pro–gun control or anti–gun control, pro-stem-cell research or anti-stem-cell research. Many people, however, are actually somewhere in the middle, taking a much more nuanced approach to complicated issues.

Consider the following statement:

> I can't believe you voted against the bill to build a wall along the southern border of the United States. Either you're for protecting our border, or you're against it.

This statement is an example of the either/or fallacy. The person who voted against the bill might be against the wall but not against all immigration restrictions. The person might favor loose restrictions for some people (for example, migrant workers) and strong restrictions for others (for example, drug smugglers). By limiting the options to just two, the speaker oversimplifies the situation and attempts to force the listener to accept a fallacious argument.

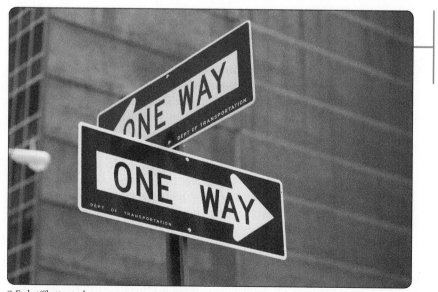

© Ferhat/Shutterstock.com

The either/or fallacy occurs when a writer presents just two choices when there are actually more.

Equivocation

The fallacy of **equivocation** occurs when a key term has one meaning in one part of an argument and another meaning in another part. (When a term is used **unequivocally**, it has the same meaning throughout the argument.) Consider the following old joke:

> The sign said, "Fine for parking here," so because it was fine, I parked there.

Obviously, the word *fine* has two different meanings in this sentence. The first time it is used, it means "money paid as a penalty." The second time, it means "good" or "satisfactory."

Most words have more than one meaning, so it is important not to confuse the various meanings. For an argument to work, a key term has to have the same meaning every time it appears in the argument. If the meaning shifts during the course of the argument, then the argument cannot be sound.

Consider the following statement:

> This is supposed to be a free country, but nothing worth having is ever free.

In this statement, the meaning of a key term shifts. The first time the word *free* is used, it means "not under the control of another." The second time, it means "without charge."

Red Herring

This fallacy gets its name from the practice of dragging a smoked fish across the trail of a fox to mask its scent during a fox hunt. As a result, the hounds lose the scent and are thrown off the track. The **red herring** fallacy occurs when a person raises an irrelevant side issue to divert attention from the real issue. Used skillfully, this fallacy can distract an audience and change the focus of an argument.

Political campaigns are good sources of examples of the red herring fallacy. Consider this example from the 2016 presidential race:

> I know that Donald Trump says that he is for the "little guy," but he lives in a three-story penthouse in the middle of Manhattan. How can we believe that his policies will help the average American?

The focus of his argument should have been on Trump's policies, not on the fact that he lives in a penthouse.

Here is another red herring fallacy from the 2016 political campaign:

Person trying to follow the argument.

The actual issue being argued.

Red herring, a distraction not related to the argument.

Hillary Clinton wants us to vote for her, but she will be sixty-nine when she becomes president. I think that this is a problem.

Again, the focus of these remarks should have been on Clinton's qualifications, not on her age.

Slippery Slope

The **slippery-slope** fallacy occurs when a person argues that one thing will inevitably result from another. (Other names for the slippery-slope fallacy are the **foot-in-the-door fallacy** and the **floodgates fallacy**.) Both these names suggest that once you permit certain acts, you inevitably permit additional acts that eventually lead to disastrous consequences. Typically, the slippery-slope fallacy presents a series of increasingly unacceptable events that lead to an inevitable, unpleasant conclusion. (Usually, there is no evidence that such a sequence will actually occur.)

We encounter examples of the slippery-slope fallacy almost daily. During a debate on same-sex marriage, for example, an opponent advanced this line of reasoning:

If we allow gay marriage, then there is nothing to stop polygamy. And once we allow this, where will it stop? Will we have to legalize incest—or even bestiality?

Whether or not you support same-sex marriage, you should recognize the fallacy of this slippery-slope reasoning. By the last sentence of the passage above, the assertions have become so outrageous that they approach parody. People can certainly debate this issue, but not in such a dishonest and highly emotional way.

© Lon C. Diehl/Photoedit, Inc.

Beware the slippery-
slope fallacy

You Also (Tu Quoque)

The **you also** fallacy asserts that a statement is false because it is inconsistent with what the speaker has said or done. In other words, a person is attacked for doing what he or she is arguing against. Parents often encounter this fallacy when they argue with their teenage children. By introducing an irrelevant point— "You did it too"—the children attempt to distract parents and put them on the defensive:

- How can you tell me not to smoke when you used to smoke?

- Don't yell at me for drinking. I bet you had a few beers before you were twenty-one.

- Why do I have to be home by midnight? Didn't you stay out late when you were my age?

Arguments such as these are irrelevant. People fail to follow their own advice, but that does not mean that their points have no merit. (Of course, not following their own advice does undermine their credibility.)

Appeal to Doubtful Authority

Writers of research papers frequently use the ideas of recognized authorities to strengthen their arguments. However, the sources offered as evidence need to be both respected and credible. The **appeal to doubtful authority** occurs when people use the ideas of nonexperts to support their arguments.

Not everyone who speaks as an expert is actually an authority on a particular issue. For example, when movie stars or recording artists give their opinions about politics, climate change, or foreign affairs— things they may know little about—they are not speaking as experts; therefore, they have no authority. (They *are* experts, however, when they discuss the film or music industries.) A similar situation occurs with the pundits who appear on television news shows. Some of these individuals have solid credentials in the fields they discuss, but others offer opinions even though they know little about the subjects. Unfortunately, many viewers accept the pronouncements of these "experts" uncritically and think it is acceptable to cite them to support their own arguments.

How do you determine whether a person you read about or hear is really an authority? First, make sure that the person actually has expertise in the field he or she is discussing. You can do this by checking his

SCHUMER & SCHUMER:
"ENOUGH IS ENOUGH"

GUN
VIOLENCE

Comedian/actor Amy
Schumer boosts her
credibility on the issue
of gun control by
appearing with her
cousin, Senator
Charles Schumer.

© Andrew Burton/Getty Images

or her credentials on the Internet. Second, make sure that the person is not biased. No one is entirely free from bias, but the bias should not be so extreme that it undermines the person's authority. Finally, make sure that you can confirm what the so-called expert says or writes. Check one or two pieces of information in other sources, such as a basic reference text or encyclopedia. Determine if others—especially recognized experts in the field—confirm this information. If there are major points of discrepancy, dig further to make sure you are dealing with a legitimate authority.

Misuse of Statistics

The **misuse of statistics** occurs when data are misrepresented. Statistics can be used persuasively in an argument, but sometimes they are distorted—intentionally or unintentionally—to make a point. For example, a classic ad for toothpaste claims that four out of five dentists recommend Crest toothpaste. What the ad neglects to mention is the number of dentists who were questioned. If the company surveyed several thousand dentists, then this statistic would be meaningful. If the company surveyed only ten, however, it would not be.

Misleading statistics can be much subtler (and much more complicated) than the example above. For example, one year, there were 16,653 alcohol-related deaths in the United States. According to the National Highway Traffic Safety Administration (NHTSA), 12,892 of these 16,653 alcohol-related deaths involved at least one driver or passenger

"That's what I want to say. See if you can find some statistics to prove it."

who was legally drunk. Of the 12,892 deaths, 7,326 were the drivers themselves, and 1,594 were legally drunk pedestrians. The remaining 3,972 fatalities were nonintoxicated drivers, passengers, or nonoccupants. These 3,972 fatalities call the total number into question because the NHTSA does not indicate which drivers were at fault. In other words, if a sober driver ran a red light and killed a legally drunk driver, the NHTSA classified this death as alcohol-related. For this reason, the original number of alcohol-related deaths—16,653—is somewhat misleading. (The statistic becomes even more questionable when you consider that a person is automatically classified as intoxicated if he or she refuses to take a sobriety test.)

Post Hoc, Ergo Propter Hoc (*After This, Therefore Because of This*)

The **post hoc** fallacy asserts that because two events occur closely in time, one event must cause the other. Professional athletes commit the post hoc fallacy all the time. For example, one major league pitcher wears the same shirt every time he has an important game. Because he has won several big games while wearing this shirt, he believes it brings him luck.

Many events seem to follow a sequential pattern even though they actually do not. For example, some people refuse to get a flu shot because they say that the last time they got one, they came down with the flu. Even though there is no scientific basis for this link, many people insist that it is true. (The more probable explanation for this situation is that the flu vaccination takes at least two weeks to take effect, so it is possible for someone to be infected by the flu virus before the vaccine starts working.)

Another health-related issue also illustrates the post hoc fallacy. Recently, the U.S. Food and Drug Administration (FDA) studied several natural supplements that claim to cure the common cold. Because the study showed that these products were not effective, the FDA ordered the manufacturers to stop making false claims. Despite this fact, however, many people still buy these products. When questioned, they say the medications actually work. Again, the explanation for this phenomenon is simple. Most colds last just a few days. As the FDA pointed out in its report, people who took the medications would have begun feeling better with or without them.

Non Sequitur (It Does Not Follow)

The **non sequitur** fallacy occurs when a conclusion does not follow from the premises. Frequently, the conclusion is supported by weak or irrelevant evidence—or by no evidence at all. Consider the following statement:

> Megan drives an expensive car, so she must be earning a lot of money.

Megan might drive an expensive car, but this is not evidence that she has a high salary. She could, for example, be leasing the car or paying it off over a five-year period, or it could have been a gift.

Non sequiturs are common in political arguments. Consider this statement:

> Gangs, drugs, and extreme violence plague today's prisons. The only way to address this issue is to release all nonviolent offenders as soon as possible.

This assessment of the prison system may be accurate, but it doesn't follow that because of this situation, all nonviolent offenders should be released immediately.

Scientific arguments also contain non sequiturs. Consider the following statement that was made during a debate on climate change:

> Recently, the polar ice caps have thickened, and the temperature of the oceans has stabilized. Obviously, we don't need to do more to address climate change.

A non sequitur
fallacy

Even if you accept the facts of this argument, you need to see more evidence before you can conclude that no action against climate change is necessary. For example, the cooling trend could be temporary, or other areas of the earth could still be growing warmer.

Bandwagon Fallacy

The **bandwagon fallacy** occurs when you try to convince people that something is true because it is widely held to be true. It is easy to see the problem with this line of reasoning. Hundreds of years ago, most people believed that the sun revolved around the earth and that the earth was flat. As we know, the fact that many people held these beliefs did not make them true.

The underlying assumption of the bandwagon fallacy is that the more people who believe something, the more likely it is to be true. Without supporting evidence, however, this form of argument cannot be valid. For example, consider the following statement made by a driver who was stopped by the police for speeding:

> Officer, I didn't do anything wrong. Everyone around me was going the same speed.

As the police officer was quick to point out, the driver's argument missed the point: he was doing fifty-five miles an hour in a thirty-five-mile-an-hour zone, and the fact that other drivers were also speeding was irrelevant. If the driver had been able to demonstrate that the police officer was mistaken—that he was driving more slowly or that the speed limit was actually sixty miles an hour—then his argument would have had merit. In this case, the fact that other drivers were going the same speed would be relevant because it would support his contention.

The bandwagon fallacy

Cartoonstock.com

Since most people want to go along with the crowd, the bandwagon fallacy can be very effective. For this reason, advertisers use it all the time. For example, a book publisher will say that a book has been on the *New York Times* bestseller list for ten weeks, and a pharmaceutical company will say that its brand of aspirin outsells other brands four to one. These appeals are irrelevant, however, because they don't address the central questions: Is the book actually worth reading? Is one brand of aspirin really better than other brands?

⊜ EXERCISE 5.10

Determine which of the following statements are logical arguments and which are fallacies. If the statement is not logical, identify the fallacy that best applies.

1. Almost all the students I talked to said that they didn't like the senator. I'm sure he'll lose the election on Tuesday.

2. This car has a noisy engine; therefore, it must create a lot of pollution.

3. I don't know how Professor Resnick can be such a hard grader. He's always late for class.

4. A vote for the bill to limit gun sales in the city is a vote against the Second Amendment.

5. It's only fair to pay your fair share of taxes.

6. I had an internship at a government agency last summer, and no one there worked very hard. Government workers are lazy.

7. It's a clear principle of law that people are not allowed to yell "Fire!" in a crowded theater. By permitting protestors to hold a rally downtown, Judge Cohen is allowing them to do just that.

8. Of course this person is guilty. He wouldn't be in jail if he weren't a criminal.

9. Schools are like families; therefore, teachers (like parents) should be allowed to discipline their kids.

10. Everybody knows that staying out in the rain can make you sick.

11. When we had a draft in the 1960s, the crime rate was low. We should bring back the draft.

12. I'm not a doctor, but I play one on TV. I recommend Vicks Formula 44 cough syrup.

13. Some people are complaining about public schools, so there must be a problem.

14. If you aren't part of the solution, you're part of the problem.

15. All people are mortal. James is a person. Therefore, James is mortal.

16. I don't know why you gave me an F for handing in someone else's essay. Didn't you ever copy something from someone else?

17. First, the government stops us from buying assault rifles. Then, it limits the number of handguns we can buy. What will come next? Soon, they'll try to take away all our guns.

18. Shakespeare was the world's greatest playwright; therefore, *Macbeth* must be a great play.

19. Last month, I bought a new computer. Yesterday, I installed some new software. This morning, my computer wouldn't start up. The new software must be causing the problem.

20. Ellen DeGeneres is against testing pharmaceutical and cosmetics products on animals, and that's good enough for me.

◆ EXERCISE 5.11

Read the following essay, and identify as many logical fallacies in it as you can. Make sure you identify each fallacy by name and are able to explain the flaws in the writer's arguments.

This essay is from Buchanan.org, where it appeared on October 31, 1994.

IMMIGRATION TIME-OUT
PATRICK J. BUCHANAN

Proposition 187 "is an outrage. It is unconstitutional. It is nativist. It is racist."

—AL HUNT, *Capital Gang*, CNN

That outburst by my columnist colleague, about California's Prop. 187— 1 which would cut off social welfare benefits to illegal aliens—suggests that this savage quarrel is about more than just money. Indeed, the roots of this dispute over Prop. 187 are grounded in the warring ideas that we Americans hold about the deepest, most divisive issues of our time: ethnicity, nation, culture.

What do we want the America of the years 2000, 2020, and 2050 to 2 be like? Do we have the right to shape the character of the country our grandchildren will live in? Or is that to be decided by whoever, outside America, decides to come here?

By 2050, we are instructed by the chancellor of the University of California at Berkeley, Chang Lin-Tin, "the majority of Americans will trace their roots to Latin America, Africa, Asia, the Middle East, and Pacific Islands." 3

Now, any man or woman, of any nation or ancestry can come here—and become a good American. 4

We know that from our history. But by my arithmetic, the chancellor is saying Hispanics, Asians, and Africans will increase their present number of 65 million by at least 100 million in 60 years, a population growth larger than all of Mexico today. 5

What will that mean for America? Well, South Texas and Southern California will be almost exclusively Hispanic. Each will have tens of millions of people whose linguistic, historic, and cultural roots are in Mexico. Like Eastern Ukraine, where 10 million Russian-speaking "Ukrainians" now look impatiently to Moscow, not Kiev, as their cultural capital, America could see, in a decade, demands for Quebec-like status for Southern California. Already there is a rumbling among militants for outright secession. A sea of Mexican flags was prominent in that L.A. rally against Prop. 187, and Mexican officials are openly urging their kinsmen in California to vote it down. 6

If no cutoff is imposed on social benefits for those who breach our borders, and break our laws, the message will go out to a desperate world: America is wide open. All you need do is get there, and get in. 7

Consequences will ensue. Crowding together immigrant and minority populations in our major cities must bring greater conflict. We saw that in the 1992 L.A. riot. Blacks and Hispanics have lately collided in D.C.'s Adams-Morgan neighborhood, supposedly the most tolerant and progressive section of Washington. The issue: bilingual education. Unlike 20 years ago, ethnic conflict is today on almost every front page. 8

Before Mr. Chang's vision is realized, the United States will have at least two official languages. Today's steady outmigration of "Anglos" or "Euro-Americans," as whites are now called, from Southern Florida and Southern California, will continue. The 50 states will need constant redrawing of political lines to ensure proportional representation. Already we have created the first "apartheid districts" in America's South. 9

Ethnic militancy and solidarity are on the rise in the United States; the old institutions of assimilation are not doing their work as they once did; the Melting Pot is in need of repair. On campuses we hear demands for separate dorms, eating rooms, clubs, etc., by black, white, Hispanic, and Asian students. If this is where the campus is headed, where are our cities going? 10

> "Ethnic militancy and solidarity are on the rise."

If America is to survive as "one nation, one people," we need to call a 11 "time-out" on immigration, to assimilate the tens of millions who have lately arrived. We need to get to know one another, to live together, to learn together America's language, history, culture, and traditions of tolerance, to become a new national family, before we add a hundred million more. And we need soon to bring down the curtain on this idea of hyphenated-Americanism.

If we lack the courage to make the decisions—as to what our country will 12 look like in 2050—others will make those decisions for us, not all of whom share our love of the America that seems to be fading away.

○ EXERCISE 5.12

Choose three of the fallacies that you identified in "Immigration Time-Out" for Exercise 5.11. Rewrite each statement in the form of a logical argument.

 LaunchPad For more practice, see the LearningCurve on
macmillan learning Reasoning and Logical Fallacies in the Launchpad for *Practical Argument*.

How Free Should Free Speech Be?

SAVE FREEDOM OF SPEECH

BUY WAR BONDS

Printed by permission of the
Norman Rockwell Family Agency.
Copyright 1943 the Norman
Rockwell Family Entities.

Go back to page 123, and reread the At Issue box that gives background on how free free speech should be. As the following sources illustrate, this question has a number of possible answers.

As you read this source material, you will be asked to answer questions and to complete some simple activities. This work will help you understand both the content and the structure of the sources. When you are finished, you will be ready to write an argument—either inductive or deductive—that takes a new position on how free free speech should actually be.

SOURCES

Thane Rosenbaum, "Should Neo-Nazis Be Allowed Free Speech?," p. 165

Sol Stern, "The Unfree Speech Movement," p. 168

American Association of University Professors, "On Freedom of Expression and Campus Speech Codes," p. 172

Wendy Kaminer, "Progressive Ideas Have Killed Free Speech on Campus," p. 175

Judith Shulevitz, "In College and Hiding from Scary Ideas," p. 178

Eric Posner, "Universities Are Right to Crack Down on Speech and Behavior," p. 183

This article originally appeared on TheDailyBeast.com on January 1, 2014.

SHOULD NEO-NAZIS BE ALLOWED FREE SPEECH?

THANE ROSENBAUM

Over the past several weeks, free speech has gotten costlier—at least in France 1 and Israel.

In France, Dieudonne M'Bala M'Bala, an anti-Semitic stand-up comic 2 infamous for popularizing the quenelle, an inverted Nazi salute, was banned from performing in two cities. M'Bala M'Bala has been repeatedly fined for hate speech, and this was not the first time his act was perceived as a threat to public order.

Meanwhile, Israel's parliament is soon to pass a bill outlawing the word 3 Nazi for non-educational purposes. Indeed, any slur against another that invokes the Third Reich could land the speaker in jail for six months with a fine of $29,000. The Israelis are concerned about both the rise of anti-Semitism globally, and the trivialization of the Holocaust—even locally.

To Americans, these actions in France and Israel seem positively un- 4 democratic. The First Amendment would never prohibit the quenelle, regardless of its symbolic meaning. And any lover of *Seinfeld* would regard banning the "Soup Nazi" episode as scandalously un-American. After all, in 1977 a federal court upheld the right of neo-Nazis to goose-step right through the town of Skokie, Illinois, which had a disproportionately large number of Holocaust survivors as residents. And more recently, the Supreme Court upheld the right of a church group opposed to gays serving in the military to picket the funeral of a dead marine with signs that read, "God Hates Fags."

While what is happening in France and Israel is wholly foreign to Ameri- 5 cans, perhaps it's time to consider whether these and other countries may be right. Perhaps America's fixation on free speech has gone too far.

Actually, the United States is an outlier among democracies in granting 6 such generous free speech guarantees. Six European countries, along with Brazil, prohibit the use of Nazi symbols and flags. Many more countries have outlawed Holocaust denial. Indeed, even encouraging racial discrimination in France is a crime. In pluralistic nations like these with clashing cultures and historical tragedies not shared by all, mutual respect and civility helps keep the peace and avoids unnecessary mental trauma.

Yet, even in the United States, free speech is not unlimited. Certain pro- 7 scribed categories have always existed—libel, slander and defamation, obscenity, "fighting words," and the "incitement of imminent lawlessness"—where the First Amendment does not protect the speaker, where the right to speak is curtailed for reasons of general welfare and public safety. There is no freedom to shout "fire" in a crowded theater. Hate crime statutes exist in many jurisdictions where bias-motivated crimes are given more severe penalties. In 2003, the Supreme Court held that speech intended to intimidate, such as cross burning, might not receive First Amendment protection.

Yet, the confusion is that in placing limits on speech we privilege physical 8 over emotional harm. Indeed, we have an entire legal system, and an attitude toward speech, that takes its cue from a nursery rhyme: "Sticks and stones can break my bones but names can never hurt me."

All of us know, however, and despite what we tell our children, names do, 9 indeed, hurt. And recent studies in universities such as Purdue, UCLA, Michigan, Toronto, Arizona, Maryland, and Macquarie University in New South Wales show, among other things, through brain scans and controlled studies with participants who were subjected to both physical and emotional pain, that emotional harm is equal in intensity to that experienced by the body, and is even more long-lasting and traumatic. Physical pain subsides; emotional pain, when recalled, is relived.

Pain has a shared circuitry in the human brain, and it makes no distinc- 10 tion between being hit in the face and losing face (or having a broken heart) as a result of bereavement, betrayal, social exclusion, and grave insult. Emotional distress can, in fact, make the body sick. Indeed, research has shown that pain relief medication can work equally well for both physical and emotional injury.

We impose speed limits on driving and regulate food and drugs because we know that the costs of not doing so can lead to accidents and harm. Why should speech be exempt from public welfare concerns when its social costs can be even more injurious? 11

> "We impose speed limits on driving and regulate food and drugs because we know that the costs of not doing so can lead to accidents and harm."

In the marketplace of ideas, there is a difference between trying to persuade and trying to injure. One can object to gays in the military without ruining the one moment a father has to bury his son; 12 neo-Nazis can long for the Third Reich without re-traumatizing Hitler's victims; one can oppose Affirmative Action without burning a cross on an African-American's lawn.

Of course, everything is a matter of degree. Juries are faced with similar 13 ambiguities when it comes to physical injury. No one knows for certain whether the plaintiff wearing a neck brace can't actually run the New York Marathon. We tolerate the fake slip and fall, but we feel absolutely helpless in evaluating whether words and gestures intended to harm actually do cause harm. Jurors are as capable of working through these uncertainties in the area of emotional harms as they are in the realm of physical injury.

Free speech should not stand in the way of common decency. No right 14 should be so freely and recklessly exercised that it becomes an impediment to civil society, making it so that others are made to feel less free, their private space and peace invaded, their sensitivities cruelly trampled upon.

⊘ AT ISSUE: HOW FREE SHOULD FREE SPEECH BE?

1. Rosenbaum waits until the end of paragraph 6 to state his thesis. Why? What information does he include in paragraphs 1–5? How does this material set the stage for the rest of the essay?

2. Rosenbaum develops his argument with both inductive and deductive reasoning. Where does he use each strategy?

3. What evidence does Rosenbaum use to support his thesis? Should he have included more evidence? If so, what kind?

4. In paragraph 11, Rosenbaum makes a comparison between regulating free speech and regulating driving and food and drugs. How strong is this **analogy**? At what points (if any) does this comparison break down?

5. Where does Rosenbaum address arguments against his position? Does he refute these arguments? What other opposing arguments could he have addressed?

6. What point does Rosenbaum reinforce in his conclusion? What other points could he have emphasized?

This op-ed originally ran in the *Wall Street Journal* on September 24, 2014.

THE UNFREE SPEECH MOVEMENT

SOL STERN

This fall the University of California at Berkeley is celebrating the 50th anni- 1 versary of the Free Speech Movement, a student-led protest against campus restrictions on political activities that made headlines and inspired imitators around the country. I played a small part in the Free Speech Movement, and some of those returning for the reunion were once my friends, but I won't be joining them.

Though the movement promised greater intellectual and political free- 2 dom on campus, the result has been the opposite. The great irony is that while Berkeley now honors the memory of the Free Speech Movement, it exercises more thought control over students than the hated institution that we rose up against half a century ago.

We early-1960s radicals believed ourselves anointed as a new "tell it like it 3 is" generation. We promised to transcend the "smelly old orthodoxies" (in George Orwell's phrase) of Cold War liberalism and class-based, authoritarian leftism. Leading students into the university administration building for the first mass protest, Mario Savio, the Free Speech Movement's brilliant leader from Queens, New York, famously said: "There's a time when the operation of the machine becomes so odious—makes you so sick at heart—that you can't take part. . . . And you've got to indicate to the people who run it, to the people who own it that unless you're free, the machine will be prevented from working at all."

The Berkeley "machine" now promotes Free Speech Movement kitsch. 4 The steps in front of Sproul Hall, the central administration building where more than 700 students were arrested on Dec. 2, 1964, have been renamed the Mario Savio Steps. One of the campus dining halls is called the Free Speech Movement Cafe, its walls covered with photographs and mementos of the glorious semester of struggle. The university requires freshmen to read an admiring biography of Savio, who died in 1996, written by New York University professor and Berkeley graduate Robert Cohen.

Yet intellectual diversity is hardly embraced. Every undergraduate under- 5 goes a form of indoctrination with a required course on the "theoretical or analytical issues relevant to understanding race, culture, and ethnicity in American society," administered by the university's Division of Equity and Inclusion.

How did this Orwellian inversion occur? It happened in part because the 6 Free Speech Movement's fight for free speech was always a charade. The struggle was really about using the campus as a base for radical politics. I was a

27-year-old New Left graduate student at the time. Savio was a 22-year-old sophomore. He liked to compare the Free Speech Movement to the civil-rights struggle—conflating the essentially liberal Berkeley administration with the Bull Connors of the racist South.

During one demonstration Savio suggested that the campus cops who 7 had arrested a protesting student were "poor policemen" who only "have a job to do." Another student then shouted out: "Just like Eichmann." "Yeah. Very good. It's very, you know, like Adolf Eichmann," Savio replied. "He had a job to do. He fit into the machinery."

I realized years later that this moment may have been the beginning of the 8 1960s radicals' perversion of ordinary political language, like the spelling "Amerika" or seeing hope and progress in Third World dictatorships.

Before that 1964–65 academic year, most of us radical students could not 9 have imagined a campus rebellion. Why revolt against an institution that until then offered such a pleasant sanctuary? But then Berkeley administrators made an incredibly stupid decision to establish new rules regarding political activities on campus. Student clubs were no longer allowed to set up tables in front of the Bancroft Avenue campus entrance to solicit funds and recruit new members.

The clubs had used this 40-foot strip of sidewalk for years on the 10 assumption that it was the property of the City of Berkeley and thus constitutionally protected against speech restrictions. But the university claimed ownership to justify the new rules. When some students refused to comply, the administration compounded its blunder by resorting to the campus police. Not surprisingly, the students pushed back, using civil-disobedience tactics learned fighting for civil rights in the South.

The Free Speech Movement was born on Oct. 1, 1964, when police tried 11 to arrest a recent Berkeley graduate, Jack Weinberg, who was back on campus after a summer as a civil-rights worker in Mississippi. He had set up a table on the Bancroft strip for the Berkeley chapter of the Congress of Racial Equality (CORE). Dozens of students spontaneously sat down around the police car, preventing it from leaving the campus. A 32-hour standoff ensued, with hundreds of students camped around the car.

Mario Savio, also back from Mississippi, took off his shoes, climbed onto 12 the roof of the police car, and launched into an impromptu speech explaining why the students had to resist the immoral new rules. Thus began months of sporadic protests, the occupation of Sproul Hall on Dec. 2 (ended by mass arrests), national media attention, and Berkeley's eventual capitulation.

That should have ended the matter. Savio soon left the political arena, saying that he had no interest in becoming a permanent student leader. But others had mastered the new world of political theater, understood the weakness of American liberalism, and soon turned their ire on the Vietnam War.

"But others had mastered the new world of political theater, understood the weakness of American liberalism, and soon turned their ire on the Vietnam War." 13

169

Mario Savio at a
victory rally on the
University of
California campus in
Berkeley (December 9,
1964)

AP Photo.

The radical movement that the Free Speech Movement spawned eventu- 14
ally descended into violence and mindless anti-Americanism. The movement
waned in the 1970s as the war wound down—but by then protesters had begun
their infiltration of university faculties and administrations they had once
decried. "Tenured radicals," in *New Criterion* editor Roger Kimball's phrase,
now dominate most professional organizations in the humanities and social
studies. Unlike our old liberal professors, who dealt respectfully with the ideas
advanced by my generation of New Left students, today's radical professors
insist on ideological conformity and don't take kindly to dissent by conservative students. Visits by speakers who might not toe the liberal line—recently
including former Secretary of State Condoleezza Rice and Islamism critic
Ayaan Hirsi Ali—spark protests and letter-writing campaigns by students in
tandem with their professors until the speaker withdraws or the invitation is
canceled.

On Oct. 1 at Berkeley, by contrast, one of the honored speakers at the Free 15
Speech Movement anniversary rally on Sproul Plaza will be Bettina Aptheker, who
is now a feminist-studies professor at the University of California at Santa Cruz.

Writing in the Berkeley alumni magazine about the anniversary, Ms. 16
Aptheker noted that the First Amendment was "written by white, propertied
men in the 18th century, who never likely imagined that it might apply to
women, and/or people of color, and/or all those who were not propertied, and
even, perhaps, not citizens, and/or undocumented immigrants. . . . In other
words, freedom of speech is a Constitutional guarantee, but who gets to exer-

cise it without the chilling restraints of censure depends very much on one's location in the political and social cartography. We [Free Speech Movement] veterans were too young and inexperienced in 1964 to know this, but we do now, and we speak with a new awareness, a new consciousness, and a new urgency that the wisdom of a true freedom is inexorably tied to who exercises power and for what ends." Read it and weep—for the Free Speech Movement anniversary, for the ideal of an intellectually open university, and for America.

⊘ AT ISSUE: HOW FREE SHOULD FREE SPEECH BE?

1. In your own words, summarize Stern's thesis. Where does he state it?

2. At what point (or points) in the essay does Stern appeal to *ethos*? How effective is this appeal?

3. In paragraph 4, Stern says, "The Berkeley 'machine' now promotes Free Speech Movement kitsch." First, look up the meaning of *kitsch*. Then, explain what Stern means by this statement.

4. Stern supports his points with examples drawn from his own experience. Is this enough? What other kinds of evidence could he have used?

5. In paragraph 5, Stern says that every undergraduate at Berkeley "undergoes a form of indoctrination." What does he mean? Does Stern make a valid point, or is he **begging the question**?

6. Why does Stern discuss Bettina Aptheker in paragraphs 15–16? Could he be accused of making an **ad hominem** attack? Why or why not?

This code came out of a June 1992 meeting of the American Association of University Professors.

ON FREEDOM OF EXPRESSION AND CAMPUS SPEECH CODES

AMERICAN ASSOCIATION OF UNIVERSITY PROFESSORS

Freedom of thought and expression is essential to any institution of higher 1 learning. Universities and colleges exist not only to transmit existing knowledge. Equally, they interpret, explore, and expand that knowledge by testing the old and proposing the new.

This mission guides learning outside the classroom quite as much as in 2 class, and often inspires vigorous debate on those social, economic, and political issues that arouse the strongest passions. In the process, views will be expressed that may seem to many wrong, distasteful, or offensive. Such is the nature of freedom to sift and winnow ideas.

On a campus that is free and open, no idea can be banned or forbidden. 3 No viewpoint or message may be deemed so hateful or disturbing that it may not be expressed.

> "On a campus that is free and open, no idea can be banned or forbidden."

Universities and colleges are also 4 communities, often of a residential character. Most campuses have recently sought to become more diverse, and more reflective of the larger community, by attracting students, faculty, and staff from groups that were historically excluded or underrepresented. Such gains as they have made are recent, modest, and tenuous. The campus climate can profoundly affect an institution's continued diversity. Hostility or intolerance to persons who differ from the majority (especially if seemingly condoned by the institution) may undermine the confidence of new members of the community. Civility is always fragile and can easily be destroyed.

In response to verbal assaults and use of hateful language some campuses 5 have felt it necessary to forbid the expression of racist, sexist, homophobic, or ethnically demeaning speech, along with conduct or behavior that harasses. Several reasons are offered in support of banning such expression. Individuals and groups that have been victims of such expression feel an understandable outrage. They claim that the academic progress of minority and majority alike may suffer if fears, tensions, and conflicts spawned by slurs and insults create an environment inimical to learning. These arguments, grounded in the need to foster an atmosphere respectful of and welcome to all persons, strike a deeply responsive chord in the academy. But, while we can acknowledge both the weight of these concerns and the thoughtfulness of those persuaded of the need for regulation, rules that ban or punish speech based upon its content cannot be justified. An institution of higher learning fails to fulfill its mission if it asserts the power to proscribe ideas—and racial or ethnic slurs, sexist epithets, or homophobic insults almost always express ideas, however repugnant. Indeed, by proscribing any ideas, a university sets an example that profoundly disserves its academic mission. Some may seek to defend a distinction between the regulation of the content of speech and the regulation of the manner (or style) of speech. We find this distinction untenable in practice because offensive style or opprobrious phrases may in fact have been chosen precisely for their expressive power. As the United States Supreme Court has said in the course of rejecting criminal sanctions for offensive words: Words are often chosen as much for their emotive as their cognitive force. We cannot sanction the view that the Constitution, while solicitous of the cognitive content of individual speech, has little or no regard for that emotive function which, practically speaking, may often be the more important element of the overall message sought to be communicated. The line between substance and style is thus too uncertain to sustain the pressure that will inevitably be brought to bear upon disciplinary rules that attempt to regulate speech. Proponents of speech codes sometimes reply that the value of emotive language of this type is of such a low order that, on balance, suppression is justified by the harm suffered by those who are directly affected, and by the general damage done to the learning environment. Yet a college or university sets a perilous course if it seeks to differentiate between high-value and low-value speech, or to choose which groups are to be protected by curbing the speech of others. A speech code unavoidably implies an institutional competence to distinguish permissible expression of hateful thought from what is proscribed as thoughtless hate. Institutions would also have to justify shielding some, but not other, targets of offensive language—not to political preference, to religious but not to philosophical creed, or perhaps even to some but not to other religious affiliations. Starting down this path creates an even greater risk that groups not originally protected may later demand similar solicitude—demands the institution that began the process of banning some speech is ill equipped to resist.

Distinctions of this type are neither practicable nor principled; their very 6 fragility underscores why institutions devoted to freedom of thought and expression ought not adopt an institutionalized coercion of silence.

Moreover, banning speech often avoids consideration of means more 7 compatible with the mission of an academic institution by which to deal with incivility, intolerance, offensive speech, and harassing behavior:

1. Institutions should adopt and invoke a range of measures that penalize conduct and behavior, rather than speech, such as rules against defacing property, physical intimidation or harassment, or disruption of campus activities. All members of the campus community should be made aware of such rules, and administrators should be ready to use them in preference to speech-directed sanctions.

2. Colleges and universities should stress the means they use best—to educate—including the development of courses and other curricular and co-curricular experiences designed to increase student understanding

and to deter offensive or intolerant speech or conduct. Such institutions should, of course, be free (indeed encouraged) to condemn manifestations of intolerance and discrimination, whether physical or verbal.

3. The governing board and the administration have a special duty not only to set an outstanding example of tolerance, but also to challenge boldly and condemn immediately serious breaches of civility.

4. Members of the faculty, too, have a major role; their voices may be critical in condemning intolerance, and their actions may set examples for understanding, making clear to their students that civility and tolerance are hallmarks of educated men and women.

5. Student personnel administrators have in some ways the most demanding role of all, for hate speech occurs most often in dormitories, locker-rooms, cafeterias, and student centers. Persons who guide this part of campus life should set high standards of their own for tolerance and should make unmistakably clear the harm that uncivil or intolerant speech inflicts.

To some persons who support speech codes, measures like these—relying as 8 they do on suasion rather than sanctions—may seem inadequate. But freedom of expression requires toleration of "ideas we hate," as Justice Holmes put it. The underlying principle does not change because the demand is to silence a hateful speaker, or because it comes from within the academy. Free speech is not simply an aspect of the educational enterprise to be weighed against other desirable ends. It is the very precondition of the academic enterprise itself.

⊘AT ISSUE: HOW FREE SHOULD FREE SPEECH BE?

1. The writers of this statement rely primarily on deductive reasoning. Construct a syllogism that includes the selection's major premise, minor premise, and conclusion.

2. At what audience is this statement aimed—students, instructors, administrators, or the general public? How do you know?

3. What problem do the writers address? Where do they present their solution?

4. In paragraph 5, the writers discuss the major arguments against their position. Why do they address opposing arguments so early in the selection? How effectively do the writers refute these arguments?

5. Paragraph 7 is followed by a numbered list. What information is in this list? Why did the writers decide to set it off in this way?

6. What do the writers mean when they say that free speech "is the very precondition of the academic exercise itself" (para. 8)?

This essay first appeared in the *Washington Post* on February 20, 2015.

PROGRESSIVE IDEAS HAVE KILLED FREE SPEECH ON CAMPUS

WENDY KAMINER

Is an academic discussion of free speech potentially traumatic? A recent panel 1 for Smith College alumnae aimed at "challenging the ideological echo chamber" elicited this ominous "trigger/content warning" when a transcript appeared in the campus newspaper: "Racism/racial slurs, ableist slurs, antisemitic language, anti-Muslim/Islamophobic language, anti-immigrant language, sexist/misogynistic slurs, references to race-based violence, references to antisemitic violence."

No one on this panel, in which I participated, trafficked in slurs. So what 2 prompted the warning?

Smith President Kathleen McCartney had joked, "We're just wild and 3 crazy, aren't we?" In the transcript, "crazy" was replaced by the notation: "[ableist slur]."

One of my fellow panelists mentioned that the State Department had for a 4 time banned the words "jihad," "Islamist," and "caliphate"—which the transcript flagged as "anti-Muslim/Islamophobic language."

I described the case of a Brandeis professor disciplined for saying "wet- 5 back" while explaining its use as a pejorative. The word was replaced in the transcript by "[anti-Latin@/anti-immigrant slur]." Discussing the teaching of *Huckleberry Finn*, I questioned the use of euphemisms such as "the n-word" and, in doing so, uttered that forbidden word. I described what I thought was the obvious difference between quoting a word in the context of discussing language, literature, or prejudice and hurling it as an epithet.

Two of the panelists challenged me. The audience of 300 to 400 people 6 listened to our spirited, friendly debate—and didn't appear angry or shocked. But back on campus, I was quickly branded a racist, and I was charged in the Huffington Post with committing "an explicit act of racial violence." McCartney subsequently apologized that "some students and faculty were hurt" and made to "feel unsafe" by my remarks.

Unsafe? These days, when students talk about threats to their safety and 7 demand access to "safe spaces," they're often talking about the threat of unwelcome speech and demanding protection from the emotional disturbances sparked by unsettling ideas. It's not just rape that some women on campus fear: It's discussions of rape. At Brown University, a scheduled debate between two feminists about rape culture was criticized for, as the *Brown Daily Herald* put it, undermining "the University's mission to create a safe and supportive environment for survivors." In a school-wide e-mail, Brown President Christina Paxon emphasized her belief in the existence of rape culture and invited students to an alternative lecture, to be given at the same time as the debate. And the *Daily Herald* reported that students who feared being "attacked by the viewpoints" offered at the debate could instead "find a safe space" among "sexual assault peer educators, women peer counselors and staff" during the same time slot. Presumably they all shared the same viewpoints and could be trusted not to "attack" anyone with their ideas.

How did we get here? How did a verbal defense of free speech become 8 tantamount to a hate crime and offensive words become the equivalent of physical assaults?

> "How did a verbal defense of free speech become tantamount to a hate crime and offensive words become the equivalent of physical assaults?"

You can credit—or blame—progres- 9 sives for this enthusiastic embrace of censorship. It reflects, in part, the influence of three popular movements dating back decades: the feminist anti-porn crusades, the pop-psychology recovery movement, and the emergence of multiculturalism on college campuses.

In the 1980s, law professor Catharine 10 MacKinnon and writer Andrea Dworkin showed the way, popularizing a view of free speech as a barrier to equality. These two impassioned feminists framed pornography—its production, distribution, and consumption—as an assault on women. They devised a novel definition of pornography as a violation of women's civil rights, and championed a model anti-porn ordinance that would authorize civil actions by any woman "aggrieved" by pornography. In 1984, the city of Indianapolis adopted the measure, defining pornography as a "discriminatory practice," but it was quickly struck down in federal court as unconstitutional. "Indianapolis justifies the ordinance on the ground that pornography affects thoughts," the court noted. "This is thought control."

So MacKinnnon and Dworkin lost that battle, but their successors are 11 winning the war. Their view of allegedly offensive or demeaning speech as a civil rights violation, and their conflation of words and actions, have helped shape campus speech and harassment codes and nurtured progressive hostility toward free speech.

The recovery movement, which flourished in the late '80s and early '90s, 12 adopted a similarly dire view of unwelcome speech. Words wound, anti-porn feminists and recovering co-dependents agreed. Self-appointed recovery experts, such as the best-selling author John Bradshaw, promoted the belief that most of us are victims of abuse, in one form or another. They broadened the definition of abuse to include a range of common, normal childhood experiences, including being chastised or ignored by your parents on occasion. From this perspective, we are all fragile and easily damaged by presumptively hurtful speech, and censorship looks like a moral necessity.

These ideas were readily absorbed on college campuses embarking on a 13 commendable drive for diversity. Multiculturalists sought to protect historically disadvantaged students from speech considered racist, sexist, homophobic or otherwise discriminatory. Like abuse, oppression was defined broadly. I remember the first time, in the early '90s, that I heard a Harvard student describe herself as oppressed, as a woman of color. She hadn't been systematically deprived of fundamental rights and liberties. After all, she'd been admitted to Harvard. But she had been offended and unsettled by certain attitudes and remarks. Did she have good reason to take offense? That was an irrelevant question. Popular therapeutic culture defined verbal "assaults" and other forms of discrimination by the subjective, emotional responses of self-proclaimed victims.

This reliance on subjectivity, in the interest of equality, is a recipe for 14 arbitrary, discriminatory enforcement practices, with far-reaching effects on individual liberty. The tendency to take subjective allegations of victimization at face value—instrumental in contemporary censorship campaigns—also leads to the presumption of guilt and disregard for due process in the progressive approach to alleged sexual assaults on campus.

This is a dangerously misguided approach to justice. "Feeling realities" 15 belong in a therapist's office. Incorporated into laws and regulations, they lead to the soft authoritarianism that now governs many American campuses. Instead of advancing equality, it's teaching future generations of leaders the "virtues" of autocracy.

⟳ AT ISSUE: HOW FREE SHOULD FREE SPEECH BE?

1. Should Kaminer have given more background information about the problem she discusses? What additional information could she have provided?

2. Kaminer devotes the first six paragraphs of her essay to describing a panel discussion. Why do you think she begins her essay in this way? How does this discussion prepare readers for the rest of the essay?

3. In paragraph 8, Kaminer asks two questions. What is the function of these questions?

4. According to Kaminer, what are "feeling realities" (para. 15)? In what sense are "feeling realities" harmful?

5. Does Kaminer ever establish that the situation she discusses is widespread enough to be a problem? Could she be accused of setting up a **straw man**?

6. What does Kaminer want to accomplish? Is her purpose to convince readers of something? To move them to action? What is your reaction to her essay?

This opinion piece was originally published on March 21, 2015, in the *New York Times*.

IN COLLEGE AND HIDING FROM SCARY IDEAS

JUDITH SHULEVITZ

Katherine Byron, a senior at Brown University and a member of its Sexual 1 Assault Task Force, considers it her duty to make Brown a safe place for rape victims, free from anything that might prompt memories of trauma.

So when she heard last fall that a student group had organized a debate about 2 campus sexual assault between Jessica Valenti, the founder of feministing.com, and Wendy McElroy, a libertarian, and that Ms. McElroy was likely to criticize the term "rape culture," Ms. Byron was alarmed. "Bringing in a speaker like that could serve to invalidate people's experiences," she told me. It could be "damaging."

Ms. Byron and some fellow task force members secured a meeting with 3 administrators. Not long after, Brown's president, Christina H. Paxson, announced that the university would hold a simultaneous, competing talk to provide "research and facts" about "the role of culture in sexual assault." Meanwhile, student volunteers put up posters advertising that a "safe space" would be available for anyone who found the debate too upsetting.

The safe space, Ms. Byron explained, was intended to give people who 4 might find comments "troubling" or "triggering," a place to recuperate. The room was equipped with cookies, coloring books, bubbles, Play-Doh, calming music, pillows, blankets, and a video of frolicking puppies, as well as students and staff members trained to deal with trauma. Emma Hall, a junior, rape survivor, and "sexual assault peer educator" who helped set up the room and worked in it during the debate, estimates that a couple of dozen people used it. At one point she went to the lecture hall—it was packed—but after a while, she had to return to the safe space. "I was feeling bombarded by a lot of viewpoints that really go against my dearly and closely held beliefs," Ms. Hall said.

Safe spaces are an expression of the conviction, increasingly prevalent 5 among college students, that their schools should keep them from being "bombarded" by discomfiting or distressing viewpoints. Think of the safe space as the live-action version of the better-known trigger warning, a notice put on top of a syllabus or an assigned reading to alert students to the presence of potentially disturbing material.

Some people trace safe spaces back to the feminist consciousness-raising 6 groups of the 1960s and 1970s, others to the gay and lesbian movement of the early 1990s. In most cases, safe spaces are innocuous gatherings of like-minded people who agree to refrain from ridicule, criticism, or what they term microaggressions—subtle displays of racial or sexual bias—so that everyone can relax enough to explore the nuances of, say, a fluid gender identity. As long as all parties consent to such restrictions, these little islands of self-restraint seem like a perfectly fine idea.

> "As long as all parties consent to such restrictions, these little islands of self-restraint seem like a perfectly fine idea." 7

But the notion that ticklish conversations must be scrubbed clean of controversy has a way of leaking out and spreading. Once you designate some spaces as safe, you imply that the rest are unsafe. It follows that they should be made safer.

This logic clearly informed a campaign undertaken this fall by a Colum- 8 bia University student group called Everyone Allied Against Homophobia that consisted of slipping a flier under the door of every dorm room on campus. The headline of the flier stated, "I want this space to be a safer space." The text below instructed students to tape the fliers to their windows. The group's vice president then had the flier published in the *Columbia Daily Spectator*, the student newspaper, along with an editorial asserting that "making spaces safer is about learning how to be kind to each other."

A junior named Adam Shapiro decided he didn't want his room to be a 9 safer space. He printed up his own flier calling it a dangerous space and had that, too, published in the *Columbia Daily Spectator*. "Kindness alone won't allow us to gain more insight into truth," he wrote. In an interview, Mr. Shapiro said, "If the point of a safe space is therapy for people who feel victimized by traumatization, that sounds like a great mission." But a safe-space mentality has begun infiltrating classrooms, he said, making both professors and students loath to say anything that might hurt someone's feelings. "I don't see how you can have a therapeutic space that's also an intellectual space," he said.

I'm old enough to remember a time when college students objected to 10 providing a platform to certain speakers because they were deemed politically unacceptable. Now students worry whether acts of speech or pieces of writing may put them in emotional peril. Two weeks ago, students at Northwestern University marched to protest an article by Laura Kipnis, a professor in the university's School of Communication. Professor Kipnis had criticized— O.K., ridiculed—what she called the sexual paranoia pervading campus life.

The protesters carried mattresses and demanded that the administration 11 condemn the essay. One student complained that Professor Kipnis was "erasing the very traumatic experience" of victims who spoke out. An organizer of the demonstration said, "we need to be setting aside spaces to talk" about "victim-blaming." Last Wednesday, Northwestern's president, Morton O. Schapiro, wrote an op-ed article in the *Wall Street Journal* affirming his commitment to academic freedom. But plenty of others at universities are willing to dignify students' fears, citing threats to their stability as reasons to cancel debates, disinvite commencement speakers, and apologize for so-called mistakes.

At Oxford University's Christ Church college in November, the college cen- 12 sors (a "censor" being more or less the Oxford equivalent of an undergraduate dean) canceled a debate on abortion after campus feminists threatened to disrupt it because both would-be debaters were men. "I'm relieved the censors have made this decision," said the treasurer of Christ Church's student union, who had pressed for the cancellation. "It clearly makes the most sense for the safety—both physical and mental—of the students who live and work in Christ Church."

A year and a half ago, a Hampshire College student group disinvited an 13 Afrofunk band that had been attacked on social media for having too many white musicians; the vitriolic discussion had made students feel "unsafe."

Last fall, the president of Smith College, Kathleen McCartney, apologized 14 for causing students and faculty to be "hurt" when she failed to object to a racial epithet uttered by a fellow panel member at an alumnae event in New York. The offender was the free-speech advocate Wendy Kaminer, who had been arguing against the use of the euphemism "the n-word" when teaching American history or *The Adventures of Huckleberry Finn*. In the uproar that followed, the Student Government Association wrote a letter declaring that "if Smith is unsafe for one student, it is unsafe for all students."

"It's amazing to me that they can't distinguish between racist speech and 15 speech about racist speech, between racism and discussions of racism," Ms. Kaminer said in an email.

The confusion is telling, though. It shows that while keeping college-level 16 discussions "safe" may feel good to the hypersensitive, it's bad for them and for everyone else. People ought to go to college to sharpen their wits and broaden their field of vision. Shield them from unfamiliar ideas, and they'll never learn the discipline of seeing the world as other people see it. They'll be unprepared for the social and intellectual headwinds that will hit them as soon as they step off the campuses whose climates they have so carefully controlled. What will they do when they hear opinions they've learned to shrink from? If they want to change the world, how will they learn to persuade people to join them?

Only a few of the students want stronger anti-hate-speech codes. Mostly 17 they ask for things like mandatory training sessions and stricter enforcement of existing rules. Still, it's disconcerting to see students clamor for a kind of intrusive supervision that would have outraged students a few generations ago. But those were hardier souls. Now students' needs are anticipated by a small army of service professionals—mental health counselors, student-life deans, and the like. This new bureaucracy may be exacerbating students' "self-infantilization," as Judith Shapiro, the former president of Barnard College, suggested in an essay for *Inside Higher Ed*.

But why are students so eager to self-infantilize? Their parents should 18 probably share the blame. Eric Posner, a professor at the University of Chicago Law School, wrote on *Slate* last month that although universities cosset students more than they used to, that's what they have to do, because today's undergraduates are more puerile than their predecessors. "Perhaps overprogrammed children engineered to the specifications of college admissions offices no longer experience the risks and challenges that

> "Their parents should probably share the blame."

breed maturity," he wrote. But "if college students are children, then they should be protected like children."

Another reason students resort to the quasi-medicalized terminology of 19 trauma is that it forces administrators to respond. Universities are in a double bind. They're required by two civil-rights statutes, Title VII and Title IX, to ensure that their campuses don't create a "hostile environment" for women and other groups subject to harassment. However, universities are not supposed to go too far in suppressing free speech, either. If a university cancels a talk or punishes a professor and a lawsuit ensues, history suggests that the university will lose. But if officials don't censure or don't prevent speech that may inflict psychological damage on a member of a protected class, they risk fostering a hostile environment and prompting an investigation. As a result, students who say they feel unsafe are more likely to be heard than students who demand censorship on other grounds.

The theory that vulnerable students should be guaranteed psychological 20 security has roots in a body of legal thought elaborated in the 1980s and 1990s and still read today. Feminist and anti-racist legal scholars argued that the First Amendment should not safeguard language that inflicted emotional injury through racist or sexist stigmatization. One scholar, Mari J. Matsuda, was particularly insistent that college students not be subjected to "the violence of the word" because many of them "are away from home for the first time and at a vulnerable stage of psychological development." If they're targeted and the university does nothing to help them, they will be "left to their own resources in coping with the damage wrought." That might have, she wrote, "lifelong repercussions."

Perhaps. But Ms. Matsuda doesn't seem to have considered the possibility 21 that insulating students could also make them, well, insular. A few weeks ago, Zineb El Rhazoui, a journalist at *Charlie Hebdo*, spoke at the University of Chicago, protected by the security guards she has traveled with since supporters of the Islamic State issued death threats against her. During the question-and-answer period, a Muslim student stood up to object to the newspaper's apparent disrespect for Muslims and to express her dislike of the phrase "I am Charlie."

Ms. El Rhazoui replied, somewhat irritably, "Being Charlie Hebdo means 22 to die because of a drawing," and not everyone has the guts to do that (although she didn't use the word guts). She lives under constant threat, Ms. El Rhazoui said. The student answered that she felt threatened, too.

A few days later, a guest editorialist in the student newspaper took Ms. El 23 Rhazoui to task. She had failed to ensure "that others felt safe enough to express dissenting opinions." Ms. El Rhazoui's "relative position of power," the writer continued, had granted her a "free pass to make condescending attacks on a member of the university." In a letter to the editor, the president and the vice president of the University of Chicago French Club, which had sponsored the talk, shot back, saying, "El Rhazoui is an immigrant, a woman, Arab, a human-rights activist who has known exile, and a journalist living in very real fear of death. She was invited to speak precisely because her right to do so is, quite literally, under threat."

You'd be hard-pressed to avoid the conclusion that the student and her 24 defender had burrowed so deep inside their cocoons, were so overcome by their own fragility, that they couldn't see that it was Ms. El Rhazoui who was in need of a safer space.

⊃ AT ISSUE: HOW FREE SHOULD FREE SPEECH BE?

1. What are "safe spaces"? According to Shulevitz, what is the problem of designating "some spaces as safe" (para. 7)?

2. In paragraph 9, Shulevitz quotes Adam Shapiro, a student, who says, "I don't see how you can have a therapeutic space that's also an intellectual space." What does Shapiro mean? Do you agree with him?

3. Does Shulevitz use inductive or deductive reasoning to make her case? Why do you think that she chose this strategy?

4. Where does Shulevitz discuss arguments against her position? Does she present these arguments fairly? Explain.

5. Does Shulevitz appeal mainly to *ethos, pathos,* or *logos*?

6. In paragraph 17, Shulevitz says, "Only a few of the students want stronger anti-hate-speech codes." Does this admission undercut her argument? Why or why not?

This essay was posted on Slate.com on February 12, 2015.

UNIVERSITIES ARE RIGHT TO CRACK DOWN ON SPEECH AND BEHAVIOR

ERIC POSNER

Lately, a moral panic about speech and sexual activity in universities has 1 reached a crescendo. Universities have strengthened rules prohibiting offensive speech typically targeted at racial, ethnic, and sexual minorities; taken it upon themselves to issue "trigger warnings" to students when courses offer content that might upset them; banned sexual acts that fall short of rape under criminal law but are on the borderline of coercion; and limited due process protections of students accused of violating these rules.

Most liberals celebrate these developments, yet with a certain uneasiness. 2 Few of them want to apply these protections to society at large. Conservatives and libertarians are up in arms. They see these rules as an assault on free speech and individual liberty. They think universities are treating students like children. And they are right. But they have also not considered that the justification for these policies may lie hidden in plain sight: that students *are* children. Not in terms of age, but in terms of maturity. Even in college, they must be protected like children while being prepared to be adults.

There is a popular, romantic notion that students receive their university 3 education through free and open debate about the issues of the day. Nothing could be farther from the truth. Students who enter college know hardly anything at all—that's why they need an education. Classroom teachers know students won't learn anything if they blab on about their opinions. Teachers are dictators who carefully control what students say to one another. It's not just that sincere expressions of opinion about same-sex marriage or campaign finance reform are out of place in chemistry and math class. They are out of place even in philosophy and politics classes, where the goal is to educate students (usually about academic texts and theories), not to listen to them spout off. And while professors sometimes believe there is pedagogical value in allowing students to express their political opinions in the context of some text, professors (or at least, good professors) carefully manipulate their students so that the discussion serves pedagogical ends.

That's why the contretemps about a recent incident at Marquette Univer- 4 sity is far less alarming than libertarians think. An inexperienced instructor was teaching a class on the philosophy of John Rawls, and a student in the class argued that same-sex marriage was consistent with Rawls' philosophy. When another student told the teacher outside of class that he disagreed, the teacher responded that she would not permit a student to oppose same-sex marriage in class because that might offend gay students.

While I believe that the teacher mishandled the student's complaint, 5 she was justified in dismissing it. The purpose of the class was to teach Rawls' theory of justice, not to debate the merits of same-sex marriage. The fact that a student injected same-sex marriage into the discussion does not mean that the class was required to discuss it. The professor might reasonably have believed that the students would gain a better understanding of Rawls' theory if they thought about how it applied to issues less divisive and hence less likely to distract students from the academic merits of the theory.

Teaching is tricky. Everyone understands that a class is a failure if stu- 6 dents refuse to learn because they feel bullied or intimidated, or if ideological arguments break out that have nothing to do with understanding an idea. It is the responsibility of the professor to conduct the class in such a way that maximal learning occurs, not maximal speech. That's why no teacher would permit students to launch into anti-Semitic diatribes in a class about the Holocaust, however sincerely the speaker might think that Jews were responsible for the Holocaust or the Holocaust did not take place. And even a teacher less scrupulous about avoiding offense to gay people would draw a line if a student in the Rawls class wanted to argue that Jim Crow or legalization of pedophilia is entailed by the principles of justice. While advocates of freedom of speech like to claim that falsehoods get squeezed out in the "marketplace of ideas," in classrooms they just receive an F.

> "It is the responsibility of the professor to conduct the class in such a way that maximal learning occurs, not maximal speech."

Most of the debate about speech codes, which frequently prohibit stu- 7 dents from making offensive comments to one another, concerns speech outside of class. Two points should be made. First, students who are unhappy with the codes and values on campus can take their views to forums outside of campus—to the town square, for example. The campus is an extension of the classroom, and so while the restrictions in the classroom are enforced less vigorously, the underlying pedagogical objective of avoiding intimidation remains intact.

Second, and more important—at least for libertarian partisans of the free 8 market—the universities are simply catering to demand in the marketplace for education. While critics sometimes give the impression that lefty professors and clueless administrators originated the speech and sex codes, the truth is that universities adopted them because that's what most students want. If students want to learn biology and art history in an environment where they needn't worry about being offended or raped, why shouldn't they? As long as universities are free to choose whatever rules they want, students with different views can sort themselves into universities with different rules. Indeed, students who want the greatest speech protections can attend public universities, which (unlike private universities) are governed by the First Amendment.

184

Libertarians might reflect on the irony that the private market, in which they normally put faith, reflects a preference among students for speech restrictions.

And this brings me to the most important overlooked fact about speech 9 and sex code debates. Society seems to be moving the age of majority from 18 to 21 or 22. We are increasingly treating college-age students as quasi-children who need protection from some of life's harsh realities while they complete the larval stage of their lives. Many critics of these codes discern this transformation but misinterpret it. They complain that universities are treating adults like children. The problem is that universities have been treating children like adults.

A lot of the controversies about campus life become clearer from this 10 perspective. Youngsters do dumb things. They suffer from lack of impulse control. They fail to say no to a sexual encounter they do not want, or they misinterpret a *no* as *yes*, or in public debate they undermine their own arguments by being needlessly offensive. Scientific research confirms that brain development continues well into a person's 20s. High schools are accustomed to dealing with the cognitive limitations of their charges. They see their mission as advancing the autonomy of students rather than assuming that it is already in place. They socialize as well as educate children to act civilly by punishing them if they don't. Universities have gradually realized that they must take the same approach to college students.

One naturally wonders why this has become necessary. Perhaps over- 11 programmed children engineered to the specifications of college admissions offices no longer experience the risks and challenges that breed maturity. Or maybe in our ever-more technologically advanced society, the responsibilities of adulthood must be delayed until the completion of a more extended period of education.

Yet college students have not always enjoyed so much autonomy. The 12 modern freedoms of college students date back only to the 1960s, when a wave of anti-authoritarianism, inspired by the Vietnam War and the civil rights movement, swept away strict campus codes in an era of single-sex dorms. The modern speech and sex codes have surfaced as those waters recede back to sea. What is most interesting is that this reaction comes not from parents and administrators, but from students themselves, who, apparently recognizing that their parents and schools have not fully prepared them for independence, want universities to resume their traditional role *in loco parentis*.

If all this is true, then maybe we can declare a truce in the culture wars 13 over education. If college students are children, then they should be protected like children. Libertarians should take heart that the market in private education offers students a diverse assortment of ideological cultures in which they can be indoctrinated. Conservatives should rejoice that moral instruction and social control have been reintroduced to the universities after a 40-year drought. Both groups should be pleased that students are kept from harm's way, and kept from doing harm, until they are ready to accept the responsibilities of adults.

⊙ AT ISSUE: HOW FREE SHOULD FREE SPEECH BE?

1. This article begins with a series of examples. Are these examples self-evident, or does Posner need to supply more material—for example, source information or evidence that the policies he mentions are widespread?

2. In paragraph 2, Posner says, "Most liberals celebrate these developments." He then goes on to talk about conservatives and libertarians. What logical fallacy does he seem to be committing?

3. In paragraph 3, Posner says, "Teachers are dictators who carefully control what students say to one another." Do you agree? How could you refute this statement?

4. What is Posner's purpose in writing this essay? Does he want to present information, change people's ideas, or move readers to action? Do you think that he achieves his purpose? Explain.

5. Posner makes a number of unsupported general statements in this essay. For example, in paragraph 8, he says that universities adopted speech and sex codes "because that's what most students want." Identify two or three of these general statements, and determine what kinds of evidence Posner would need to support them.

6. In his conclusion, Posner speculates on why universities should assume the responsibility of socializing students. Do you agree? Why or why not?

TEMPLATE FOR WRITING A DEDUCTIVE ARGUMENT

Write a one-paragraph **deductive** argument in which you argue *against* your school imposing speech codes. Follow the template below, filling in the blanks to create your argument.

One of the basic principles of the United States government is the constitutional guarantee of freedom of speech. With few exceptions, all Americans _____. In college _____.

For example, _____. By having the right to express themselves freely, _____. Therefore, _____.

Not everyone agrees with this view, however. Some people argue that _____. This argument misses the point. When a university limits the speech of some students because others may be upset by their comments, _____.

For this reason, colleges should _____.

TEMPLATE FOR WRITING AN INDUCTIVE ARGUMENT

Write a one-paragraph **inductive** argument in which you argue *in favor of* your school imposing speech codes. Follow the template below, filling in the blanks to create your argument.

The number of students demanding protection from distasteful ideas is growing yearly. Some students complain that _____

_____

_____ . These students want _____

_____ .

A number of studies have shown that so-called safe spaces and trigger warnings go a long way toward calming students' fears and creating a hospitable learning environment. For example, some students _____

_____ . As a result, _____

_____

_____ . The best way for colleges to deal with this

problem is to _____

_____ .

Free speech advocates, however, argue that _____

_____

_____

_____ . Although this may be true, _____

_____

_____ .

For this reason, it would make sense to _____

_____

_____

⊙ EXERCISE 5.13

Interview several of your classmates as well as one or two of your instructors about how free free speech should be. Then, edit the deductive and inductive arguments you wrote using the templates above so that they include some of these comments.

⊙ EXERCISE 5.14

Write an essay in which you take a position on the question, "Should Universities Be Able to Place Limits on Free Speech?" Make sure that your essay is organized primarily as either a deductive argument or an inductive argument. Use the readings on pages 165–186 as source material, and be sure to document all information that you get from these sources. (See Chapter 10 for information on documenting sources.)

⊙ EXERCISE 5.15

Review the logical fallacies discussed on pages 147–160. Then, reread the essay you wrote for Exercise 5.14, and check to see if it contains any fallacies. Underline any fallacies you find, and identify them by name. Then, rewrite each statement so it expresses a logical argument. Finally, revise your draft to eliminate any fallacies you found.

⊙ EXERCISE 5.16

Review the four pillars of argument discussed in Chapter 1. Does your essay include all four elements of an effective argument? Add anything that is missing. Then, label the key elements of your essay.

6

Rogerian Argument, Toulmin Logic, and Oral Arguments

AT ISSUE

Is Online Education Better Than Classroom Education?

Chances are good that you have either taken an online course, or that you know someone who has. The National Center for Education Statistics found that as of 2014, one in four undergraduate students took at least one online course, and that number is expected to more than double in the coming years. In fact, from 2012 to 2013, online courses accounted for nearly three-quarters of the increase in enrollment for colleges in the United States. Given these facts, some educators wonder if students in online courses are getting what they pay for. Is online instruction as effective as meeting regularly on campus?

The appeal of online education is clear. For students, online education offers flexible scheduling, more time for work or family, and extra money, because online courses eliminate the need to commute to and from school. For colleges and universities, online education programs are cost-effective and profitable because they enable schools to reach new student populations, both nationally and internationally, without the expense of classrooms, offices, libraries, and bookstores.

But despite the advantages of online education, questions remain about its efficacy. For example, some educators ask if virtual classrooms are able to duplicate the dynamic educational atmosphere of face-to-face instruction. Others question whether students learn as well from education delivered by technology as they do from classroom instruction. Still others point out that because online instruction requires more self-discipline than on-campus classes, students find it easy to procrastinate and fall behind on their work.

Later in this chapter, you will be asked to think more about this issue. You will be given several sources to consider and asked to write an argument—using one of the three approaches discussed in this chapter—that takes a position on whether online education is better than classroom instruction.

A confrontational
argument

BloomImage/Getty Images

Understanding Rogerian Argument

The traditional model of argument is **confrontational**—characterized by conflict and opposition. This has been the tradition since Aristotle wrote about argument in ancient Greece. The end result of this model of argument is that someone is a winner and someone is a loser or someone is right and someone is wrong.

Arguments do not always have to be confrontational, however. In fact, the twentieth-century psychologist Carl Rogers contended that in many situations, this method of arguing can actually be counterproductive, making it impossible for two people to reach agreement. According to Rogers, attacking opponents and telling them that they are wrong or misguided puts them on the defensive. The result of this tactic is frequently ill will, anger, hostility—and conflict. If you are trying to negotiate an agreement or convince someone to do something, these are exactly the responses that you do not want. To solve this problem, Rogers developed a new approach to argument—one that emphasizes cooperation over confrontation.

Rogerian argument begins with the assumption that people of good will can find solutions to problems that they have in common. Rogers recommends that you consider those with whom you disagree as colleagues, not opponents. Instead of entering into the adversarial relationship that is assumed in classical argument, Rogerian argument encourages you to enter into a cooperative relationship in which both you and your readers search for **common ground**—points of agreement about a problem. By taking this approach, you are more likely to find a solution that will satisfy everyone.

Structuring Rogerian Arguments

Consider the following situation. Assume that you bought a video game console that stopped working one week after the warranty expired. Also assume that the manager of the store where you purchased the game console has refused to exchange it for another console. His point is that because the warranty has expired, the store has no obligation to take the product back. As a last resort, you write a letter to the game console's manufacturer. If you were writing a traditional argument, you would state your thesis—"It is clear that I should receive a new game console"—and then present arguments to support your position. You would also refute opposing arguments, and you would end your letter with a strong concluding statement.

Because Rogerian arguments begin with different assumptions, however, they are structured differently from classical arguments. In a Rogerian argument, you would begin by establishing common ground—by pointing out the concerns you and the video game console's manufacturer share. For example, you could say that as a consumer, you want to buy merchandise that will work as advertised. If the company satisfies your needs, you will continue to buy its products. This goal is shared by the manufacturer. Therefore, instead of beginning with a thesis statement that demands a yes or no response, you would point out that you and the manufacturer share an interest in solving your problem.

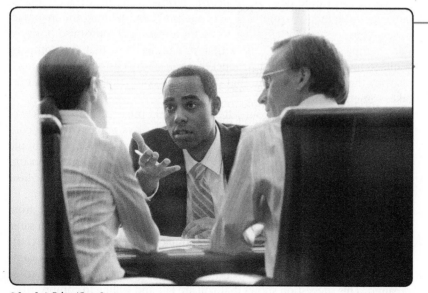

Establishing common ground

© Jose Luis Pelaez/Getty Images

Rogerian argument
could resolve
your problem.

© shvili/iStock/Getty Images

Next, you would describe *in neutral terms*—using impartial, unbiased language—the manufacturer's view of the problem, defining the manufacturer's concerns and attempting to move toward a compromise position. For example, you would explain that you understand that the company wants to make a high-quality product that will satisfy customers. You would also say that you understand that despite the company's best efforts, mistakes sometimes happen.

In the next section of your letter, you would present your own view of the problem fairly and objectively. This section plays a major role in convincing the manufacturer that your position has merit. Here, you should also try to concede the strengths of the manufacturer's viewpoint. For example, you can say that although you understand that warranties have time limits, your case has some unique circumstances that justify your claim.

Then you would explain how the manufacturer would benefit from granting your request. Perhaps you could point out that you have been satisfied with other products made by this manufacturer and expect to purchase more in the future. You could also say that instead of requesting a new game console, you would be glad to send the console back to the factory to be repaired. This suggestion shows that you are fair and willing to compromise.

Finally, your Rogerian argument would reinforce your position and end with a concluding statement that emphasizes the idea that you are certain that the manufacturer wants to settle this matter fairly.

⊃ EXERCISE 6.1

Read through the At Issue topics listed in this book's table of contents. Choose one topic, and then do the following:

1. Summarize your own position on the issue.

2. In a few sentences, summarize the main concerns of someone who holds the opposite position.

3. Identify some common ground that you and someone who holds the opposite position might have.

4. Write a sentence that explains how your position on the issue might benefit individuals (including those who hold opposing views) or society in general.

Writing Rogerian Arguments

Rogerian arguments are typically used to address issues that are open to compromise. By making it clear that you understand and respect the opinions of others, you avoid an "I win / you lose" situation and demonstrate empathy and respect for all points of view. In this sense, Rogerian arguments are more like negotiations than classical arguments. Thus, in a Rogerian argument, you spend a good deal of time defining the common ground that exists between you and those with whom you disagree. Ideally, you demonstrate that it is possible to reach a consensus, one that represents the common ground that exists between opposing sides. The more successful you are in accomplishing this goal, the more persuasive your argument will be. Of course with some issues—usually the most polarizing—a consensus is difficult or even impossible to achieve. In these cases, the best you can hope for is to convince people to agree on just one or two points. With other issues, however, you will be able to demonstrate to readers how they would benefit by moving toward your position.

> **NOTE**
>
> Although the Rogerian approach to argument can be used to develop a whole essay, it can also be part of a more traditional argument. In this case, it frequently appears in the refutation section, where opposing arguments are addressed.

In general, a Rogerian argument can be structured in the following way:

INTRODUCTION	Introduces the problem, pointing out how both the writer and reader are affected (establishes common ground)
BODY	Presents the reader's view of the problem
	Presents the writer's view of the problem (includes evidence to support the writer's viewpoint)
	Shows how the reader would benefit from moving toward the writer's position (includes evidence to support the writer's viewpoint)
	Lays out possible compromises that would benefit both reader and writer (includes evidence to support the writer's viewpoint)
CONCLUSION	Strong concluding statement reinforces the thesis and emphasizes compromise

⊘ EXERCISE 6.2

The following student essay includes all the elements of a Rogerian argument. This essay was written in response to the question, "Is it fair for instructors to require students to turn off their cell phones in class?" After you read the essay, answer the questions on page 199, consulting the outline above if necessary.

WHY CELL PHONES DO NOT BELONG IN THE CLASSROOM

ZOYA KAHN

Some college students think it is unfair for instructors to require   1
them to turn off their cell phones during class. Because they are accustomed to constant cell phone access, they don't understand how such a rule is justified. Granted, a strict, no-exceptions policy requiring that cell phones be turned off all over campus is not fair, but neither is a policy that prevents instructors from imposing restrictions ("Official Notices").

Common ground   Both students and instructors know that cell phone use—including

texting—during class can be disruptive. In addition, most would agree that the primary goal of a university is to create a respectful learning environment and that cell phone use during class undercuts this goal. For this reason, it is in everyone's interest for instructors to institute pol- Thesis statement
icies that require students to turn off cell phones during class.

Many students believe that requiring them to turn off their cell   2
phones is unfair because it makes them feel less safe. Students are   Reader's view of the
understandably concerned that, with their phones turned off, they will   problem
be unreachable during an emergency. For example, text message alerts are part of the emergency response system for most universities. Simi-larly, cell phones are a way for friends and family to contact students if there is an emergency. For these reasons, many students think that they should be free to make their own decisions concerning cell use. They believe that by turning their phones to vibrate or silent mode, they are showing respect for their classmates. As one student points out, "Only a small percentage of students will misuse their phones. Then, why should every student have to sacrifice for someone's mistakes?" (SchoolBook). After all, most students are honest and courteous. How-ever, those few students who are determined to misuse their phones will do so, regardless of the school's phone policy.

To protect the integrity of the school's learning environment,   3 Writer's view of the
instructors are justified in requiring students to turn off their phones.   situation
Recent studies have shown how distracting cell phones can be during a class. For example, a ringing cell phone significantly impairs students' performance, and a vibrating phone can be just as distracting (End et al. 56–57). In addition, texting in class decreases students' ability to focus, lowers test performance, and lessens students' retention of class mate-rial (Tindell and Bohlander 2). According to a recent study, most stu-dents believe that texting causes problems, "including a negative impact on classroom learning for the person who is texting, and distrac-tion for those sitting nearby" (Tindell and Bohlander 4). Even more dis-turbing, cell phones enable some students to cheat. Students can use cell phones to text test questions and answers, to search the Web, and to photograph exams. Although asking students to turn off their phones will not prevent all these problems, it will reduce the abuses, and this will benefit the majority of students.

Benefits for reader of
writer's position

Students have good reasons for wanting to keep their phones on,   4
but there are even better reasons for accepting some reasonable restrictions. First, when students use cell phones during class, they distract
themselves (as well as their classmates) and undermine everyone's ability to learn. Second, having their cell phones on gives students a false
sense of security. A leading cell phone company has found that cell
phones can actually "detract from school safety and crisis prepared-
ness" in numerous ways. For example, the use of cell phones during a
crisis can overload the cell phone system and make it useless. In addition, cell phones make it easy for students to spread rumors and, in
some cases, cell phone use has created more panic than the incidents
that actually caused the rumors ("Cell Phones").

Possible compromise

One possible compromise is for instructors to join with students to   5
create cell phone policies that take into consideration various situations
and settings. For example, instructors could require students to turn off
their phones only during exams. Instructors could also try to find ways
to engage students by using cell phone technology in the classroom.
For example, in some schools teachers take advantage of the various
functions available on most cell phones—calculators, cameras, diction-
aries, and Internet browsers ("Cell Phones"). In addition, schools should
consider implementing alternative emergency alert systems. Such com-
promises would ensure safety, limit possible disruptions, reduce the
potential for academic dishonesty, and enhance learning.

It is understandable that students want instructors to permit the   6
use of cell phones during class, but it is also fair for instructors to ask
students to turn them off. Although instructors should be able to
restrict cell phone use, they should also make sure that students understand the need for this policy. It is in everyone's best interest to protect
the integrity of the classroom and to make sure that learning is not

Concluding statement

compromised by cell phone use. To ensure the success of their education, students should be willing to turn off their phones.

Works Cited

"Cell Phones and Text Messaging in Schools." *National School Safety
and Security Services*, 2012, www.schoolsecurity.org/trends/cell
-phones-and-text-messaging-in-schools/.

End, Christian M., Shaye Worthman, Mary Bridget Mathews, and Katharina Wetterau. "Costly Cell Phones: The Impact of Cell Phone Rings on Academic Performance." *Teaching of Psychology*, vol. 37, no. 1, 2010, pp. 55–57. *Academic Search Complete*, doi: 10.1080/00986280903425912.

"Official Notices." UCLA Registrar's Office, Department of Student Affairs, 24 Oct. 2011, www.registrar.ucla.edu/soc/notices.htm.

SchoolBook. "Time to Repeal the Cell Phone Ban, Students Say." New York Public Radio, 2 Nov. 2011, www.wnyc.org/story/303205-time -to-repeal-the-cellphone-ban-students-say/.

Tindell, Deborah R., and Robert W. Bohlander. "The Use and Abuse of Cell Phones and Text Messaging in the Classroom: A Survey of College Students." *College Teaching*, vol. 60, no. 1, 2012, pp. 1–9. *ERIC Institute of Education Services*, eric.ed.gov/?id=EJ951966.

Identifying the Elements of a Rogerian Argument

1. How does the writer attempt to establish common ground? Do you think she is successful?

2. What evidence does the writer supply to support her position?

3. Other than reinforcing the writer's position, what else is the conclusion trying to accomplish?

4. How does the concluding statement reinforce agreement and compromise?

5. How would this essay be different if it were written as a traditional (as opposed to a Rogerian) argument?

Understanding Toulmin Logic

Another way of describing the structure of argument was introduced by the philosopher Stephen Toulmin in his book *The Uses of Argument* (1958). Toulmin observed that although formal logic is effective for analyzing classical arguments, it is inadequate for describing the arguments you encounter in everyday life. Although Toulmin was primarily concerned with the structures of arguments at the level of sentences or paragraphs, his model is also useful when dealing with longer arguments.

In its simplest terms, a **Toulmin argument** has three parts—the *claim*, the *grounds*, and the *warrant*. The **claim** is the main point of the essay—usually stated as the thesis. The **grounds** are the evidence that a writer uses to support the claim. The **warrant** is the **inference**—either stated or implied—that connects the claim to the grounds.

A basic argument using Toulmin logic would have the following structure.

CLAIM	Online education should be a part of all students' education.
GROUNDS	Students who take advantage of online education get better grades and report less stress than students who do not.
WARRANT	Online education is a valuable educational option.

Notice that the three-part structure above resembles the **syllogism** that is the backbone of classical argument. (See pp. 125–129 for a discussion of syllogisms.)

> NOTE
>
> When you use Toulmin logic to construct an argument, you still use deductive and inductive reasoning. You arrive at your claim inductively from facts, observations, and examples, and you connect the grounds and the warrant to your claim deductively.

Constructing Toulmin Arguments

Real arguments—those you encounter in print or online every day—are not as simple as the three-part model above implies. To be convincing, arguments often contain additional parts. To account for the demands of everyday debates, Toulmin expanded his model to include the following six interconnected elements.

CLAIM	The **claim** is the main point of your essay. It is a debatable statement that the rest of the essay will support.
	Online education should be a part of all students' education.
GROUNDS	The **grounds** are the concrete evidence that a writer uses to support the claim. These are the facts and observations that support the thesis. They can also be the opinions of experts that you locate when you do research.
	Studies show that students who take advantage of online education often get better grades than students who do not.

Research indicates that students who take advantage of online education are under less stress than those who are not.

WARRANT

The **warrant** is the inference that links the claim with the grounds. The warrant is often an unstated assumption. Ideally, the warrant should be an idea with which your readers will agree. (If they do not agree with it, you will need to supply **backing**.)

Online education is a valuable educational option.

BACKING

The **backing** consists of statements that support the warrant.

My own experience with online education was positive. Not only did it enable me to schedule classes around my job, but it also enabled me to work at my own pace in my courses.

QUALIFIERS

The **qualifiers** are statements that limit the claim. For example, they can be the real-world conditions under which the claim is true. These qualifiers can include words such as *most, few, some, sometimes, occasionally, often,* and *usually.*

Online education should be a required part of most students' education.

REBUTTALS

The **rebuttals** are exceptions to the claim. They are counterarguments that identify the situations where the claim does not hold true.

Some people argue that online education deprives students of an interactive classroom experience, but a course chat room can give students a similar opportunity to interact with their classmates.

◆ EXERCISE 6.3

Look through this book's table of contents, and select an At Issue topic that interests you (ideally, one that you know something about). Write a sentence that states your position on this issue. (In terms of Toulmin argument, this statement is the *claim.*)

Then, supply as many of the expanded Toulmin model elements as you can, consulting the description of these elements above.

Claim: _____

_____

Grounds: _____

_____

_____

Warrant: _____

_____

_____

Backing: _____

_____

Qualifiers: _____

_____

_____

Rebuttals: _____

_____

Writing Toulmin Arguments

One of the strengths of the Toulmin model is that it emphasizes that presenting effective arguments involves more than stating ideas in absolute terms. Unlike the classical model of argument, the Toulmin model encourages writers to make realistic and convincing points by including claims and qualifiers and by addressing opposing arguments in down-to-earth and constructive ways. In a sense, this method of constructing an argument reminds writers that arguments do not exist in a vacuum. They are often quite subtle and are aimed at real readers who may or may not agree with them.

In general, a Toulmin argument can be organized in the following way:

INTRODUCTION	Introduces the problem
	States the claim (and possibly the qualifier)
BODY	Possibly states the warrant
	Presents the backing that supports the warrant
	Presents the grounds that support the claim
	Presents the conditions of rebuttal
	States the qualifiers
CONCLUSION	Brings the argument to a close
	Strong concluding statement reinforces the claim

⊖ EXERCISE 6.4

The following student essay, which includes all the elements of a Toulmin argument, was written in response to the question, "Are cheerleaders athletes?" After you read the essay, answer the questions on page 205, consulting the outline on the previous page if necessary.

COMPETITIVE CHEERLEADERS ARE ATHLETES

JEN DAVIS

Recently, the call to make competitive cheerleading an official   1
college sport and to recognize cheerleaders as athletes has gotten
stronger. Critics of this proposal maintain that cheerleading is simply
entertainment that occurs on the sidelines of real sporting events.
According to them, although cheerleading may show strength and skill,
it is not a competitive activity. This view of cheerleading, however,
misses the point. Because competitive cheerleading pits teams against
each other in physically and technically demanding athletic contests,
it should be recognized as a sport. For this reason, those who participate   Claim and qualifier
in the sport of competitive cheerleading should be considered athletes.

Acknowledging cheerleaders as athletes gives them the respect   2 Warrant
and support they deserve. Many people associate cheerleading with   Backing
pom-poms and short skirts and ignore the strength and skill competitive
cheerleading requires. Like athletes in other female-dominated sports,
cheerleaders unfortunately have had to fight to be taken seriously. For   Grounds
example, Title IX, the law that mandates gender equity in college
sports, does not recognize competitive cheerleading as a sport. This
situation demonstrates a very narrow definition of sports, one that
needs to be updated. As one women's sports advocate explains,
"What we consider sports are things that men have traditionally
played" (qtd. in Thomas). For this reason, women's versions of long-
accepted men's sports—such as basketball, soccer, and track—are easy
for people to respect and to support. Competitive cheerleading, however, departs from this model and is not seen as a sport even though

those who compete in it are skilled, accomplished athletes. As one coach points out, the athleticism of cheerleading is undeniable: "We don't throw balls, we throw people. And we catch them" (qtd. in Thomas).

Backing

Grounds

Recent proposals to rename competitive cheerleading "stunt" or   3
"team acrobatics and tumbling" are an effort to reshape people's ideas about what cheerleaders actually do. Although some cheerleading squads have kept to their original purpose—to lead fans in cheering on their teams—competitive teams practice rigorously, maintain impressive levels of physical fitness, and risk serious injuries. Like other sports, competitive cheerleading involves extraordinary feats of strength and skill. Cheerleaders perform elaborate floor routines and ambitious stunts, including flips from multilevel human pyramids. Competitive cheerleaders also do what all athletes must do: they compete. Even a critic concedes that cheerleading could be "considered a sport when cheerleading groups compete against one another" (Sandler). Competitive cheerleading teams do just that; they enter competitive contests, are judged, and emerge as winners or losers.

Rebuttal

Those in authority, however, are slow to realize that cheerleading is   4
a sport. In 2010, a federal judge declared that competitive cheerleading was "too underdeveloped and disorganized" to qualify as a legitimate varsity sport under Title IX (Tigay). This ruling was shortsighted. Before competitive cheerleading can develop as a sport, it needs to be *acknowledged* as a sport. Without their schools' financial support, cheerleading teams cannot recruit, offer scholarships, or host competitions. To address this situation, several national groups are asking the National Collegiate Athletic Association (NCAA) to designate competitive cheerleading as an "emerging sport." By doing this, the NCAA would show

Qualifiers

its support and help competitive cheerleading to develop and eventually to flourish. This does not mean, however, that all cheerleaders are athletes or that all cheerleading is a sport. In addition, the NCAA does have reason to be cautious when it comes to redefining competitive cheerleading. Some schools have taken sideline cheerleading teams and recategorized them just so they could comply with Title IX. These efforts to sidestep the purpose of the law are, as one expert puts it, "obviously transparent and unethical" (Tigay). Even so, fear of possible abuse should not keep the NCAA from doing what is right and giving legitimate athletes the respect and support they deserve.

Competitive cheerleaders are athletes in every sense of the word. 5
They are aggressive, highly skilled, physically fit competitors. For this reason, they deserve to be acknowledged as athletes under Title IX and supported by their schools and by the NCAA. Biased and outdated ideas about what is (and what is not) a sport should not keep competitive cheerleading from being recognized as the sport it is. As one proponent puts it, "Adding flexibility to the definition of college athletes is a com-   *Concluding statement*
mon sense move that everyone can cheer for" ("Bona Fide"). It is time to give competitive cheerleaders the support and recognition they deserve.

Works Cited

"Bona Fide Athletes." *USA Today*, 16 Oct. 2009, www.usatoday.com
/story/opinion/2019/10/16/bona-fide-athletes/81582044/. Editorial.

Sandler, Bernice R. "Certain Types of Competition Define Sports." *USA Today*, 22 Oct. 2009, usatoday30.usatoday.com/printedition /news/20091022/letters22_st2.art.htm.

Thomas, Katie. "Born on the Sideline, Cheering Clamors to Be a Sport." *New York Times*, 22 May 2011, www.nytimes.com/2011/05/23/sports /gender-games-born-on-sideline-cheering-clamors-to-be-sport.html.

Tigay, Chanan. "Is Cheerleading a Sport Protected by Title IX?" *CQ Researcher*, 25 Mar. 2011, p. 276. library.cqpress.com/cqresearcher /document.php?id=cqresrre2011032500.

Identifying the Elements of a Toulmin Argument

1. Summarize the position this essay takes as a three-part argument that includes the claim, the grounds, and the warrant.

2. Do you think the writer includes enough backing for her claim? What other supporting evidence could she have included?

3. Find the qualifier in the essay. How does it limit the argument? How else could the writer have qualified the argument?

4. Do you think the writer addresses enough objections to her claim? What other arguments could she have addressed?

5. Based on your reading of this essay, what advantages do you think Toulmin logic offers to writers? What disadvantages does it present?

Understanding Oral Arguments

Many everyday arguments—in school, on the job, or in your community—are presented orally. In many ways, an oral argument is similar to a written one: it has an introduction, a body, and a conclusion, and it addresses and refutes opposing points of view. In other, more subtle ways, however, an oral argument is different from a written one. Before you plan and deliver an oral argument, you should be aware of these differences.

The major difference between an oral argument and a written one is that an audience cannot reread an oral argument to clarify information. Listeners have to understand an oral argument the first time they hear it. To help your listeners, you need to design your presentation with this limitation in mind, considering the following guidelines:

- **An oral argument should contain verbal signals that help guide listeners.** Transitional phrases such as "My first point," "My second point," and "Let me sum up" are useful in oral arguments, where listeners do not have a written text in front of them. They alert listeners to information to come and signal shifts from one point to another.

- **An oral argument should use simple, direct language and avoid long sentences.** Complicated sentences that contain elevated language and numerous technical terms are difficult for listeners to follow. For this reason, your sentences should be straightforward and easy to understand.

- **An oral argument should repeat key information.** A traditional rule of thumb for oral arguments is, "Tell listeners what you're going to tell them; then tell it to them; finally, tell them what you've told them." In other words, in the introduction of an oral argument, tell your listeners what they are going to hear; in the body, discuss your points, one at a time; and finally, in your conclusion, restate your points. This intentional repetition ensures that your listeners follow (and remember) your points.

- **An oral argument should include visuals.** Visual aids can make your argument easier to follow. You can use visuals to identify your points as you discuss them. You can also use visuals—for example, charts, graphs, or tables—to clarify or reinforce key points as well as to add interest. Carefully selected visuals help increase the chances that what you are saying will be remembered.

Planning an Oral Argument

The work you do to plan your presentation is as important as the presentation itself. Here is some advice to consider as you plan your oral argument:

1. **Choose your topic wisely.** Select a topic that is somewhat controversial so listeners will want to hear your views. You can create interest in a topic, but it is easier to appeal to listeners if they are already interested in what you have to say. In addition, try to choose a topic that you know something about. Even though you will probably do some research, the process will be much easier if you are already familiar with the basic issues.

2. **Know your audience.** Consider your audience and its needs before you begin to plan your presentation. For example, how much do listeners already know about your topic? Are they well informed, or do they know little about it? If listeners are unfamiliar with your topic, you will have to supply background information and definitions of key terms. If they already know a lot, you can dispense with this material and discuss your subject in more depth. Also, assess your audience members' likely response to your presentation. Will they be receptive? Hostile? Neutral? The answers to these questions will help you decide which arguments will most likely be effective (and which will not).

3. **Know your time limit.** Most oral presentations have a time limit. If you run over your allotted time, you risk boring or annoying your listeners. If you finish too soon, it will seem as if you don't know much about your subject. As you prepare your argument, include all the information that you can cover within your time limit. Keep in mind

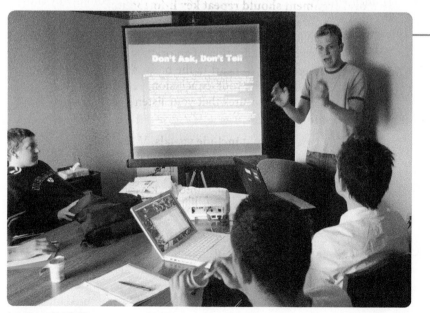

Visual aids can help listeners follow an oral presentation.

Ann Heisenfelt/AP Photo

that you will not be able to go into as much detail in a short speech as you will in a long speech, so plan accordingly.

4. **Identify your thesis statement.** Like a written argument, an oral argument should have a debatable thesis statement. Keep this statement simple, and make sure that it clearly conveys your position. Remember that in an oral argument, your listeners have to understand your thesis the first time they hear it. (See Chapter 7 for more on developing a thesis statement.)

5. **Gather support for your thesis.** Assume that your listeners are **skeptical**, that is, that they are not easily convinced. Even if you think that your audience is friendly, you still need to make a persuasive case. Don't make the mistake of thinking that listeners will automatically accept all your ideas just because they agree with your main point. For this reason, you need to support your thesis with compelling evidence if you expect listeners to conclude that your position is valid. Supporting evidence can be in the form of facts, observations, expert opinion, or statistics. Some of your support can come from your own experiences, but most will come from your research.

6. **Acknowledge your sources.** Remember that all of the information you get from your research needs to be acknowledged. As you deliver your presentation, let listeners know where the information you are using comes from—for example, "According to a 2015 editorial in the *New York Times . . .*" or "As Kenneth Davis says in his book *America's Hidden History. . . .*" This strategy enhances your credibility by showing that you are well informed about your topic. (Including source information also helps you protect yourself from unintentional **plagiarism**. See Chapter 11.)

7. **Prepare your speaking notes.** Effective speakers do not read their speeches. Instead, they prepare **speaking notes**—often on index cards—that list the points they want to make. (Microsoft's PowerPoint, as well as some other presentation software packages, has a section on each slide for speaking notes. Although the notes are displayed on the computer screen, they are not visible to the audience.) These notes guide you as you speak, so you should make sure that there are not too many of them and that they contain just key information. (If you use note cards, it is a good idea to number them so that you can be sure that they are in the correct order.)

8. **Prepare visual aids.** Visual aids help you to communicate your thesis and your supporting points more effectively. Visuals increase interest in your presentation, and they also strengthen your argument by reinforcing your points and making them easier for listeners to follow and to understand. In addition, visuals can help establish your credibility and thus improve the persuasiveness of your argument.

You can use the following types of visual aids in your presentations:

- Diagrams
- Photographs
- Slides
- Smartboards, flip charts
- Overhead transparencies
- Document cameras
- Handouts, objects

In order moving clockwise from top left:
© deomis/Shutterstock.com; © Peter Vaclavek/
Shutterstock.com; © Tarapong Siri/
Shutterstock.com; © deomis/Shutterstock.com

In addition to these kinds of visual aids, you can also use **presentation software**, such as Microsoft's PowerPoint or the Web-based application *Prezi* (Prezi.com). With presentation software, you can easily create visually appealing and persuasive slides. You can insert scanned photographs or drawings into slides, or you can cut and paste charts, graphs, and tables into them. You can even include YouTube videos and MP3 files. Keep in mind, however, that the images, videos, or sound files that you use must support your thesis; if they are irrelevant, they will distract or confuse your listeners. (See pp. 218–221 for examples of PowerPoint slides.)

9. **Practice your presentation.** As a general rule, you should spend as much time rehearsing your speech as you do preparing it. In other words, practice, practice, practice. Be sure you know the order in which you will present your points and when you will move from one visual to another. Rehearse your speech aloud with just your speaking notes and your visuals until you are confident that you can get through your presentation effectively. Try to anticipate any problems that may arise with your visuals, and solve them at this stage of the process. If possible, practice your speech in the room in which you will actually deliver it. Bring along a friend, and ask for feedback. Finally, cut or add material as needed until you are certain that you can stay within your time limit.

CHECKLIST

Designing and Displaying Visuals

☐ Use images that are large enough for your audience to see and that will reproduce clearly.

(continued)

☐ Make lettering large enough for your audience to see. Use 40- to 50-point type for titles, 25- to 30-point type for major points, and 20- to 25-point type for less important points.

☐ Use bulleted lists, not full sentences or paragraphs.

☐ Put no more than three or four points on a single visual.

☐ Make sure there is a clear contrast between your lettering and the background.

☐ Don't show your listeners the visual before you begin to speak about it. Display the visual only when you discuss it.

☐ Face your listeners when you discuss a visual. Even if you point to the screen, always look at your listeners. Never turn your back on your audience.

☐ Introduce and discuss each visual. Don't simply show or read the visual to your audience. Always tell listeners more than they can read or see for themselves.

☐ Don't use elaborate visuals or special effects that will distract your audience.

⊘ EXERCISE 6.5

Look through the table of contents of this book, and select three At Issue topics that interest you. Imagine that you are planning to deliver an oral argument to a group of college students on each of these topics. For each topic, list three visual aids you could use to enhance your presentation.

Delivering Oral Arguments

Delivery is the most important part of a speech. The way you speak, your interaction with the audience, your posture, and your eye contact all affect your overall presentation. In short, a confident, controlled speaker will have a positive impact on an audience, while a speaker who fumbles with note cards, speaks in a shaky voice, or seems disorganized will lose credibility. To make sure that your listeners see you as a credible, reliable source of information, follow these guidelines:

1. **Accept nervousness.** For most people, nervousness is part of the speech process. The trick is to convert this nervousness into energy that you can channel into your speech. The first step in dealing with nervousness is to make sure that you have rehearsed enough. If you have prepared adequately, you will probably be able to handle any problem you may encounter. If you make a mistake, you can correct it. If you forget something, you can fit it in later.

DEALING WITH NERVOUSNESS

If nervousness is a problem, the following strategies can help you to relax:

- **Breathe deeply.** Take a few deep breaths before you begin speaking. Research has shown that increased oxygen has a calming effect on the brain.

- **Use visualization.** Imagine yourself delivering a successful speech, and fix this image in your mind. It can help dispel anxiety.

- **Empty your mind.** Consciously try to eliminate all negative thoughts. Think of your mind as a room full of furniture. Imagine yourself removing each piece of furniture until the room is empty.

- **Drink water.** Before you begin to speak, take a few sips of water. Doing so will eliminate the dry mouth that is a result of nervousness. Don't, however, drink water during your speech.

- **Keep things in perspective.** Remember, your speech is a minor event in your life. Nothing that you do or say will affect you significantly.

2. **Look at your audience.** When you speak, look directly at the members of your audience. At the beginning of the speech, make eye contact with a few audience members who seem to be responding positively. As your speech progresses, look directly at as many audience members as you can. Try to sweep the entire room. Don't focus excessively on a single person or on a single section of your audience.

3. **Speak naturally.** Your presentation should sound like a conversation, not a performance. This is not to suggest that your presentation should include slang, ungrammatical constructions, or colloquialisms; it should conform to the rules of standard English. The trick is to maintain the appearance of a conversation while following the conventions of public speaking. Achieving this balance takes practice, but it is a goal worth pursuing.

4. **Speak slowly.** When you give a presentation, you should speak more slowly than you do in normal conversation. This strategy gives listeners time to process what they hear—and gives you time to think about what you are saying.

5. **Speak clearly and correctly.** As you deliver your presentation, speak clearly. Do not drop endings, and be careful to pronounce words correctly. Look up the pronunciation of unfamiliar words in a dictionary, or

ask your instructor for help. If you go though an entire speech pronouncing a key term or a name incorrectly, your listeners will question your competence.

6. **Move purposefully.** As you deliver your speech, don't pace, move your hands erratically, or play with your note cards. Try to stand in one spot, with both feet flat on the floor. Move only when necessary—for example, to point to a visual or to display an object. If you intend to distribute printed material to your listeners, do so only when you are going to discuss it. (Try to arrange in advance for someone else to give out your handouts.) If you are not going to refer to the material in your presentation, wait until you have finished your speech before you distribute it. Depending on the level of formality of your presentation and the size of your audience, you may want to stand directly in front of your audience or behind a podium.

7. **Be prepared for the unexpected.** Don't get flustered if things don't go exactly as you planned. If you forget material, work it in later. If you make a mistake, correct it without apologizing. Most of the time, listeners will not realize that something has gone wrong unless you call attention to it. If someone in the audience looks bored, don't worry. You might consider changing your pace or your volume, but keep in mind that the person's reaction might have nothing to do with your presentation. He or she might be tired, preoccupied, or just a poor listener.

Remember to project confidence and control as you speak.

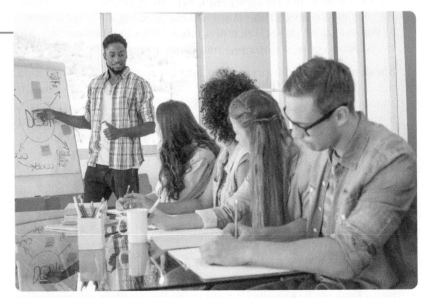

© Wavebreak Media/Agefotostock

8. **Leave time for questions.** End your presentation by asking if your listeners have any questions. As you answer questions, keep in mind the following advice:

- *Be prepared.* Make sure you have anticipated the obvious counterarguments to your position, and be prepared to address them. In addition, prepare a list of websites or other resources that you can refer your audience to for more information.

- *Repeat a question before you answer it.* This technique enables everyone in the audience to hear the question, and it also gives you time to think of an answer.

- *Keep control of interchanges.* If a questioner repeatedly challenges your answer or monopolizes the conversation, say that you will be glad to discuss the matter with him or her after your presentation is finished.

- *Be honest.* Answer questions honestly and forthrightly. If you don't know the answer to a question, say so. Tell the questioner you will locate the information that he or she wants and send it by email. Above all, do not volunteer information that you are not sure is correct.

- *Use the last question to summarize.* When you get to the last question, end your answer by restating the main point of your argument.

Composing an Oral Argument

The written text of an oral argument is organized just as any other argument is: it has an introduction that gives the background of the issue and states the thesis, it has a body that presents evidence that supports the thesis, it identifies and refutes arguments against the thesis, and it ends with a concluding statement.

In general, an oral argument can be structured in the following way:

INTRODUCTION	Presents the background of the issue
	States the thesis
BODY	Presents evidence: Point 1 in support of the thesis
	Presents evidence: Point 2 in support of the thesis
	Presents evidence: Point 3 in support of the thesis
	Refutes opposing arguments
CONCLUSION	Brings the argument to a close
	Concluding statement restates thesis
	Speaker asks for questions

⊘ EXERCISE 6.6

The following oral argument was presented by a student in a speech course in response to the assignment, "Argue for or against the advantages of a 'gap year' between high school and college." (Her PowerPoint slides appear at the end of the speech.) After you read this argument, answer the questions on page 221, consulting the outline on the previous page if necessary.

AN ARGUMENT IN SUPPORT OF THE "GAP YEAR"

CHANTEE STEELE

College: even the word sounded wonderful when I was in high   1
school. Everyone told me it would be the best time of my life. They told me that I would take courses in exciting new subjects and that I'd make lifelong friends. [Show slide 1.] What they didn't tell me was that I would be anxious, confused, and uncertain about my major and about my future. Although this is only my second year in college, I've already changed my major once, and to be honest, I'm still not sure I've made the right decision. But during the process of changing majors, my adviser gave me some reading material that included information about a "gap year." A gap year is a year off between high school and college when students focus on work or community service and learn about themselves—something that would have benefited me. Although gaining popularity in the United States, the gap year still suggests images of spoiled rich kids who want to play for a year before going to college. According to educator Christina Wood, however, in the United Kingdom a gap year is common; it is seen as a time for personal growth that helps students mature (36). [Show slide 2.] In fact, 230,000 British students take a gap year before going to college. As the rest of my speech

Thesis statement   will show, a well-planned gap year gives students time to mature, to explore potential careers, and to volunteer or travel.

Evidence: Point 1 in   [Show slide 3.] Apparently I'm not alone in my uncertainty about my   2
support of thesis   major or about my future. As Holly Bull, a professional gap-year counselor, explains, "The National Research Center for College and University Admissions estimates that over 50 percent of students switch majors at

least once" (8). As they go from high school to college, most students have little time to think about what to do with their lives. A gap year before college would give them time to learn more about themselves. According to Wood, "Gap years provide valuable life experiences and maturity so students are more ready to focus on their studies when they return" (37). A year off would give some students the perspective they need to mature and to feel more confident about their decisions. Bull agrees, noting that the gap year helps students choose or confirm the area of study they want to pursue, that it makes them "instantly more mature," and that it "boosts their excitement about learning" (7–8).

The gap year gives students many options to explore before going to college. [Show slide 4.] This slide shows just some of the resources students can use as they prepare for their gap year. As you can see, they can explore opportunities for employment, education, and volunteer work. There are even resources for students who are undecided. As David Lesesne, the dean of admissions at Sewanee, says, "Some students do very interesting and enriching things: hike the Appalachian Trail, herd sheep in Crete, play in a rock band, [or even] attend school in Guatemala" (qtd. in Wood 37). Many other students, especially in these economic hard times, use the gap year to earn money to offset the high cost of their education (Wood 35).

3 Evidence: Point 2 in support of thesis

Taking a gap year can also help students to get into better colleges. According to an article by the dean of admissions at Harvard, "Occasionally students are admitted to Harvard or other colleges in part because they accomplished something unusual during a year off" (Fitzsimmons, McGrath, and Ducey). Depending on the scope of their service or work, a gap year could enable students to earn scholarships that they were not eligible for before. In fact, some colleges actually recommend that students take time off after high school. Harvard is one of several U.S. colleges that "encourages admitted students to defer enrollment for one year to travel, pursue a special project or activity, work, or spend time in another meaningful way" (Fitzsimmons, McGrath, and Ducey). Furthermore, evidence shows that a gap year can help students to be more successful after they begin in college. One Middlebury College admissions officer has calculated that "a single gap semester was the strongest predictor of academic success at his school"

4 Evidence: Point 3 in support of thesis

(Bull 7). Given this support for the gap year and given the resources that are now available to help students plan it, the negative attitudes about it in the United States are beginning to change.

Refutation of opposing arguments

In spite of these benefits, parental concerns about "slackerdom" and money are common. Supporters of the gap year acknowledge that students have to be motivated to make the most of their experiences. Clearly, the gap year is not for everyone. For example, students who are not self-motivated may not benefit from a gap year. In addition, parents worry about how much money the gap year will cost them. This is a real concern when you add the year off to the expense of four years of college (Wood 37). However, if finances are a serious concern, students can spend their gap year working in their own communities or taking advantage of a paid experience like AmeriCorps—which, as the AmeriCorps website shows, covers students' room and board *and* offers an educational stipend after students complete the program. [Show slide 5.] Additionally, parents and students should consider the time and money that is wasted when a student who is not ready for college starts school and then drops out. 5

After considering the benefits of a gap year, I have concluded that more students should postpone college for a year. Many students (like me) are uncertain about their goals. We welcome new opportunities and are eager to learn from new experiences and may find a year of service both emotionally and intellectually rewarding. Given another year to mature, many of us would return to school with a greater sense of purpose, focus, and clarity. In some cases, the gap year could actually help us get into better schools and possibly get more financial aid. If we intend to take the college experience seriously, spending a gap year learning about our interests and abilities would help us to become better, more confident, and ultimately more focused students. [Show slide 6.] 6

Concluding statement

Are there any questions? 7

Works Cited

Bull, Holly. "Navigating a Gap Year." *TeenLife*, Feb. 2011, pp. 6–9.

Fitzsimmons, William, et al. "Time Out or Burn Out for the Next Generation." *Harvard College Office of Admissions*, 2011, college.harvard .edu/admissions/preparing-college/should-i-take-time.

Wood, Christina. "Should You Take a 'Gap Year'?" *Careers and Colleges*, Fall 2007, pp. 36–37.

Slide 1

© Ana Blazic/istockphoto.com

Slide 2

230,000 students between 18 and 25 take a Gap Year in the U.K.

—Tom Griffiths, founder and director of GapYear.com

(qtd. in Christina Wood, "Should You Take a 'Gap Year'?," *Careers and Colleges*, Fall 2007)

Slide 3

> **50%** of students change their major at least once.
>
> —National Research Center for College
> and University Admissions

Slide 4

A Few Links for the Potential "Gapster"

(links from Holly Bull, "The Possibilities of the Gap
Year," *Chronicle of Higher Education* 52.44 [2006])

Employment

Cool Works: CoolWorks.com (domestic jobs)

Working Abroad: WorkingAbroad.org (jobs overseas)

Education

Global Routes: GlobalRoutes.org (semester-long courses)

Sea-mester: Seamester.com (sea voyage programs)

Volunteer Work

AmeriCorps: AmeriCorps.gov

City Year: CityYear.org

Thoughtful Texts for Fence Sitters

Karl Haigler and Rae Nelson, *The Gap-Year
  Advantage* (Macmillan, 2005)

Colin Hall, *Taking Time Off* (Princeton Review, 2003)

Charlotte Hindle and Joe Bindloss, *The Gap Year
  Book* (Lonely Planet, 2005)

Slide 5

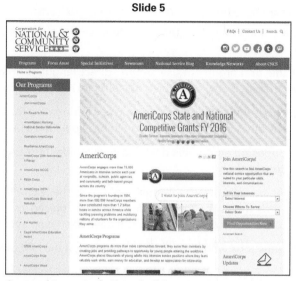

Courtesy of Corporation for National and Community Service. Reproduced by permission.

Slide 6

In order moving clockwise from top left: © Roger Cracknell 01/classic/Alamy; © Ben Blankenburg/iStock/Getty Images; © Steve Stock/Alamy; David Cordner/Getty Images

Identifying the Elements of an Oral Argument

1. Where does this oral argument include verbal signals to help guide readers?

2. Does this oral argument use simple, direct language? What sections of the speech, if any, could be made simpler?

3. Where does this oral argument repeat key information for emphasis? Is there any other information that you think should have been repeated?

4. What opposing arguments does the speaker identify? Does she refute them convincingly?

5. How effective are the visuals that accompany the text of this oral argument? Are there enough visuals? Are they placed correctly? What other information do you think could have been displayed in a visual?

6. What questions would you ask this speaker at the end of her speech?

Is Online Education Better Than Classroom Education?

© Karl Dolenc/iStock/Getty Images

Go back to page 191, and reread the At Issue box, which gives background about whether online education is better than classroom instruction. As the following sources illustrate, this question has a number of possible answers.

After you review the sources listed below, you will be asked to answer some questions and to complete some simple activities. This work will help you to understand both the content and the structure of the sources. When you are finished, you will be ready to develop an argument—using one of the three alternative approaches to argument discussed in this chapter—that takes a position on whether online education is better than classroom learning.

SOURCES

"The Evolution of Online Schooling" (infographic), p. 222
www.collegedegreesearch.net

Chris Bustamante, "The Risks and Rewards of Online Learning," p. 224

David Smith, "Reliance on Online Materials Hinders Learning Potential for Students," p. 228

Elena Kadvany, "Online Education Needs Connection," p. 231

John Crisp, "Short Distance Learning," p. 233

Scott L. Newstok, "A Plea for Close Learning," p. 236

Ray McNulty, "Old Flames and New Beacons," p. 241

Pete Rorabaugh, "Trading Classroom Authority for Online Community," p. 246

The Evolution of Online Schooling

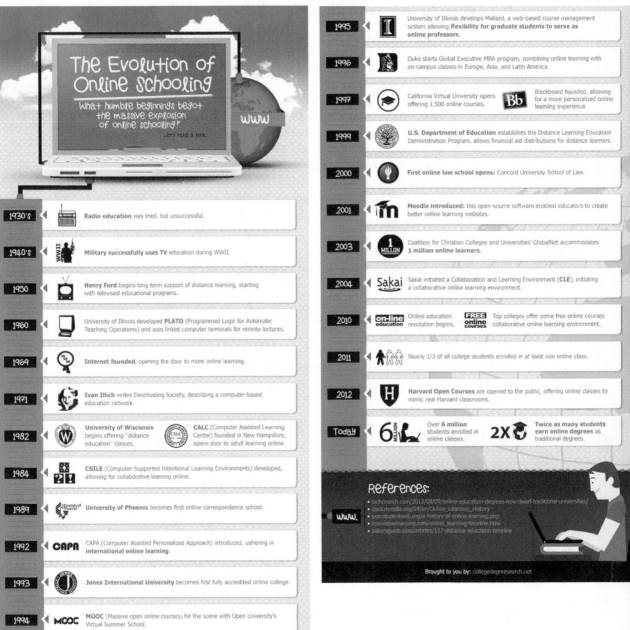

The Evolution of Online Schooling

What humble beginnings begot the massive explosion of online schooling? Let's take a look.

1930's — Radio education was tried, but unsuccessful.

1940's — Military successfully uses TV education during WWII.

1950 — Henry Ford begins long-term support of distance learning, starting with televised educational programs.

1960 — University of Illinois developed PLATO (Programmed Logic for Automatic Teaching Operations) and uses linked computer terminals for remote lectures.

1969 — Internet founded, opening the door to more online learning.

1971 — Ivan Illich writes Deschooling Society, describing a computer-based education network.

1982 — University of Wisconsin begins offering "distance education" classes. CALC (Computer Assisted Learning Center) founded in New Hampshire, opens door to adult learning online.

1984 — CSILE (Computer-Supported Intentional Learning Environments) developed, allowing for collaborative learning online.

1989 — University of Phoenix becomes first online correspondence school.

1992 — CAPA (Computer Assisted Personalized Approach) introduced, ushering in international online learning.

1993 — Jones International University becomes first fully accredited online college.

1994 — MOOC (Massive open online courses) hit the scene with Open University's Virtual Summer School.

1995 — University of Illinois develops Mallard, a web-based course management system allowing flexibility for graduate students to serve as online professors.

1996 — Duke starts Global Executive MBA program, combining online learning with on-campus classes in Europe, Asia, and Latin America.

1997 — California Virtual University opens offering 1,500 online courses. Blackboard founded, allowing for a more personalized online learning experience.

1999 — U.S. Department of Education establishes the Distance Learning Education Demonstration Program, allows financial aid distributions for distance learners.

2000 — First online law school opens: Concord University School of Law.

2001 — Moodle introduced: this open-source software enabled educators to create better online learning websites.

2003 — Coalition for Christian Colleges and Universities' GlobalNet accommodates 1 million online learners.

2004 — Sakai initiated a Collaboration and Learning Environment (CLE), initiating a collaborative online learning environment.

2010 — Online education revolution begins. Top colleges offer some free online courses collaborative online learning environment.

2011 — Nearly 1/3 of all college students enrolled in at least one online class.

2012 — Harvard Open Courses are opened to the public, offering online classes to mimic real Harvard classrooms.

Today — Over 6 million students enrolled in online classes. Twice as many students earn online degrees as traditional degrees.

References:
- techcrunch.com/2012/08/09/online-education-degrees-now-dwarf-traditional-universities/
- docs.moodle.org/24/en/Online_Learning_History
- seacstudentweb.org/a-history-of-online-learning.php
- innovativelearning.com/online_learning/timeline.html
- bakersguide.com/articles/127-distance-education-timeline

Brought to you by: collegedegreesearch.net

www.collegedegreesearch.net

⊙ AT ISSUE: SOURCES FOR USING ALTERNATIVE APPROACHES TO ARGUMENT

1. What is the purpose of this infographic? How successful is it in achieving this purpose?

2. What kind of audience does this infographic seem to be addressing? How can you tell?

3. What is this infographic's main idea or message? Write a one-sentence summary of this main idea.

4. Where does the infographic appeal to *ethos*? Is this appeal necessary? Why or why not?

5. How clear is this infographic? What other arrangement (or arrangements) of words, numbers, color, and spacing could have been used?

6. If you were going to write an argumentative essay in favor of online education, which information in this infographic would you find most useful? Which information would you find least useful? Explain.

This essay is from the online newspaper *Community College Times*. It appeared on November 16, 2011.

THE RISKS AND REWARDS OF ONLINE LEARNING

CHRIS BUSTAMANTE

In 2008, investors wanted to buy Rio Salado College, the nation's largest online 1 public community college headquartered in Tempe, Ariz. The offer was more than $400 million with plans to convert it into a national, for-profit, online school.

Rio Salado wasn't for sale, but the offer proved how much demand exists 2 for serving students who find traditional education systems inconvenient and need the flexibility of online formats.

Online learning may not be the first thing that comes to mind when com- 3 munity colleges consider providing support for student success. But that mindset is changing. It has to. The 2011 Sloan Survey of Online Learning reported that more than six million college students in the fall of 2010 took at least one online course, comprising nearly one-third of all college and university students. The growth rate in online course enrollment far exceeds the growth rate of the overall higher education student population.

Still, there is healthy skepticism about the proliferation of online learning 4 and views still differ about its value. According to surveys by the Pew Research Center and the *Chronicle of Higher Education*, less than 30 percent of the public believes that online and classroom courses provide the same educational value. Half of college presidents share that belief.

Any way you look at it, online learning is an increasingly vital part of pro- 5 ducing the number of qualified graduates needed to meet future workforce demands—when it is done correctly.

A Calculated Risk

In 1996, Rio Salado, one of 10 Maricopa Community Colleges, took a calculated 6 risk and began offering courses online—16 to start—just when the Internet was taking off. Critics at the time challenged the quality of online education and claimed that students wouldn't adjust well to such a radical change in their learning environment. But Maricopa and Rio Salado pushed ahead, determined to create an innovative, nontraditional, and nimble approach that is responsive to and supportive of changing student needs.

The risks have proven to be worth it. While no one could have predicted 7 the economic environment that students and higher education face today, making the decision to move online proved to be provident for the college and students. Rio Salado extended educational access to students who found traditional college to be out of reach in Arizona, nationwide, and around the world.

The college currently serves nearly 70,000 students each year, with more than 41,000 enrolled in 600-plus online courses.

Keeping Costs Down

To keep costs down, Rio Salado supports more than 60 certificate and degree 8 programs with just 22 residential faculty and more than 1,400 adjunct faculty. Our "one-course, many sections" model uses a master course approved by the resident faculty and taught by adjunct faculty in more than 6,000 course sections. The college's cost to educate students is as much as 48 percent less than peer institutions nationwide.

Without the expense of a traditional campus, Rio Salado has been able to 9 focus on building and improving its RioLearn platform, a customized learning management system that provides access to course-related resources, instructors, fellow students, and other support services.

Focused on Student Support

Meeting students' needs means providing access to robust, comprehensive 10 support services that are customized for their complex lifestyles, whether they are a working adult, an active military student accessing their coursework online, or someone taking in-person classes in adult basic education, incarcerated reentry, early college, or workforce training programs. Today's students need the resources of round-the-clock instructional and technology helpdesks, tutoring, and virtual library services. Additionally, we never cancel an online class and offer the flexibility of 48 start dates a year.

Students also need real-time support to keep them on track. Predictive 11 analytic technology allows the college to monitor online student engagement and predict by the eighth day of class the level of success students will have in a course. When needed, instructors facilitate interventions to minimize risks and support successful course completion.

Building a culture of unified support focused on completion won't hap- 12 pen overnight. It took 30 years for Rio Salado to get to this point. Our upside-down faculty model has made it possible for the college to adapt a corporate "systems approach," and all Rio Salado staff and faculty participate in a training program to instill a unified commitment to helping students complete their degree programs.

Technical Challenges

Staying ahead of the online curve comes with its share of challenges. Rio Salado 13 had to build its own learning management system because there wasn't one available that would support all of the features that our faculty and students wanted. In partnership with Microsoft and Dell, RioLearn was designed to be scalable to more than 100,000 students.

However, a few years ago, it didn't fully support Mac users. Although stu- 14 dents could access their coursework, they had to switch Internet browsers to do so. A new version of RioLearn was launched in 2010 to help students access their courses, regardless of the platform they are using.

We've also learned that many of our students are co-enrolled in traditional 15
colleges and universities. They come to Rio Salado for flexibility, affordability,
and convenience to accelerate their degree on their terms. They bank credits and
ultimately transfer those credits to complete their degrees at another institution.

A recent report examines Rio Salado's efforts and the experience and per- 16
spectives of more than 30 institutions throughout the U.S. addressing similar
challenges to ensure student success—especially for low-income, minority,
and adult students—and pursuing promising approaches to increase college
completion rates.

Reimagining the System

Our country can't continue to allow millions of people who are college mate- 17
rial to fall through the cracks. We must find new, convenient, and high-quality
educational options for students who might
otherwise have missed out on a college education. That means serving more students in
more places—especially where college enroll-
ments have been capped—through efforts
such as online early college initiatives, by cre-
ating cohorts at the high-school level and developing open-source courses.

> "We must find new, convenient, and high-quality educational options for students."

With tuition rising faster than the rate of inflation, and the best-paying jobs 18
requiring some form of postsecondary degree, specialized certification, or licen-
sure, we have to find solutions that lower costs for students. We need to innovate. We need new models of education to leverage public resources through
private and public partnerships and increase the capacity to serve nontraditional
students through productive and cost-efficient means.

It's encouraging to see the rapid growth in affordable online learning. It 19
has broken down the barriers of time, distance, and affordability without sac-
rificing high-quality academics. But shoring up its credibility and value for
students means heeding some of the lessons learned over the past 15 years.
The stakes for getting it right are certainly high and getting higher.

⊘ AT ISSUE: SOURCES FOR USING ALTERNATIVE APPROACHES TO ARGUMENT

1. According to Bustamante, "[T]here is healthy skepticism about the proliferation of online learning" (para. 4). What does he mean? What reservations, if any, do you have about the rise of online education?

2. In this essay, where does the claim appear? How is this claim quali-fied? How does the qualifier set up the rest of the essay?

3. Bustamante's article focuses on the development of one school's online education program. Do you think the risks and rewards he dis-cusses also apply to other schools' online offerings? What factors might account for any differences in other schools' experiences with online learning?

4. What is Bustamante's purpose? What does he want readers to take away from his essay?

5. Does Bustamante ever address opposing arguments? If he does, where? If he does not, should he have addressed them? Explain.

6. What does Bustamante mean when he says that we must reimagine the system of higher education? What problems does he see with the current educational system? How will online education help solve these problems?

This essay was published in the *Daily Nebraskan*, the student newspaper of the University of Nebraska, on November 29, 2011.

RELIANCE ON ONLINE MATERIALS HINDERS LEARNING POTENTIAL FOR STUDENTS

DAVID SMITH

1   Students of today should be thankful for the . . . plethora of ways available for them to learn. Compared to our grandparents, parents, and even older siblings, we have access to modes of communication and education that would not have been possible even 10 years ago.

2   Students today, not just in college but in high school, middle school, and elementary school, take in and process astounding amounts of information on a daily basis. We have access to TV and the Internet, social media outlets such as Twitter and Facebook, and a nearly inexhaustible supply of ways to keep in contact with and learn about one another.

3   This variety has begun to work its way into academia, as well; more and more, it seems, organized instruction is moving beyond the classroom and into cyberspace. Pencils and paper, once the sole staples of the educational experience, are slowly being ousted by keyboards, webcams, and online dropboxes.

4   Here at the University of Nebraska–Lincoln, this growing prevalence is easy to see. Just look at Blackboard and how some courses are completely dependent upon it. Blackboard has everything from grade tracking and homework assignments to the administration of quizzes and exams.

5   Look at MyRED, which now handles everything from class enrollment and scheduling to residence hall contracts and meal plans.

6   Look at things such as the Love Library's EBSCO search engine, which gives students access to a greater wealth of information than even the most practiced scholar would know what to do with, and online courses such as the Keller Plan, which allow students to complete coursework and earn credit without having to leave their dorm rooms.

> "While the Internet has certainly made learning easier, has it made it better?"

7   It's clear to even the most casual observer that taking in and processing information is far easier for the students of today than it was for the students of 100, 50, or even 10 years ago.

8   But it begs the question: While the Internet has certainly made learning easier, has it made it better? Not necessarily.

9   Think for a moment about the fundamental differences between a traditional course, taught in a classroom, and one conducted entirely via Blackboard's online services.

In the former, students are bound by structure and organization. They 10 must attend class on a regular basis or suffer the consequences, typically (though not always) complete regular homework assignments for points, and are constantly reminded of the work that needs to be done by the ever-present figure (or specter) of the professor.

Such is not the case with classes taken outside the classroom. The 11 instructions for such courses are, at least in my experience, pared down to the following: "Read this by this date, this by this date, and this by this date. There are quizzes on Day X, Day Y, and Day Z, and the final exam can be taken at any time during finals week in the testing center. Have a nice semester."

Now, I know that college is supposed to be a place of greater expectations, 12 of increased responsibilities and better time management skills. I get that, I really do. But the sad truth is that all too often, giving a student that kind of freedom doesn't end well.

By removing the sense of structure from a course, you remove the stu- 13 dent's notion that he or she is under any sort of pressure, any sort of time constraint. By removing a constantly present instructor, you remove what is, in many cases, the sole source of motivation students have to do well in a class. You take away the sense of urgency, the sense of immediate requirement, and by extension the student's drive.

Readings are put off or forgotten, material review sessions (if there are 14 any) are blown off or missed, and quizzes and exams are ultimately bombed. More often than not, the student will get caught up with work from the other, more traditional courses on their schedule—the ones they remember they have homework in because it was assigned in class this afternoon or the ones they have to study for because the professor reminded them about the upcoming exam the other day. Unfortunately, another marked difference between traditional and online courses is that the latters are typically far less forgiving when it comes to things such as deadlines and extensions, making it next to impossible for students to get out of the holes they dig themselves into.

The Internet is a powerful tool. It allows us to share, distribute, and 15 absorb more information in a single year than our ancestors absorbed in a lifetime, and its capacity to do those things is constantly growing. What people, educators in particular, need to realize is that no matter how power-ful a tool it becomes, the Internet should never become anything more than that: a tool.

There will never be an adequate online substitute for the watchful eye 16 and the stern voice of a professor, or the pressure of an exam time limit that is about to expire, or the dismay and subsequent motivation to improve that can come from a handed-back assignment with a failing grade scrawled on it.

Now . . . off to class. 17

⊙ AT ISSUE: SOURCES FOR USING ALTERNATIVE APPROACHES TO ARGUMENT

1. Paragraph 8 expresses Smith's thesis in the form of a question and answer. Paraphrase this thesis statement in one sentence.

2. Why does Smith spend his first seven paragraphs discussing the amount of information currently available to students?

3. In paragraph 8, Smith says that his previous statement "begs the question." What does he mean? Is this statement actually an example of **begging the question**? Explain.

4. How, according to Smith, is online education different from classroom learning? What problems does Smith identify with online learning?

5. In paragraph 13, Smith says that online courses remove "the sense of structure from a course." What evidence does he present to support this statement?

6. What does Smith mean in paragraph 15 when he says that what we "need to realize is that no matter how powerful a tool it becomes, the Internet should never become anything more than that: a tool"? What is he warning against here?

7. Where does Smith use the techniques of Rogerian argument? Does he use these techniques often enough? Does he use them effectively? Explain.

8. In paragraph 16, Smith says, "There will never be an adequate online substitute for the watchful eye and the stern voice of a professor." Do you agree? Do you think this highlights a disadvantage of online education (as Smith intends) or an advantage?

This essay is from the October 9, 2011, edition of the *Daily Trojan*, the student newspaper of the University of Southern California.

ONLINE EDUCATION NEEDS CONNECTION

ELENA KADVANY

From the most trivial of issues (who went to what party this weekend?) to the most traditional of society's establishments (newspapers, music and book industries, Postal Service), the Internet has transformed our lives. But one area remains to be revolutionized digitally: education. 1

Online education is on the rise, pitting those who support the idea of a virtual university for its ability to increase access and revenue against those who believe there is no substitute for real-time, traditional educational experiences. 2

There's one thing wrong with the entire conversation, however: Viewing online education as a new higher-education business model that must supplant the current system is a close-minded view. Why not look at it as a means by which we can strengthen and innovate education by blending digital and traditional elements? 3

Online education began mostly as distance-learning programs for graduate degrees that lend themselves to the medium like engineering or business. 4

USC's Viterbi School of Engineering has a well-established Distance Education Network that offers more than 30 master's degree programs. 5

Now, in times of financial crisis, schools across the country, especially in California, are searching for ways to reinvent themselves. This has led to an expansion of digital courses into the undergraduate sphere. 6

But there is a distinct danger in allowing finance-driven ideas to dominate the dialogue about schools' futures and education in general, especially for undergraduates whose educational experiences and life tracks are so defined by their first four years on a campus. 7

> "[T]here is a distinct danger in allowing finance-driven ideas to dominate."

This is not to say that universities should completely reject online learning. It's great to be able to listen to lectures at home or gain access to classes you can't physically attend or afford. 8

Higher learning, however, is about a level of personal interaction and commitment that can't be re-created online. 9

Before transferring to USC, I spent a semester at the University of San Francisco, where I took a hybrid service-learning Spanish class. It combined conventional in-class instruction twice a week with a once-a-week class online with Blackboard, in addition to a requirement of outside community service hours. 10

This kind of blending shows the innovative potential universities should 11 recognize and seize. The idea of a virtual university should not replace the traditional, but instead should merge with it.

For undergraduates, hybrid classes could be incredibly valuable and much 12 more engaging for a generation that spends so much time online.

Some of the University of California schools have submitted courses in 13 response to an online education pilot project proposed by the University's Office of the President.

Sebastian Thrun, a professor at Stanford University renowned for leading 14 the team that built Google's self-driving car, now offers a free online course, "Introduction to Artificial Intelligence." Enrollment in this class has jumped from 58,000 to 130,000 across the world in the past month, according to the *New York Times*. USC is lucky enough to have generous alumni that keep it more than afloat financially. But as many universities choose to go digital, USC might want to follow suit.

The potential of all things online is vast. And there's no match for the 15 value of real-time, person-to-person educational experiences.

There's no reason universities can't take advantage of both. 16

⊙ AT ISSUE: SOURCES FOR USING ALTERNATIVE APPROACHES TO ARGUMENT

1. In paragraph 2, Kadvany says that online education pits those who support virtual education against those who support traditional classroom education. Do the essays in this At Issue section confirm or challenge Kadvany's point? Explain.

2. In paragraph 3, Kadvany says that it is wrong to view online education as a "higher-education business model" that will displace classroom education. Why does she use the term "business model"? Does she expect this term to have positive or negative connotations for her readers? How can you tell?

3. How has the financial crisis helped to promote the idea of online education? According to Kadvany, what is the danger of letting "finance-driven ideas" (para. 7) dominate the conversation about education?

4. In paragraph 9, Kadvany says that the personal interaction and commitment that characterize higher learning "can't be re-created online." What evidence does she present to support this statement? How convincing is this evidence? What additional evidence could she have used?

5. Does Kadvany ever use the techniques of Rogerian argument? If so, where? If not, should she have used them?

This essay is from the December 14, 2011, edition of the *MetroWest Daily News.*

SHORT DISTANCE LEARNING
JOHN CRISP

The end of the semester at my college always inclines me toward reflection, 1
relief, and mild melancholy. I suspect my students feel the same way, with
more inclination, perhaps, toward relief. Five classes have met with me about
30 times each over the course of 15 weeks, five communities of individuals
that materialize, coalesce, and disperse in a few months.

Whatever its merits, I've never developed
much enthusiasm for online learning. Its
proponents contend that a community of
learners can develop among students scattered
by geography but connected by the Internet,
and I'm not in a position to say they're wrong.

> "I've never developed much enthusiasm for online learning."

2

In fact, my purpose isn't to disparage online education. Along with the 3
trend toward a part-time professoriate, the proliferation of online education is
probably the most prominent tendency in higher education during the last
decade.

Still, I prefer the face-to-face classroom, which seems to me to preserve a 4
fine touch of humanity that warrants reflection during this week of final
exams.

Who was in my classes this semester? Many are traditional students, fresh 5
from high school and on their way to a four-year college or university, after a
sojourn at my community college. Many are bright, capable, and articulate.
Others are shy and reserved. A few are sullen or downright surly. But they're
not always my most interesting students.

Consider the young woman who, a decade after high school, finds herself 6
slogging through a developmental writing course before she can even attempt
freshman composition. Pardon the cliché, but sometimes you do see a light go
on in a student. She begins to listen to her instructor's and classmates' every
word, to take notes and to think, to become absorbed in her writing, which
over the course of the semester really does get better.

It doesn't always work like that, by any means. Other students are tak- 7
ing my developmental writing class for the second or third time. I like
them, but they miss too much class. Some of them have tattoos that betray
their gangbanger history; some have been thieves and some have been in
prison. And how well can you learn to write amid the violence and futility
in the barrio?

Many of them say that's all in the past now, and I believe them. Will they 8
pass this semester? I'm not sure. If they don't, what will become of them?

Momentous life passages occurred as the classes proceeded: At least two 9
women in my five classes this semester were pregnant and one gave birth. Two
students died. One young man, a veteran who had survived tours in Iraq and
Afghanistan, was killed in the second week of the semester, hit by a car while
out for his morning jog.

In mid-semester, a young woman in the same class lost control of her car 10
on the way home from school and died in a one-vehicle rollover. When I told
the class the next week that she wouldn't be coming back, there were some
tears. So we learned about more than just writing this semester.

A middle-aged woman expressed conservative religious beliefs then 11
admitted that she spent two years in prison for marijuana possession. Several
veterans can't sleep at night and some of them drink too much. A young man
came to class so depressed that I took him to one of the college's counselors,
and he never came back.

Another young man and a young woman sat on opposite sides of the class 12
and never spoke up or spoke to anyone else. Then they began to sit together
and talk to each other. A lot. Now I occasionally see them around the campus
together. Does that happen in online classes?

In short, it's all there, a rich mixture of human experiences in one ephem- 13
eral microcosm: birth, mating, sickness, death, frustration, laughter, storytelling, aspiration, failure, and learning.

Good luck, students; the pleasure was mine. 14

⊘ AT ISSUE: SOURCES FOR USING ALTERNATIVE APPROACHES TO ARGUMENT

1. Where does Crisp attempt to establish his credibility? How effective is this appeal to *ethos*?

2. To whom is Crisp addressing his argument? Teachers? Students? Parents? Administrators? Others? How do you know?

3. In paragraph 3, Crisp says that his purpose "isn't to disparage online education." What is his purpose?

4. In paragraph 4, Crisp says that he prefers traditional classroom instruction because it preserves "a fine touch of humanity." What does he mean? What evidence does he present in paragraphs 5–12 to support this point? How convincing is this evidence?

5. Draw a **rhetorical triangle** (p. 19) that represents the relative importance of the various appeals in this essay. Which appeal does the longest side of the triangle represent? Which does the shortest side represent? Do you think this is a good balance?

6. In paragraph 2, Crisp briefly addresses an opposing argument. Does he accurately characterize the case for online learning? Should he have spent more time addressing opposing arguments?

7. Crisp ends his essay with a single sentence. Is this sentence an effective concluding statement? Why or why not?

8. Suppose Crisp wanted to present his ideas in a speech. What parts of his essay would you suggest he expand? What parts would you advise him to condense or delete? What visuals would you suggest he include?

This article was originally published in *Liberal Education* in the Fall 2013 issue.

A PLEA FOR CLOSE LEARNING

SCOTT L. NEWSTOK

"At the School" (1910), French postcard envisioning learning in the year 2000. Private Collection © Look and Learn/Bridgeman Images.

What an exciting year for distance learning! Cutting-edge communication 1
systems allowed universities to escape the tired confines of face-to-face education. Bold new technologies made it possible for thousands of geographically
dispersed students to enroll in world-class courses.

Innovative assessment mechanisms let professors supervise their pupils 2
remotely. All this progress was good for business, too. Private entrepreneurs
leapt at the chance to compete in the new distance-learning marketplace,
while Ivy League universities bustled to keep pace.

True, a few naysayers fretted about declining student attention spans and 3
low course-completion rates. But who could object to the expansively democratic goal of bringing first-rate education to more people than ever before?
The new pedagogical tools promised to be not only more affordable than traditional classes, but also more effective at measuring student progress. In the
words of one prominent expert, the average distance learner "knows more of
the subject, and knows it better, than the student who has covered the same
ground in the classroom." Indeed, "the day is coming when the work done [via

distance learning] will be greater in amount than that done in the class-rooms of our colleges." The future of education was finally here.

2013, right? Think again: 1885. The commentator quoted above was Yale 4 classicist (and future University of Chicago President) William Rainey Harper, evaluating *correspondence courses.* That's right: you've got (snail) mail. Journalist Nicholas Carr has chronicled the recurrent boosterism about mass mediated education over the last century: the phonograph, instructional radio, televised lectures. All were heralded as transformative educational tools in their day. This should give us pause as we recognize that massive open online courses, or MOOCs, are but the latest iteration of distance learning.

> "This should give us pause as we recognize that massive open online courses, or MOOCs, are but the latest iteration of distance learning."

In response to the current enthusiasm for MOOCs, skeptical faculty 5 (Aaron Bady, Ian Bogost, and Jonathan Rees, among many others) have begun questioning venture capitalists eager for new markets and legislators eager to dismantle public funding for American higher education. Some people pushing for MOOCs, to their credit, speak from laudably egalitarian impulses to provide access for disadvantaged students. *But to what are they being given access?* Are broadcast lectures and online discussions the sum of a liberal education? Or is it something more than "content" delivery?

"Close Learning"

To state the obvious: there's a personal, human element to liberal education, what 6 John Henry Newman once called "the living voice, the breathing form, the expressive countenance" (2001, 14). We who cherish personalized instruction would benefit from a pithy phrase to defend and promote this millennia-tested practice. I propose that we begin calling it *close learning*, a term that evokes the laborious, time-consuming, and costly but irreplaceable proximity between teacher and student. Close learning exposes the stark deficiencies of mass distance learning, such as MOOCs, and its haste to reduce dynamism, responsiveness, presence.

Techno-utopians seem surprised that "blended" or "flipped" classrooms— 7 combining out-of-class media with in-person discussions—are more effective than their online-only counterparts, or that one-on-one tutoring strengthens the utility of MOOCs. In spite of all the hype about interactivity, "lecturing" à la MOOCs merely extends the cliché of the static, one-sided lecture hall, where distance learning begins after the first row. As the philosopher Scott Samuelson (2013) suggests, "The forces driving online education, particularly MOOCs, aren't moving us toward close learning. We should begin by recognizing that close learning is the goal and then measure all versions of our courses by that standard. Many giant lecture-hall courses are going to be found wanting, as will many online courses, and all (or almost all) MOOCs. In the end, we're still going to need a lot of face-to-face learning if we want to promote close learning."

The old-fashioned Socratic seminar is where we actually find interactive 8
learning and open-ended inquiry. In the close learning of the live seminar, spontaneity rules. Both students and teachers are always at a crossroads, collaboratively deciding where to go and where to stop; how to navigate and how to detour; and how to close the distance between a topic and the people discussing it. For the seminar to work, certain limits are required (most centrally, a limit in size). But these finite limits enable the infinity of questioning that is close learning. MOOCs claim to abolish those limits, while they paradoxically reinstate them. Their naïve model assumes that there is always total transparency, that passively seeing (watching a lecture or a virtual simulation) is learning.

A Columbia University neuroscientist, Stuart Firestein, recently published a 9
polemical book titled *Ignorance: How It Drives Science*. Discouraged by students regurgitating his lectures without internalizing the complexity of scientific inquiry, Firestein created a seminar to which he invited his colleagues to discuss what they don't know. As Firestein repeatedly emphasizes, it is informed ignorance, not information, that is the genuine "engine" of knowledge. His seminar reminds us that mere data transmission from teacher to student doesn't produce liberal learning. It's the ability to interact, to think hard thoughts alongside other people.

In a seminar, a student can ask for clarification, and challenge a teacher; a 10
teacher can shift course when spirits are flagging; a stray thought can spark a new insight. Isn't this the kind of nonconformist "thinking outside the box" that business leaders adore? So why is there such a rush to freeze knowledge and distribute it in a frozen form? Even Coursera cofounder Andrew Ng concedes that the real value of a college education "isn't just the content. . . . The real value is the interactions with professors and other, equally bright students" (quoted in Oremus 2012).

The business world recognizes the virtues of proximity in its own human 11
resource management. (The phrase "corporate campus" acknowledges as much.) Witness, for example, Yahoo's controversial decision to eliminate telecommuting and require employees to be present in the office. CEO Marissa Mayer's memo reads as a mini-manifesto for close learning: "To become the absolute best place to work, communication and collaboration will be important, so we need to be working side-by-side. That is why it is critical that we are all present in our offices. Some of the best decisions and insights come from hallway and cafeteria discussions, meeting new people, and impromptu team meetings. Speed and quality are often sacrificed when we work from home. We need to be one Yahoo!, and that starts with physically being together" (quoted in Swisher 2013).

Why do boards of directors still go through the effort of convening in 12
person? Why, in spite of all the fantasies about "working from anywhere" are "creative classes" still concentrating in proximity to one another: the entertainment industry in Los Angeles, information technology in the Bay Area, financial capital in New York City? The powerful and the wealthy are well aware that computers can accelerate the exchange of information and facilitate "training," but not the development of knowledge, much less wisdom.

Close learning transcends disciplines. In every field, students must incline 13
toward their subjects: leaning into a sentence, to craft it most persuasively; leaning

into an archival document, to determine an uncertain provenance; leaning into a musical score, to poise the body for performance; leaning into a data set, to discern emerging patterns; leaning into a laboratory instrument, to interpret what is viewed. MOOCs, in contrast, encourage students and faculty to lean back, not to cultivate the disciplined attention necessary to engage fully in a complex task. Low completion rates for MOOCs (still hovering around 10 percent) speak for themselves.

Technology as Supplement

Devotion to close learning should not be mistaken for an anti-technology 14 stance. (Contrary to a common misperception, the original Luddites simply wanted machines that made high-quality goods, run by trained workers who were adequately compensated.) I teach Shakespeare, supposedly one of the mustiest of topics. Yet my students navigate the vast resources of the Internet, evaluate recorded performances, wrestle with facsimiles of original publications, listen to pertinent podcasts, survey decades of scholarship in digitized form, circulate their drafts electronically, explore the cultural topography of early modern London, and contemplate the historical richness of the English language. Close learning is entirely compatible with engaging in meaningful conversations outside the classroom: faculty can correspond regularly with students via e-mail and keep in close contact via all kinds of new media. But this is all in service of close learning, and the payoff comes in the classroom.

Teachers have always employed "technology"—including the book, one 15 of the most flexible and dynamic learning technologies ever created. But let's not fixate upon technology for technology's sake, or delude ourselves into thinking that better technology overcomes bad teaching. At no stage of education does technology, no matter how novel, ever replace human attention. Close learning can't be automated or scaled up.

As retrograde as it might sound, gathering humans in a room with real 16 time for dialogue still matters. As educators, we must remind ourselves—not to mention our legislators, our boards, our administrators, our alumni, our students, and our students' parents—of the inescapable fact that our "product" is close learning. This is why savvy parents have always invested in intensive human interaction for their children. (Tellingly, parents from Silicon Valley deliberately restrict their children's access to electronic distractions, so that they might experience the free play of mind essential to human development.)

What remains to be seen is whether we value this kind of close learning at 17 all levels of education enough to defend it, and fund it, for a wider circle of Americans—or whether we will continue to permit the circle to contract, excluding a genuinely transformative intellectual experience from those without means. Proponents of distance education have always boasted that they provide access, but are they providing access to *close learning*?

References

Firestein, S. 2012. *Ignorance: How It Drives Science*. New York: Oxford University Press.

Newman, J. H. 2001. "What Is a University?" In *Rise and Progress of Universities and Benedictine Essays,* edited by M. K. Tilman, 6–17. Notre Dame, IN: University of Notre Dame Press.

Oremus, W. 2014. "The New Public Ivies: Will Online Education Startups like Coursera End the Era of Expensive Higher Education?" *Slate*, July 17, http://www.slate.com/articles/technology/future_tense/2012/07/coursera_udacity_edx_will_free_online_ivy_league_courses_end_the_era_of_expensive_higher_ed_.html.

Swisher, K. 2013. " 'Physically Together': Here's the Internal Yahoo No-Work-from-Home Memo for Remote Workers and Maybe More." *AllThingsD*, February 22. http://allthingsd.com/20130222/physically-together-heres-the-internal-yahoo-no-work-from-home-memo-which-extends-beyond-remote-workers.

⊙ AT ISSUE: SOURCES FOR USING ALTERNATIVE APPROACHES TO ARGUMENT

1. What effect does Newstok want his introduction to have on readers? How can you tell? In your opinion, is his strategy successful?

2. In paragraph 5, Newstok asks whether an education "is something more than 'content' delivery." What does he mean?

3. According to Newstok, what is "close learning" (para. 6)? What are its advantages over online education?

4. Where does Newstok address the major arguments against his position? How effectively does he refute them?

5. Use Toulmin logic to analyze Newstok's essay, identifying the argument's claim, its grounds, and its warrant. Does Newstok appeal only to *logos*, or does he also appeal to *pathos* and *ethos*? Explain.

6. Is Newstok's argument primarily deductive or inductive? Why do you think that he chose this structure?

This essay originally appeared in the January 2013 issue of *Techniques*.

OLD FLAMES AND NEW BEACONS

RAY MCNULTY

A few years ago, I saw a video of a pop concert. It looked just like concerts of 1 my youth: a well-lit stage amid a darkened crowd flecked with small wavering lights. I laughed when I realized, however, that the swaying glow was coming not from cigarette lighters but from LCD screens.

This juxtaposition of old flames and new beacons reminds me of distance 2 learning. Once the realm of correspondence schools, whose matchbook cover advertisements promised the chance to learn from home, distance learning has evolved into myriad interactive opportunities that cater to the spectrum of learners' needs. Striking a match on the correspondence school model, technology has ignited a virtual wildfire of prospects for education.

Educators have long pondered the technology question. Most of their stu- 3 dents know nothing firsthand about, or can scarcely remember, a time before laptops and cellphones. Yet, though they recognize the value of technology, many educators still do not take full advantage of it in their teaching. They are flummoxed by what they perceive as an all-or-nothing choice. If they integrate virtual learning strategies, will they work themselves into obsolescence? If they maintain the status quo, will they be able to fully engage students? These are understandable questions, but I do not believe the answer is mutually exclusive.

> "They are flummoxed by what they perceive as an all-or-nothing choice."

Light Sources

Emerging teaching models combine the best of classroom methods with the 4 litheness of online learning to offer more pathways to learning for more students. Three particularly strong new models of this ilk are gaining popularity in American education: flipped classroom, blended classroom, and supported distance learning. Technology-infused, these learning models suit all types of curricula, including career and technical education (CTE), which leads the way in applied learning by keeping current with technological advances across disciplines. They also echo CTE's core goal of providing learners with relevant skills and knowledge to prepare them for successful careers.

The flipped classroom model reverses the traditional lecture/application 5 cycle. Educators post recorded lectures online and assign digital materials to further students' understanding. Pre-class work by students frees teachers to focus class meetings on discussions to reinforce understanding and hands-on activities for practice in application. Continuous access to lectures supports rigor in learning by enabling students to review lessons, in whole or in part, as many times as needed to grasp content. Relevancy is heightened through increased opportunities for hands-on activities. Further, when students have greater responsibility for content, they practice essential skills, such as self-motivation and time management, which become additional assets for employability and career success.

The blended classroom model involves mixing in-class lectures with online assignments, giving students opportunities for both group and independent learning. Classroom and online activities are balanced depending on content and learning goals. This model works particularly well for large or especially diverse groups of learners because it supports differentiated instruction to ensure that all students not only meet expectations but are also stretched in their learning. 6

Supported distance learning—technology-delivered coursework with low or no classroom residency requirements—is education's fastest growing sector. The National Center for Education Statistics reports that between 2005 and 2010, distance learning course enrollment among American public high school students increased by 77 percent to 1.3 million students, representing 53 percent of public high school districts. An estimated 18 percent of undergraduates will enroll in distance learning for 80 percent or more of their coursework by 2013, according to coursehero.com. 7

Snuffing Out the Myths

The rising popularity of online learning models invites a hard look at the myths and realities of what these approaches offer. 8

First, there is the erroneous perception that distance learning is only for adults. Distance and hybrid learning options are relevant across levels, from high school to graduate to career advancement programs, and capture more nontraditional students. The flexibility appeals to learners for many reasons. Some are encouraged—sometimes subsidized—by employers, others are self-motivated for career entry, advancement, or change. Others are pursuing new dreams. Learners who struggle in traditional programs find that asynchronous delivery and other elements of distance learning allow them to eliminate obstacles and forge pathways to learning success. 9

A recent Penn Foster blog asked students for feedback about why they had chosen distance learning. Some responses were expected: people with jam-packed lives sought portability and flexibility, employers were paying the fees, and lower costs. Others revealed simple but important personal reasons. One student shared that fluorescent classroom lighting gave her headaches; working at home eliminated the issue. Many respondents mentioned that music—from classical to classic rock—helped them concentrate. Several posters were happy to leave behind noisy classrooms, social pressures, and bullying. For many students, learning had become joyful and purposeful instead of forced. 10

Another myth: when it comes to employability, online learning cre- 11 dentials are not valid or valuable. Every consumer service sector has highs and lows in quality. Some remote courses are designed well and led by great teachers; some are not. Some programs are accredited; others are not. Wise students research options to ensure that courses or programs support their academic needs and professional goals. Industries often work on content development with reputable programs—traditional and online—to ensure courses align with industry standards in many fields. Some top-rated companies now look to online learning to enhance employees' credentials while keeping them engaged in the workforce. Employers also recognize the value in skills required to successfully complete online programs, such as self-motivation, task focus, ability to work independently, and time management.

Then there is the idea that hybrid and distance learning work only for 12 purely "academic" subjects, not for courses or programs that require hands-on time in labs, practicums, or internships for credentialing. A good example of success in distance learning for a hands-on profession is Penn Foster's veterinary technician program. Our vet tech students complete accredited coursework online with support from peers and advisors. When they are ready for internships, an advisor helps connect them with an onsite learning position with one of the school's many partners. The approach works: 100 percent of Penn Foster's vet tech students have passed the independent credentialing exams required for employment in the field.

The vet tech program debunks the notion that distance learners must go 13 it alone, without the valuable and vibrant dialog with teachers and peers or well-appointed libraries and other learning resources available on traditional campuses. Flipped and blended classrooms feature classroom or campus time, so these concerns are irrelevant to those models.

Students enrolled in well-supported distance learning need not worry 14 about isolation either. Quality distance learning programs provide many options for students to engage with peers and teachers through online forums, via email, by phone, and, sometimes, in person with local classmates. In the vet tech program, students regularly connect with peers in online forums, and they work closely, if remotely, with advisors throughout the program, especially when it comes time to arrange for internships.

Tending to the Future

The go-it-alone myth strikes a chord with many educators. If students have 15 the main responsibility for their learning, what is the teacher's role? Changes in teaching theory and practice do not change the qualities of a good teacher. The most effective teachers are still those who are most inspired by the possibility and responsibility of helping to shape the future and who aspire to inspire their students. Certainly, distance and hybrid learning models change the educator's role, but they do not negate it. High-quality programs and courses rely on good teachers who continually seek ways to engage all types of learners so they can succeed not only in the world they live in now, but also in the one they are only beginning to dream up.

Teaching distance or hybrid model classes is different, but it offers some unique advantages. 16

In distance learning, the biggest practical differences for teachers tend 17 to be asynchronistic teaching cycles and limited (or no) face-to-face time. Because distance learners set their own pace, teachers may find they are working with more students concurrently than is possible in a classroom. Staggered learning timelines make this possible, and many educators enjoy simultaneously teaching various stages of their lessons rather than following a sequential path for a set term. Although in-person contact is reduced, there are many opportunities for one-to-one contact by phone and online.

Flipped and blended classrooms shift the educator's role from a "sage on 18 the stage" to one of an applied learning coach. With students taking on more pre-class prep, educators have more time to facilitate discussions and hands-on activities.

One of the most exciting advantages these dynamic models have for 19 teachers is the flexibility to explore "next practices," innovative and sometimes as-yet untested ideas that may (or may not) evolve into best practices. Next practices speak to the ideals of what education can accomplish, and these teaching models support the creativity educators need to think ahead to those ideals.

In fact, it's a bit like switching from cigarette lighters to LCD screens at a 20 concert. The old flame was good in its time, but technology offers a new beacon. As an educator, how will you choose to light up learning?

⊘ AT ISSUE: SOURCES FOR USING ALTERNATIVE APPROACHES TO ARGUMENT

1. Explain the essay's title.

2. Regarding technology, how does McNulty characterize students? How does he characterize instructors? Based on your experiences, are these characterizations fair? Accurate? Explain.

3. Define the following terms that McNulty introduces in paragraph 4.

   ■ Flipped classroom

   ■ Blended classroom

   ■ Supported distance learning

   Why does he discuss these new models of instruction? How does his discussion prepare readers for the rest of his essay?

4. Much of this essay involves "snuffing out the myths" (para. 8) associated with online learning. What are these myths? How successfully does McNulty refute them?

5. Throughout his essay, McNulty uses headings. What is the purpose of these headings? Do they help readers, or do they just get in the way? Explain.

6. Who is McNulty's intended audience? How can you tell?

This piece first appeared online at HybridPedagogy.com on January 5, 2012.

TRADING CLASSROOM AUTHORITY FOR ONLINE COMMUNITY

PETE RORABAUGH

Early web commenters referred to the Internet as a primitive, lawless place like the "Wild West." Plenty still needs to change to make certain parts of the web more civil and useful, but some aspect of the "Wild West" spirit is applicable to a discussion of student-directed learning. Too much civilization and society makes us compartmentalized and complacent. The West was a challenging place for European immigrants because it required an expansive sense of responsibility. You could no longer be just an apothecary or a cobbler. You had to provide for your own food and shelter from the resources around you; you had to decide just "what to do" with all this freedom. 1

Digital culture is having a similar effect on the practice of education, and that's a good thing. Students have to own their learning more. They can't just follow the dotted line on the ground that leads to their assignment, their grade, their degree. 2

Consider four core values for the classroom in general and the online classroom: **show up**, **be curious**, **collaborate**, and **contribute**. The online classroom is more student-directed in the sense that students are more "on their own" than they are in a traditional classroom. With more authors, contexts, and platforms to consider, digital media literacy insists that students filter, evaluate, and prioritize information with more critical proficiency than traditional students. Traditional students could trust the stability of the worksheet and the textbook. Digital education by its mere existence insists on more progressive practices for teachers and students. Digital culture has already started affecting dominant cultural epistemology° by shifting some focus away from experts and giving it to participants. 3

A type of philosophy focused on the study of knowledge

Students in the digital environment, whether in a hybrid or fully online classroom, carry more responsibility for their own progress. To succeed, they have to monitor their own progress more directly, engage with the insights of their peers, and ponder the external relevance of their work. A revolution is growing online that takes this trend to an extreme—digital citizens are building educational communities without institutions. "Learning" no longer means, or needs to mean, "going to school." It can just mean developing good observation and critical thinking skills. 4

> "A revolution is growing online that takes this trend to an extreme—digital citizens are building educational communities without institutions."

What this means for the online classroom is twofold: **1.** We recognize and communicate the shift from a follow-the-leader framework to a framework in 5 which the authority is more equally distributed between teacher and students. **2.** We have to model this new approach to learning in our classrooms (whether analog or digital). Students might be happy to see the culture of experts and talking heads dissolve, but if they want to be part of the revolution then they have to be ready to share the work that the experts used to do. For example, we might have students blogging publicly instead of submitting their work to the instructor as a one-to-one transaction. In this move, students become content creators, instead of content consumers—creators of their own educations instead of consumers—textbook creators instead of consumers.

Traditional classrooms, the ones inspired by factories, create ideal students 6 who follow instructions well. ("Changing Education Paradigms," a video from RSA animate, offers a cogent argument for this shift in thinking about education.) The web and digital culture create ideal citizens who investigate things "just because." These students reach for *Wikipedia* or Google Maps on their iPhones to get immediate clarification when they need help. Our online classrooms should harness this educational holster mentality. Don't understand something? Ask the class, email a group of professionals, call the company, interview your grandmother. And this is the beauty of digital and critical pedagogy; when it's done right, it connects us to each other and to the world.

⊖ AT ISSUE: SOURCES FOR USING ALTERNATIVE APPROACHES TO ARGUMENT

1. Rorabaugh begins his essay by comparing the Internet to the Wild West. In what respects is this **analogy** valid? In what respects is it not?

2. Where in this essay does the claim appear? How is the claim qualified? How does the qualifier set up the rest of the essay?

3. Rorabaugh makes a number of statements that he assumes are self-evident. For example, in paragraph 2 he says that in the online classroom "[s]tudents have to own their learning more," and in paragraph 3 he says, "The online classroom is more student-directed." Identify other statements like these. Are they really self-evident, or do they require support?

4. Rorabaugh is clearly a supporter of online learning. Does this prevent him from seeing problems associated with online learning? Explain.

5. What preconceptions about online learning does Rorabaugh assume his readers have? How do you know?

6. Suppose Rorabaugh wanted to rewrite his essay as a Rogerian argument. What changes in his essay's tone and emphasis would he have to make?

TEMPLATE FOR WRITING A ROGERIAN ARGUMENT

Write a one-paragraph **Rogerian** argument in which you argue that the drawbacks of online education have to be addressed before it can be successful. Follow the template below, filling in the blanks to create your argument.

> With more and more students taking online courses, both the students and the colleges benefit. For example, _____
> _____
> _____. In addition, _____
> _____.
> However, online education does have some drawbacks. For instance, _____
> _____
> _____.
> These problems could be easily solved. First, _____
> _____. Second, _____
> _____.
> If these problems are addressed, both students and colleges would benefit because _____
> _____.

TEMPLATE FOR WRITING A TOULMIN ARGUMENT

Write a one-paragraph **Toulmin** argument in which you argue in favor of online education. Follow the template below, filling in the blanks to create your argument.

Many colleges and universities have instituted online education programs. These programs are the best way _____

_____.

If colleges are going to meet the rising demand for education, they _____

_____

_____.

The online course I took _____

_____

_____.

Recent studies show that _____

_____. In addition, _____

_____. However, some people argue that _____

_____

_____. They also say that _____

_____.

These arguments _____

_____.

For this reason, online education is _____

_____

_____.

⊜ EXERCISE 6.7

Discuss your ideas about online learning with one or two of your classmates. Consider both the strengths and the limitations of this method of teaching. What types of classes do you think it is best suited for? Which classes do you think it would not work for? Then, edit the Rogerian and Toulmin arguments that you wrote on the previous templates so that they include some of these comments.

➲ EXERCISE 6.8

Write an argumentative essay on the topic, "Is Online Education Better Than Classroom Education?" Use the principles of either Rogerian argument or Toulmin logic to structure your essay. Cite sources in the Reading and Writing about the Issue section on pages 222–247, and be sure to document the sources you use and to include a works-cited page. (See Chapter 10 for information on documenting sources.)

➲ EXERCISE 6.9

Review the four pillars of argument that are discussed in Chapter 1. Does your essay include all four elements of an effective argument? Add anything that is missing. Then, label the elements of your argument.

➲ EXERCISE 6.10

Assume that you have been asked to present the information in the essay you wrote for Exercise 6.8 as an oral argument. What information would you include? What information would you eliminate? Find two or three visuals that you would use when you deliver your speech. Then, make an outline of your speech and indicate at what points you would display these visuals.

Writing an Argumentative Essay

free!

2014/2015
UC SANTA CRUZ

Campus Food & Garden Guide

Where to find sustainable food at UC Santa Cruz and discover ways to engage in your campus and community food system!

FOOD SYSTEMS WORKING GROUP

DINING HALLS • CAMPUS EATERIES • CAMPUS GARDENS • FOOD SYSTEMS RELATED ACADEMIC COURSES • STUDENT AND COMMUNITY ORGANIZATIONS • VOLUNTEER OPPORTUNITIES • STUDENT INTERNSHIPS & PROJECTS • FARMERS' MARKETS

9TH EDITION

7

Planning, Drafting, and Revising an Argumentative Essay

AT ISSUE

Should College Campuses Go Green?

In recent years, more and more American colleges and universities have become "green campuses," emphasizing **sustainability**—the use of systems and materials that will not deplete the earth's natural resources. Various schools have taken steps such as the following:

- Placing an emphasis on recycling and reducing nonbiodegradable waste

- Creating green buildings and using eco-friendly materials in construction projects

- Instituting new curricula in environmental science

- Monitoring their greenhouse gas emissions and evaluating their carbon footprint

- Growing crops on campus to feed students

- Hiring full-time "sustainability directors"

- Encouraging students to use bikes instead of cars

- Purchasing wind-generated electricity to supply the campus's energy

- Eliminating trays in college cafeterias

Although many schools have launched ambitious programs and projects to reduce their energy dependence, some have been more cautious, citing the high cost of such programs and the need to allocate resources elsewhere. Moreover, some critics of the green movement object to the notion that colleges should help to make students "sustainability literate." Such critics consider the green movement to be an expression of political correctness that at best does no more than pay lip service to the problem and at worst threatens academic freedom by furthering a political agenda.

The question remains whether the green movement that is spreading rapidly across college campuses is here to stay or just a fad—or something between these two extremes. This chapter takes you through the process of writing an argumentative essay on the topic of whether college campuses should go green. (Exercises guide you through the process of writing your own argumentative essay on a topic of your choice.)

Before you can write a convincing argumentative essay, you need to understand the **writing process**. You are probably already familiar with the basic outline of this process, which includes *planning, drafting,* and *revising.* This chapter reviews this familiar process and explains how it applies to the specific demands of writing an argument.

Choosing a Topic

The first step in planning an argumentative essay is to choose a topic you can write about. Your goal is to select a topic that you have some emotional stake in—not simply one that interests you. If you are going to spend hours planning, writing, and revising an essay, then you should care about your topic. At the same time, you should be able to keep an open mind about your topic and be willing to consider various viewpoints. Your topic also should be narrow enough to fit the boundaries of your assignment—the time you have to work on the essay and its length and scope.

Typically, your instructor will give you a general assignment, such as the following.

Assignment
Write a three- to five-page argumentative essay on a topic related to college services, programs, facilities, or curricula.

The first thing you need to do is narrow this general assignment to a topic, focusing on one particular campus service, program, facility, or curriculum. You could choose to write about any number of topics—financial aid, the writing center, athletics, the general education curriculum—taking a position, for example, on who should receive financial aid, whether to expand the mission of the writing center, whether college athletes should receive a salary, or why general education requirements are important for business majors.

If you are interested in the environment, however, you might decide to write about the green movement that is spreading across college campuses, perhaps using your observations of your own campus's programs and policies to support your position.

Topic
The green movement on college campuses

TOPICS TO AVOID

Certain kinds of topics are not appropriate for argumentative essays. For one thing, some topics are just not arguable. For example, you could not write an argumentative essay on a statement of fact, such as the fact that many colleges saw their endowments decline after the financial crisis of 2008. (A fact is not debatable, so there can be no argument.)

Some familiar topics also present problems. These issues—the death penalty, abortion rights, and so on—are important (after all, that's why they are written about so often), but finding an original argument on either side of the debate can be a challenge. For example, you might have a hard time finding something new to say that would convince some readers that the death penalty is immoral or that abortion is a woman's right. In many people's minds, these issues are "settled." When you write on topics such as these, some readers' strong religious or cultural beliefs are likely to prevent them from considering your arguments, however well supported they might be.

Finally, topics that are very narrow or depend on subjective value judgments—or that take a stand on issues readers simply will not care much about, such as whether one particular video game or TV reality show is more entertaining than another—are unlikely to engage your audience (even if these topics are compelling to you and your friends).

⊘ EXERCISE 7.1

In response to the boxed assignment on the previous page, list ten topics that you could write about. Then, cross out any that do not meet the following criteria:

- The topic interests you.
- You know something about the topic.
- You care about the topic.
- You are able to keep an open mind about the topic.
- The topic fits the boundaries of your assignment.

Now, choose one topic to write an essay about.

LaunchPad
macmillan learning

For more practice, see the LearningCurve on Recognizing Topics and Main Ideas in the LaunchPad for *Practical Argument*.

Thinking about Your Topic

Before you can start to do research, develop a thesis statement, or plan the structure of your argument, you need to think a bit about the topic you have chosen. You can use *invention strategies,* such as **freewriting** (writing without stopping for a predetermined time), **brainstorming** (making quick notes on your topic), or **clustering** (creating a diagram to map out your thoughts) to help you discover ideas you might write about. You can also explore ideas in a writing journal or in conversations with friends, classmates, family members, or instructors.

Freewriting

> People say green is good, but I'm not sure why. Do we really need a separate, smelly container for composting? Won't the food decompose just as fast in a landfill? In middle school, we learned about the "three Rs" to save the environment—one was Recycle, but I forget the other two. Renew? Reuse? Remember? Whatever. OK, I know not to throw trash on the ground, and I know we're supposed to separate trash and recycling, etc. I get that. But does all this time and effort really do any good?

Brainstorming

TOPIC: THE GREEN MOVEMENT ON COLLEGE CAMPUSES

When started? Why? (Real need — or just a fad?) ——→ Could help recruit students

Background on our campus

Help environment

• Recycling
• Styrofoam take-out containers in cafeteria
• Paperless classes

Hurt environment

✱ Students' responsibility vs. school's responsibility

Do green campuses save money or waste money?

FUTURE — more special courses? new majors?
(Could strict green rules lead to police-state atmosphere on campus?)

(Possible Drawback)   (Does it really help?)

Clustering

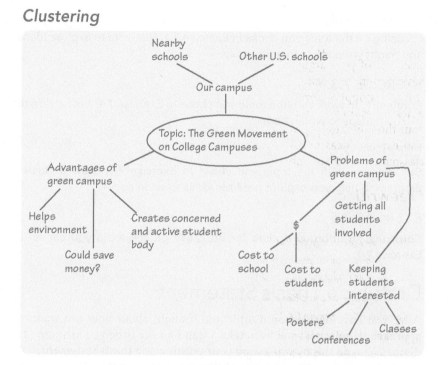

When you finish exploring ideas, you should be able to construct a quick **informal outline** that lists the ideas you plan to discuss.

Informal Outline

Topic: The Green Movement on College Campuses
  History/background
    National
    Our campus
  Positive aspects
    Helps environment
    Attracts new students
  Negative aspects
    Cost
    Enforcement
  Future

By grouping your ideas and arranging them in a logical order, an informal outline like the one above can help lead you to a thesis statement that expresses the position you will take on the issue.

❯ EXERCISE 7.2

Focusing on the topic you chose in Exercise 7.1, freewrite to explore ideas you might write about in your essay.

❯ EXERCISE 7.3

Continuing to work with the topic you chose in Exercise 7.1, brainstorm to discover ideas to write about.

❯ EXERCISE 7.4

Still working with the topic you chose in Exercise 7.1, draw a cluster diagram to help you explore possible ideas to write about.

❯ EXERCISE 7.5

Construct an informal outline for an essay on the topic you chose in Exercise 7.1.

Drafting a Thesis Statement

After you have decided on a topic and thought about how you want to approach it, your next step is to take a stand on the issue you are going to discuss. You do this by expressing your position as a **thesis statement**.

A thesis statement is the central element of any argumentative essay. It tells readers what your position is and perhaps also indicates why you are taking this position and how you plan to support it. As you draft your thesis statement, keep the following guidelines in mind:

- An argumentative thesis statement is not simply a statement of your topic; rather, it expresses the point you will make about your topic.

    TOPIC   The green movement on college campuses

    THESIS STATEMENT   College campuses should go green.

- An argumentative thesis statement should be specific, clearly indicating to readers exactly what position you will take in your essay.

    TOO GENERAL   Colleges need to do more to get students involved in environmental issues.

    REVISED   Colleges should institute programs and classes to show students the importance of using sustainable resources.

- An argumentative thesis statement should get right to the point, avoiding wordy, repetitive language.

WORDY   Because issues that revolve around the environment are so crucial and important, colleges should
do more to increase student involvement in campus projects that are concerned with sustainability.

REVISED   Because environmental issues are so important,
colleges should take steps to involve students in
campus sustainability projects.

■ Many argumentative thesis statements include words such as *should*
and *should not*.

- College campuses should _____.
- Because _____, colleges should _____.
- Even though _____, colleges should not _____.

> **NOTE**
>
> At this point, any thesis that you come up with is tentative. As you think
> about your topic and as you read about it, you will very likely modify
> your thesis statement, perhaps expanding or narrowing its scope,
> rewording it to make it more precise, or even changing your position.
> Still, the thesis statement that you decide on at this point can help you
> focus your exploration of your topic.

TENTATIVE THESIS STATEMENT

College campuses should go green.

⊙ EXERCISE 7.6

List five possible thesis statements for the topic you chose in Exercise 7.1.
(To help you see your topic in several different ways, you might experiment
by drafting at least one thesis statement that evaluates, one that considers
causes and/or effects, and one that proposes a solution to a problem.)
Which thesis statement seems most promising for your essay? Why?

Understanding Your Purpose and Audience

When you write an argument, your primary purpose is to convince your
audience to accept your position. Sometimes you will have other goals as
well. For example, you might want to change readers' ideas about an issue,
perhaps by challenging a commonly held assumption, or even to move
readers to take some action in support of your position.

To make the best possible case to your audience, you need to understand who your audience is—what knowledge, values, beliefs, and opinions your readers might have. You will also need to have some idea whether your audience is likely to be receptive, hostile, or neutral to the ideas you propose.

In most cases, it makes sense to assume that your readers are receptive but **skeptical**—that they have open minds but still need to be convinced. However, if you are writing about a topic that is very controversial, you will need to assume that at least some of your readers will not support your position and may, in fact, be hostile to it. If this is the case, they will be scrutinizing your arguments very carefully, looking for opportunities to argue against them. Your goal in this case is not necessarily to win readers over but to make them more receptive to your position—or at least to get them to admit that you have made a good case even though they may disagree with you. At the same time, you also have to work to convince those who probably agree with you or those who are neutral (perhaps because the issue you are discussing is something they haven't thought much about).

An audience of first-year college students who are used to the idea that sound environmental practices make sense might find the idea of a green campus appealing—and, in fact, natural and obvious. An audience of faculty or older students might be more skeptical, realizing that the benefits of green practices might be offset by the time and expense they could involve. College administrators might find the long-term goal of a green campus attractive (and see it as a strong recruitment tool), but they might also be somewhat hostile to your position, anticipating the considerable expense that would be involved. If you wrote an argument on the topic of green campuses, you would need to consider these positions—and, if possible, address them.

◑ EXERCISE 7.7

Consider how different audiences might respond to the thesis statement you found the most promising in Exercise 7.6. Identify five possible groups of readers on your college campus—for example, athletes, history majors, or part-time faculty. Would you expect each group to be receptive, hostile, or neutral to your position? Why?

 LaunchPad
macmillan learning

For more practice, see the LearningCurve on Topic, Purpose, and Audience in the Launch-Pad for *Practical Argument*.

Gathering Evidence

After you have a sense of who your audience will be and how these readers might react to your thesis, you can begin to collect **evidence** to support your thesis. As you look for evidence, you need to evaluate the usefulness and relevance of each of your sources, and you need to be alert for possible bias.

Evaluating the Evidence in Your Sources

As you read each potential source, consider the quality of the supporting evidence that the writer marshals to support his or her position. The more compelling the evidence, the more willing you should be to accept the writer's ideas—and, perhaps, to integrate these ideas into your own essay.

> **NOTE**
>
> Don't forget that if you use any of your sources' ideas, you must document them. See Chapter 10 for information on MLA documentation format and Appendix B for information on APA documentation format.

To be convincing, the evidence that is presented in the sources you review should be *accurate*, *relevant*, *representative*, and *sufficient*:

- **Accurate** evidence comes from reliable sources that are quoted carefully—and not misrepresented by being quoted out of context.

- **Relevant** evidence applies specifically (not just tangentially) to the topic under discussion.

- **Representative** evidence is drawn from a fair range of sources, not just those that support the writer's position.

- **Sufficient** evidence is enough facts, statistics, expert opinion, and so on to support the essay's thesis.

(For more detailed information on evaluating sources, see Chapter 8.)

> **NOTE**
>
> Remember, the evidence you use to support your own arguments should also satisfy the four criteria listed above.

Detecting Bias in Your Sources

As you select sources, you should be alert for **bias**—a writer's use of preconceived ideas (rather than factual evidence) as support for his or her arguments. A writer who demonstrates bias may not be trustworthy, and you should approach such a writer's arguments with skepticism. To determine whether a writer is biased, follow these guidelines:

- *Consider what a writer explicitly tells you* about his or her beliefs or opinions. For example, if a writer mentions that he or she is a lifelong member of the Sierra Club, a vegan, and the owner of a house heated by solar energy, then you should consider the possibility that he or she might downplay (or even disregard) valid arguments against a green campus rather than presenting a balanced view.

- *Look for slanted language.* For example, a writer who mocks supporters of environmental issues as *politically correct* or uses pejorative terms such as *hippies* for environmentalists should not earn your trust.

- *Consider the supporting evidence* the writer chooses. Does the writer present only examples that support his or her position and ignore valid opposing arguments? Does the writer quote only those experts who agree with his or her position—for example, only pro- (or only anti-) environmental writers? A writer who does this is presenting an unbalanced (and therefore biased) case.

- *Consider the writer's tone.* A writer whose tone is angry, bitter, or sarcastic should be suspect.

- *Consider any overtly offensive statements or characterizations* that a writer makes. A writer who makes negative assumptions about college students (for example, characterizing them as selfish and self-involved and therefore dismissing their commitment to campus environmental projects) should be viewed with skepticism.

> **NOTE**
>
> Be aware of any biases you hold that might affect the strength or logic of your own arguments. See "Being Fair," page 268.

⊖ EXERCISE 7.8

What evidence might you use to support the thesis statement you decided on in Exercise 7.6?

⊖ EXERCISE 7.9

In writing an essay that supports the thesis statement you have been working with in this chapter, you might find it difficult to remain objective. What biases do you have that you might have to watch for as you research and write about your topic?

⊖ EXERCISE 7.10

Gather evidence to support your thesis statement, evaluating each source carefully (consulting Chapter 8 as necessary). Be on the lookout for bias in your sources.

> ### USING ANALOGIES AS EVIDENCE
>
> An **analogy** is an extended comparison between two items, situations, or concepts on the basis of a number of shared characteristics. This kind of comparison explains a difficult or unfamiliar concept in terms of something more familiar. **Argument by analogy** is a strategy that makes the case that a position about an issue is valid because it is analogous to a comparable position on another issue—a position you expect your readers to accept. For example, you could develop a comparison between the relatively recent green campus movement and the earlier movement to make campuses fully accessible for students with disabilities.
>
> However, this kind of argument has limitations. For more information, see the discussion of weak analogy in Chapter 5.

Refuting Opposing Arguments

As you plan your essay and read sources that will supply your supporting evidence, you will encounter evidence that contradicts your position. You may be tempted to ignore this evidence, but if you do, your argument will not be very convincing. Instead, as you review your sources, identify the most convincing arguments against your position and prepare yourself to **refute** them (that is, disprove them or call them into question), showing them to be illogical, unfair, or untrue. Indicating to readers that you are willing to address these arguments—and that you can respond effectively to them—will help convince them to accept your position.

Of course, simply saying that your opponent's position is "wrong" or "stupid" is not convincing. You need to summarize opposing arguments accurately and clearly identify their weaknesses. In the case of a strong opposing argument, be sure to acknowledge its strengths before you refute it; if you do not, readers may see you as uninformed or unfair. For example, you could refute the argument that a green campus is too expensive by acknowledging that although expenditures are high at first, in the long run, a green campus is not all that costly considering its benefits. Also be careful not to create a **straw man**—that is, do not distort an opposing argument by oversimplifying it so it can be easily refuted (for example, claiming that environmentalists believe that sustainability should always be a college's first priority in its decisions about allocating resources). This unfair tactic will discourage readers from trusting you and thus will undermine your credibility.

Strategies for Refuting Opposing Arguments

In order to do a convincing job of refuting an argument that challenges your position, you need to consider where such an argument might be weak and on what basis you could refute it.

WEAKNESS IN OPPOSING ARGUMENT	REFUTATION STRATEGY
Factual errors or contrary-to-fact statements	Identify and correct the errors, perhaps explaining how they call the writer's credibility into question
Insufficient support	Point out that more facts and examples are needed; note the kind of support (for example, statistics) that is missing.
Illogical reasoning	Identify fallacies in the writer's argument, and explain why the logic is flawed. For example, is the writer setting up a straw man or employing the either/or fallacy? (See Chapter 5 for more on logic.)
Exaggerated or overstated claims	Identify exaggerated statements, and explain why they overstate the case.
Biased statements	Identify biased statements, and show how they exhibit the writer's bias. (See page 261, "Detecting Bias in Your Sources.")
Irrelevant arguments	Identify irrelevant points and explain why they are not pertinent to the writer's argument.

⊘ EXERCISE 7.11

Read paragraphs 7 and 8 of the student essay on page 283. Summarize the opposing argument presented in each of these paragraphs. Then, consulting the list above, identify the specific weakness of each opposing argument. Finally, explain the strategy the student writer uses to refute the argument.

Revising Your Thesis Statement

Before you can begin to draft your argumentative essay and even before you can start to arrange your ideas, you need to revise your tentative thesis statement so it says exactly what you want it to say. After you have gathered and evaluated evidence to support your position and considered the merits of opposing ideas, you are ready to refocus your thesis and state it in more definite terms. Although a tentative thesis statement such as

"College campuses should go green" is a good start, the thesis that guides your essay's structure should be more specific. In fact, it will be most useful as a guide if its phrasing actually acknowledges opposing arguments.

> **REVISED THESIS STATEMENT**
>
> Despite the expense, colleges should make every effort to create green campuses because doing so improves their own educational environment, ensures their own institution's survival, and helps solve the global climate crisis.

⊘ EXERCISE 7.12

Consulting the sources you gathered in Exercise 7.10, list all the arguments against the position in your thesis statement. Then, list possible refutations of each of these arguments. When you have finished, revise your thesis statement so that it is more specific, acknowledging the most important argument against your position.

After you have revised your thesis statement, you will have a concise blueprint for the essay you are going to write. At this point, you will be ready to plan your essay's structure and write a first draft.

Structuring Your Essay

As you learned in Chapter 1, an argumentative essay, like other essays, includes an introduction, a body, and a conclusion. In the introduction of an argumentative essay, you state your thesis; in the body paragraphs, you present evidence to support your thesis and you address opposing arguments; and in your conclusion, you bring your argument to a close and reinforce your thesis with a strong concluding statement. As you have seen, these four elements—thesis, evidence, refutation, and concluding statement—are like the four pillars of the ancient Greek temple, supporting your argument so that it will stand up to scrutiny.

> ### SUPPLYING BACKGROUND INFORMATION
>
> Depending on what you think your readers know—and what you think they need to know—you might decide to include a background paragraph that supplies information about the issue you are discussing. For example, in an essay about green campuses, you might briefly sum up the history of the U.S. environmental movement and trace its rise on college campuses. If you decide to include a background paragraph, it should be placed right after your introduction, where it can prepare readers for the discussion to follow.

Understanding basic essay structure can help you as you shape your essay. You should also know how to use induction and deduction, how to identify a strategy for your argument, and how to construct a formal outline.

Using Induction and Deduction

Many argumentative essays are structured either **inductively** or **deductively**. (See Chapter 5 for explanations of induction and deduction.) For example, the body of an essay with the thesis statement that is shown on page 265 could have either of the following two general structures:

INDUCTIVE STRUCTURE

- Colleges are taking a number of steps to follow green practices.
- Through these efforts, campuses have become more environmentally responsible, and their programs and practices have made a positive difference.
- Because these efforts are helping to save the planet, they should be expanded.

DEDUCTIVE STRUCTURE

- Saving the planet is vital.
- Green campuses can help to save the planet.
- Therefore, colleges should create green campuses.

These structures offer two options for arranging material in your essay. Many argumentative essays, however, combine induction and deduction or use other strategies to shape their ideas.

Identifying a Strategy for Your Argument

There are a variety of different ways to structure an argument, and the strategy you use depends on what you want your argument to accomplish. In this text, we discuss five options for presenting material: *definition arguments, cause-and-effect arguments, evaluation arguments, proposal arguments,* and *ethical arguments.*

Any of the five options listed above could guide you as you develop an essay on green campuses:

- You could structure your essay as a **definition argument**, explaining the concept of a green campus and giving examples to show how it operates.
- You could structure your essay as a **cause-and-effect argument**, showing how establishing a green campus could have positive results for students and for the campus.

- You could structure your essay as an **evaluation argument**, assessing the strengths and weaknesses of various programs and policies designed to create and sustain a green campus.

- You could structure your essay as a **proposal argument**, recommending a particular program, service, or course of action and showing how it can support a green campus.

- You could structure your essay as an **ethical argument**, explaining why creating a green campus is the right thing to do from a moral or ethical standpoint.

Constructing a Formal Outline

If you like, you can construct a **formal outline** before you begin your draft. (Later on, you can also construct an outline of your finished paper to check the logic of its structure.) A formal outline, which is more detailed and more logically organized than the informal outline shown on page 257, presents your main points and supporting details in the order in which you will discuss them.

A formal outline of the first body paragraph of the student essay on page 280 would look like this:

I. Background of the term *green*
   A. 1960s environmental movement
      1. Political agenda
      2. Environmental agenda
   B. Today's movements
      1. Eco-friendly practices
      2. Green values

Following a formal outline makes the drafting process flow smoothly, but many writers find it hard to predict exactly what details they will use for support or how they will develop their arguments. In fact, your first draft is likely to move away from your outline as you develop your ideas. Still, if you are the kind of writer who prefers to know where you are going before you start on your way, you will probably consider the time you devote to outlining to be time well spent.

⊗ EXERCISE 7.13

Look back at the thesis you decided on earlier in this chapter, and review the evidence you collected to support it. Then, construct a formal outline for your argumentative essay.

Establishing Credibility

Before you begin drafting your essay, you need to think about how to approach your topic and your audience. The essay you write will use a combination of logical, emotional, and ethical appeals, and you will have to be careful to use these appeals reasonably. (See pp. 14–21 for information on these appeals.) As you write, you will concentrate on establishing yourself as well-informed, reasonable, and fair.

Being Well-Informed

If you expect your readers to accept your ideas, you will need to establish yourself as someone they should believe and trust. This involves showing your audience that you have a good command of your material—that is, that you know what you are talking about.

If you want readers to listen to what you are saying, you need to earn their respect by showing them that you have done your research, that you have collected evidence that supports your argument, and that you understand the most compelling arguments against your position. For example, discussing your own experiences as a member of a campus or community environmental group, your observations at a Greenpeace convention, and essays and editorials that you have read on both sides of the issue will encourage your audience to accept your ideas on the subject of green campuses.

Being Reasonable

Even if your evidence is strong, your argument will not be convincing if it does not seem reasonable. One way to present yourself as a reasonable person is to **establish common ground** with your readers, stressing possible points of agreement instead of attacking those who might disagree with your position. For example, saying, "We all want our planet to survive" is a more effective strategy than saying, "Those who do not support the concept of a green campus are out to destroy our planet." (For more on establishing common ground, see the discussion of Rogerian argument in Chapter 6.)

Another way to present yourself as a reasonable person is to **maintain a reasonable tone**. Try to avoid absolutes (words like *always* and *never*); instead, use more conciliatory language (*in many cases, much of the time,* and so on). Try not to use words and phrases like *obviously* or *as anyone can see* to introduce points whose strength may be obvious only to you. Do not brand opponents of your position as misguided, uninformed, or deluded; remember, some of your readers may hold opposing positions and will not appreciate your unfavorable portrayal of them.

Finally, be very careful to treat your readers with respect, addressing them as your intellectual equals. Avoid statements that might insult them or their beliefs ("Although some ignorant or misguided people may still think . . ."). And never assume that your readers know less about your topic than you do; they may actually know a good deal more.

Being Fair

If you want readers to respect your point of view, you need to demonstrate respect for them by being fair. It is not enough to support your ideas convincingly and maintain a reasonable tone. You also need to avoid unfair tactics in your argument and take care to avoid **bias**.

In particular, you should be careful not to *distort evidence, quote out of context, slant evidence, make unfair appeals,* or *use logical fallacies.* These unfair tactics may influence some readers in the short term, but in the long run such tactics will alienate your audience.

- **Do not distort evidence. Distorting** (or misrepresenting) **evidence** is an unfair tactic. It is not ethical or fair, for example, to present your opponent's views inaccurately or to exaggerate his or her position and then argue against it. If you want to argue that green programs on college campuses are a good idea, it is not fair to attack someone who expresses reservations about their cost by writing, "Mr. McNamara's concerns about cost reveal that he has basic doubts about saving the planet." (His concerns reveal no such thing.) It is, however, fair to acknowledge your opponent's reasonable concerns about cost and then go on to argue that the long-term benefits of such programs justify their expense.

- **Do not quote out of context.** It is perfectly fair to challenge someone's stated position. It is not fair, however, to misrepresent that position by **quoting out of context**—that is, by taking the words out of the original setting in which they appeared. For example, if a college dean says, "For schools with limited resources, it may be more important to allocate resources to academic programs than to environmental projects," you are quoting the dean's remarks out of context if you say, "According to Dean Levering, it is 'more important to allocate resources to academic programs than to environmental projects.'"

- **Do not slant evidence.** An argument based on slanted evidence is not fair. **Slanting** involves choosing only evidence that supports your position and ignoring evidence that challenges it. This tactic makes your position seem stronger than it actually is. Another kind of slanting involves using biased language to unfairly characterize your opponents or their positions—for example, using a dismissive term such as *tree hugger* to describe a concerned environmentalist.

- **Do not make unfair appeals.** If you want your readers to accept your ideas, you need to avoid **unfair appeals** to the emotions, such as appeals to your audience's fears or prejudices. For example, if you try to convince readers of the importance of using green building materials by saying, "Construction projects that do not use green materials doom future generations to a planet that cannot sustain itself," you are likely to push neutral (or even receptive) readers to skepticism or to outright hostility.

- **Do not use logical fallacies.** Using **logical fallacies** (flawed arguments) in your writing will alienate your readers. (See Chapter 5 for information about logical fallacies.)

> ## MAINTAINING YOUR CREDIBILITY
>
> Be careful to avoid phrases that undercut your credibility ("Although this is not a subject I know much about") and to avoid apologies ("This is just my opinion"). Be as clear, direct, and forceful as you can, showing readers you are confident as well as knowledgeable. And, of course, be sure to proofread carefully: grammatical and mechanical errors and typos will weaken your credibility.

Drafting Your Essay

Once you understand how to approach your topic and your audience, you will be ready to draft your essay. At this point, you will have selected the sources you will use to support your position as well as identified the strongest arguments against your position (and decided how to refute them). You may also have prepared a formal outline (or perhaps just a list of points to follow).

As you draft your argumentative essay, keep the following guidelines in mind:

- **Follow the general structure of an argumentative essay.** State your thesis in your first paragraph, and discuss each major point in a separate paragraph, moving from least to most important point to emphasize your strongest argument. Introduce each body paragraph with a clearly worded topic sentence. Discuss each opposing argument in a separate paragraph, and be sure your refutation appears directly after your mention of each opposing argument. Finally, don't forget to include a strong concluding statement in your essay's last paragraph.

- **Decide how to arrange your material.** As you draft your essay, you may notice that it is turning out to be an ethical argument, an evaluation argument, or another kind of argument that you recognize. If this is the case, you might want to ask your instructor how you can arrange your material so it is consistent with this type of argument.

- **Use evidence effectively.** As you make your points, select the evidence that supports your argument most convincingly. As you write, summarize or paraphrase relevant information from your sources, and respond to this information in your own voice, supplementing material that you find in your sources with your own original ideas and conclusions. (For information on finding and evaluating sources, see Chapter 8; for information on integrating source material, see Chapter 9.)

- **Use coordination and subordination to make your meaning clear.** Readers shouldn't have to guess how two points are connected; you should use coordination and subordination to show them the relationship between ideas.

Choose **coordinating conjunctions**—*and, but, or, nor, for, so,* and *yet*—carefully, making sure you are using the right word for your purpose. (Use *and* to show addition; *but, for,* or *yet* to show contradiction; *or* to present alternatives; and *so* to indicate a causal relationship.)

Choose **subordinating conjunctions**—*although, because,* and so on—carefully, and place them so that your emphasis will be clear. Consider the following two sentences.

> Achieving a green campus is vitally important. Creating a green campus is expensive.

If you want to stress the idea that green measures are called for, you would connect the two sentences like this:

> Although creating a green campus is expensive, achieving a green campus is vitally important.

If, however, you want to place emphasis on the high cost, you would connect the two sentences as follows:

> Although achieving a green campus is vitally important, creating a green campus is expensive.

■ **Include transitional words and phrases.** Be sure you have enough transitions to guide your readers through your discussion. Supply signals that move readers smoothly from sentence to sentence and paragraph to paragraph, and choose signals that make sense in the context of your discussion.

SUGGESTED TRANSITIONS FOR ARGUMENT

■ To show causal relationships: *because, as a result, for this reason*

■ To indicate sequence: *first, second, third; then; next; finally*

■ To introduce additional points: *also, another, in addition, furthermore, moreover*

■ To move from general to specific: *for example, for instance, in short, in other words*

■ To identify an opposing argument: *however, although, even though, despite*

■ To grant the validity of an opposing argument: *certainly, admittedly, granted, of course*

■ To introduce a refutation: *however, nevertheless, nonetheless, still*

GRAMMAR IN CONTEXT

Using Parallelism

As you draft your argumentative essay, you should express corresponding words, phrases, and clauses in **parallel** terms. The use of matching parts of speech to express corresponding ideas strengthens your argument's impact because it enables readers to follow your line of thought.

In particular, use parallelism in sentences that highlight *paired items* or *items in a series*.

- **Paired Items**

    UNCLEAR   Creating a green campus is important because <u>it sets</u> an example for students and the <u>environment will be protected</u>.

    PARALLEL   Creating a green campus is important because it <u>sets</u> an example for students and <u>protects</u> the environment.

- **Items in a Series**

    UNCLEAR   Students can do their part to support a green campus in four ways—by <u>avoiding</u> bottled water, use of electricity <u>should be limited</u>, and they <u>can recycle</u> packaging and also <u>educating</u> themselves about environmental issues is a good strategy.

    PARALLEL   Students can do their part to support a green campus in four ways—by <u>avoiding</u> bottled water, by <u>limiting</u> use of electricity, by <u>recycling</u> packaging, and by <u>educating</u> themselves about environmental issues.

- **Define your terms.** If the key terms of your argument have multiple meanings—as *green* does—be sure to indicate what the term means in the context of your argument. Terms like *environmentally friendly, climate change, environmentally responsible, sustainable,* and *sustainability literacy* may mean very different things to different readers.

- **Use clear language.** An argument is no place for vague language or wordy phrasing. If you want readers to understand your points, your writing should be clear and direct. Avoid vague words like *good, bad, right,* and *wrong,* which are really just unsupported judgments that do nothing to help you make your case. Also avoid wordy phrases such as *revolves around* and *is concerned with,* particularly in your thesis statement and topic sentences.

- **Finally, show your confidence and your mastery of your material.** Avoid qualifying your statements with phrases such as *I think, I* *believe, it seems to me,* and *in my opinion.* These qualifiers weaken your argument by suggesting that you are unsure of your material or that the statements that follow may not be true.

 LaunchPad For more practice, see the LearningCurve on Parallelism in the LaunchPad for *Practical Argument.*
macmillan learning

⊘ EXERCISE 7.14

Keeping the above guidelines in mind, write a draft of an argumentative essay that develops the thesis statement you have been working with.

Revising Your Essay

After you have written a draft of your essay, you will need to revise it. **Revision** is "re-seeing"—looking carefully and critically at the draft you have written. Revision is different from editing and proofreading (discussed on p. 278), which focus on grammar, punctuation, mechanics, and the like. In fact, revision can involve substantial reworking of your essay's structure and content. The strategies discussed on the pages that follow can help you revise your arguments.

Asking Questions

Asking some basic questions, such as those in the three checklists that follow, can help you as you revise.

CHECKLIST

Questions about Your Essay's Purpose and Audience

☐ What was your primary purpose in writing this essay? What other purposes did you have?

☐ What appeals, strategies, and evidence did you use to accomplish your goals?

☐ Who is the audience for your essay? Do you see your readers as receptive, hostile, or neutral to your position?

☐ What basic knowledge do you think your readers have about your topic? Did you provide enough background for them?

☐ What biases do you think your readers have? Have you addressed these biases in your essay?

☐ What do you think your readers believed about your topic before reading your essay?

☐ What do you want readers to believe now that they have read your essay?

Questions about Your Essay's Structure and Style

- ☐ Do you have a clearly stated thesis?
- ☐ Are your topic sentences clear and concise?
- ☐ Do you provide all necessary background and definitions?
- ☐ Do you refute opposing arguments effectively?
- ☐ Do you include enough transitional words and phrases to guide readers smoothly through your discussion?
- ☐ Have you avoided vague language and wordy phrasing?
- ☐ Do you have a strong concluding statement?

Questions about Your Essay's Supporting Evidence

- ☐ Do you support your opinions with *evidence*—facts, observations, examples, statistics, expert opinion, and so on?
- ☐ Do you have enough evidence to support your thesis?
- ☐ Do the sources you rely on present information accurately and without bias?
- ☐ Are your sources' discussions directly relevant to your topic?
- ☐ Have you consulted sources that represent a wide range of viewpoints, including sources that challenge your position?

The answers to the questions in the checklists may lead you to revise your essay's content, structure, and style. For example, you may want to look for additional sources that can provide the kind of supporting evidence you need. Or, you may notice you need to revise the structure of your essay, perhaps rearranging your points so that the most important point is placed last, for emphasis. You may also want to revise your essay's introduction and conclusion, sharpening your thesis statement or adding a stronger concluding statement. Finally, you may decide to add more background material to help your readers understand the issue you are writing about or to help them take a more favorable view of your position.

Using Outlines and Templates

To check the logic of your essay's structure, you can prepare a revision outline or consult a template.

- To make sure your essay's key points are arranged logically and supported convincingly, you can construct a **formal outline** of your draft. (See p. 267 for information on formal outlines.) This outline will indicate whether you need to discuss any additional points, add supporting evidence, or refute an opposing argument more fully. It will also show you if paragraphs are arranged in a logical order.

- To make sure your argument flows smoothly from thesis statement to evidence to refutation of opposing arguments to concluding statement, you can refer to one of the paragraph **templates** that appear throughout this book. These templates can help you to construct a one-paragraph summary of your essay.

Getting Feedback

After you have done as much as you can on your own, it is time to get feedback from your instructor and (with your instructor's permission) from your school's writing center or from other students in your class.

Instructor Feedback You can get feedback from your instructor in a variety of different ways. For example, your instructor may ask you to email a draft of your paper to him or her with some specific questions ("Do I need paragraph 3, or do I have enough evidence without it?" "Does my thesis statement need to be more specific?"). The instructor will then reply with corrections and recommendations. If your instructor prefers a traditional face-to-face conference, you may still want to email your draft ahead of time to give him or her a chance to read it before your meeting.

Writing Center Feedback You can also get feedback from a writing center tutor, who can be either a student or a professional. The tutor can give you another point of view about your paper's content and organization and also help you focus on specific questions of style, grammar, punctuation, and mechanics. (Keep in mind, however, that a tutor will not edit or proofread your paper for you; that is your job.)

Peer Review Finally, you can get feedback from your classmates. **Peer review** can be an informal process in which you ask a classmate for advice, or it can be a more structured process, involving small groups working with copies of students' work. Peer review can also be conducted electronically. For example, students can exchange drafts by email or respond to one another's drafts that are posted on the course website. They can also use Word's comment tool, as illustrated in the following example.

DRAFT

Colleges and universities have no excuse for ignoring the threat of global climate change. Campus leaders need to push beyond efforts to recycle or compost and instead become models of sustainability. Already, many universities are hard at work demonstrating that reducing their institution's environmental impact is not only possible but worthwhile. They are overhauling their entire infrastructure, their buildings, systems, and even curriculum. While many students, faculty, staff, and administrators are excited by these new challenges, some still question this need to go green. Is it worth the money? Is it promoting "a moral and behavioral agenda rather than an educational one"? (Butcher). In fact, greening will ultimately save institutions money while providing their students with a good education. Colleges should make every effort to create green campuses because by doing so they will help solve the global climate crisis.

Comment [LB]: Your first two sentences are a little abrupt. Maybe you could ease into your argument more slowly?

Comment [KS]: I like these two questions. They really got me thinking.

Comment [PL]: Could you be more specific? I'm not sure what you mean.

Comment [PL]: You definitely talk about this in your paper, but you also talk about other reasons to go green. You might consider revising this thesis statement so it matches your argument.

FINAL VERSION

Over the last few years, the pressure to go green has led colleges and universities to make big changes. The threats posed by global climate change are inspiring campus leaders to push beyond efforts to recycle to become models of sustainability. Today, in the interest of reducing their environmental impact, many campuses are seeking to overhaul their entire infrastructure—their buildings, their systems, and even their curriculum. While many students, faculty, staff, and administrators are excited by these new challenges, some question this need to go green. Is it worth the money? Is it promoting "a moral and behavioral agenda rather than an educational one"? (Butcher). In fact, greening will ultimately save institutions money while providing their students with the educational opportunities necessary to help them solve the crisis of their generation. Despite the expense, colleges should make every effort to create green campuses because by doing so they will improve their own educational environment, ensure their own institution's survival, and help solve the global climate crisis.

GUIDELINES FOR PEER REVIEW

Remember that the peer-review process involves *giving* feedback as well as receiving it. When you respond to a classmate's work, follow these guidelines:

- Be very specific when making suggestions, clearly identifying errors, inconsistencies, redundancy, or areas that need further development.

- Be tactful and supportive when pointing out problems.

- Give praise and encouragement whenever possible.

- Be generous with your suggestions for improvement.

⮞ EXERCISE 7.15

Following the guidelines for revision discussed earlier, get some feedback from others, and then revise your argumentative essay.

Adding Visuals

After you have gotten feedback about the ideas in your paper, you might want to consider adding a **visual**—such as a chart, graph, table, photo, or diagram—to help you make a point more forcefully. For example, in a paper on the green campus movement, you could include anything from photos of students recycling to a chart comparing energy use at different schools. Sometimes a visual can be so specific, so attractive, or so dramatic that its impact will be greater than words would be. At other times, a visual can expand and support a verbal argument.

You can create a visual yourself, or you can download one from the Internet, beginning your search with Google Images. If you download a visual and paste it into your paper, be sure to include a reference to the visual in your discussion to show readers how it supports your argument.

> **NOTE**
>
> Don't forget to label your visual with a figure number, to use proper documentation, and to include a caption explaining what the visual shows, as the student paper that begins on page 280 does. (For information on how to document visuals, see Chapter 10.)

Polishing Your Essay

The final step in the writing process is putting the finishing touches on your essay. At this point, your goal is to make sure that your essay is well organized, convincing, and clearly written, with no distracting grammatical or mechanical errors.

Editing

When you **edit** your revised draft, you review your essay's overall struc-ture, style, and sentence construction, but you focus on grammar, punc-tuation, and mechanics. Editing is an important step in the writing process because an interesting, logically organized argument will not be convinc-ing if readers are distracted by run-ons and fragments, confusingly placed modifiers, or incorrect verb forms. (Remember, your grammar checker will spot some grammatical errors, but it will miss many others.)

GRAMMAR IN CONTEXT

Pronoun-Antecedent Agreement

A pronoun must always agree in number with its **antecedent**, the word to which it refers. Every pronoun must clearly refer to a particular antecedent.

CONFUSING	College administrators, faculty members, and staff members must work hard to show every student that a green campus will benefit <u>them</u>.
REVISED	College administrators, faculty members, and staff members must work hard to show every student that a green campus will benefit <u>him or her</u>.

 LaunchPad
macmillan learning

For more practice, see the LearningCurve on Nouns and Pronouns in the LaunchPad for *Practical Argument.*

Proofreading

When you **proofread** your revised and edited draft, you carefully read every word, trying to spot any remaining punctuation or mechanical errors, as well as any typographical errors (typos) or misspellings that your spell checker may have missed. (Remember, a spell checker will not flag a correctly spelled word that is used incorrectly.)

GRAMMAR IN CONTEXT

Contractions versus Possessive Pronouns

Be especially careful not to confuse the contractions *it's, who's, they're,* and *you're* with the possessive forms *its, whose, their,* and *your.*

INCORRECT	<u>Its</u> not always clear <u>who's</u> responsibility it is to promote green initiatives on campus.
CORRECT	<u>It's</u> not always clear <u>whose</u> responsibility it is to promote green initiatives on campus.

Choosing a Title

After you have edited and proofread your essay, you need to give it a title. Ideally, your title should create interest and give readers clear information about the subject of your essay. It should also be appropriate for your topic. A serious topic calls for a serious title, and a thoughtfully presented argument deserves a thoughtfully selected title.

A title does not need to surprise or shock readers. It also should not be long and wordy or something many readers will not understand. A simple statement of your topic ("Going Green") or of your position on the issue ("College Campuses Should Go Green") is usually all that is needed. If you like, you can use a quotation from one of your sources as a title ("Green Is Good").

⊘ EXERCISE 7.16

Evaluate the suitability and effectiveness of the following titles for an argumentative essay on green campuses. Be prepared to explain the strengths and weaknesses of each title.

- Green Campuses
- It's Not Easy Being Green
- The Lean, Clean, Green Machine
- What Students Can Do to Make Their Campuses More Environmentally Responsible
- Why All Campuses Should Be Green Campuses
- Planting the Seeds of the Green Campus Movement
- The Green Campus: An Idea Whose Time Has Come

Checking Format

Finally, make sure that your essay follows your instructor's guidelines for documentation style and manuscript format. (The student paper on p. 280 follows MLA style and manuscript format. For additional sample essays illustrating MLA and APA documentation style and manuscript format, see Chapter 10 and Appendix B, respectively.)

⊙ The following student essay, "Going Green," argues that colleges should make every effort to create green campuses.

GOING GREEN

SHAWN HOLTON

Introduction

Over the last few years, the pressure to go green has led colleges   1
and universities to make big changes. The threats posed by climate
change are encouraging campus leaders to push beyond early efforts,
such as recycling, to become models of sustainability. Today, in the
interest of reducing their environmental impact, many campuses are
seeking to overhaul their entire infrastructure. Although many students,
faculty, staff, and administrators are excited by these new challenges,
some question this need to go green. Is it worth the money? Is it
promoting "a moral and behavioral agenda rather than an educational
one"? (Butcher). In fact, greening will ultimately save institutions money
while providing their students with the educational opportunities
necessary to help them solve the crisis of their generation. Colleges

Thesis statement

should make every effort to create green campuses because by doing so
they will improve their own educational environment, ensure their own
institution's survival, and help solve the global climate crisis.

Body paragraph:
Background of green
movement

Although the green movement has been around for many years,   2
green has become a buzzword only relatively recently. Green political
parties and groups began forming in the 1960s to promote environmentalist goals ("Environmentalism"). These groups fought for "grassroots
democracy, social justice, and nonviolence" in addition to environmental protections and were "self-consciously activist and unconventional"
in their strategies ("Environmentalism"). Today, however, *green* denotes
much more than a political movement; it has become a catchall word
for anything eco-friendly. People use *green* to describe everything from
fuel-efficient cars to fume-free house paint. Green values have become
more mainstream in response to evidence that human activities, particularly those that result in greenhouse-gas emissions, may be causing
global warming at a dramatic rate ("Call for Climate Leadership" 4). To
fight this climate change, many individuals, businesses, and organizations are choosing to go green, making sustainability and preservation
of the environment a priority.

Greening a college campus means moving toward a sustainable campus that works to conserve the earth's natural resources. It means reducing the university's carbon footprint by focusing on energy efficiency in every aspect of campus life. This is no small task. Although replacing incandescent light bulbs with compact fluorescent ones and offering more locally grown food in dining halls are valuable steps, meaningful sustainability requires more comprehensive changes. For example, universities also need to invest in alternative energy sources, construct new buildings and remodel old ones, and work to reduce campus demand for nonrenewable products. Although these changes will eventually save universities money, in most cases, the institutions will need to spend money now to reduce costs in the long term. To achieve this transformation, many colleges are—individually or in cooperation with other schools—establishing formal "climate commitments," setting specific goals, and developing tools to track their investments and evaluate their progress.

3   Body paragraph: Definition of *green* as it applies to colleges

Despite these challenges, there are many compelling reasons to act now. Saving money on operating costs, thus making the school more competitive in the long term, is an appealing incentive. In fact, many schools have made solid and sometimes immediate gains by greening some aspect of their campus. For example, by changing its parking and transit systems to encourage more carpooling, biking, and walking, Cornell University has saved 417,000 gallons of fuel and cut costs by $36 million over the last twelve years ("Call for Climate Leadership" 10). By installing geothermal wells and replacing its old power plant with a geothermal pump system, the University of Central Missouri is saving 31 percent in energy costs, according to a case study in *Climate Neutral Campus Report* (Trane). These changes were not merely a social, or even a political, response, but a necessary part of updating the campus. Betty Roberts, the UCM vice president for administration, was faced with the problem of how to "make a change for the benefit of the institution . . . with no money." After saving several million dollars by choosing to go green, Roberts naturally reported that the school was "very happy!" with its decision (qtd. in Trane). There is more to be gained than just savings, however. Oberlin College not only saves money by generating its own solar energy (as shown in Fig. 1) but also makes money by selling its excess electricity back to the local power company (Petersen). Many other schools have taken similar steps, with similarly positive results.

4   Body paragraph: First argument in support of thesis

AP Photo/The Morning Journal/Paul M. Walsh.

Fig. 1. Solar panels on the roof of the
Adam Joseph Lewis Center for
Environmental Studies, Oberlin
College. 2008. Oberlin.edu.

Attracting the attention of the   5
media, donors, and—most significantly—
prospective students is another practical
reason for schools to go green. As one
researcher explains, "There is enough
evidence nationwide to detect an arms-
race of sorts among universities competing for green status" (Krizek et al. 27).
The *Princeton Review* now includes a
"green rating," and according to recent
studies, more than two thirds of college
applicants say that they consider green
ratings when choosing a school (Krizek
et al. 27). A school's commitment to the
environment can also bring in large private donations. For example, Carnegie
Mellon University attracted $1.7 million
from the National Science Foundation
for its new Center for Sustainable Engineering (Egan). The University of Cali-
fornia, Davis, will be receiving up to $25 million from the Chevron Corpo-
ration to research biofuel technology ("Call for Climate Leadership" 10).
While greening certainly costs money, a green commitment can also
help a school remain financially viable.

In addition to these practical reasons for going green, universities   6
also have another, perhaps more important, reason to promote and model
sustainability: doing so may help solve the climate crisis. Although an
individual school's reduction of emissions may not noticeably affect global
warming, its graduates will be in a position to make a huge impact. College is a critical time in most students' personal and professional development. Students are making choices about what kind of adults they will be,
and they are also receiving the training, education, and experience that
they will need to succeed in the working world. If universities can offer
time, space, and incentives—both in and out of the classroom—to help
students develop creative ways to live sustainably, these schools have the
potential to change the thinking and habits of a whole generation.

Many critics of greening claim that becoming environmentally friendly is too expensive and will result in higher tuition and fees. However, often a very small increase in fees, as little as a few dollars a semester, can be enough to help a school institute significant change. For example, at the University of Colorado–Boulder, a student-initiated $1 increase in fees allowed the school to purchase enough wind power to reduce its carbon emissions by 12 million pounds ("Call for Climate Leadership" 9). Significantly, the students were the ones who voted to increase their own fees to achieve a greener campus. Although university faculty and administrators' commitment to sustainability is critical for any program's success, few green initiatives will succeed without the enthusiastic support of the student body. Ultimately, students have the power. If they think their school is spending too much on green projects, then they can make a change or choose to go elsewhere.

7   Refutation of first opposing argument

Other critics of the trend toward greener campuses believe that schools with commitments to sustainability are dictating how students should live rather than encouraging free thought. As one critic says, "Once [sustainability literacy] is enshrined in a university's public pronouncements or private articles, then the institution has diminished its commitment to academic inquiry" (Butcher). This kind of criticism overlooks the fact that figuring out how to achieve sustainability requires and will continue to require rigorous critical thinking and creativity. Why not apply the academic skills of inquiry, analysis, and problem solving to the biggest problem of our day? Not doing so would be irresponsible and would confirm the perception that universities are ivory towers of irrelevant knowledge. In fact, the presence of sustainability as both a goal and a subject of study has the potential to reaffirm academia's place at the center of civil society.

8   Refutation of second opposing argument

Creating a green campus is a difficult task, but universities must rise to the challenge or face the consequences. If they do not commit to changing their ways, they will become less and less able to compete for students and for funding. If they refuse to make a comprehensive commitment to sustainability, they also risk irrelevance at best and institutional collapse at worst. Finally, by not rising to the challenge, they will be giving up the opportunity to establish themselves as leaders in addressing the climate crisis. As the coalition of American College and

9   Conclusion

University Presidents states in its Climate Commitment, "No other institution has the influence, the critical mass and the diversity of skills needed to successfully reverse global warming" ("Call for Climate Leadership" 13). Now is the time for schools to make the choice and pledge to go green.

Concluding statement

Works Cited

Butcher, Jim. "Keep the Green Moral Agenda off Campus." *Times Higher Education*, 19 Oct. 2007, www.timeshighereducation.com/news /keep-the-green-moral-agenda-off-campus/310853.article.

"A Call for Climate Leadership." *American College and University Presidents Climate Commitment*, Aug. 2009, www2 .presidentsclimatecommitment.org/html/documents/ACUPCC _InfoPacketv2.pdf

Egan, Timothy. "The Greening of America's Campuses." *New York Times*, 8 Jan. 2006, www.nytimes.com/2006/01/08/education /edlife/egan_environment.html?scp=1&amp%3Bsq=The&_r=0.

"Environmentalism." *Encyclopaedia Britannica Online*, 2015, www.britannica.com/topic/environmentalism.

Krizek, Kevin J., Dave Newport, James White, and Alan R. Townsend. "Higher Education's Sustainability Imperative: How to Practically Respond?" *International Journal of Sustainability in Higher Education*, vol. 13, no. 1, 2012, pp. 1 -33. DOI: 10.1108/14676371211190281.

Petersen, John. "A Green Curriculum Involves Everyone on Campus." *Chronicle of Higher Education*, vol. 54, no. 41, 2008, p. A25. *ERIC Institute of Education Services*, eric.ed.gov/?id=EJ801316.

Trane. "University of Central Missouri." *Climate Neutral Campus Report*, Kyoto Publishing, 14 Aug. 2009, secondnature.org/wp-content /uploads/09-8-14_ClimateNeutralCampusReportReleased.pdf.

⊙ EXERCISE 7.17

Find a visual that will strengthen your argument, and add it to your essay. Be sure to document it appropriately and to include a descriptive caption. Then, edit and proofread your paper, paying special attention to parenthetical documentation and your works-cited page. When you have finished, add a title, and print out a final copy of your essay.

4

Using Sources to Support Your Argument

8

Finding and Evaluating Sources

Is Technology a Serious Threat to Our Privacy?

It is increasingly common to share personal details on social media and online dating sites. The number of people who have profiles on online sites is staggering: Facebook currently has over 1.44 billion users worldwide, Twitter has over 236 million users, and Instagram has 300 million. Even newer apps like Yik Yak have millions of users, and one in five adults between the ages of twenty-five and thirty-four have used an online dating site. Studies have shown that the longer people use these sites, the more information they reveal without thinking about the possible consequences.

According to a 2015 Huffington Post report, 25 percent of Facebook users don't bother using their privacy settings. In addition, 63 percent of Facebook profiles are set on "visible to the public," meaning that anyone can access information. Even more disturbing is that every time a user visits a site with a "like" button, Facebook gets a notice, even if the user doesn't push the button. Not

surprisingly, the Internet has become the primary tool for those who want to access personal information: employers routinely use social-networking sites to find out about job candidates, advertisers buy their data to target consumers, and cybercriminals use information from these sites to steal users' identities.

In response to complaints, the federal government has begun to focus on the issue of cyberprivacy. As a result of pressure from the Federal Trade Commission, Facebook, Twitter, and Google have agreed to submit to privacy audits, and in response to complaints by users, Mark Zuckerberg, creator of Facebook, has repeatedly revised the site's privacy policies. Although privacy audits expose important weaknesses, critics claim that the only way to absolutely ensure privacy is for people to disengage from social media entirely and to avoid sharing personal information online. Others disagree, saying that social networks are a fact of

(continued)

(*continued*)

life and that people have to learn to use them responsibly. In other words, people should have no expectation of privacy when they post information about themselves online.

Later in this chapter, you will be asked to evaluate a number of research sources to determine if they are acceptable for an argumentative essay on the topic of technology and privacy. In Chapter 9, you will learn how to integrate sources into an essay on this general topic. In Chapter 10, you will see an MLA paper on one aspect of the topic: whether it is ethical for employers to access information posted on job applicants' social-networking sites. Finally, in Chapter 11, you will learn how to use sources responsibly while considering the question "Where should we draw the line with plagiarism?"

Finding Sources

In some argumentative essays, you can use your own ideas as evidence in support of your position. In many others, however, you have to do **research**—collect information (in both print and electronic form) from magazines, newspapers, books, journals, and other sources—to supplement your own ideas.

The obvious question is, "How does research help you to construct better arguments?" The answer is that research enables you to explore the ideas of others, consider multiple points of view, and expand your view of your subject. As you do so, you get a sense of the issues surrounding your topic, and as a result, you are able to develop a strong thesis and collect the facts, examples, statistics, quotations, and expert opinion that you will need to support your points. In addition, by taking the time to find reliable, up-to-date sources, you demonstrate to readers that your discussion is credible and that you are someone worth listening to. In short, doing research enables you to construct intelligent, authoritative, and convincing arguments.

Finding Information in the Library

When most students do research, they immediately go to the Internet—or, more specifically, to the Web. Unfortunately, by doing this, they ignore the most reliable source of high-quality information available to them: their college library.

Your college library contains both print and electronic resources that you cannot find anywhere else. Although the Internet gives you access to an almost unlimited amount of material, it does not offer the consistently high level of reliable information found in your college library. For this reason, you should always begin your research by surveying the resources of the library.

The best way to access your college library is to visit its website, which is the gateway to a great deal of information—for example, its online catalog, electronic databases, and reference works.

> **The Online Catalog:** The **online catalog** lists all the books, journals, newspapers, magazines, and other material housed in the library. Once you gain access to this catalog, you can type in keywords that will lead you to sources related to your topic.

NOTE

Many libraries have a **discovery service** that enables you to use a single search box to access a wide variety of content—for example, the physical items held by a library, content from e-books, journal articles, government documents, and electronic databases. Most discovery services return high-quality results quickly and (like Google) rank them according to relevancy.

> **Online Databases:** All college libraries subscribe to **databases**—collections of digital information that you access through a keyword search. The library's online databases enable you to retrieve bibliographic citations as well as the full text of articles from hundreds of publications. Some of these databases—for example, *Expanded Academic ASAP* and *Proquest Research Library*—provide information on a wide variety of topics. Others—for example, *Business Source Premier* and *Sociological Abstracts*—provide information on a particular subject area. Before selecting a database, check with the reference librarian to determine which will be most useful for your topic.
>
> **Reference Works:** All libraries contain **reference works**—sources of accurate and reliable information such as dictionaries, encyclopedias, and almanacs. These reference works are available both in print and in electronic form. **General encyclopedias**—such as the *New Encyclopaedia Britannica* and the *Columbia Encyclopedia*—provide general information on a wide variety of topics. **Specialized reference works**—such as *Facts on File* and the *World Almanac*—and **special encyclopedias**—such as the *Encyclopedia of Law and Economics*—offer detailed information on specific topics.

NOTE

Although a general encyclopedia can provide an overview of your topic, encyclopedia articles do not usually treat topics in enough depth for college-level research. Be sure to check your instructor's guidelines before you use a general encyclopedia in your research.

Finding Information on the Internet

Although the Internet gives you access to a vast amount of information, it has its limitations. For one thing, because anyone can publish on the Web, you cannot be sure if the information found there is trustworthy, timely, or authoritative. Of course, there are reliable sources of information on the Web. For example, the information on your college library's website is reliable. In addition, Google Scholar provides links to some scholarly sources that are as good as those found in a college library's databases. Even so, you have to approach this material with caution; some articles accessed through Google Scholar are pay-per-view, and others are not current or comprehensive.

A **search engine**—such as Google or Bing—helps you to locate and to view documents that you search for with keywords. Different types of search engines are suitable for different purposes:

- **General-Purpose Search Engines: General-purpose search engines** retrieve information on a great number of topics. They cast the widest possible net and bring in the widest variety of information. The disadvantage of general-purpose search engines is that you get a great deal of irrelevant material. Because each search engine has its own unique characteristics, you should try a few of them to see which you prefer. The most popular general-purpose search engines are Google, Bing, Yahoo!, Ask, and AOL Search.

- **Specialized Search Engines: Specialized search engines** focus on specific subject areas or on a specific type of content. The advantage of specialized search engines is that they eliminate the need for you to wade through pages of irrelevant material. By focusing your search on a specific subject area, you are more likely to locate information on your particular topic. (You are able to narrow your search to a specific subject area when you use a general-purpose search engine, but a specialized search engine narrows your search for you.) You can find a list of specialized search engines on the Search Engine List (thesearchenginelist.com).

- **Metasearch Engines:** Because each search engine works differently, results can (and do) vary. For this reason, if you limit yourself to a single search engine, you can miss a great deal of useful information. **Metasearch engines** solve this problem by taking the results of several search engines and presenting them in a simple, no-nonsense format. The most popular metasearch engines are Dogpile, Kartoo, Mamma, Surfwax, Yippy, and Zoo.

Evaluating Sources

Whenever you locate a source—print or electronic—you should always take the time to evaluate it. When you **evaluate** a source, you assess the

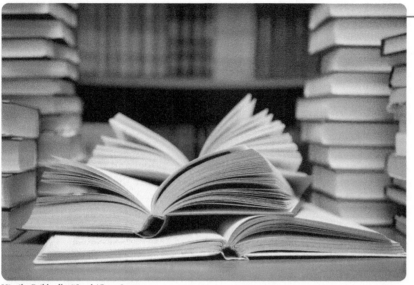

Sources must be evaluated carefully.

Viorika Prikhodko/iStock/Getty Images

objectivity of the author, the credibility of the source, and its relevance to your argument. (Although a librarian or an instructor has screened the print and electronic sources in your college library for general accuracy and trustworthiness, you cannot simply assume that these sources are suitable for your particular writing project.)

Material that you access online presents particular problems. Because anyone can publish on the Internet, the information you find there has to be evaluated carefully for accuracy. Although some material on the Internet (for example, journal articles that are published in both print and digital format) is reliable, other material (for example, personal websites and blogs) may be unreliable and unsuitable for your research. To be reasonably certain that the information you are accessing is appropriate, you have to approach it critically.

As you locate sources, make sure that they are suitable for your research. (Remember, if you use an untrustworthy source, you undercut your credibility.)

To evaluate sources, you use the same process that you use when you evaluate anything else. For example, if you are thinking about buying a laptop computer, you use several criteria to help you make your decision—for example, price, speed, memory, reliability, and availability of technical support. The same is true for evaluating research sources. You can use the following criteria to decide whether a source is appropriate for your research:

- Accuracy
- Credibility

- Objectivity

- Currency

- Comprehensiveness

- Authority

The illustrations on page 293 show where to find information that can help you evaluate a source.

Accuracy   A source is **accurate** when it is factual and free of errors. One way to judge the accuracy of a source is to compare the information it contains to that same information in several other sources. If a source has factual errors, then it probably includes other types of errors as well. Needless to say, errors in spelling and grammar should also cause you to question a source's general accuracy.

You can also judge the accuracy of a source by checking to see if the author cites sources for the information that is discussed. Documentation can help readers determine both the quality of information in a source and the range of sources used. It can also show readers what sources a writer has failed to consult. (Failure to cite an important book or article should cause you to question the writer's familiarity with a subject.) If possible, verify the legitimacy of some of the books and articles that a writer cites by seeing what you can find out about them online. If a source has caused a great deal of debate or if it is disreputable, you will probably be able to find information about the source by researching it on Google.

Credibility   A source is **credible** when it is believable. You can begin checking a source's credibility by determining where a book or article was published. If a university press published the book, you can be reasonably certain that it was **peer reviewed**—read by experts in the field to confirm the accuracy of the information. If a commercial press published the book, you will have to consider other criteria—the author's reputation and the date of publication, for example—to determine quality. If your source is an article, see if it appears in a **scholarly journal**—a periodical aimed at experts in a particular field—or in a **popular magazine**—a periodical aimed at general readers. Journal articles are almost always acceptable research sources because they are usually documented, peer reviewed, and written by experts. (They can, however, be difficult for general readers to understand.) Articles in high-level popular magazines, such as the *Atlantic* and the *Economist*, may also be suitable—provided experts wrote them. However, articles in lower-level popular magazines—such as *Sports Illustrated* and *Time*—may be easy to understand, but they are seldom acceptable sources for research.

You can determine how well respected a source is by reading reviews written by critics. You can find reviews of books by consulting *Book*

TOMMIE SHELBY ———————————— Author

We Who Are Dark

**The Philosophical Foundations
of Black Solidarity**

Publisher

The Belknap Press of
Harvard University Press
Cambridge, Massachusetts
London, England 2005

Copyright © 2005 by the President and Fellows of Harvard College
All rights reserved
Printed in the United States of America

Library of Congress Cataloging-in-Publication Data

Shelby, Tommie, 1967–
We who are dark: the philosophical foundations of
Black solidarity/Tommie Shelby.
p. cm.

Date of publication

Sources cited ——————— Includes bibliographical references and index.
Contents: Two conceptions of Black nationalism—Class, poverty, and
shame—Black power nationalism—Black solidarity after Black power—Race,
culture, and politics—Social identity and group solidarity.

ISBN 0-674-01936-9 (alk. paper)

1. African Americans—Politics and government. 2. African Americans—
Race identity. 3. African Americans—Social conditions—1975–
4. Black nationalism—United States. 5. Black power—United States.
6. Ethnicity—Political aspects—United States. 7. Racism—Political
aspects—United States. 8. United States—Race relations—Political aspects.
I. Title.

E185.615.S475 2005
305.896'073—dc22   2005045329

Review Digest—either in print or online—which lists books that have been reviewed in at least three magazines or newspapers and includes excerpts of reviews. In addition, you can consult the *New York Times Book Review* website—www.nytimes.com/pages/books/index.html—to access reviews printed by the newspaper since 1981. (Both professional and reader reviews are also available at Amazon.com.)

Finally, you can determine how well respected a source is by seeing how often other scholars in the field refer to it. **Citation indexes** indicate how often books and articles are mentioned by other sources in a given year. This information can give you an idea of how important a work is in a particular field. Citation indexes for the humanities, the social sciences, and the sciences are available online and in your college library.

Objectivity   A source is **objective** when it is not unduly influenced by personal opinions or feelings. Ideally, you want to find sources that are objective, but to one degree or another, all sources are **biased**. In short, all sources—especially those that take a stand on an issue—reflect the opinions of their authors, regardless of how hard they may try to be impartial. (Of course, an opinion is perfectly acceptable—as long as it is supported by evidence.)

As a researcher, you should recognize that bias exists and ask yourself whether a writer's assumptions are justified by the facts or are simply the result of emotion or preconceived ideas. You can make this determination by looking at a writer's choice of words and seeing if the language is slanted or by reviewing the writer's points and seeing if his or her argument is one-sided. Get in the habit of asking yourself whether you are being offered a legitimate point of view or simply being fed propaganda.

The covers of the liberal and conservative magazines shown here suggest different biases.

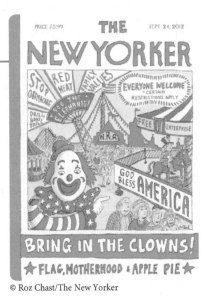

© Roz Chast/The New Yorker

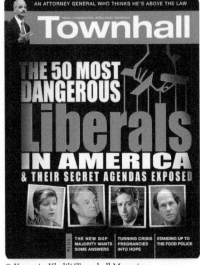

© Yasamin Khalili/Townhall Magazine

Currency A source is **current** when it is up-to-date. (For a book, you can find the date of publication on the copyright page, as above. For an article, you can find the date on the front cover of the magazine or journal.) If you are dealing with a scientific subject, the date of publication can be very important. Older sources might contain outdated information, so you want to use the most up-to-date source that you can find. For other sub-jects—literary criticism, for example—the currency of the information may not be as important as it is in the sciences.

Comprehensiveness A source is **comprehensive** when it covers a sub-ject in sufficient depth. The first thing to consider is whether the source deals specifically with your subject. (If it treats your subject only briefly, it will probably not be useful.) Does it treat your subject in enough detail? Does the source include the background information that you need to understand the discussion? Does the source mention other important sources that discuss your subject? Are facts and interpretations supported by the other sources you have read, or are there major points of disagree-ment? Finally, does the author include documentation?

How comprehensive a source needs to be depends on your purpose and audience as well as on your writing assignment. For a short essay for an introductory course, editorials from the *New York Times* or the *Wall Street Journal* might give you enough information to support your argu-ment. If you are writing a longer essay, however, you might need to con-sult journal articles (and possibly books) about your subject.

Authority A source has **authority** when a writer has the expertise to write about a subject. Always try to determine if the author is a recognized author-ity or simply a person who has decided to write about a particular topic. For example, what other books or articles has the author written? Has your instructor ever mentioned the author's name? Is the author mentioned in your textbook? Has the author published other works on the same subject or on related subjects? (You can find this information on Amazon.com.)

You should also determine if the author has an academic affiliation. Is he or she a faculty member at a respected college or university? Do other established scholars have a high opinion of the author? You can often find this information by using a search engine such as Google or by consulting one of the following directories:

Contemporary Authors
Directory of American Scholars
International Who's Who
National Faculty Directory
Who's Who in America
Wilson Biographies Plus Illustrated

⊙ EXERCISE 8.1

Assume that you are preparing to write an argumentative essay on the topic of whether information posted on social-networking sites threatens privacy. Read the sources that follow, and evaluate each source for accuracy, credibility, objectivity, currency, comprehensiveness, and authority.

- Nicholas Thompson, "Bigger Brother: The Exponential Law of Privacy Loss"

- *USA Today* editorial board, "Time to Enact 'Do Not Track'"

- Rebecca MacKinnon, "Privacy and Facebook"

This essay appeared in the December 5, 2011, edition of the *New Yorker*.

BIGGER BROTHER: THE EXPONENTIAL LAW OF PRIVACY LOSS

NICHOLAS THOMPSON

This past Tuesday, Facebook made a deal with the F.T.C.: from now on, the   1
social-networking company can no longer humbug us about privacy. If we're told that something we post on the site will be private, it will stay that way, unless we give Facebook permission to make it public. Or at least sort of. For a while. Facebook has been relentless in its effort to make more of what it knows about us—the music we listen to, the photos we take, the friends we have—available to more people, and it will surely figure out creative ways, F.T.C. or no F.T.C., to further that campaign. The company's leadership sincerely believes that the more we share the better the world will be. Mark Zuckerberg, the C.E.O., has said that in ten years we'll share a thousand times as much as we do now. That seems to be both an observation and a goal.

Meanwhile, Zynga has announced that it's going to raise about a billion   2
dollars in an impending I.P.O. Zynga makes social games like *FarmVille*, in which people harvest and sell virtual tomatoes. The games sound inane to non-players, and Zynga employees claim that their workplace is run like a labor camp; yet the company is worth perhaps ten billion dollars. Why? Partly because they collect and analyze fifteen terabytes of data a day from their users. They watch carefully in order to learn how to hook people and what enticements to offer someone frustrated about his slow-growing tomato crop. (There's a segment from *Bloomberg West* in which an analyst compares Zynga to a drug dealer.) According to Zynga's recent S.E.C. filings, its total

number of players is stagnant, but the amount of money it can extract from each one is growing. Data is the currency of the Web right now. Whoever has the most detailed data about you will get rich. Zynga has great data, and Zynga is about to get very rich.

> "Whoever has the most detailed data about you will get rich."

Last week also brought the news that a company called Carrier IQ has   3 installed software on about a hundred and fifty million phones that lets it and its customers—such as Sprint, A.T. & T., and Apple—know an awful lot about you. It tracks location, stores the numbers you dial, and even records the Websites you browse when you're not connected to a cell network. The point of the software is to help the phone companies improve their networks and serve you better. But this is done in a mysterious (and perhaps nefarious) way. Most people don't know they have it, and it's not easy to remove. It's also not clear exactly what it's recording, though a bevy of new lawsuits and government investigations will now try to figure that out. At the very least, there's one more company that you've never heard of that knows a heck of a lot about you. "The excuse proffered thus far—improved service—is at best feeble when compared to the extent of the potential invasion of privacy," Stephen Wicker, a professor in electrical and computer engineering at Cornell, told me.

These are just three stories from the past seven days. There'll surely be   4 more soon. Together, they've made me think of something I'll call The Exponential Law of Privacy Loss (or TELPL, pronounced "tell people"). The more we do online, the better companies get at tracking us, and the more accurate and detailed the data they glean from us becomes. The amount of data that they have grows exponentially over time.

It's impossible to exactly measure what percent of our time is spent con-   5 nected to the Internet: texting, shopping, surfing, browsing, sleeping. But, my best estimation is that, a few years ago, we lived roughly ten percent of our lives online, and companies captured about ten percent of what we did. Now it's about thirty percent, and the companies capture thirty percent of that—which means roughly nine times as much as a few years ago. Eventually, when we live seventy percent of our lives online, digital companies will capture and store about seventy percent of that. I'm not sure what will happen to the formula when we spend our entire lives online. Ideally, we won't get there.

This tracking isn't all bad; it may not even be mostly bad. People keep   6 letting Facebook broadcast more of their preferences and habits, and they love it. The more that advertisers know about you, the more willing they are to do things like buy advertisements on Websites, supporting journalism such as this. Carrier IQ makes our phones more efficient, and I have yet to hear of any specific harm done to any specific person by their system. Still, the Law is real. The F.T.C. can slow things down, but only a little. All of us are still becoming corporate data at an ever faster rate, for better and for worse.

This editorial was published in *USA Today* on December 11, 2011.

TIME TO ENACT "DO NOT TRACK"

USA TODAY EDITORIAL BOARD

Facebook's 800 million users are probably feeling a little more secure since the social media giant agreed to privacy measures forced by the Federal Trade Commission (FTC) late last month. But they'd be wise to stay cautious. Plenty of incentive for mischief remains, and not only on Facebook.   1

The agreement requires Facebook to stop letting users mark their profile information as private and then making it public without their permission. Facebook also promised that it will warn users of privacy policy changes before enacting them.   2

But the agreement won't stop Facebook from monitoring and sharing users' Web-browsing habits, which is a way for the company and others like it to make money. It's an unsatisfying ending to a two-year investigation, but more important, it's a marker of how difficult it will be to maintain privacy in an increasingly wired world.   3

The weakness in the FTC's agreement is that it didn't establish any guidelines about Internet tracking, the method by which Facebook collects data about its users even when they're not on the network itself. As company representatives recently acknowledged to *USA Today,* Facebook automatically compiles a log of every Web page its users visit that has a Facebook plug-in, such as the ubiquitous "like" button.   4

Other online giants, such as Google and Yahoo, use similar methods to monitor users' Web-browsing. This lets them tailor their pages and advertisements to appeal to different visitors.   5

Online tracking companies, which help sites compile these browsing records, claim that your personal details are not connected to your name, meaning your privacy is not compromised when they share information with advertisers or others. But as the *Wall Street Journal* discovered last year, at least one tracking company collected Web surfers' names and other personally identifiable information and passed it on to clients.   6

The implication is that tracking companies and advertisers could know your name, e-mail address, hometown, medical history, political affiliation, and more. Such information could be used in troubling ways. A health insurance company, for example, could guess your medical conditions. Or a potential employer could find out whether you spend your time gambling online.   7

> "Such information could be used in troubling ways."

If you don't like that prospect, your only option is to use a Web browser that ₈ offers a "Do Not Track" mechanism, such as Mozilla Firefox or Internet Explorer 9. Once you activate the feature, it signals websites you visit indicating that you do not want your data tracked by third parties. But existing Do Not Track mechanisms can't control what websites do; they can only communicate your preference.

That's why the FTC has called for a tougher and more universal version of ₉ Do Not Track, a move that the online advertising industry argues would hamper Internet innovation. These fears are overblown. Behavioral advertising, which targets viewers based on their Web-browsing history, is large and growing, but it still accounts for less than 5% of all online advertising. So ads that rely on tracking are hardly the Internet's only revenue stream.

Measures that would create a legally enforceable Do Not Track mechanism ₁₀ or otherwise address privacy concerns are languishing in Congress. Lawmakers should give Web users more tools to control their personal information. Until that happens, your online habits will reveal much more about you than just what you put on your Facebook profile.

This essay is from MacKinnon's book *Consent of the Networked* (2012).

PRIVACY AND FACEBOOK

REBECCA MACKINNON

As protests mounted in reaction to Iran's presidential elections on June 12, ₁ 2009, Facebook actively encouraged members of the pro-opposition Green Movement to use the social networking platform. By mid-June, more than four hundred members of Facebook's fast-growing Farsi-speaking community volunteered their time to create a Farsi version of Facebook. Thanks to efforts by Facebook enthusiasts all around the world, the platform has been made accessible in seventy languages—including many languages spoken in countries where regimes are known not to tolerate dissent.

Then in December 2009, Facebook made a sudden and unexpected alteration ₂ of its privacy settings. On December 9, to be precise, people who logged in got an automatic pop-up message announcing major changes. Until that day, it was possible to keep one's list of Facebook "friends" hidden not only from the general Internet-surfing public but also from one another. That changed overnight without warning. An array of information that Facebook previously had treated as private, suddenly and without warning became publicly available information by default. This included a user's profile picture, name, gender, current city, what professional and regional "networks" one belonged to within Facebook, the "causes" one had signed on to support, and one's entire list of Facebook friends.

The changes were driven by Facebook's need to monetize the service ₃ but were also consistent with founder Mark Zuckerberg's strong personal conviction that people everywhere should be open about their lives and actions. In Iran, where authorities were known to be using information and contacts obtained from people's Facebook accounts while interrogating Green Movement activists detained from the summer of 2009 onward, the implications of the new privacy settings were truly frightening. Soon after the changes were made, an anonymous commenter on the technology news site ZDNet confirmed that Iranian users were deleting their accounts in horror:

> A number of my friends in Iran are active student protesters of the government. They use Facebook extensively to organize protests and meetings, but they had no choice but to delete their Facebook accounts today. They are terrified that their once private lists of friends are now available to "everyone" that wants to know. When that "everyone" happens to include the Iranian Revolutionary Guard and members of the Basij militia, willing to kidnap, arrest, or murder to stifle dissent, the consequences seem just a bit more serious than those faced from silly pictures and status updates. I realize this may not be an issue for the vast majority of American Facebook users, but it's just plain irresponsible to do this without first asking consent. It's even more egregious because Facebook threw out the original preference (the one that requested Facebook keep the list of friends private) and replaced it with a mandate, publicizing what was once private information—with no explicit consent. If given the choice to remain a Facebook user with those settings, or quit, my friends would have quit rather than risk that information being seen by the wrong people. Instead, Facebook published it anyways. It's a betrayal of trust for the sake of better targeted advertising.

The global outcry over the exposure of people's friend lists in December   4
2009 was so strong that within roughly a day after the dramatic change, Facebook made an adjustment so that users could once again hide their friend lists from public view. People's friends could still see one another, however, and there was no way to hide them. Everybody's "causes" and "pages" were still publicly exposed by default, another serious vulnerability for activists. People kept complaining—many by creating protest groups within Facebook itself, where hundreds of thousands of people from all around the world posted angry messages. The groups had names like "Facebook! Fix the Privacy Settings!" and "Hide Friend List and Fan Pages! We Need Better Privacy Controls!" and "We Want Our Old Privacy Settings Back!" Scrolling through these pages, you see people posting from all over the world, with large numbers of Arab, Persian, Turkish, Eastern European, and Chinese names.

> "People's friends could still see one another, however, and there was no way to hide them."

Eventually Facebook fixed this problem as well, adjusting the privacy   5
options so that information about what pages users follow, or groups they

have joined, can be made private. Meanwhile, however, lives of people around the world had been endangered unnecessarily—not because any government pressured Facebook to make changes, but because Facebook had its own reasons and did not fully consider the implications for the service's most vulnerable users, in democratic and authoritarian countries alike.

⊙ EXERCISE 8.2

Write a one- or two-paragraph evaluation of each of the three sources you read for Exercise 8.1. Be sure to support your evaluation with specific references to the sources.

Evaluating Websites

The Internet is like a freewheeling frontier town in the old West. Occasionally, a federal marshal may pass through, but for the most part, there is no law and order, so you are on your own. On the Internet, literally anything goes—exaggerations, misinformation, errors, and even complete fabrications. Some websites contain reliable content, but many do not. The main reason for this situation is that there is no authority—as there is in a college library—who evaluates sites for accuracy and trustworthiness. That job falls to you, the user.

Another problem is that websites often lack important information. For example, a site may lack a date, a sponsoring organization, or even the name of the author of the page. For this reason, it is not always easy to evaluate the material you find there.

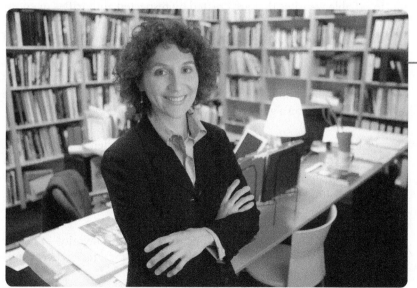

Most sources found in a college library have been evaluated by a reference librarian for their suitability as research sources.

© Steve Hix/Somos Images/Corbis

When you evaluate a website (especially when it is in the form of a blog or a series of posts), you need to begin by viewing it skeptically—unless you know for certain that it is reliable. In other words, assume that its information is questionable until you establish that it is not. Then apply the same criteria you use to evaluate any sources—*accuracy, credibility, objectivity, currency, comprehensiveness,* and *authority.*

The Web page pictured on page 303 shows where to find information that can help you evaluate a website.

Accuracy Information on a website is **accurate** when it is factual and free of errors. Information in the form of facts, opinions, statistics, and interpretations is everywhere on the Internet, and in the case of Wiki sites, this information is continually being rewritten and revised. Given the volume and variety of this material, it is a major challenge to determine its accuracy. You can assess the accuracy of information on a website by asking the following questions:

- **Does the site contain errors of fact?** Factual errors—inaccuracies that relate directly to the central point of the source—should immediately disqualify a site as a reliable source.

- **Does the site contain a list of references or any other type of documentation?** Reliable sources indicate where their information comes from. The authors know that people want to be sure that the information they are using is accurate and reliable. If a site provides no documentation, you should not trust the information it contains.

- **Does the site provide links to other sites?** Does the site have links to reliable websites that are created by respected authorities or sponsored by trustworthy institutions? If it does, then you can conclude that your source is at least trying to maintain a certain standard of quality.

- **Can you verify information?** A good test for accuracy is to try to verify key information on a site. You can do this by checking it in a reliable print source or on a good reference website such as *Encyclopedia.com.*

Credibility Information on a website is **credible** when it is believable. Just as you would not naively believe a stranger who approached you on the street, you should not automatically believe a site that you randomly encounter on the Web. You can assess the credibility of a website by asking the following questions:

- **Does the site list authors, directors, or editors?** Anonymity—whether on a website or on a blog—should be a red flag for a researcher who is considering using a source.

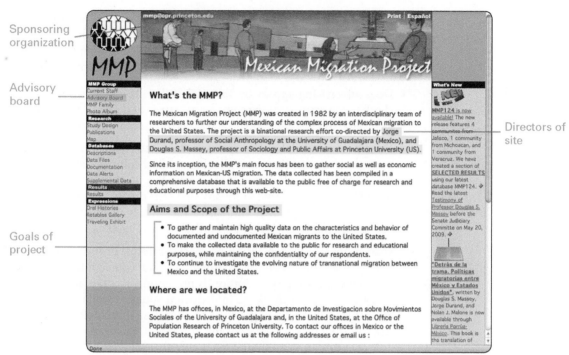

Courtesy from the Mexican Migration Project, mmp.opr.princeton.edu

- **Is the site refereed?** Does a panel of experts or an advisory board decide what material appears on the website? If not, what standards are used to determine the suitability of content?

- **Does the site contain errors in grammar, spelling, or punctuation?** If it does, you should be on the alert for other types of errors. If the people maintaining the site do not care enough to make sure that the site is free of small errors, you have to wonder if they will take the time to verify the accuracy of the information presented.

- **Does an organization sponsor the site?** If so, do you know (or can you find out) anything about the sponsoring organization? Use a search engine such as Google to determine the purpose and point of view of the organization.

Objectivity Information on a website is **objective** when it limits the amount of **bias** that it displays. Some sites—such as those that support a particular political position or social cause—make no secret of their biases. They present them clearly in their policy statements on their home pages. Others, however, try to hide their biases—for example, by referring only to sources that support a particular point of view and not mentioning those that do not.

Keep in mind that bias does not automatically disqualify a source. It should, however, alert you to the fact that you are seeing only one side of an issue and that you will have to look further to get a complete picture. You can assess the objectivity of a website by asking the following questions:

- **Does advertising appear on the site?** If the site contains advertising, check to make sure that the commercial aspect of the site does not affect its objectivity. The site should keep advertising separate from content.

- **Does a commercial entity sponsor the site?** A for-profit company may sponsor a website, but it should not allow commercial interests to determine content. If it does, there is a conflict of interest. For example, if a site is sponsored by a company that sells organic products, it may include testimonials that emphasize the virtues of organic products and ignore information that is skeptical of their benefits.

- **Does a political organization or special-interest group sponsor the site?** Just as you would for a commercial site, you should make sure that the sponsoring organization is presenting accurate information. It is a good idea to check the information you get from a political site against information you get from an educational or a reference site— *Ask.com* or *Encyclopedia.com*, for example. Organizations have specific agendas, and you should make sure that they are not bending the truth to satisfy their own needs.

- **Does the site link to strongly biased sites?** Even if a site seems trustworthy, it is a good idea to check some of its links. Just as you can judge people by the company they keep, you can also judge websites by the sites they link to. Links to overly biased sites should cause you to reevaluate the information on the original site.

USING A SITE'S URL TO ASSESS ITS OBJECTIVITY

A website's **URL** (uniform resource locator) can give you information that can help you assess the site's objectivity.

Look at the domain name to identify sponsorship. Knowing a site's purpose can help you determine whether a site is trying to sell you something or just trying to provide information. The last part of a site's URL can tell you whether a site is a commercial site (.com and .net), an educational site (.edu), a nonprofit site (.org), or a governmental site (.gov, .mil, and so on).

See if the URL has a tilde (~) in it. A tilde in a site's URL indicates that information was published by an individual and is unaffiliated with the sponsoring organization. Individuals can have their own agendas, which may be different from the agenda of the site on which their information appears or to which it is linked.

AVOIDING CONFIRMATION BIAS

Confirmation bias is a tendency that people have to accept information that supports their beliefs and to ignore information that does not. For example, people see false or inaccurate information on websites, and because it reinforces their political or social beliefs, they forward it to others. Eventually, this information becomes so widely distributed that people assume that it is true. Numerous studies have demonstrated how prevalent confirmation bias is. Consider the following examples:

- A student doing research for a paper chooses sources that support her thesis and ignores those that take the opposite position.

- A prosecutor interviews witnesses who establish the guilt of a suspect and overlooks those who do not.

- A researcher includes statistics that confirm his hypothesis and excludes statistics that do not.

When you write an argumentative essay, do not accept information just because it supports your thesis. Realize that you have an obligation to consider all sides of an issue, not just the side that reinforces your beliefs.

Currency Information on a website is **current** when it is up-to-date. Some sources—such as fiction and poetry—are timeless and therefore are useful whatever their age. Other sources, however—such as those in the hard sciences—must be current because advances in some disciplines can quickly make information outdated. For this reason, you should be aware of the shelf life of information in the discipline you are researching and choose information accordingly. You can assess the currency of a website by asking the following questions:

- **Does the website include the date when it was last updated?** As you look at Web pages, check the date on which they were created or updated. (Some websites automatically display the current date, so be careful not to confuse this date with the date the page was last updated.)

- **Are all links on the site live?** If a website is properly maintained, all the links it contains will be **live**—that is, a click on the link will take you to other websites. If a site contains a number of links that are not live, you should question its currency.

- **Is the information on the site up-to-date?** A site might have been updated, but this does not necessarily mean that it contains the most up-to-date information. In addition to checking when a website was last updated, look at the dates of the individual articles that appear on the site to make sure they are not outdated.

Comprehensiveness   Information on a website is **comprehensive** when it covers a subject in depth. A site that presents itself as a comprehensive source should include (or link to) the most important sources of information that you need to understand a subject. (A site that leaves out a key source of information or that ignores opposing points of view cannot be called comprehensive.) You can assess the comprehensiveness of a website by asking the following questions:

- **Does the site provide in-depth coverage?** Articles in professional journals—which are available both in print and online—treat subjects in enough depth for college-level research. Other types of articles—especially those in popular magazines and in general encyclopedias, such as *Wikipedia*—are often too superficial (or untrustworthy) for college-level research.

- **Does the site provide information that is not available elsewhere?** The website should provide information that is not available from other sources. In other words, it should make a contribution to your knowledge and do more than simply repackage information from other sources.

- **Who is the intended audience for the site?** Knowing the target audience for a website can help you to assess a source's comprehensiveness. Is it aimed at general readers or at experts? Is it aimed at high school students or at college students? It stands to reason that a site that is aimed at experts or college students will include more detailed information than one that is aimed at general readers or high school students.

Authority   Information on a website has **authority** when you can establish the legitimacy of both the author and the site. You can determine the authority of a source by asking the following questions:

- **Is the author an expert in the field that he or she is writing about?** What credentials does the author have? Does he or she have the expertise to write about the subject? Sometimes you can find this information on the website itself. For example, the site may contain an "About the Author" section or links to other publications by the author. If this information is not available, do a Web search with the author's name as a keyword. If you cannot confirm the author's expertise (or if the site has no listed author), you should not use material from the site.

- **What do the links show?** What information is revealed by the links on the site? Do they lead to reputable sites, or do they take you to sites that suggest that the author has a clear bias or a hidden agenda? Do other reliable sites link back to the site you are evaluating?

- **Is the site a serious publication?** Does it include information that enables you to judge its legitimacy? For example, does it include a statement of purpose? Does it provide information that enables you to determine the criteria for publication? Does the site have a board of advisers? Are these advisers experts? Does the site include a mailing address and a phone number? Can you determine if the site is the domain of a single individual or the effort of a group of individuals?

- **Does the site have a sponsor?** If so, is the site affiliated with a reputable institutional sponsor, such as a governmental, educational, or scholarly organization?

⊘ EXERCISE 8.3

Consider the following two home pages—one from the website for the *Chronicle of Higher Education*, a publication aimed at college instructors and administrators, and the other from the website for *Glamour*, a publication aimed at general readers. Assume that on both websites, you have found articles about privacy and social-networking sites. Locate and label the information on each home page that would enable you to determine the suitability of using information from the site in your paper.

Courtesy of The Chronicle of Higher Education, www.chronicle.com; © Nabil K. Mark Photography; © Mark Leong/Redux

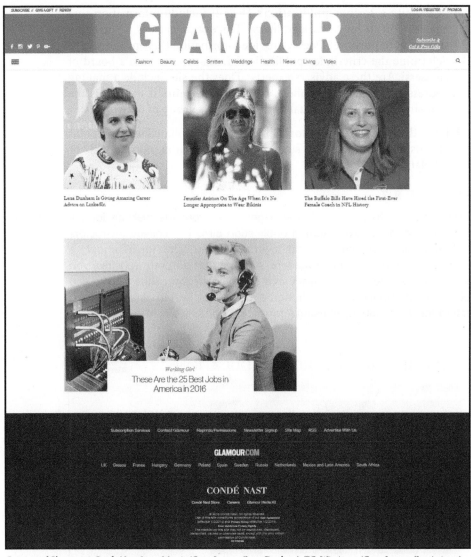

Courtesy of Glamour, © Conde Nast; Jason Merritt/Getty Images (Lena Dunham); TC: Wireimage/Getty Images (Jen Aniston); TR: AP/Wire Photo (Kathryn Smith); Bottom: Superstock/Getty Images (phone operator)

⊘ EXERCISE 8.4

Here are the **mission statements**—statements of the organizations' purposes—from the websites for the *Chronicle of Higher Education* and *Glamour*, whose home pages you considered in Exercise 8.3. What additional information can you get from these mission statements? How do they help you to evaluate the sites as well as the information that might appear on the sites?

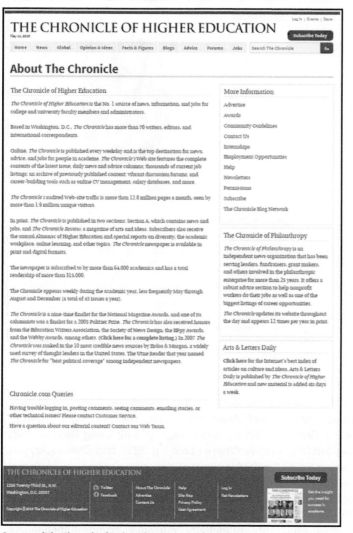

Courtesy of The Chronicle of Higher Education, www.chronicle.com

Glamour

About
Editor-in-chief Bio
Publisher, Chief Revenue Officer Bio
Brand News
Media Kit
Contacts
Product Licensing
International

Subscribe

Live the life, fill it with *Glamour*

Glamour is for the woman who sets the direction of her own life and lives it to its fullest and chicest. Her point-of-view is unmistakably American, unwavering in its optimism and wide open to the possibilities ahead. The dream job, the perfect look, the right guy: All are in her reach.

Glamour makes them reality. Its inspiration, ideas and guidance help her conquer her world with confidence and style. One in eight American women fill their lives with *Glamour*.

With *Glamour*, she looks her best and does her best every day, every night and **everywhere**.

Cover Photo by: Steven Pan/Glamour; © Conde Nast

⊙EXERCISE 8.5

Each of the following sources was found on a website: Jonathan Mahler, "Who Spewed That Abuse? Anonymous Yik Yak App Isn't Telling," p. 310; Jennifer Golbeck, "All Eyes on You," p. 316; Craig Desson, "My Creepy Instagram Map Knows Where I Live," p. 322; and Sharon Jayson, "Is Online Dating Safe?," p. 324.

Assume that you are preparing to write an essay on the topic of whether information posted on social-networking sites threatens privacy. First, visit the websites on which the articles appear, and evaluate each site for accuracy, credibility, objectivity, currency, comprehensiveness, and authority. Then, using the same criteria, evaluate each source.

This article originally ran in the *New York Times* on March 8, 2015.

WHO SPEWED THAT ABUSE? ANONYMOUS YIK YAK APP ISN'T TELLING

JONATHAN MAHLER

During a brief recess in an honors course at Eastern Michigan University last 1
fall, a teaching assistant approached the class's three female professors. "I think you need to see this," she said, tapping the icon of a furry yak on her iPhone.

The app opened, and the assistant began scrolling through the feed. 2
While the professors had been lecturing about post-apocalyptic culture,
some of the 230 or so freshmen in the auditorium had been having a separate conversation about them on a social media site called Yik Yak. There
were dozens of posts, most demeaning, many using crude, sexually explicit
language and imagery.

After class, one of the professors, Margaret Crouch, sent off a flurry of 3
emails—with screenshots of some of the worst messages attached—to various university officials, urging them to take some sort of action. "I have been defamed, my
reputation besmirched. I have been sexually harassed and verbally abused," she
wrote to her union representative. "I am about ready to hire a lawyer."

In the end, nothing much came of Ms. Crouch's efforts, for a simple rea- 4
son: Yik Yak is anonymous. There was no way for the school to know who was
responsible for the posts.

Eastern Michigan is one of a number of universities whose campuses have 5
been roiled by offensive "yaks." Since the app was introduced a little more
than a year ago, it has been used to issue threats of mass violence on more than
a dozen college campuses, including the University of North Carolina, Michigan State University, and Penn State. Racist, homophobic, and misogynist
"yaks" have generated controversy at many more, among them Clemson,
Emory, Colgate, and the University of Texas. At Kenyon College, a "yakker"
proposed a gang rape at the school's women's center.

In much the same way that Facebook swept through the dorm rooms of 6
America's college students a decade ago, Yik Yak is now taking their smart-
phones by storm. Its enormous popularity on campuses has made it the most
frequently downloaded anonymous social app in Apple's App Store, easily
surpassing competitors like Whisper and Secret. At times, it has been one of
the store's 10 most downloaded apps.

Like Facebook or Twitter, Yik Yak is a social media network, only without 7
user profiles. It does not sort messages according to friends or followers but by
geographic location or, in many cases, by university. Only posts within a 1.5-mile
radius appear, making Yik Yak well suited to college campuses. Think of it as a
virtual community bulletin board—or maybe a virtual bathroom wall at the
student union. It has become the go-to social feed for college students across
the country to commiserate about finals, to find a party, or to crack a joke
about a rival school.

Much of the chatter is harmless. Some of it is not.   8

"Yik Yak is the Wild West of anonymous   9
social apps," said Danielle Keats Citron, a law
professor at University of Maryland and the
author of *Hate Crimes in Cyberspace*. "It is
being increasingly used by young people in a
really intimidating and destructive way."

> "Much of the
> chatter is harmless.
> Some of it is not."

Colleges are largely powerless to deal with the havoc Yik Yak is wreak- 10
ing. The app's privacy policy prevents schools from identifying users

without a subpoena, court order, or search warrant, or an emergency request from a law-enforcement official with a compelling claim of imminent harm. Schools can block access to Yik Yak on their Wi-Fi networks, but banning a popular social media network is controversial in its own right, arguably tantamount to curtailing freedom of speech. And as a practical matter, it doesn't work anyway. Students can still use the app on their phones with their cell service.

Yik Yak was created in late 2013 by Tyler Droll and Brooks Buffington, fraternity brothers who had recently graduated from Furman University in South Carolina. Mr. Droll majored in information technology and Mr. Buffington in accounting. Both 24, they came up with the idea after realizing that there were only a handful of popular Twitter accounts at Furman, almost all belonging to prominent students, like athletes. With Yik Yak, they say, they hoped to create a more democratic social media network, one where users didn't need a large number of followers or friends to have their posts read widely. 11

"We thought, 'Why can't we level the playing field and connect everyone?'" said Mr. Droll, who withdrew from medical school a week before classes started to focus on the app. 12

"When we made this app, we really made it for the disenfranchised," Mr. Buffington added. 13

Just as Mark Zuckerberg and his roommates introduced Facebook at Harvard, Mr. Buffington and Mr. Droll rolled out their app at their alma mater, relying on fraternity brothers and other friends to get the word out. 14

Within a matter of months, Yik Yak was in use at 40 or so colleges in the South. Then came spring break. Some early adopters shared the app with college students from all over the country at gathering places like Daytona Beach and Panama City. "And we just exploded," Mr. Buffington said. 15

Mr. Droll and Mr. Buffington started Yik Yak with a loan from Mr. Droll's parents. (His parents also came up with the company's name, which was inspired by the 1958 song, "Yakety Yak.") In November, Yik Yak closed a $62 million round of financing led by one of Silicon Valley's biggest venture capital firms, Sequoia Capital, valuing the company at hundreds of millions of dollars. 16

The Yik Yak app is free. Like many tech start-ups, the company, based in Atlanta, doesn't generate any revenue. Attracting advertisers could pose a challenge, given the nature of some of the app's content. For now, though, Mr. Droll and Mr. Buffington are focused on extending Yik Yak's reach by expanding overseas and moving beyond the college market, much as Facebook did. 17

Yik Yak's popularity among college students is part of a broader reaction against more traditional social media sites like Facebook, which can encourage public posturing at the expense of honesty and authenticity. 18

"Share your thoughts with people around you while keeping your privacy," Yik Yak's home page says. It is an attractive concept to a generation of smartphone users who grew up in an era of social media—and are thus 19 inclined to share—but who have also been warned repeatedly about the permanence of their digital footprint.

In a sense, Yik Yak is a descendant of JuicyCampus, an anonymous online college message board that enjoyed a brief period of popularity several years ago. Matt Ivester, who founded JuicyCampus in 2007 and shut it in 2009 after it became a hotbed of gossip and cruelty, is skeptical of the claim that Yik Yak does much more than allow college students to say whatever they want, publicly and with impunity. "You can pretend that it is serving an important role on college campuses, but you can't pretend that it's not upsetting a lot of people and doing a lot of damage," he said. "When I started JuicyCampus, cyberbullying wasn't even a word in our vernacular. But these guys should know better." 20

Yik Yak's founders say the app's overnight success left them unprepared for some of the problems that have arisen since its introduction. In response to complaints, they have made some changes to their product, for instance, adding filters to prevent full names from being posted. Certain keywords, like "Jewish," or "bomb," prompt this message: "Pump the brakes, this yak may contain threatening language. Now it's probably nothing and you're probably an awesome person but just know that Yik Yak and law enforcement take threats seriously. So you tell us, is this yak cool to post?" 21

In cases involving threats of mass violence, Yik Yak has cooperated with authorities. Most recently, in November, local police traced the source of a yak—"I'm gonna [gun emoji] the school at 12:15 p.m. today"—to a dorm room at Michigan State University. The author, Matthew Mullen, a freshman, was arrested within two hours and pleaded guilty to making a false report or terrorist threat. He was spared jail time but sentenced to two years' probation and ordered to pay $800 to cover costs connected to the investigation. 22

In the absence of a specific, actionable threat, though, Yik Yak zealously protects the identities of its users. The responsibility lies with the app's various communities to police themselves by "upvoting" or "downvoting" posts. If a yak receives a score of negative 5, it is removed. "Really, what it comes down to is that we try to empower the communities as much as we can," Mr. Droll said. 23

When Yik Yak appeared, it quickly spread across high schools and middle schools, too, where the problems were even more rampant. After a rash of complaints last winter at a number of schools in Chicago, Mr. Droll and Mr. Buffington disabled the app throughout the city. They say they have since built virtual fences—or "geo-fences"—around about 90 percent of the nation's high schools and middle schools. Unlike barring Yik Yak from a Wi-Fi network, which has proved ineffective in limiting its use, these fences actually make it impossible to open the app on school grounds. Mr. Droll and Mr. Buffington also changed Yik Yak's age rating in the App Store from 12 and over to 17 and over. 24

Toward the end of last school year, almost every student at Phillips Exeter Academy in New Hampshire had the app on his or her phone and checked it constantly to read the anonymous attacks on fellow students, faculty members, and deans. 25

"Please stop using Yik Yak immediately," Arthur Cosgrove, the dean of residential life, wrote in an email to the student body. "Remove it from your phones. It is doing us no good." 26

At Exeter's request, the company built a geo-fence around the school, but it covered only a few buildings. Students continued using the app on different parts of the sprawling campus. 27

"We made the app for college kids, but we quickly realized it was getting into the hands of high schoolers, and high schoolers were not mature enough to use it," Mr. Droll said. 28

The widespread abuse of Yik Yak on college campuses, though, suggests that the distinction may be artificial. Last spring, Jordan Seman, then a sophomore at Middlebury College, was scrolling through Yik Yak in the dining hall when she happened across a post comparing her to a "hippo" and making a sexual reference about her. "It's so easy for anyone in any emotional state to post something, whether that person is drunk or depressed or wants to get revenge on someone," she said. "And then there are no consequences." 29

In this sense, the problem with Yik Yak is a familiar one. Anyone who has browsed the comments of an Internet post is familiar with the sorts of intolerant, impulsive language that the cover of anonymity tends to invite. But Yik Yak's particular design can produce especially harmful consequences. 30

"It's a problem with the Internet culture in general, but when you add this hyper-local dimension to it, it takes on a more disturbing dimension," says Elias Aboujaoude, a Stanford psychiatrist and the author of *Virtually You*. "You don't know where the aggression is coming from, but you know it's very close to you." 31

Jim Goetz, a partner at Sequoia Capital who recently joined Yik Yak's board, said the app's history of misuse was a concern when his firm considered investing in the company. But he said he was confident that Mr. Droll and Mr. Buffington were committed to ensuring more positive interactions on Yik Yak, and that over time, the constructive voices would overwhelm the destructive ones. 32

"It's certainly a challenge to the company," Mr. Goetz said. "It's not going to go away in a couple of months." 33

Ms. Seman wrote about her experience being harassed on Yik Yak in the school newspaper, the *Middlebury Campus*, prompting a schoolwide debate over what to do about the app. Unable to reach a consensus, the paper's editorial board wrote two editorials, one urging a ban, the other arguing that the problem wasn't Yik Yak but the larger issue of cyberbullying. (Middlebury has not taken any action.) 34

Similar debates have played out at other schools. At Clemson, a group of African-American students unsuccessfully lobbied the university to ban Yik Yak when some racially offensive posts appeared after a campus march to protest the grand jury's decision not to indict a white police officer in the fatal shooting of an unarmed black teenager in Ferguson, Mo. "We think that in the educational community, First Amendment rights are very important," said 35

Leon Wiles, the school's chief diversity officer. "It's just problematic because you have young people who use it with no sense of responsibility."

During the fall, Maxwell Zoberman, the sophomore representative to the student government at Emory, started noticing a growing number of yaks singling out various ethnic groups for abuse. "Fave game to play while driving around Emory: not hit an Asian with a truck," read one.   36

"Guys stop with all this hate. Let's just be thankful we arn't black," read another.   37

After consulting the university's code, Mr. Zoberman discovered that statements deemed derogatory to any particular group of people were not protected by the school's open expression policy, and were in fact in violation of its discriminatory harassment rules. Just because the statements were made on an anonymous social-media site should not, in his mind, prevent Emory from acting to enforce its own policies. "It didn't seem right that the school took one approach to hate speech in a physical medium and another one in a digital medium," he said.   38

Mr. Zoberman drafted a resolution to have Yik Yak disabled on the school's Wi-Fi network. He recognized that this would not stop students from using the app, but he nevertheless felt it was important for the school to take a stand.   39

After Mr. Zoberman formally proposed his resolution to the student government, someone promptly posted about it on Yik Yak. "The reaction was swift and harsh," he said. "I seem to have redirected all of the fury of the anonymous forum. Yik Yak was just dominated with hateful and other aggressive posts specifically about me." One compared him to Hitler.   40

A few colleges have taken the almost purely symbolic step of barring Yik Yak from their servers. John Brown University, a Christian college in Arkansas, did so after its Yik Yak feed was overrun with racist commentary during a march connected to the school's World Awareness Week. Administrators at Utica College in upstate New York blocked the app in December in response to a growing number of sexually graphic posts aimed at the school's transgender community.   41

In December, a group of 50 professors at Colgate University—which had experienced a rash of racist comments on the app earlier in the fall—tried a different approach, flooding the app with positive posts.   42

Generally speaking, though, the options are limited. A student who felt that he or she had been the target of an attack on Yik Yak could theoretically pursue defamation charges and subpoena the company to find out who had written the post. But it is a difficult situation to imagine, given the cost and murky legal issues involved. Schools will probably just stand back and hope that respect and civility prevail, that their communities really will learn to police themselves.   43

Yik Yak's founders say their start-up is just experiencing some growing pains. "It's definitely still a learning process for us," Mr. Buffington said, "and we're definitely still learning how to make the community more constructive."   44

> "Yik Yak's founders say their start-up is just experiencing some growing pains."

Golbeck's essay appeared in the September/October 2014 issue of *Psychology Today*.

ALL EYES ON YOU

JENNIFER GOLBECK

Every day, nearly everywhere I go, I'm being followed. That's not paranoia. It's 1
a fact. Consider:

On my local Washington, D.C., streets, I am constantly watched. The city 2
government alone has hundreds of traffic and surveillance cameras. And then
there are the cameras in parks, office buildings, ATM lobbies, and, of course,
around every federal building and landmark. On an average day, my image is
captured by well over 100 cameras.

When I'm online and using social media, a wealth of information about 3
my interests and routines is collected behind the scenes. I employ an add-on
on my browser that blocks companies from tracking my searches and visits. In
just one recent month, it reported blocking nearly 16,000 separate attempts to
access my data online.

I'm monitored offline, too. Anytime I use a reward card at a supermarket, 4
department store, or other retail outlet, my purchase is recorded, and the data
either sold to other marketers or used to predict my future purchases and guide
me to make them in that store. Department store tracking based on purchase
records can even conclude that a woman is pregnant and roughly when she is due.

My own devices report on me. I carry an iPhone, which tracks and records 5
my every movement. This will help me find my phone if I ever lose it (I haven't
yet), but it also provides Apple with a treasure trove of data about my daily habits.

Data on any call I place or email I send may be collected by the National 6
Security Agency. Recent news reports have revealed that the federal intelligence arm may be collecting metadata on phone and Internet traffic—when
Americans communicate and with whom, if not the actual content of those
communications. As Barton Gellman, Pulitzer Prize–winning intelligence
reporter for the *Washington Post*, said during a recent panel discussion, it's
not that the NSA knows everything about everyone, but that "it *wants* to be
able to know anything about anybody."

Thirty years after 1984, Big Brother is here. He's everywhere. In many 7
cases, we've invited him in. So the question we have to ask now is, How does
this constant surveillance affect us and what, if anything, can we do about it?

"Get Over It."

There's no question our privacy has been eroded with the help of technology. 8
There's also little question that those most responsible aren't much inclined to
retreat. As Scott McNealy, cofounder of Sun Microsystems, famously said:
"You have zero privacy anyway. Get over it."

Privacy is an intangible asset. If we never think about it, we may not realize it's gone. Does it still matter? Elias Aboujaoude, a professor of psychiatry at Stanford University and the author of *Virtually You: The Dangerous Powers of the E-Personality*, insists that it does. "We cannot afford to just 'get over it,' for nothing short of our self-custody seems to be at stake," he says. "At its heart, this is about our psychological autonomy and the maintenance of some semblance of control over the various little details that make us us."

"Does it still matter?"   9

In the modern surveillance environment, with so much personal information accessible by others—especially those with whom we have not chosen to share that information—our sense of self is threatened, as is our ability to manage the impression others have of us, says Ian Brown, senior research fellow at the Oxford Internet Institute.   10

If people treat us differently based on what they have discovered online, if the volume of data available about us eradicates our ability to make a first impression on a date or a job interview, the result, Brown believes, is reduced trust, increased conformity, and even diminished civic participation. The impact can be especially powerful when we know that our information was collected and shared without our consent.   11

To be sure, we are responsible for much of this. We're active participants in creating our surveillance record. Along with all of the personal information we voluntarily, often eagerly, share on social networks and shopping sites— and few of us take advantage of software or strategies to limit our digital footprint—we collectively upload 144,000 hours of video footage a day to You-Tube. And with tech enthusiasts trumpeting personal drones as the next hot item, we may soon be equipped to photograph ourselves and, just as easily, our neighbors, from above.   12

Most of us try to curate the public identities we broadcast—not only through the way we dress and speak in public, but also in how we portray ourselves on social-media platforms. The problem arises when we become conscious that uninvited observers are also tuning in. "The most fundamental impact surveillance has on identity," Brown says, "is that it reduces individuals' control over the information they disclose about their attributes in different social contexts, often to such powerful actors as the state or multinational corporations." When we discover that such entities—and third parties to which our information may be sold or shared—make decisions about us based on that data, our sense of self can be altered.   13

The Right to Be Forgotten

There are existential threats to our psyches in a world where nothing we do can be forgotten, believes Viktor Mayer-Schönberger, professor of Internet governance and regulation at the Oxford Internet Institute. His book, *Delete: The Virtue of Forgetting in the Digital Age*, relates the experiences of people whose lives were negatively affected because of information available about them online.   14

In 2006, for example, psychotherapist Andrew Feldmar drove from his   15
Vancouver home to pick up a friend flying in to Seattle. At the United States
border, which Feldmar had crossed scores of times, a guard decided to do an
Internet search on him. The query returned an article Feldmar had written for
an academic journal five years earlier, in which he revealed that he'd taken
LSD in the 1960s. The guard held Feldmar for four hours, fingerprinted him,
and asked him to sign a statement that he had taken drugs almost 40 years
earlier. He was barred from entry into the U.S.

Aboujaoude relates the story of "Rob," a nurse in a public hospital emer-   16
gency room chronically short on staff. His willingness to fill in when the ER
needed extra hands led to significant overtime pay. When a website published
an "exposé" of seemingly overpaid public employees, Rob's name and salary
were posted as an example. He was then hounded by hate mail—both paper
and electronic. People called his house, and his daughter was harassed at
school. Eventually the stress and constant criticism made him feel as if he were
becoming paranoid and led him to Aboujaoude as a therapy patient.

The ability to forget past events, Mayer-Schönberger says, or at least to let   17
them recede in our minds, is critical for decision making. Psychologists often
note that our ability to forget is a valuable safety valve. As we naturally forget
things over time, we can move on and make future choices without difficult or
embarrassing episodes clouding our outlook. But when our decisions are tan-
gled up in the perfect memory of the Internet—when we must factor in the
effect of our online footprint before every new step—"we may lose a fundamental human capacity: to live and act firmly in the present," he says.

The result can be demoralizing and even paranoia-inducing. Lacking the   18
power to control what, when, and with whom we share, Mayer-Schönberger
explains, our sense of self may be diminished, leading to self-doubt internally
and self-censorship externally, as we begin to fixate on what others will think
about every potentially public action and thought, now and in the future.

Under normal circumstances, the passage of time allows us to shape our nar-   19
rative, cutting out or minimizing less important (or more embarrassing) details to
form a more positive impression. When we can't put the past behind us, it can
affect our behavior and intrude on our judgment. Instead of making decisions
fully in the present, we make them while weighed down by every detail of our past.

The effects are not trivial. A range of people, from a long-reformed crimi-   20
nal seeking a fresh slate to a sober former college party girl in the job market,
can find that the omnipresence of public
records and posted photos permanently
holds them back. At its worst, these
weights can inhibit one's desire to
change. If we can never erase the record
of one mistake we made long ago, if we're
convinced it will only continue to hinder

> "With easily accessible digital reminders, bygones cannot be bygones."

our progress, what motivation do we have to become anyone different from
the person who made that mistake? For that matter, why bother moving

beyond conflicts with others if the sources of those disputes remain current online? With easily accessible digital reminders, bygones cannot be bygones. It's no accident that the most successful legal campaign yet against permanent digital records hinges on "the right to be forgotten."

A Spanish lawyer, Mario Costeja González, sued Google over search results that prominently returned a long-ago news article detailing a government order that he sell his home to cover unpaid debts. The European Court of Justice ruled in his favor, asserting, based on an older legal concept allowing ex-convicts to object to the publication of information related to their crimes, that each of us has the right to be forgotten. Even if the information about the man's foreclosure is true, the court ruled, it is "irrelevant, or no longer relevant," and should be blocked from Google's (and other browsers') searches. 21

Google is now working to implement a means for European users to request that certain information be removed from their searches, a process it is finding to be more complicated than many observers had imagined. No similar verdict has been handed down in the U.S., and privacy experts believe that Congress is unlikely to take up the issue anytime soon. 22

Do Cameras Make Us More Honorable, or Just Paranoid?

Trust is perennially strained in our workplaces, where more employees than ever are being overseen via cameras, recorded phone calls, location tracking, and email monitoring. Studies dating back two decades have consistently found that employees who were aware that they were being surveilled found their working conditions more stressful and reported higher levels of anxiety, anger, and depression. More recent research indicates that, whatever productivity benefits management hopes to realize, increased surveillance on the office floor leads to poorer performance, tied to a feeling of loss of control as well as to lower job satisfaction. 23

Outside the workplace, we expect more freedom and wider opportunity to defend our privacy. But even as we become more savvy about online tracking, we're beginning to realize just how little we can do about so-called "passive" surveillance—the cameras recording our movements as we go about our business—especially because so much of this observation is covert. The visual range of surveillance cameras has expanded even as their physical size has shrunk, and as satellites and drones become more accurate from increasing distances, social scientists have begun to explore how near-constant surveillance, at least in the public sphere, affects our behavior. The research so far identifies both concerns and potential benefits. We tend, for example, to be more cooperative and generous when we suspect someone is watching—a recent Dutch study found that people were more likely to intervene when witnessing a (staged) crime if they knew they were being watched, either by others or by a camera. But we don't become more generous of spirit. Pierrick Bourrat, a graduate student at the University of Sydney, and cognitive scientist Nicolas Baumard of the École Normale Supérieure in Paris, recently published a study on how we judge other people's bad behavior. They found that when subjects believed they were being watched, they rated others' actions more severely. A possible 24 explanation: When we think we're being observed, we adjust our behavior to project an image of moral uprightness through harsher-than-usual judgment of others.

But adjusting our behavior in the presence of cameras to project an 25 image aligned with presumed social norms can have a downside. The Oxford Internet Institute's Brown sees a cooling effect on public discourse, because when people think they're being watched, they may behave, consciously or not, in ways that comply with what they presume governmental or other observers want. That doesn't mean we trust the watchers. A recent Gallup poll found that only 12 percent of Americans have "a lot of trust" that the government will keep their personal information secure; we trust banks three times as much.

When Users Strike Back

What would happen if we really tried to root out all of the surveillance in our life 26 and took action to erase ourselves from it? We think such knowledge would equal power, but it may just bring on paranoia. Pulitzer Prize–winning investigative journalist Julia Angwin tried for a year to prevent her life from being monitored. She used a disposable cell phone. She installed encryption software on her email accounts. She even developed a fake identity ("Ida Tarbell") to prevent her online and commercial activities from being tied to her true self.

Angwin detailed these efforts in her book, *Dragnet Nation*, which, while 27 ultimately hopeful, relates a draining journey during which she lost trust in nearly every institution that holds her data. Even with her resources and single-mindedness, Angwin could achieve only partial success: Her past personal data, after all, were stored in bits and pieces by hundreds of brokers that traffic in information, and she had no means of turning back the clock.

The efforts also affected her worldview: "I wasn't happy with the toll that 28 my countersurveillance techniques had taken on my psyche. The more I learned about who was watching me, the more paranoid I became. By the end of my experiment, I was refusing to have digital conversations with my close friends without encryption. I began using my fake name for increasingly trivial transactions; a friend was shocked when we took a yoga class together and I casually registered as Ida Tarbell."

The Next Level

Modern surveillance does have some clear benefits. Cameras in public spaces 29 help the authorities detect crime and catch perpetrators, though they catch us in the dragnet as well. Cell phone tracking and networked late-model cars allow us to be found if we become lost or injured, and mapping apps are incredibly useful for directing us where we want to go. These features save lives—but all of them constantly transmit our location and generate a precisely detailed record of our movements. Our social media history helps providers put the people and content we prefer front and center when we log on, and our online searches and purchase records allow marketers to offer us discounts at the places we shop most, all the while collecting data on our personal preferences and quirks. Given the difficulty of completely avoiding the monitoring, it may be somewhat reassuring to acknowledge this tradeoff.

Laura Brandimarte of Carnegie Mellon University and her colleagues have 30 studied people's willingness to disclose personal information. They found that when entities give people more control over the publication of their information, people disclose more about themselves—even if it is also clear that the information will be accessed and seen by others more often than it currently is.

Their work demonstrates the concept of illusion of control. In many situa- 31 tions, we tend to overestimate the control we have over events, especially when we get cues that our actions matter. The risk to our private information comes not just from what we've shared but from how much of it is sold or made available to others. And yet when we feel that we have been given more control over our information's dissemination, our privacy concerns decrease and our disclosure increases, even though that apparent control does not actually diminish the possibility that our data will be shared. "The control people perceive over the publication of personal information makes them pay less attention to the lack of control they have over access by others," Brandimarte says.

In other words, we are simply not very sophisticated when it comes to 32 making choices about what to share.

When it comes to privacy-protection, the first issue for social-media users 33 to grapple with is inertia: According to a range of surveys of U.S. Facebook users, for example, as many as 25 percent have never checked or adjusted their privacy settings to impose even the most basic restriction on their postings: not making them public.

There is a growing availability of privacy fixes for homes, cell phones, and 34 computers. Whether they will be able to keep up with tracking mechanisms is unclear. But evidence suggests that even if they work as advertised, we may not be savvy enough to use them.

So we have limited options to protect our privacy, and few of us take 35 advantage even of those. What's the ultimate cost? Aboujaoude argues that our need for privacy and true autonomy is rooted in the concept of individuation, the process by which we develop and maintain an independent identity. It's a crucial journey that begins in childhood, as we learn to separate our own identity from that of our parents, and continues through adulthood.

Many psychologists emphasize that maintaining self-identity requires a 36 separation from others, and Aboujaoude believes that, in today's environment, control over personal information is a critical piece of the process. "You are a psychologically autonomous individual," he says, "if you have the option to keep your person to yourself and dole out the pieces as you see fit."

And who do we become if we don't have that option? We may soon find out. 37

I Married a P.I.

When we worry about who might be watching us, we tend to focus our con- 38 cern on Facebook, the NSA, or marketers. But we may want to consider our own partners as well.

Sue Simring, an associate professor at Columbia University's School of   39
Social Work and a psychotherapist with four decades of experience working
primarily with couples, says the ease with which people can now monitor each
other has radically changed her work. "It used to be that, unless you literally
discovered them [in flagrante], there was no way to know for sure that people
were having an affair," she says.

No more.   40

When spouses stray today, their digital trail inevitably provides clues for   41
the amateur sleuth with whom they share a bed. Simring describes one case in
which a man had carried on an affair for years while traveling for work. He
managed to keep it secret until a technical glitch started sending copies of his
text messages to his wife's iPad.

But the easy availability of tools to track a partner can cut both ways.   42
In the case of another couple that Simring worked with, the husband was
convinced that his wife was having an affair. Determined to catch her, he
undertook increasingly complex and invasive surveillance efforts, eventually monitoring all of her communications and installing spy cameras in
their home to catch her in the act. The more he surveilled, the more his
paranoia grew. It turned out that the wife was not having an affair, but
because of the trauma the husband's surveillance caused her, she ended the
marriage.

This essay was posted to the online newspaper *The Start* on February 27, 2015.

MY CREEPY INSTAGRAM
MAP KNOWS WHERE I LIVE

CRAIG DESSON

U.S. Congressman Aaron Schock's reputation took a hit this week when the   1
Associated Press used geo-location data from his Instagram account to show
how he was flying on private jets provided by campaign donors, expensed
massages, and bought Katy Perry tickets for his interns.

The reporters involved explained that "the AP extracted location data   2
associated with each image, then correlated it with flight records showing air-
port stopovers and expenses later billed for air travel against Schock's office
and campaign records."

To track somebody on Instagram the way AP did for the Schock story   3
isn't difficult. There is a program called Creepy that will create a Google map
showing where you've been, based on what you've shared on Instagram, Twitter,
and Flickr.

I ran Creepy on my own Instagram account and found it wouldn't be   4
hard for a stranger to figure out where I live in the Annex.

This is the map the program made about my account, and with a bit of 5 deductive logic it's clear I live just north of Bloor and Spadina.

The photos taken around Front St. are all interiors of offices, because that's 6 where I've worked for the past two and a half years. The photos taken along major streets such as King and Bloor portray me hanging out with friends.

Then there is the funny collection of dots north of Bloor in the Annex 7 that link to Instagram photos of an apartment's interior.

You don't need to be Sherlock Holmes to guess that's my home. 8

It's true that 20 years ago, a phonebook might have led a stranger to my 9 home address. But I would at least know that I had a listed number. The trouble with Instagram tracking is that most users have no idea their photo-sharing app is also building a detailed history of where they work and live.

If Aaron Schock, a congressman with paid communications people, 10 couldn't figure this out, then it's likely most members of the public have no idea this is going on.

USA Today posted this article to its website on March 27, 2014.

IS ONLINE DATING SAFE?

SHARON JAYSON

Change may be coming to the rapidly growing dating industry as concern 1 mounts about the privacy and safety of all online and mobile users.

Sen. Al Franken, D-Minn., introduced legislation Thursday requiring 2 companies to get customers' permission before collecting location data off their mobile devices and sharing it with others.

It's a move that would greatly affect dating websites and apps. As mobile dating proliferates, the focus no longer is just on daters leery of scams or sexual predators, but on keeping their locations confidential. 3

"This stuff is advancing at a faster and faster rate, and we've got to try and catch up," Franken says. "This is about Americans' right to privacy and one of the most private things is your location." 4

> "As mobile dating proliferates, the focus no longer is just on daters leery of scams or sexual predators, but on keeping their locations confidential."

Illinois, New York, New Jersey, and Texas have laws that require Internet 5 dating sites to disclose whether they conduct criminal background checks on users and to offer advice on keeping safe.

"I see more regulation about companies stating what kind of information 6 they actually use and more about their specific operation(s)," says analyst Jeremy Edwards, who authored a report on the industry last fall for IBIS-World, a Santa Monica, Calif.–based market research company. "I expect them to have to be more explicit in what they do with their data and what they require of users."

According to a Pew Research Center report in October, 11% of American 7 adults—and 38% of those currently "single and looking" for a partner—say they've used online dating sites or mobile dating apps.

"We entrust some incredibly sensitive information to online dating sites," 8 says Rainey Reitman of the San Francisco, Calif.–based Electronic Frontier Foundation, a nonprofit that advocates for user privacy amid technology development. "People don't realize how much information they're exposing even by doing something as slight as uploading a photograph."

He adds, "Many online apps are very cavalier about collecting that 9 information and perhaps exposing it in a way that would make you uncomfortable."

Dating services eHarmony, Match.com, and Spark Networks and 10 ChristianMingle signed an agreement in 2012 with the California attorney general's office to protect customers with online safety tools. These include companies checking subscribers against national sex offender registries and providing a rapid abuse reporting system for members.

However, cyberdating expert Julie Spira of Los Angeles says such reports 11 are sometimes little more than revenge.

"When people get reported, sometimes it's because they got jilted," she 12 says. "How do you quantify when someone feels rejected and pushes the report button, and when somebody really feels scared?"

Match.com, which has 1.9 million paid subscribers, has been screening all 13 subscribers against sexual offender registries since the summer of 2011, according to spokesman Matthew Traub. Earlier that year, a woman sued the dating site saying she was assaulted by someone she met through it.

Edwards believes dating sites are doing what they can to help users 14 be safe.

"It's difficult for these companies to do much else than provide information 15 and tips," he says. "Meeting someone through one of these websites does not present any greater risk than meeting someone in a bar or any other setting. There's no real added risk because you don't know who anyone is when you meet them for the first time."

⊘ EXERCISE 8.6

Read the blog post below and then answer the questions on page 327.

Read the blog post below and then answer the questions on page 327.

This article first appeared on Mashable.com on February 6, 2012.

SHOULD ATHLETES HAVE SOCIAL MEDIA PRIVACY? ONE BILL SAYS YES

SAM LAIRD

Should universities be allowed to force student athletes to have their Facebook and Twitter accounts monitored by coaches and administrators? 1

No, says a bill recently introduced into the Maryland state legislature. 2

The bill would prohibit institutions "from requiring a student or an applicant for admission to provide access to a personal account or service through an electronic communications device"—by sharing usernames, passwords, or unblocking private accounts, for example. 3

Introduced on Thursday, Maryland's Senate Bill 434 would apply to all students but particularly impact college sports. Student-athletes' social media accounts are frequently monitored by authority figures for instances of indecency or impropriety, especially in high-profile sports like football and men's basketball. 4

> "Student-athletes' social media accounts are frequently monitored. . . ."

In one example, a top football recruit reportedly put his scholarship hopes in jeopardy last month after a series of inappropriate tweets. 5

The bill's authors say that it is one of the first in the country to take on the issue of student privacy in the social media age, according to the *New York Times*. 6

Bradley Shear is a Maryland lawyer whose work frequently involves sports and social media. In a recent post to his blog, Shear explained his support for Senate Bill 434 and a similar piece of legislation that would further extend students' right to privacy on social media. 7

"Schools that require their students to turn over their social media user names and/or content are acting as though they are based in China and not in the United States," Shear wrote. 8

But legally increasing student-athletes' option to social media privacy could also help shield the schools themselves from potential lawsuits. 9

On his blog, Shear uses the example of Yardley Love, a former University of Virginia women's lacrosse player who was allegedly murdered by her ex-boyfriend, who played for the men's lacrosse team. 10

If the university was monitoring the lacrosse teams' social media accounts 11 and missed anything that could have indicated potential violence, it "may have had significant legal liability for negligent social media monitoring because it failed to protect Love," Shear wrote.

On the other hand, if the school was only monitoring the accounts of its 12 higher-profile football and basketball players, Shear wrote, then that could have been considered discrimination and the university "may have been sued for not monitoring the electronic content of all of its students."

Do you think universities should be allowed to force their athletes into 13 allowing coaches and administrators to monitor their Facebook and Twitter accounts?

Questions

1. What steps would you take to determine whether Laird's information is accurate?

2. How could you determine whether Laird is respected in his field?

3. Is Laird's blog written for an audience that is knowledgeable about his subject? How can you tell?

4. Do you think this blog post is a suitable research source? Why or why not?

5. This blog post was written in 2012. Do you think it is still relevant today? Why or why not?

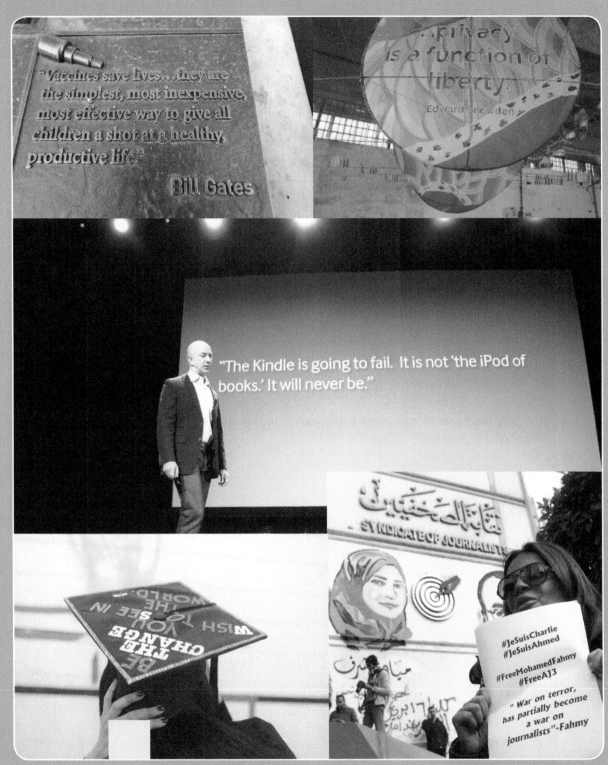

Summarizing, Paraphrasing, Quoting, and Synthesizing Sources

AT ISSUE

Is Technology a Serious Threat to Our Privacy? (continued)

In Chapter 8, you learned how to evaluate sources for an essay about the dangers of posting personal information online. In this chapter, you will learn how to take notes from various sources that address this issue.

As you saw in Chapter 8, before you can decide which material to use to support your arguments, you need to evaluate a variety of potential sources. After you decide which sources you will use, you can begin thinking about where you might use each source and about how to integrate information from the sources you have chosen into your essay in the form of *summary, paraphrase,* and *quotation.* When you actually write your argument, you will *synthesize* the sources into your paper, blending them with your own ideas and interpretations (as the student writer did when she wrote the MLA research paper in Chapter 10).

Summarizing Sources

A **summary** restates the main idea of a passage (or even of an entire book or article) in concise terms. Because a summary does not cover the examples or explanations in the source, and because it omits the original source's rhetorical strategies and stylistic characteristics, it is always much shorter than the original. Usually, in fact, it consists of just a sentence or two.

WHEN TO SUMMARIZE

Summarize when you want to give readers a general sense of a passage's main idea or a source's position on an issue.

When you summarize information, you do not include your own opinions, but you do use your own words and phrasing, not those of your source. If you want to use a particularly distinctive word or phrase from your source, you may do so—but you must always place such words in quotation marks and **document** them. If you do not, you will be committing **plagiarism**. (See Chapter 10 for information on documenting sources; see Chapter 11 for information on using sources responsibly.)

The following paragraph appeared in a newspaper opinion essay.

ORIGINAL SOURCE

When everyone has a blog, a MySpace page, or Facebook entry, everyone is a publisher. When everyone has a cellphone with a camera in it, everyone is a paparazzo. When everyone can upload video on YouTube, everyone is a filmmaker. When everyone is a publisher, paparazzo, or filmmaker, everyone else is a public figure. We're all public figures now. The blogosphere has made the global discussion so much richer—and each of us so much more transparent. ("The Whole World Is Watching," Thomas L. Friedman, *New York Times*, June 27, 2007, p. 23)

The following effective summary conveys a general but accurate sense of the original paragraph without using the source's phrasing or including the writer's own opinions. (One distinctive and hard-to-reword phrase is placed in quotation marks.) Parenthetical documentation indicates the source of the material.

EFFECTIVE SUMMARY

The popularity of blogs, social-networking sites, cell phone cameras, and YouTube has enhanced the "global discussion" but made it very hard for people to remain anonymous (Friedman 23).

Notice that this one-sentence summary is much shorter than the original passage and that it does not include all the original's examples. Still, it accurately communicates a general sense of the source's main idea.

The following summary is not acceptable. Not only does it express the student writer's opinion, but it also uses the source's exact words without putting them in quotation marks or providing documentation. (This constitutes plagiarism.)

UNACCEPTABLE SUMMARY

It seems to me that blogs, social-networking sites, cell phone cameras, and YouTube are everywhere, and what this means is that we're all public figures now.

SUMMARIZING SOURCES

Do

- Convey the main idea of the original passage.

- Be concise.

- Use your own original words and phrasing.

- Place any words borrowed from your source in quotation marks.

- Include documentation.

Do not

- Include your own analysis or opinions.

- Include digressions.

- Argue with your source.

- Use your source's syntax or phrasing (unless you are quoting).

⬦ EXERCISE 9.1

Write a two-sentence summary of the following passage. Then, edit your summary so that it is only one sentence long. Be sure your summary conveys the main idea of the original passage and includes proper documentation.

We're living at a time when attention is the new currency: with hundreds of TV channels, billions of Web sites, podcasts, radio shows, music downloads, and social networking, our attention is more fragmented than ever before.

Those who insert themselves into as many channels as possible look set to capture the most value. They'll be the richest, the most successful, the most connected, capable, and influential among us. We're all publishers now, and the more we publish, the more valuable connections we'll make.

Twitter, Facebook, Flickr, Foursquare, Fitbit, and the SenseCam give us a simple choice: participate or fade into a lonely obscurity. (Pete Cashmore, "Privacy Is Dead, and Social Media Hold Smoking Gun," *CNN.com*, October 28, 2009)

Paraphrasing Sources

A **paraphrase** is different from a summary. While a summary gives a general overview of the original, a paraphrase presents the source's ideas in detail, including its main idea, its key supporting points, and perhaps even its examples. For this reason, a paraphrase is longer than a summary. In fact, it may be as long as the original.

WHEN TO PARAPHRASE

Paraphrase when you want to communicate the key points discussed in a source—particularly a complex or complicated passage—in clear, accessible language.

Like a summary, a paraphrase uses your own words and phrasing, not the language and syntax of the original. Any words or phrases from your source must be placed in quotation marks. When you paraphrase, you may not always follow the order of the original source's ideas, but you should try to convey the writer's emphasis and most important points.

The following paragraph is from an editorial that appeared in a student newspaper.

ORIGINAL SOURCE

Additionally, as graduates retain their Facebook accounts, employers are increasingly able to use Facebook as an evaluation tool when making hiring decisions. Just as companies sometimes incorporate social functions into their interview process to see if potential hires can handle themselves responsibly, they may also check out a student's Facebook account to see how the student chooses to present him or herself. This may seem shady and underhanded, but one must understand that social networks are not anonymous; whatever one chooses to post will be available to all. Even if someone goes to great pains to keep an employer-friendly profile, his or her friends may still tag pictures of him or her which will be available to whoever wants to see them. Not only can unexpected Facebook members get information by viewing one's profile, but a user's personal information can also leak out by merely registering for the service. Both the user agreement and the privacy policy indicate that Facebook can give information to third parties and can supplement its data with information from newspapers, blogs, and instant messages. ("Beware What You Post on Facebook," *The Tiger*, Clemson University, August 4, 2006)

The following paraphrase reflects the original paragraph's emphasis and clearly communicates its key points.

EFFECTIVE PARAPHRASE

Because students keep their accounts at social-networking sites after they graduate, potential employers can use the information they find there to help them evaluate candidates' qualifications. This process is comparable to the way a company might evaluate an applicant in person in a social situation. Some people may see the practice of employers checking applicants' Facebook pages as "shady and underhanded," but these sites are not intended to be anonymous or private. For example, a person may try to maintain a profile that will be appropriate for employers, but friends may post inappropriate pictures. Also, people can reveal personal information not only in profiles but also simply by registering with Facebook. Finally, as Facebook states in its membership information, it can supply information to others as well as provide data from other sources. ("Beware")

Notice that this paraphrase includes many of the details presented in the original passage and quotes a distinctive phrase, but its style and sentence structure are different from those of the original.

The following paraphrase is not acceptable because its phrasing and sentence structure are too close to the original. It also borrows words and phrases from the source without attribution or documentation.

UNACCEPTABLE PARAPHRASE

As more and more college graduates keep their Facebook accounts, employers are increasingly able to use them as evaluation tools when they decide whom to hire. Companies sometimes set up social functions during the interview process to see how potential hires handle themselves; in the same way, they can consult a Facebook page to see how an applicant presents himself or herself. This may seem underhanded, but after all, Facebook is not anonymous; its information is available to all. Many people try to keep their profiles employer friendly, but their friends sometimes tag pictures of them that employers will be able to see. Besides, students' personal information is available not just on their profiles but also in the form they fill out when they register. Finally, according to their user agreement and their privacy policy, Facebook can give information to third parties and also add data from other sources.

PARAPHRASING SOURCES

Do

- Convey the source's ideas fully and accurately.
- Use your own words and phrasing.
- Convey the emphasis of the original.
- Simplify and clarify complex language and syntax.
- Put any words borrowed from the source in quotation marks.
- Include documentation.

Do not

- Use the exact words or phrasing of your source (unless you are quoting).
- Include your own analysis or opinions.
- Argue with or contradict your source.
- Wander from the topic of the source.

⊘ EXERCISE 9.2

Write a paraphrase of the passage you summarized in Exercise 9.1. How is your paraphrase different from your summary?

⊘ EXERCISE 9.3

The following paragraph is from the same Clemson University student newspaper article that was excerpted on pages 332–333. Read the paragraph, and then write a paraphrase that communicates its key ideas. Before you begin, circle any distinctive words and phrases that might be difficult to paraphrase, and consider whether you should quote them. Be sure to include documentation.

> All these factors make clear the importance of two principles: Responsibility and caveat emptor. First, people should be responsible about how they portray themselves and their friends, and employers, authorities, and the owners must approach this information responsibly and fairly. Second, "let the buyer beware" applies to all parties involved. Facebook users need to understand the potential consequences of the information they share, and outside viewers need to understand that the material on Facebook is often only a humorous, lighthearted presentation of one aspect of a person. Facebook is an incredibly valuable communications tool that will link the college generation more tightly than any before it, but users have to understand that, like anything good in life, they have to be aware of the downsides.

Quoting Sources

When you **quote** words from a source, you need to quote accurately—that is, every word and every punctuation mark in your quotation must match the source *exactly*. You also need to be sure that your quotation conveys the meaning its author intended and that you are not distorting the meaning by **quoting out of context** or by omitting an essential part of the passage you are quoting.

WHEN TO QUOTE

Quote a source's words only in the following situations:

- Quote when your source's words are distinctive or memorable.

- Quote when your source's words are so direct and concise that a paraphrase would be awkward or wordy.

- Quote when your source's words add authority or credibility to your argument (for example, when your source is a well-known expert on your topic).

- Quote an opposing point when you will go on to refute it.

Remember, quoting from a source adds interest to your paper—but only when the writer's words are compelling. Too many quotations—especially long quotations—distract readers and make it difficult for them to follow your discussion. Quote only when you must. If you include too many quotations, your paper will be a patchwork of other people's words, not an original, unified whole.

QUOTING SOURCES

Do

- Enclose borrowed words in quotation marks.
- Quote accurately.
- Include documentation.

Do not

- Quote out of context.
- Distort the source's meaning.
- Include too many quotations.

○ EXERCISE 9.4

Read the following paragraphs from a newspaper column that appeared in the *Calgary Herald*. (The full text of this column appears in Exercise 9.5.) If you were going to use these paragraphs as source material for an argumentative essay, which particular words or phrases do you think you might want to quote? Why?

> How do users not know that a server somewhere is recording where you are, what you ate for lunch, how often you post photos of your puppy, what you bought at the supermarket for dinner, the route you drove home, and what movie you watched before you went to bed?
>
> So why do we act so surprised and shocked about the invasion of the privacy we so willingly relinquish, and the personal information we forfeit that allows its captors to sell us products, convict us in court, get us fired, or produce more of the same banality that keeps us logging on?
>
> We, all of us, are digital captives. (Shelley Fralic, "Don't Fall for the Myths about Online Privacy," *Calgary Herald*, October 17, 2015.)

○ EXERCISE 9.5

Read the newspaper column that follows, and highlight it to identify its most important ideas. (For information on highlighting, see Chapter 2.) Then, write a summary of one paragraph and a paraphrase of another paragraph. Assume that this column is a source for an essay you are writing on the topic, "Is Technology a Serious Threat to Our Privacy?" Be sure to include documentation.

This column is from the *Calgary Herald*, where it appeared on October 17, 2015.

DON'T FALL FOR THE MYTHS ABOUT ONLINE PRIVACY

SHELLEY FRALIC

If you are a Facebooker—and there are 1.5 billion of us on the planet, so chances are about one in five that you are—you will have noticed yet another round of posts that suggest in quasi-legalese that you can somehow block the social network's invasion of your privacy.   1

This latest hoax cautions that Facebook will now charge $5.99 to keep privacy settings private, and the copyright protection disclaimers making the   2 rounds this week typically begin like this: "As of date-and-time here, I do not give Facebook or any entities associated with Facebook permission to use my pictures, information, or posts, both past and future. By this statement, I give notice to Facebook it is strictly forbidden to disclose, copy, distribute, or take any other action against me based on this profile and/or its contents. The content of this profile is private and confidential information."

Well, no, it's not.   3

This is a new-age version of an old story, oft-told. No one reads the   4
fine print. Not on contracts, not on insurance policies, and not on social media sites that are willingly and globally embraced by perpetually plugged-in gossipmongers, lonely hearts, news junkies, inveterate sharers, and selfie addicts.

Facebook's fine print, like that of many Internet portals, is specific and   5
offers users a variety of self-selected "privacy" options.

But to think that any interaction with it, and its ilk, is truly private is   6
beyond absurd.

How can there still be people out there who still don't get that Netflix and   7
Facebook, Instagram and Twitter, Google and Tinder and pretty much every keystroke or communication we register on a smartphone or laptop, not to mention a loyalty card and the GPS in your car, are constantly tracking and sifting and collating everything we do?

How do users not know that a server somewhere is recording where you   8
are, what you ate for lunch, how often you post photos of your puppy, what you bought at the supermarket for dinner, the route you drove home, and what movie you watched before you went to bed?

So why do we act so surprised and shocked about the invasion of the pri-   9
vacy we so willingly relinquish, and the personal information we forfeit that allows its captors to sell us products, convict us in court, get us fired, or produce more of the same banality that keeps us logging on?

We, all of us, are digital captives.   10

But do we have to be so stupid about it?   11

And the bigger question is this: If we, the adults who should know better,   12
don't get it, what are we teaching our kids about the impact and repercussions of their online lives? What are they learning about the voluntary and wholesale abandonment of their privacy? What are we teaching them about "sharing" with strangers?

Worried about future generations not reading books or learning how to   13
spell properly or write in cursive? Worry more, folks, that Internet ignorance is the new illiteracy.

Meantime, when another Facebook disclaimer pops up with a plea to   14
share, consider this clever post from a user who actually read the fine print:

"I hereby give my permission to the police, the NSA, the FBI and CIA,   15
the Swiss Guard, the Priory of Scion, the inhabitants of Middle Earth,

Agents Mulder and Scully, the Goonies, ALL the Storm Troopers and Darth Vader, the Mad Hatter, Chuck Norris, S.H.I.E.L.D., The Avengers, The Illuminati . . . to view all the amazing and interesting things I publish on Facebook. I'm aware that my privacy ended the very day that I created a profile on Facebook."

Yes, it did.   16

Working Source Material into Your Argument

When you use source material in an argumentative essay, your goal is to integrate the material smoothly into your discussion, blending summary, paraphrase, and quotation with your own ideas.

To help readers follow your discussion, you need to indicate the source of each piece of information clearly and distinguish your own ideas from those of your sources. Never simply drop source material into your discussion. Whenever possible, introduce quotations, paraphrases, and summaries with an **identifying tag** (sometimes called a *signal phrase*), a phrase that identifies the source, and always follow them with documentation. This practice helps readers identify the boundaries between your own ideas and those of your sources.

It is also important that you include clues to help readers understand why you are using a particular source and what the exact relationship is between your source material and your own ideas. For example, you may be using a source to support a point you are making or to disagree with another source.

Using Identifying Tags

Using identifying tags to introduce your summaries, paraphrases, or quotations will help you to accomplish the goals discussed above (and help you to avoid accidental plagiarism).

> **SUMMARY WITH IDENTIFYING TAG**
> <u>According to Thomas L. Friedman</u>, the popularity of blogs, social-networking sites, cell phone cameras, and YouTube has enhanced the "global discussion" but made it hard for people to remain anonymous (23).

Note that you do not always have to place the identifying tag at the beginning of the summarized, paraphrased, or quoted material. You can also place it in the middle or at the end:

IDENTIFYING TAG AT THE BEGINNING

<u>Thomas L. Friedman notes</u> that the popularity of blogs, social-networking sites, cell phone cameras, and YouTube has enhanced the "global discussion" but made it hard for people to remain anonymous (23).

IDENTIFYING TAG IN THE MIDDLE

The popularity of blogs, social-networking sites, cell phone cameras, and YouTube, <u>Thomas L. Friedman observes</u>, has enhanced the "global discussion" but made it hard for people to remain anonymous (23).

IDENTIFYING TAG AT THE END

The popularity of blogs, social-networking sites, cell phone cameras, and YouTube has enhanced the "global discussion" but made it hard for people to remain anonymous, <u>Thomas L. Friedman points out</u> (23).

TEMPLATES FOR USING IDENTIFYING TAGS

To avoid repeating phrases like *he says* in identifying tags, try using some of the following verbs to introduce your source material. (You can also use "According to . . . ," to introduce a source.)

For Summaries or Paraphrases

[Name of writer]	notes	acknowledges	proposes	that [summary or paraphrase].
The writer	suggests	believes	observes	
The article	explains	comments	warns	
The essay	reports	points out	predicts	
	implies	concludes	states	

For Quotations

As [name of writer]	notes,	acknowledges,	proposes,	"_____[quotation]_____."
As the writer	suggests,	believes,	observes,	
As the article	warns,	reports,	points out,	
As the essay	predicts,	implies,	concludes,	
	states,	explains,		

Working Quotations into Your Sentences

When you use quotations in your essays, you may need to edit them to provide context or to make them fit smoothly into your sentences. If you do edit a quotation, be careful not to distort the source's meaning.

Adding or Changing Words When you add or change words in a quotation, use **brackets** to indicate your edits.

ORIGINAL QUOTATION
"Twitter, Facebook, Flickr, FourSquare, Fitbit, and the SenseCam give us a simple choice: participate or fade into a lonely obscurity." (Cashmore)

WORDS ADDED FOR CLARIFICATION
As Cashmore observes, "Twitter, Flickr, FourSquare, Fitbit, and the SenseCam [as well as similar social-networking sites] give us a simple choice: participate or fade into a lonely obscurity."

ORIGINAL QUOTATION
"The blogosphere has made the global discussion so much richer—and each of us so much more transparent" (Friedman 23).

WORDS CHANGED TO MAKE VERB TENSE LOGICAL
As Thomas L. Friedman explains, increased access to cell phone cameras, YouTube, and the like continues to "[make] the global discussion so much richer—and each of us so much more transparent" (23).

Deleting Words When you delete words from a quotation, use **ellipses**—three spaced periods—to indicate your edits. However, never use ellipses to indicate a deletion at the beginning of a quotation.

ORIGINAL QUOTATION
"Just as companies sometimes incorporate social functions into their interview process to see if potential hires can handle themselves responsibly, they may also check out a student's Facebook account to see how the student chooses to present him or herself" ("Beware").

UNNECESSARY WORDS DELETED
"Just as companies sometimes incorporate social functions into their interview process, . . . they may also check out a student's Facebook account . . ." ("Beware").

DISTORTING QUOTATIONS

Be careful not to distort a source's meaning when you add, change, or delete words from a quotation. In the following example, the writer intentionally deletes material from the original quotation that would weaken his argument.

Original Quotation

"This incident is by no means an isolated one. Connecticut authorities are investigating reports that seven girls were sexually assaulted by older men they met on MySpace" ("Beware").

Distorted

"This incident is by no means an isolated one. [In fact,] seven girls were sexually assaulted by older men they met on MySpace" ("Beware").

⊙ EXERCISE 9.6

Look carefully at the quotations that accompany this chapter's opening images (p. 328). Select three quotations, and summarize each quotation in one sentence. Then, compose an original sentence that quotes each statement. Be sure to acknowledge each source in an identifying tag and to integrate the borrowed material smoothly into each sentence.

⊙ EXERCISE 9.7

Reread the summary you wrote for Exercise 9.1 and the paraphrase you wrote for Exercise 9.3. Add three different identifying tags to each, varying the verbs you use and the position of the tags. Then, check to make sure you have used correct parenthetical documentation. (If the author's name is included in the identifying tag, it should not also appear in the parenthetical citation.)

Synthesizing Sources

In a **synthesis**, you combine summary, paraphrase, and quotation from several sources with your own ideas to support an original conclusion. A synthesis sometimes identifies similarities and differences among ideas, indicating where sources agree and disagree and how they support or challenge one another's ideas. Transitional words and phrases identify points of similarity (*also*, *like*, *similarly*, and so on) or difference (*however*, *in contrast*, and so on). When you write a synthesis, you include identifying tags and parenthetical documentation to identify each piece of information you get from a source and to distinguish your sources' ideas from one another and from your own ideas.

The following effective synthesis is excerpted from the student paper in Chapter 10. Note how the synthesis blends information from three sources with the student's own ideas to support her point about how the Internet has affected people's concepts of "public" and "private."

EFFECTIVE SYNTHESIS

Student's original point

Paraphrase

Student's own ideas

Quotation

Student's evaluation of source

Quotation

Part of the problem is that the Internet has fundamentally altered our notions of "private" and "public" in ways that we are only just beginning to understand. As Shelley Fralic observes in "Don't Fall for the Myths about Online Privacy," Facebook's privacy options do not really protect its users' privacy. On sites like Facebook, people often reveal intimate details of their lives to hundreds—perhaps even thousands—of strangers. This situation is unprecedented and, at least for the foreseeable future, irreversible. As *New York Times* columnist Thomas L. Friedman observes, "When everyone has a blog, a MySpace page, or Facebook entry, everyone is a publisher. . . . When everyone is a publisher, paparazzo, or filmmaker, everyone else is a public figure." Given the public nature of the Internet, the suggestion that we should live our lives by the same rules we lived by twenty years ago simply does not make sense. As Friedman notes, in the Internet age, more and more of "what you say or do or write will end up as a digital fingerprint that never gets erased" (23).

Compare the effective synthesis above with the following unacceptable synthesis.

UNACCEPTABLE SYNTHESIS

"The sheer volume of personal information that people are publishing online—and the fact that some of it could remain visible permanently—is changing the nature of personal privacy." On sites like Facebook, people can reveal the most intimate details of their lives to millions of total strangers. This development is unprecedented and, at least for the foreseeable future, irreversible. "When everyone has a blog, a MySpace page, or Facebook entry, everyone is a publisher. . . . When everyone is a publisher, paparazzo, or filmmaker, everyone else is a public figure" (Friedman 23). Given the changes in our understanding of privacy and the essentially public nature of the Internet, the analogy that Hall makes between a MySpace post and a private conversation seems of limited use. In the Internet age, more and more of "what you say or do or write will end up as a digital fingerprint that never gets erased."

Unlike the effective synthesis, the unacceptable synthesis above does not begin with a topic sentence that states the point the source material in the paragraph will support. Instead, it opens with an out-of-context quotation whose source is not identified. This quotation could have been paraphrased—

its wording is not particularly memorable—and, more important, it should have been accompanied by documentation. (If source information is not provided, the writer is committing plagiarism even if the borrowed material is set in quotation marks.) The second quotation, although it includes parenthetical documentation (Friedman 23), is dropped into the paragraph without an identifying tag; the third quotation, also from the Friedman article, is not documented at all, making it appear to be from Hall. All in all, the paragraph is not a smoothly connected synthesis but a string of unconnected ideas. It does not use sources effectively and responsibly, and it does not cite them appropriately.

⊙ EXERCISE 9.8

Write a synthesis that builds on the paraphrase you wrote for Exercise 9.2. Add your own original ideas—examples and opinions—to the paraphrase, and also blend in information from one or two of the other sources that appear in this chapter. Use identifying tags and parenthetical documentation to introduce your sources and to distinguish your own ideas from ideas expressed in your sources.

Documenting Sources: MLA

When you are building an argument, you use sources for support. To acknowledge the material you borrow and to help readers evaluate your sources, you need to supply documentation. In other words, you need to tell readers where you found your information. If you use documentation responsibly, you will also avoid **plagiarism**, an ethical offense with serious consequences. (See Chapter 11 for more on plagiarism.)

WHY DOCUMENT SOURCES?

- To acknowledge the debt that you owe to your sources

- To demonstrate that you are familiar with the conventions of academic discourse

- To enable readers to judge the quality of your research

- To avoid plagiarism

- To make your argument more convincing

MLA documentation consists of two parts: **parenthetical references** in the text of your paper and a **works-cited list** at the end of the paper. (The references are keyed to the works-cited list.)

Using Parenthetical References

The basic parenthetical citation consists of the author's last name and a page number:

(Fielding 213)

If the author is referred to in the sentence, include only the page number in the parenthetical reference.

> According to environmental activist Brian Fielding, the number of species affected is much higher (213).

Here are some other situations you may encounter:

- When referring to a work by two authors, include both authors' names.

  > (Stange and Hogarth 53)

- When citing a work with no listed author, include a short version of the title.

  > ("Small Things" 21)

- When citing a source that is quoted in another source, indicate this by including the abbreviation *qtd. in.*

  > According to Kevin Kelly, this narrow approach is typical of the "hive mind" (qtd. in Doctorow 168).

- When citing two or more works by the same author, include a short title after the author's name.

  > (Anderson, *Long Tail* 47)

- If a source does not include page numbers, or if you are referring to the entire source rather than to a specific page, cite the author's name in the text of your paper rather than in a parenthetical reference.

You must document *all* information that is not **common knowledge**, whether you are summarizing, paraphrasing, or quoting. (See p. 374 for an explanation of common knowledge.) With direct quotations, include the parenthetical reference and a period *after* the closing quotation marks.

> According to Doctorow, this is "authorship without editorship. Or authorship fused with editorship" (166).

When quoting a passage of more than four lines, indent the entire passage half an inch from the left margin, and do not use quotation marks. Place the parenthetical reference *after* the final punctuation mark.

Doctorow points out that *Wikipedia*'s history pages can be extremely informative:

> This is a neat solution to the problem of authority—if you want to know what the fully rounded view of opinions on any controversial subject looks like, you need only consult its entry's history page for a blistering eyeful of thorough debate on the subject. (170)

Preparing the Works-Cited List

Start your works-cited list on a new page following the last page of your paper. Center the heading Works Cited at the top of the page. List entries alphabetically by the author's last name—or by the first word (other than an article such as *a* or *the*) of the title if an author is not given. Double-space within and between entries. Each entry should begin at the left-hand margin, with subsequent lines indented one-half inch. (This format can be automatically generated if you use the "hanging indent" option in your word processing program.)

Here are some additional guidelines:

- Italicize all book and periodical titles.

- Use a short version of a publisher's name (Penguin rather than Penguin Books), and abbreviate *University Press* (as in Princeton UP or U of Chicago P).

- If you are listing more than one work by the same author, include the author's name in the first entry, and substitute three unspaced hyphens followed by a period for the second and subsequent entries.

- Put quotation marks around the title of a periodical article or a section of an edited book or anthology, and provide the inclusive page numbers: 44–99. For page numbers larger than 99, give the last two digits of the second number if the first is the same: 147–69 (but 286–301).

When you have completed your list, double-check your parenthetical references to make sure they match the items in your works-cited list.

The following models illustrate the most common kinds of references.

Periodicals

For periodical articles found online or through a full-text database, see page 355.

Guidelines for Citing a Periodical Article

To cite a print article in MLA style, include the following:

1. Author, last name first

2. Title of the article, in quotation marks

3. Title of the periodical, in italics

4. Volume and issue numbers

5. Date or year of publication

6. Page number(s) of the article

(See images on page 349.)

Carton, Evan. "American Scholars: Ralph Waldo Emerson, Joseph

Smith, John Brown, and the Springs of Intellectual Schism."

New England Quarterly, vol. 85, no. 1, 2012, pp. 5–37.

Journals

Journals are periodicals published for experts in a field. Cite both volume number and issue number when available. In cases where only an issue number is available, cite just the issue.

> Minkler, Lanse. "Economic Rights and Political Decision-Making."
> *Human Rights Quarterly*, vol. 31, no. 2, 2009, pp. 369–93.
> Picciotto, Joanna. "The Public Person and the Play of Fact."
> *Representations*, no. 105, 2009, pp. 85–132.

Magazines

Magazines are periodicals published for a general audience. Do not include a magazine's volume and issue number, but do include the date (day, month, and year for weekly publications; month and year for those published less frequently). If pages are not consecutive, give the first page followed by a plus sign.

> Aviv, Rachel. "The Death Treatment." *The New Yorker,* 22 June
> 2015, pp. 56–65.
> Rice, Andrew. "Mission from Africa." *The New York Times Magazine,*
> 12 Apr. 2009, pp. 30+.

Copyright Page

THE NEW ENGLAND QVARTERLY

— Title of periodical

A Historical Review of New England Life and Letters

Registered in the U.S. Patent and Trademark Office

EDITORS

Edmund S. Morgan	Robert L. Middlekauff
David Brion Davis	William M. Fowler Jr.
Andrew Delbanco	Robert D. Richardson
Bernard Bailyn	Daniel R. Coquillette
Louis Menand	Laura Dassow Walls
Mary Kelley	Richard D. Brown
Neil Harris	Michael Kammen
Nina Baym	Mary Loeffelholz

Editor
Linda Smith Rhoads

Editorial Assistant
Anna Kimball Williams

Volume and issue number — Volume LXXXV   Number 1

March 2012

Date of publication

Copyright 2012 by The New England Quarterly
ISSN 0028–4866

Title of article

Author

Page numbers

First Page of Article

⊠+⊠+⊠+⊠+⊠+⊠+⊠+⊠+⊠+⊠+⊠+⊠+⊠+⊠+⊠+⊠+⊠+⊠+

American Scholars: Ralph Waldo Emerson,
Joseph Smith, John Brown, and the Springs
of Intellectual Schism

EVAN CARTON

Every man, woman, and child was more or less a theologian.
—Harriet Beecher Stowe

THE literary intellectual, the Christian evangelical, and the political radical are, according to our contemporary civic understanding, denizens of distinctly separate spheres, spheres bounded and policed, to the extent that they come into contact at all, by mutual distrust or disdain. I propose to advance a counter-claim (for which I will begin to muster evidence and assess implications): to wit, that the seemingly divergent cultural icons of the American scholar, prophet, and revolutionary in fact share a common milieu and moment of origin in the social, spiritual, and epistemological ferment of the early nineteenth century. Thus, I contend, the icons' apparently incommensurable vocations and commitments are better viewed as variations on the volatile "American synthesis" of scriptural, rational, and ideological authority that historian of religion Mark Noll describes in his magisterial *America's God* or, rather, as schismatic expressions of what political scientist Hugh Heclo calls the "mutual and tensioned embrace between the democratic and Christian faiths."[1]

[1]Mark Noll, *America's God: From Jonathan Edwards to Abraham Lincoln* (New York: Oxford University Press, 2002), p. 9; Hugh Heclo, *Christianity and American Democracy* (Cambridge: Harvard University Press, 2007), p. 5.

The New England Quarterly, vol. LXXXV, no. 1 (March 2012). © 2012 by The New England Quarterly. All rights reserved.

5

Newspapers

Include both the letter of the section and the page number. If an article continues on to a nonconsecutive page, give just the first page followed by a plus sign.

> Darlin, Damon. "Software That Monitors Your Work, Wherever You Are." *The New York Times*, 12 Apr. 2009, pp. B2+.

Editorial, Letter to the Editor, or Review

Include authors and titles where available as well as a descriptive label—for example Editorial, Letter, or Review. In the case of reviews, include the title and author of the work that is reviewed.

> Bernath, Dan. "Letter to the Editor." *The Washington Post*, 12 Apr. 2009, p. A16. Letter.
>
> Franklin, Nancy. "Whedon's World." Review of *Dollhouse*, directed by Joss Whedon. *The New Yorker*, 2 Mar. 2009, p. 45.
>
> "World Bank Responsibility." *The Wall Street Journal*, 28 Mar. 2009, p. A10. Editorial.

Political Cartoon or Comic Strip

Include the author and title (if available) of the cartoon or comic strip, followed by a descriptive label and publication information.

> Adams, Scott. "Dilbert." *The Chicago Tribune*, 10 Mar. 2012, p. C9. Comic strip.
>
> Pett, Joel. *Lexington Herald-Leader,* 30 Apr. 2012, p. A12. Cartoon.

Advertisement

Cite the name of the product or company that is advertised, followed by the descriptive label and the publication information.

> Maxwell House. *Rolling Stone,* 18 June 2015, p. 35. Advertisement.

Books

Guidelines for Citing a Book

To cite a book in MLA style, include the following:

1. Author, last name first

2. Title, in italics

3. Full publisher's name

4. Date of publication

$$\underbrace{\hspace{3cm}}_{1} \quad \underbrace{\hspace{3cm}}_{2} \quad \underbrace{\hspace{3cm}}_{3} \; \underbrace{\hspace{0.5cm}}_{4}$$

Kahneman, Daniel. *Thinking, Fast and Slow*. Farrar, Straus and Grioux, 2011.

Copyright Page

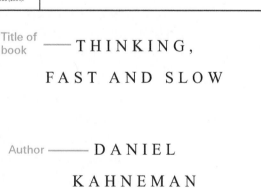

Farrar, Straus and Giroux
18 West 18th Street, New York 10011

Copyright © 2011 by Daniel Kahneman
All rights reserved
Printed in the United States of America
First edition, 2011

Date of publication

Grateful acknowledgment is made for permission to reprint the following previously published material:
"Judgment Under Uncertainty: Heuristics and Biases" from Science, New Series. Vol. 185, No. 4157, copyright
© 1974 by Amos Tversky and Daniel Kahneman. Reprinted by permission of Science. "Choices, Values, and
Frames" from The American Psychologist, copyright © 1983 by Daniel Kahneman and Amos Tversky. Reprinted
by permission of the American Psychological Association.

Grateful acknowledgment is made for permission to reprint the following images: Image on page 19 courtesy of
Paul Ekman Group, LLC. Image on page 57 from "Cues of Being Watched Enhance Cooperation in a
Real-World Setting" by Melissa Bateson, Daniel Nettle, and Gilbert Roberts, Biology Letters (2006); reprinted
by permission of Biology Letters. Image on page 100 from Mind Sights by Roger N. Shepard (New York: W.H.
Freeman and Company, 1990); reprinted by permission of Henry Holt and Company. Image on page 300 from
"Human Amygdala Responsivity to Masked Fearful Eye Whites" by Paul J. Whalen et al., Science 306 (2004).
Reprinted by permission of Science.

Library of Congress Cataloging-in-Publication Data
Kahneman, Daniel, 1934–
    Thinking, fast and slow / Daniel Kahneman. — 1st ed.
        p.   cm.
    Includes bibliographical references and index.
    ISBN 978-0-374-27563-1 (alk. paper)
    1. Thought and thinking.   2. Decision making.   3. Intuition.   4. Reasoning.   1. Title.

BF441 .K238 2011
153.4'2—dc23

Designed by Abby Kagan

www.fsgbooks.com

1   3   5   7   9   10   8   6   4   2

Title Page

Title of book ——— THINKING,

FAST AND SLOW

Author ——— DANIEL

KAHNEMAN

Publisher

FARRAR, STRAUS AND GIROUX   NEW YORK

Book by One Author

List the author, last name first, followed by the title (italicized). Include the full publisher's name, abbreviated when called for, and end with the date of publication.

> Skinner, Quentin. *Forensic Shakespeare*. Oxford UP, 2014.

Book by Two Authors

List authors in the order in which they are listed on the book's title page. List the first author with last name first, but list the second author with first name first.

> Singer, Peter, and Jim Mason. *The Way We Eat: Why Our Food Choices Matter*. Rodale, 2006.

Book by Three or More Authors

List only the first author, last name first, followed by the abbreviation et al. ("and others").

> Gould, Harvey, et al. *Advanced Computer Simulation Methods*. Pearson Education, 2009.

Two or More Books by the Same Author

List the entries alphabetically by title. In each entry after the first, substitute three unspaced hyphens, followed by a period, for the author's last name.

> Friedman, Thomas L. *Hot, Flat, and Crowded: Why We Need a Green Revolution—and How It Can Renew America*. Farrar, Strauss and Giroux, 2008.
>
> ---. *The World Is Flat: A Brief History of the Twenty-First Century*. Farrar, Strauss and Giroux, 2005.

Edited Book

If your focus is on the *author*, include the name of the editor (or editors) after the title, preceded by the abbreviation Ed. (for "edited by"). If the book is an edited collection of essays by different authors, treat it as an anthology.

> Whitman, Walt. *The Portable Walt Whitman*. Edited by Michael Warner, Penguin Classics, 2004.

If your focus is on the *editor*, begin with the editor's name followed by editor or editors.

> Michael Warner, editor. *The Portable Walt Whitman*. Penguin
>   Classics, 2004.

Translation

> Bolaño, Roberto. *The Savage Detectives*. Translated by Natasha
>   Wimmer, Picador, 2008.

Revised Edition

> Smith, Steven S., et al., *The American Congress*. 4th ed., Cambridge
>   UP, 2006.

Anthology

Include the name of the editor (or editors) of the anthology, followed by editor or editors.

> Browning, John Edgar, and Caroline Joan S. Picart, editors.
>   *Speaking of Monsters*, Palgrave, 2012.

Work in an Anthology

> Malone, Dan. "Immigration, Terrorism, and Secret Prisons."
>   *Keeping Out the Other: Immigration Enforcement Today*,
>   edited by David C. Brotherton and Philip Kretsedemas,
>   Columbia UP, 2008, pp. 44–62.

More Than One Work in the Same Anthology

To avoid repeating the entire anthology entry, you may provide a cross-reference from individual essays to the entire anthology.

> Adelson, Glenn et al., editors. *Environment: An Interdisciplinary
>   Anthology*, Yale UP, 2008.
> Lesher, Molly. "Seeds of Change." Adelson, pp. 131–37.
> Marshall, Robert. "The Problem of the Wilderness." Adelson,
>   pp. 288–92.

Section or Chapter of a Book

Leavitt, Steven D., and Stephen J. Dubner. "Why Do Drug Dealers
Still Live with Their Moms?" *Freakonomics: A Rogue
Economist Explores the Hidden Side of Everything,* Morrow,
2006, pp. 49-78.

Introduction, Preface, Foreword, or Afterword

Christiano, Thomas, and John Christman. Introduction.
Contemporary Debates in Political Philosophy. Edited by
Thomas Christiano and John Christman, Wiley, 2009, pp. 1–20.

Multivolume Work

McNeil, Peter, editor. *Fashion: Critical and Primary Sources.* Berg
Publishers, 2009. 4 vols.

Article in a Reference Work

A **reference work** is a book (print or electronic)—such as an encyclopedia, a dictionary, a bibliography, an almanac, or a handbook—that contains factual information. If the entries in a reference work are arranged
alphabetically, do not include page numbers or volumes. When citing a
familiar encyclopedia that publishes new editions regularly, include only
the edition (if given) and year. If the article's author is given, include that
as well. For less well-known reference encyclopedias, include publication
information.

"Human Rights." *Encyclopedia Americana.* 2003 ed.
"Seagrass Beds." *Ocean: A Visual Encyclopedia.* DK Publishing,
2015.

> **NOTE**
>
> Keep in mind that many instructors do not consider encyclopedia
> articles acceptable research sources. Before including a citation for
> an encyclopedia article in your works-cited list, check with your
> instructor.

Audiovisual Sources

TV Show

"A Desperate Man." *NCIS,* written by Nicole Mirante-Matthews,
directed by Leslie Libman, CBS, 10 Jan. 2012.

Film

The Tree of Life. Directed by Terrence Malick, performances by Brad
Pitt, Sean Penn, and Jessica Chastain, Fox Searchlight, 2011.

Internet Sources

Citing Internet sources can be problematic because they sometimes lack
basic information—for example, dates of publication or authors' names.
When citing Internet sources, include all the information you can find.

- For sites that are online editions of printed works, include as much of
  the original print information as is available, as well as the URL.

- For sites that exist only online, include (when available) the author,
  title, overall website title (if part of a larger project), the date it was last
  updated, and the URL.

- For works that are accessed through a library database, include the
  name of the database (in italics) and the URL or Digital Object Identifier (DOI). A DOI is a unique series of numbers assigned to electronic
  documents. The DOI remains the same regardless of where on the
  Internet a document is located.

For particularly long URLs (three lines or greater), you may use the
URL for the main website on which you found the content instead of the
URL for the specific page which you are referencing. However, your
instructor may not require a URL, so be sure to confirm their preference.
It is always a good idea, however, to keep a record of the URLs for yourself
in case you need to revisit your source.

If you type a URL into a works-cited entry that carries over to the next
line, make sure that you break it at an appropriate place—for example,
after a slash or a hyphen. If you paste a URL into a works-cited entry,
Word will do this for you.

Guidelines for Citing a Website

To cite a website in MLA style, follow these guidelines:

1. Author (if any)

2. Title (if any)

3. Name of website or sponsor

4. Date the site was last updated

5. DOI or URL

Author

Foodsafety.gov
Your Gateway to Federal Food Safety Information

Blog   Multimedia   News   Español

Search   [GO]

Home | Recalls & Alerts | Keep Food Safe | Who's at Risk | Food Poisoning | Report a Problem | Ask the Experts

Home > Recalls & Alerts > See Recent Recalls

Text Size: A A A

Share

Recalls & Alerts:

See Recent Recalls

Get Automatic Alerts

Get Food Safety Widget

See Recent Recalls

This page lists notices of recalls and alerts from both the U.S. Food and Drug Administration (FDA) and the U.S. Department of Agriculture (USDA).

Click the title of a recall to display the recall notice on the FDA or USDA website.

If the product details in the recall notice match the details on the food product you have at home, **do not open or consume the product**. Instead, do one of the following:

- Return the product to the place of purchase for a refund.
- Dispose of the product following the instructions provided in the recall notice to assure it will not be consumed by anyone.

For more information, see What to do if you have a recalled food product.

Bellisio Foods, Inc. Recalls Boneless Pork Rib Frozen Entree Products Due To Possible Foreign Matter Adulteration

Dec 22, 2015 3:51 PM

Bellisio Foods, Inc., a Jackson, Ohio establishment, is recalling approximately 285,264 pounds of boneless pork rib shaped patty frozen entree products that may be adulterated with extraneous materials.

The Cure House Recalls Pork Products Produced Without Benefit Of Inspection ——— Title

Dec 19, 2015 3:38 PM

The Cure House, a Louisville, Ky. establishment, is recalling an undetermined amount of cured pork products that were produced without the benefit of federal inspection.

Bonavista Foods Inc. Recalls Pork Products Produced Without Benefit Of Import Inspection

Dec 18, 2015 8:42 PM

Bonavista Foods Inc., Ovid, N.Y. establishment, is recalling approximately 4,338 pounds of cured pork products that were not presented at the U.S. point of entry for inspection.

Stay Connected

Our Partners

City of
publication

USDA   FDA   CDC

About FoodSafety.gov   Accessibility   Privacy Policy   FOIA   Disclaimers   Plain Writing

Contact Us   No FEAR   Viewers & Players   WhiteHouse.gov   USA.gov   GobiernoUSA.gov   Give Feedback

December 30, 2015   U.S. Department of Health & Human Services - 200 Independence Avenue, S.W. - Washington, D.C. 20201

January 7, 2016

Date of last
update

Sponsor

Foodsafety.gov

```
   ┌─────1─────┐ ┌────────────2────────────────┐
Foodsafety.gov. "The Cure House Recalls Pork Products without
   ┌────────────┐ ┌──────────3──────────┐
   Benefit of Inspection." US Dept of Health and Human
   ┌──────┐┌────4────┐ ┌─────────5─────────┐
   Services, 30 Dec. 2015. www.fsis.usda.gov/wps/wcm/connect
   ┌─────────────5──────────────┐
   /FSIS-Content/internet/main/topics/recalls-and-public-health
   ┌──────────────5──────────────┐
   -alerts/recall-case-archive/archive/2015/recall-148-2015-release.
```

Entire Website

Include (if available) the author, title of the website, date of last update, and the URL.

Document within a Website

"Uniform Impunity: Mexico's Misuse of Military Justice to Prosecute
    Abuses in Counternarcotics and Public Security Operations."
    Human Rights Watch, Apr. 2009, www.hrw.org/report/2009/04/29
    /uniform-impunity/mexicos-misuse-military-justice-prosecute
    -abuses-counternarcotics.

Online Video

Baggs, Amanda. "In My Language." *YouTube*, 14 Jan. 2007,
    www.youtube.com/watch?v=JnyIM1hl2jc.

Blog Posts and Blog Comments

Caryl, Christian. "Burma: How Much Change?" *NYR Daily*, NYREV,
    17 Nov. 2015, www.nybooks.com/daily/2015/11/17/burma
    -election-how-much-change/.

Cimons, Marlene. "Why Cities Could Be the Key to Solving the
    Climate Crisis." *Thinkprogress.org*, Center for American
    Progress Action Fund, 10 Dec. 2015, thinkprogress.org
    /climate/2015/12/10/3730938/cities-key-to-climate-crisis/.

Tweet

Begin with the author's real name, followed by the user name in parentheses. Include only the user name if the real name is unknown. Next, include the entire text of the tweet in quotation marks, followed by the date, the time, and the medium (Tweet).

Curiosity Rover. "Can you see me waving? How to spot #Mars
in the night sky: https://youtu.be/hv8hVvJlcJQ." *Twitter*,
5 Nov. 2015, 11:00 a.m., twitter.com/marscuriosity/status
/672859022911889408.

Podcast

Koenig, Sarah. "The Alibi." *Serial,* Chicago Public Radio,
3 Oct. 2014, serialpodcast.org/season-one/1/the-alibi.

Ogg, Erica. "Google Tries to Rehab Its Antitrust Image." *CNET News
Daily Podcast*, CBS Interactive, 8 May 2009, www.cnet.com
/news/cnet-news-daily-podcast-google-tries-to-rehab-its
-antitrust-image/.

Online Book

Doctorow, Cory. *Content: Selected Essays on Technology,
Creativity, Copyright, and the Future of the Future,* Tachyon,
2008. *Craphound.com.*

Part of an Online Book

Zittrain, Jonathan L. "The Lessons of *Wikipedia*." *The Future of the
Internet and How to Stop It,* Yale UP, 2008. *futureoftheinternet.org.*

Article in an Online Scholarly Journal

Johnston, Rebecca. "Salvation or Destruction: Metaphors
of the Internet." *First Monday*, vol. 14, no. 4, 2009,
firstmonday.org/article/view/2370/2158.

Magazine Article Accessed Online

Marantz, Andrew. "What to Do When Your App Is Racist." *The New
Yorker*, 29 Jul. 2015, www.newyorker.com/business/currency
/what-to-do-when-your-app-is-racist.

Newspaper Article Accessed Online

Possley, Maurice, and Ken Armstrong. "The Verdict: Dishonor."
Chicago Tribune, 11 Jan. 1999, www.chicagotribune.com/news
/watchdog/chi-020103trial1-story.html.

Article from a Library Database

Hartley, Richard D. "Sentencing Reform and the War on Drugs: An
Analysis of Sentence Outcomes for Narcotics Offenders
Adjudicated in the US District Courts on the Southwest
Border." *Criminal Justice Policy Review,* vol. 19, no. 4, 2008,
pp. 414-37. *Sage Premier,* doi: 10.1177/1043986208323264.

Legal Case

When citing a court opinion, provide the plaintiffs' names, the legal
citation (volume, abbreviation of the source, page numbers), the name
of the court, the year of the decision, and any relevant information
about where you found it. In many cases, online versions of the opinions will include only the first page; in those cases, supply that page
number followed by a plus sign.

Miranda v. Arizona, 384 US 436+. Supreme Court of the US. 1966.
FindLaw, Thompson Reuters, caselaw.findlaw.com
/us-supreme-court/384/436.html.

Government Document

Include the government agency or body issuing the document, followed by
publication information.

United States, Department of Homeland Security, *Estimates of the
Unauthorized Immigrant Population Residing in the United
States, Office of Immigration Policy,* Feb. 2009, www.dhs.gov
/sites/default/files/publications/ois_ill_pe_2011_0.pdf.

LaunchPad
macmillan learning

For more practice, see the LearningCurve on
Working with Sources (MLA) in the LaunchPad
for *Practical Argument.*

⬇The following student research paper, "Should Data Posted on
Social-Networking Sites Be 'Fair Game' for Employers?" by Erin Blaine,
follows MLA documentation style as outlined in the preceding pages.

MLA PAPER GUIDELINES

- An MLA paper should have a one-inch margin all around and be double-spaced.

- Indent the first line of every paragraph. Number all pages, including the first, consecutively. Type your name, followed by the page number, in the upper right-hand corner.

- An MLA paper does not typically have a title page. Type the following information at the top of the paper, one inch from the left-hand margin:

    Name

    Instructor

    Course

    Date submitted

- Center the title of the paper. Capitalize all important words of the title, except prepositions, articles, coordinating conjunctions, and the *to* in infinitives—unless the word is the first or last word of the title. Titles should never be italicized, underlined, or followed by a period.

- Begin the **works-cited list** on a new numbered page, after the body of the paper. (See page 347 for a discussion of the works-cited list.)

- Citations should follow MLA documentation style.

> **NOTE**
>
> In the student essay that follows, note that the green annotations explain the student's choice of sources and the orange annotations highlight features of the student's use of documentation.

Blaine 1

Erin Blaine

Professor Adams

Humanities 101

4 March 2015

Should Data Posted on Social-Networking Sites

Be "Fair Game" for Employers?

The popularity of social-networking sites such as 　　　　1

Facebook and Twitter has increased dramatically over the last

several years, especially among college students and young

professionals. These sites provide valuable opportunities for

networking and for connecting socially. At the same time, how-

ever, potential employers, human resources professionals, and

even college admissions officers routinely use these sites to

evaluate applicants. Because it is so easy to access social-

networking sites and because they provide valuable information,

this trend is certain to continue. Some people are concerned

about this development, arguing that social-networking sites

should be off-limits to potential employers because they do not

have the context they need to evaluate information. As long as

applicants have freely posted information in a public forum,

however, there is no reason for an employer not to consult this

information during the hiring process.

The number of employers and universities using social- 　　2

networking sites to evaluate candidates is growing every year.

A recent survey found that 24 percent of college admissions

officers acknowledged visiting sites like Facebook to learn more

about applicants, and 12 percent said that the information they

found "negatively impacted the applicant's admissions chances"

("Online Behavior"). This practice also occurs in the business

world, where the numbers are even more striking. A study con-

ducted by CareerBuilder found that 43 percent of employers use

This source and the following one supply statistics that support the main point of the paragraph.

Parenthetical reference identifies the source, which is included in the works-cited list.

Blaine 2

social-networking sites such as Facebook, Twitter, and LinkedIn to help them evaluate potential employees ("Number of Employers"). According to the *New York Times,* 75 percent of recruiters are required by their companies to research applicants online, and 70 percent of recruiters have rejected applicants because of information they found. The practice of checking social media is so common that some employers use outside companies, such as Social Intelligence Corp., to do Internet background checks on job candidates (Preston).

Not everyone is happy with this practice, though, and some have strong objections. Becca Bush, a college student in Chicago, argues that employers should not have the right to use social media to evaluate potential employees. "It's a violation of privacy," she says. "Twenty years ago, people still did the same things as now," but the information "wasn't as widespread" (qtd. in Cammenga). Marc S. Rotenberg, president of the Electronic Privacy Information Center, agrees, saying, "Employers should not be judging what people in their private lives do away from the workplace" (qtd. in Preston). Rotenberg goes on to say that privacy settings on sites like Facebook are often misunderstood. According to him, "People are led to believe that there is more limited disclosure than there actually is" (qtd. in Preston). Some people mistakenly think that looking at an applicant's Facebook page is illegal (Cammenga). Even though it is not, this practice can lead to discrimination, which *is* illegal. An online search can reveal characteristics that an applicant is not required to disclose to employers—for example, race, age, religion, sex, national origin, marital status, or disability (Preston).

Given the realities of the digital age, however, admissions committees and job recruiters are acting reasonably when they access social-networking sites. As a practical matter, it would be

3

4

Blaine 3

almost impossible to prevent employers from reviewing online sites as part of informal background and reference checks. Moreover, those who believe that it is unethical for recruiters to look at the online profiles of prospective job candidates seem willing to accept the benefits of social-networking sites but unwilling to acknowledge that these new technologies bring new responsibilities and liabilities. Finally, the problems associated with employers' use of social-networking sites would not be an issue in the first place if users of social-networking sites took full advantage of the available measures to protect themselves.

Part of the problem is that the Internet has fundamentally altered our notions of "private" and "public" in ways that we are only just beginning to understand. As Shelley Fralic observes in "Don't Fall for the Myths about Online Privacy," Facebook's privacy options do not really protect its users' privacy, and thinking they do "is beyond absurd" (1). On sites like Facebook, people can reveal intimate details of their lives to millions of strangers. This situation is unprecedented and, at least for the foreseeable future, irreversible. As *New York Times* columnist Thomas L. Friedman observes, "When everyone has a blog, a MySpace page, or Facebook entry, everyone is a publisher. . . . When everyone is a publisher, paparazzo, or film-maker, everyone else is a public figure." Given the changes in our understanding of privacy and the public nature of the Internet, the suggestion that we should live our lives by the same rules we lived by twenty years ago simply does not make sense. As Friedman notes, in the Internet age, more and more of "what you say or do or write will end up as a digital fingerprint that never gets erased" (23).

5

Because the source and the author are named in an identifying tag, only the page numbers are needed parenthetically.

Ellipses indicate that words have been left out of a quotation.

Including a recognized authority, such as Friedman, adds credibility.

Blaine 4

Rather than relying on outdated notions of privacy, 6
students and job seekers should accept these new conditions
and take steps to protect themselves. Most college and career
counseling services have easy-to-follow recommendations for
how to maintain a positive online reputation. First on almost
everyone's list is the advice, "Adjust your privacy settings."
Northwestern University's Career Services says it simply:
"Use your settings wisely and employers will not have access
to the contents of your sites" ("Using Social Networking").
Understanding and employing these settings is a user's
responsibility; misunderstanding such protections is no excuse.
As Mariel Loveland suggests, those who want extra help can
hire an online reputation-management company such as
Reputation.com or Integrity Defenders or use services such as
those offered by Reppler. The "Reppler Image Score" enables
social-networking users to identify questionable material
"across different social networks" and to rate its "professional-
ism and consistency."

The most important way for people to protect themselves 7
against the possible misuse of personal information is for them
to take responsibility for the information they post online.
According to a recent article in *Education Week*, even middle
school students should keep their future college and career
plans in mind when they post information online ("Online
Behavior"). In preparing students to apply for college, many
high school counselors stress the "golden rule": "students
should never post anything online they wouldn't want their

Internet source includes no page number in the parenthetical documentation.

Distinctive key phrases are quoted directly.

Not every summary or paraphrase needs to include a quotation.

Blaine 5

parents to see" ("Online Behavior"). Students and job seekers must realize that a commonsense approach to the Internet requires that they develop good "digital grooming" habits (Bond). For example, one self-described "cautious Internet user" says that she "goes through the information on her [Facebook] account every few weeks and deletes statuses, messages, and other things" (Bond). She understands that a potential employer coming across an applicant's membership in a Facebook group such as "I Sold My Grandma for Crack-Cocaine!" or a picture of a student posing with an empty liquor bottle may not understand the tone, the context, or the joke. Students should also be careful about "friends" who have access to their online social networks, asking themselves whether these people really know them and would have good things to say about them if a prospective employer contacted them for a reference. According to one high school principal, 75 percent of the students at his school admitted to accepting a friend request from someone they did not know ("Online Behavior"). Getting students to consider the repercussions of this kind of choice is central to many social-media education programs.

Although social-networking sites have disadvantages, they   8
also have advantages. These sites provide an excellent opportunity for job seekers to connect with potential employers and to get their names and résumés in circulation. For example, a job seeker can search the LinkedIn networks of a company's executives or human resources staff for mutual connections. In addition, a job seeker can post information calculated to appeal to potential employers. Recruiters are just as likely to hire

Brackets indicate that a quotation has been edited for clarity.

Paraphrasing provides readers with the key points of a source.

Blaine 6

candidates based on social-media screening as they are to reject them. A recent article reports the following:

A quotation of more than four lines of text is double-spaced, indented one inch from the left margin, and typed as a block, without quotation marks. Parenthetical documentation comes after the final punctuation.

> However, one third (33 percent) of employers who research candidates on social networking sites say they've found content that made them more likely to hire a candidate. What's more, nearly a quarter (23 percent) found content that directly led to them hiring the candidate, up from 19 percent last year. ("Number of Employers")

In today's job market, people should think of their networks as extensions of themselves. They need to take an active role in shaping the image they want to project to future employers.

As Thomas L. Friedman argues in his column, "The Whole World Is Watching," access to information creates opportunities as well as problems. Quoting Dov Seidman, Friedman maintains that the most important opportunity may be the one to "out-behave your competition." In other words, just as the Internet allows negative information to travel quickly, it also allows positive information to spread. So even though students and job seekers should be careful when posting information online, they should not miss the opportunity to take advantage of the many opportunities that social-networking sites offer.

9

Blaine 7

Works Cited

Bond, Michaelle. "Facebook Timeline a New Privacy Test." *USA
 Today*, 2 Nov. 2011, www.usatoday.com/tech/news
 /internetprivacy/story/2011-11-02/facebook-timeline
 -privacy/51047658/1.

Cammenga, Michelle. "Facebook Might Be the Reason You
 Don't Get That Job." *Hub Bub*, Loyola University Chicago's
 School of Communication, 23 Feb. 2012, blogs.luc.edu
 /hubbub/reporting-and-writing/employers-screen-facebook/.

Fralic, Shelley. "Don't Fall for the Myths about Online Privacy."
 Calgary Herald, 17 Oct. 2015, p. 1.

Friedman, Thomas L. "The Whole World Is Watching." *The New
 York Times,* 27 June 2007, p. A23.

Loveland, Mariel. "Reppler Launches 'Reppler Image Score,' Rates
 Social Network Profile Content for Potential Employers."
 Scribbal, 27 Sept. 2011, www.scribbal.com/reppler-launches
 -rates-social-network-profile-content-09-27-11/.

"Number of Employers Passing on Applicants Due to Social Media
 Posts Continues to Rise." *CareerBuilder*, 26 June 2014,
 www.careerbuilder.com/share/aboutus/pressreleasesdetail
 .aspx?sd=6%2F26%2F2014&id=pr829&ed=12%2F31%2F2014.

"Online Behavior Jeopardizing College Plans; Admissions Officers
 Checking Social-Networking Sites for Red Flags." *Education
 Week,* 14 Dec. 2011, p. 11. *Academic One File*, www.edweek
 .org/ew/articles/2011/12/08/14collegeadmit.h31.html.

Preston, Jennifer. "Social Media History Becomes a New Job
 Hurdle." *The New York Times*, 20 July 2011, www.nytimes
 .com/2011/07/21/technology/social-media-history-becomes
 -a-new-job-hurdle.html?_r=0.

"Using Social Networking in Your Employment Search."
 University Career Services, Northwestern University, 2011,
 www.northwestern.edu/careers/job-intern-prep/social
 -media-advice/index.html.

The works-cited list includes full information for all sources cited in the paper.

Be sure that your data comes from recent sources.

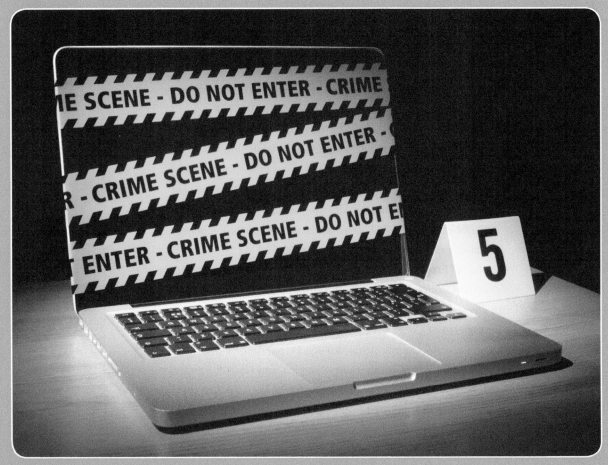

Tim Roberts/Getty Images

Using Sources Responsibly

AT ISSUE

Where Should We Draw the Line with Plagiarism?

In recent years, a number of high-profile plagiarism cases have put a spotlight on how much "borrowing" from other sources is acceptable. Some critics—and many colleges and universities—draw little distinction between intentional and unintentional plagiarism, arguing that any unattributed borrowing is theft. Others are more forgiving, accepting the fact that busy historians or scientists (or students) might not realize that a particular sentence in their notes was not their original idea or might accidentally incorporate a source's exact words (or its unique syntax or phrasing) into their own work without attribution.

In the age of the Internet, with its "cut-and-paste" culture, plagiarism has become easier to commit; however, with the development of plagiarism-detection software, it is also now much easier to detect. Still, some colleges and universities are uncomfortable with the idea of using such software, arguing that it establishes an atmosphere of distrust.

On college campuses, as in the professional world, questions like the following have arisen: What exactly constitutes plagiarism? How serious a matter is it? Is there a difference between intentional and unintentional plagiarism? Is plagiarizing a few sentences as bad as plagiarizing an entire paper? Why do people commit plagiarism? What should be done to prevent it? How should it be punished? What are its short- and long-term consequences?

These are some (although by no means all) of the questions that you might think about as you consider the sources at the end of this chapter. After reading these sources, you will be asked to write an argumentative essay that takes a position on the issue of what exactly constitutes plagiarism and how it should be dealt with.

Understanding Plagiarism

Plagiarism is the act of using the words or ideas of another person without attributing them to their rightful author—that is, presenting those borrowed words and ideas as if they are your own. When you plagiarize, you fail to use sources ethically or responsibly.

TWO DEFINITIONS OF PLAGIARISM

From *MLA Handbook* Eighth Edition (2016)

Merriam-Webster's Collegiate Dictionary defines plagiarizing as committing "literary theft." Plagiarism is presenting another person's ideas, information, expressions, or entire work as one's own. It is thus a kind of fraud: deceiving others to gain something of value. While plagiarism only sometimes has legal repercussions (e.g., when it involves copyright infringement—violating an authors' exclusive legal right to publication), it is always a serious moral and ethical offense.

From *Publication Manual of the American Psychological Association*, Sixth Edition (2009)

Researchers do not claim the words and ideas of another as their own; they give credit where credit is due (APA Ethics Code Standard 8.11, Plagiarism). Quotation marks should be used to indicate the exact words of another. *Each time* you paraphrase another author (i.e., summarize a passage or rearrange the order of a sentence and change some of the words), you need to credit the source in the text.

The key element of this principle is that authors do not present the work of another as if it were their own work. This can extend to ideas as well as written words. If authors model a study after one done by someone else, the originating author should be given credit. If the rationale for a study was suggested in the Discussion section of someone else's article, that person should be given credit. Given the free exchange of ideas, which is very important to the health of intellectual discourse, authors may not know where an idea for a study originated. If authors do know, however, they should acknowledge the source; this includes personal communications.

For many people, defining plagiarism is simple: it is not "borrowing" but stealing, and it should be dealt with severely. For others, it is a more slippery term, seen as considerably more serious if it is intentional than if it is accidental (for example, the result of careless research methods). Most colleges and universities have guidelines that define plagiarism strictly and have penalties in place for those who commit it. To avoid committing unintentional plagiarism, you need to understand exactly what it is and why it occurs. You also need to learn how to use sources responsibly and to understand what kind of information requires documentation and what kind does not.

Avoiding Unintentional Plagiarism

Even if you do not intentionally misuse the words or ideas of a source, you are still committing plagiarism if you present the work of others as your own. The most common errors that lead to unintentional plagiarism—and how to avoid them—are listed below.

COMMON ERROR	HOW TO AVOID IT
No source information is provided for borrowed material (including statistics).	Always include full parenthetical documentation and a works-cited list that make the source of your information clear to readers. (See Chapter 10.)
A source's ideas are presented as if they are your own original ideas.	Keep track of the sources you consult, and always keep full source information with your sources. Never cut and paste material from an electronic source directly into your paper.
The boundaries of borrowed material are unclear.	Be sure to use an identifying tag *before* and parenthetical documentation *after* borrowed material. (See Chapter 9.)
The language of paraphrases or summaries is still too close to that of the original source.	Be careful to use original phrasing and syntax when you write summaries and paraphrases. (See Chapter 9.)

(Continued)

COMMON ERROR	HOW TO AVOID IT
A friend's or tutor's words or ideas appear in your paper.	Any help you receive should be in the form of suggestions, not additions.
Material you wrote for another course is used in your paper.	Always get permission from *both* instructors if you want to reuse work you did for another course, and be sure the material you use is substantially revised.

To avoid unintentional plagiarism, you need to maintain control over your sources, keeping track of all the material you use so that you remember where you found each piece of information.

As you take notes, be careful to distinguish your sources' ideas from your own. If you are copying a source's words into your notes, put them in quotation marks. (If you are taking notes by hand, circle the quotation marks; if you are typing your notes, put the quotation marks in boldface.) If you photocopy material, write the full source information on the first page, and staple the pages together. When you download material from the Internet, be sure the URL appears on every page. Finally, never cut and paste material from a source directly into your paper.

INTERNET SOURCES AND PLAGIARISM

The Internet presents a particular challenge for students as they try to avoid plagiarism. Committing plagiarism (intentional or unintentional) with electronic sources is easy because it is simple to cut and paste material from online sources into a paper. However, inserting even a sentence or two from an Internet source (including a blog, an email, or a website) into a paper without quotation marks and documentation constitutes plagiarism.

It is also not acceptable to use a visual (such as a graph, chart, table, or photograph) found on the Internet without acknowledging its source. Finally, even if an Internet source does not identify its author, the words or ideas you find there are not your own original material, so you must identify their source.

As you draft your paper, be sure to quote your sources' words accurately (even punctuation must be reproduced exactly as it appears in the source). Be careful not to quote out of context, and be sure that you are presenting your sources' ideas accurately when you summarize or paraphrase. (For information on quoting, paraphrasing, and summarizing source material, see Chapter 9.)

INTENTIONAL PLAGIARISM

Deliberately plagiarizing from a source, handing in another student's paper as your own, or buying a paper from an Internet site is never acceptable. Such acts constitute serious violations of academic integrity. Creating your own original work is an important part of the educational experience, and misrepresenting someone else's work as your own undermines the goals of education.

Cartoon by Loos Diallo from Whitman Pioneer.

Knowing What to Document

Documentation is the practice of identifying borrowed material and providing the proper bibliographic information for each source. Different academic disciplines require different formats for documentation—for example, English uses MLA, and psychology uses APA. For this reason, you should be sure to check with your instructor to find out what documentation style he or she requires. (For information on MLA and APA documentation formats, see Chapter 10 and Appendix B, respectively.)

Regardless of the discipline, the following kinds of information should always be documented:

- Quotations from a source

- Summaries or paraphrases of a source's original ideas

- Opinions, judgments, and conclusions that are not your own

- Statistics from a source

- Visuals from a source

- Data from charts or graphs in a source

The following kinds of information, however, do not require documentation:

- **Common knowledge**—that is, factual information that can be found in several different sources (for example, a writer's date of birth, a scientific fact, or the location of a famous battle)

- Familiar quotations—anything from proverbs to frequently quoted lines from Shakespeare's plays—that you expect readers will recognize

- Your own original opinions, judgments, and conclusions

⊘ EXERCISE 11.1

Which of the following statements requires documentation, and why?

1. Doris Kearns Goodwin is a prize-winning historian.

2. Doris Kearns Goodwin's *The Fitzgeralds and the Kennedys* is a 900-page book with about 3,500 footnotes.

3. In 1994, Lynne McTaggart accused Goodwin of borrowing material from a book that McTaggart wrote.

4. My own review of the background suggests that Goodwin's plagiarism was unintentional.

5. Still, these accusations left Goodwin to face the "slings and arrows" of media criticism.

6. As Goodwin explains, "The more intensive and far-reaching a historian's research, the greater the difficulty of citation."

7. In her defense, Goodwin argued that the more research a historian does, the harder it is to keep track of sources.

8. Some people still remain convinced that Goodwin committed plagiarism.

9. Goodwin believes that her careful research methods, which she has described in exhaustive detail, should have prevented accidental plagiarism.

10. Some of Goodwin's critics have concluded that her reputation as a historian was hurt by the plagiarism charges.

● EXERCISE 11.2

Assume you are using the following editorial as a source. Identify two pieces of information you would need to document (for example, statistics). Then, identify two pieces of information you would *not* need to document (for example, common knowledge).

This unsigned newspaper editorial appeared on August 11, 2006.

CHEATERS NEVER WIN

AUSTIN AMERICAN-STATESMAN

We live in the era of cut and paste, thanks to the Internet, which provides students with countless materials to plagiarize. 1

If you think that's an exaggeration, do an Internet search of "free term papers." You'll find cheathouse.com, Cheater.com, Schoolsucks.com, echeat .com, and Free Essay Network (freeessay.com) among the 603 million results that turn up. 2

One site, 24hourtermpapers.com, even boasts of providing "custom term papers" within 24 hours (at $23.95 per page), targeting college students who put off writing papers until the 11th hour. A disclaimer warns that "these term papers are to be used for research purposes only. Use of these papers for any other purpose is not the responsibility of 24 Hour Term Papers." Funny that they say that, because the site provides the student with a nice package to hand directly to the professor: All term papers are "sent within the due date," with a bibliography page thrown in for no extra charge. 3

A student who pays such a steep price for a term paper is not likely to use it only as a resource. One of the perks of being a student today is unlimited access to a slew of research tools, from the library to an online research database the institution pays for the student to use. 4

Student Judicial Services at the University of Texas defines plagiarism as "representing as your own work any material that was obtained from another 5 source, regardless of how or where you acquired it." This includes borrowing ideas or even structure. And "by merely changing a few words or rearranging several words or sentences, you are not paraphrasing. Making minor revisions to borrowed text amounts to plagiarism," the Web site warns.

But those warnings go unheeded by many. The Center for Academic 6 Integrity found last year that more than 70 percent of college students admitted to having cheated at least once, more than 60 percent admitted to plagiarizing, and nearly 40 percent said they have plagiarized from the Internet.

Strict disciplinary action should follow students who are caught trying to 7 claim someone else's work as their own. The more it goes unnoticed, the easier it is for students to keep stealing. Educators should devote time and attention to properly educating students on what plagiarism is and why it's stupid to do it.

In the end, the plagiarizer has the most to lose, whether he or she gets 8 caught or not. Many of the online papers are not worthy of copying, especially if a student wants to excel in college. By stealing someone else's work and labeling it as their own, students forgo the opportunity to learn how to research, develop ideas, and translate them into quality writing. Not to mention tarnishing a reputation, if the student gets caught.

> "In the end, the plagiarizer has the most to lose, whether he or she gets caught or not."

Cheathouse.com and other sites like it might get students a passing grade 9 in a course, but it only puts them a step behind everyone else who is developing the skills needed to thrive in the workplace. Employers won't be as forgiving as teachers or disciplinary committees. The day will come when the "I'm a student. I'm still learning" excuse will fall on deaf ears.

Revising to Eliminate Plagiarism

As you revise your papers, scrutinize your work carefully to be sure you have not inadvertently committed plagiarism.

The following paragraph (from page 28 of *Hot, Flat, and Crowded* by Thomas L. Friedman) and the four guidelines that follow it will help you to understand the situations in which accidental plagiarism is most likely to occur.

> So if you think the world feels crowded now, just wait a few decades. In 1800, London was the world's largest city with one million people. By 1960, there were 111 cities with more than one million people. By 1995 there were 280, and today there are over 300, according to

UN Population Fund statistics. The number of megacities (with ten million or more inhabitants) in the world has climbed from 5 in 1975 to 14 in 1995 and is expected to reach 26 cities by 2015, according to the UN. Needless to say, these exploding populations are rapidly overwhelming infrastructure in these megacities—nineteen million people in Mumbai alone—as well as driving loss of arable land, deforestation, overfishing, water shortages, and air and water pollution.

1. **Be sure you have identified your source and provided appropriate documentation.**

   PLAGIARISM
   The world is becoming more and more crowded, and some twenty-six cities are expected to have populations of over 10 million by 2015.

This student writer does not quote directly from Friedman's discussion, but her summary of his comments does not represent her original ideas and therefore needs to be documented.

The following correct use of source material includes both an **identifying tag** (a phrase that identifies Friedman as the source of the ideas) and a page number that directs readers to the exact location of the material the student is summarizing. (Full source information is provided in the works-cited list.)

   CORRECT
   According to Thomas L. Friedman, the world is becoming more and more crowded, and twenty-six cities are expected to have populations of over 10 million by 2015 (28).

2. **Be sure you have placed quotation marks around borrowed words.**

   PLAGIARISM
   According to Thomas L. Friedman, the exploding populations of megacities around the world are overwhelming their infrastructure (28).

Although the passage above provides parenthetical documentation and includes an identifying tag indicating the source of its ideas, it uses Friedman's exact words without placing them in quotation marks.

To avoid committing plagiarism, the writer needs to either place quotation marks around Friedman's words or paraphrase his comments.

   CORRECT (BORROWED WORDS IN QUOTATION MARKS)
   According to Thomas L. Friedman, the "exploding populations" of large cities around the world are "rapidly overwhelming infrastructure in these megacities" (28).

CORRECT (BORROWED WORDS PARAPHRASED)

According to Thomas L. Friedman, the rapid rise in population of large cities around the world poses a serious threat to their ability to function (28).

3. **Be sure you have indicated the boundaries of the borrowed material.**

PLAGIARISM

The world is becoming more and more crowded, and this will lead to serious problems in the future. Soon, as many as twenty-six of the world's cities will have populations over 10 million. It is clear that "these exploding populations are rapidly overwhelming infrastructure in these megacities" (Friedman 28).

In the passage above, the student correctly places Friedman's words in quotation marks and includes appropriate parenthetical documentation. However, she does not indicate that other ideas in the passage, although not quoted directly, are also Friedman's.

To avoid committing plagiarism, the student needs to use identifying tags to indicate the boundaries of the borrowed material, which goes beyond the quoted words.

CORRECT

According to Thomas L. Friedman, the world is becoming more and more crowded, and this will lead to serious problems in the future. Soon, Friedman predicts, as many as twenty-six of the world's cities will have populations of over 10 million, and this rise in population will put a serious strain on the cities' resources, "rapidly overwhelming infrastructure in these megacities" (28).

4. **Be sure you have used your own phrasing and syntax.**

PLAGIARISM

If you feel crowded now, Thomas L. Friedman says, just wait twenty or thirty years. In 1800, London, with a million inhabitants, was the largest city in the world; over 111 cities had more than a million people by 1960. Thirty-five years later, there were 280; today, according to statistics provided by the UN Population Fund, there are more than 300. There were only five megacities (10 million people or more) in 1975 and fourteen in 1995. However, by 2015, the United Nations predicts, there might be twenty-six. These rapidly growing populations threaten to overwhelm the infrastructure of the megacities (Mumbai alone has 19 million people), destroying arable land, the forests, and fishing and causing water shortages and water and air pollution (28).

The student who wrote the paragraph on the preceding page does provide an identifying tag and parenthetical documentation to identify the source of her ideas. However, her paragraph's phrasing and syntax are almost identical to Friedman's.

In the following paragraph, the writer correctly paraphrases and summarizes Friedman's ideas, quoting a few distinctive passages. (See Chapter 9 for information on paraphrase and summary.)

CORRECT

As Thomas L. Friedman warns, the world has been growing more and more crowded and is likely to grow still more crowded in the years to come. Relying on UN population data, Friedman estimates that there will be some twenty more "megacities" (those with more than 10 million people) in 2015 than there were in 1975. (In 1800, in contrast, only one city in the world—London—had a million inhabitants.) Obviously, this is an alarming trend. Friedman believes that these rapidly growing populations are "overwhelming infrastructure in these megacities" and are bound to strain resources, leading to "loss of arable land, deforestation, [and] overfishing" and creating not only air and water pollution but water shortages as well (28).

> NOTE
>
> Do not forget to document statistics that you get from a source. For example, Thomas L. Friedman's statistics about the threat of rising population are the result of his original research, so you need to document them.

◉ EXERCISE 11.3

The following student paragraph synthesizes information from two different sources (which appear on pp. 380–381, following the student paragraph), but the student writer has not used sources responsibly. (For information on synthesis, see Chapter 9.) Read the sources and the paragraph, and then make the following changes:

- Insert quotation marks where the student has quoted a source's words.

- Edit paraphrased and summarized material if necessary so that its syntax and phrasing are not too close to those of a source.

- Add parenthetical documentation where necessary to acknowledge the use of a source's words or original ideas.

- Add identifying tags where necessary to clarify the scope of the borrowed material or to differentiate material from the two sources.

- Check every quoted passage once more to see if the quotation adds something vital to the paragraph. If it does not, summarize or paraphrase the source's words instead.

STUDENT PARAGRAPH

In recent years, psychologists have focused on the idea that girls (unlike boys) face a crisis of self-esteem as they approach adolescence. Both Carol Gilligan and Mary Pipher did research to support this idea, showing how girls lose their self-confidence in adolescence because of sexist cultural expectations. Women's groups have expressed concern that the school system favors boys and is biased against girls. In fact, boys are often regarded not just as classroom favorites but also as bullies who represent obstacles on the path to gender justice for girls. Recently, however, this impression that boys are somehow privileged while girls are shortchanged is being challenged.

Source 1

That boys are in disrepute is not accidental. For many years women's groups have complained that boys benefit from a school system that favors them and is biased against girls. "Schools shortchange girls," declares the American Association of University Women. . . . A stream of books and pamphlets cite research showing not only that boys are classroom favorites but also that they are given to schoolyard violence and sexual harassment.

In the view that has prevailed in American education over the past decade, boys are resented, both as the unfairly privileged sex and as obstacles on the path to gender justice for girls. This perspective is promoted in schools of education, and many a teacher now feels that girls need and deserve special indemnifying consideration. "It is really clear that boys are Number One in this society and in most of the world," says Patricia O'Reilly, a professor of education and the director of the Gender Equity Center, at the University of Cincinnati.

The idea that schools and society grind girls down has given rise to an array of laws and policies intended to curtail the advantage boys have and to redress the harm done to girls. That girls are treated as the second sex in school and consequently suffer, that boys are accorded privileges

and consequently benefit—these are things everyone is presumed to
know. But they are not true.

—Christina Hoff Sommers, "The War against Boys"

Source 2

Girls face an inevitable crisis of self-esteem as they approach adolescence. They are in danger of losing their voices, drowning, and facing a devastating dip in self-regard that boys don't experience. This is the picture that Carol Gilligan presented on the basis of her research at the Emma Willard School, a private girls' school in Troy, N.Y. While Gilligan did not refer to genes in her analysis of girls' vulnerability, she did cite both the "wall of Western culture" and deep early childhood socialization as reasons.

Her theme was echoed in 1994 by the clinical psychologist Mary Pipher's surprise best seller, *Reviving Ophelia* (Putnam, 1994), which spent three years on the *New York Times* best-seller list. Drawing on case studies rather than systematic research, Pipher observed how naturally outgoing, confident girls get worn down by sexist cultural expectations. Gilligan's and Pipher's ideas have also been supported by a widely cited study in 1990 by the American Association of University Women. That report, published in 1991, claimed that teenage girls experience a "free-fall in self-esteem from which some will never recover."

The idea that girls have low self-esteem has by now become part of the academic canon as well as fodder for the popular media. But is it true? No.

—Rosalind C. Barnett and Caryl Rivers, "Men Are from Earth, and So Are Women. It's Faulty Research That Sets Them Apart"

Where Should We Draw the Line with Plagiarism?

Reread the At Issue box on page 369. Then, read the sources on the following pages. As you read these sources, you will be asked to answer questions and to complete some activities. This work will help you to understand the content and structure of the material you read. When you have read the sources, you will be ready to write an argumentative essay in which you take a position on the topic, "Where Should We Draw the Line with Plagiarism?"

Tim Roberts/Getty Images

SOURCES

   Jack Shafer, "Sidebar: Comparing the Copy," p. 383

   Lawrence M. Hinman, "How to Fight College Cheating," p. 386

   Trip Gabriel, "Plagiarism Lines Blur for Students in Digital Age," p. 389

   Elizabeth Minkel, "Too Hard *Not* to Cheat in the Internet Age?," p. 393

   Richard A. Posner, "The Truth about Plagiarism," p. 395

   Dylan Byers, "Plagiarism and BuzzFeed's Achilles' Heel," p. 398

   K. Balibalos and J. Gopalakrishnan, "OK or Not?," p. 401

   Dan Ariely, "Essay Mills: A Coarse Lesson in Cheating," p. 406

   Term Papers for Sale Advertisement (Web page), p. 409

In this *Slate* article, Shafer accuses a *New York Times* reporter of plagiarism. As evidence, he presents the opening paragraphs from the source (a *Bloomberg News* story), the accused reporter's *New York Times* article, and—for contrast—two other newspaper articles that report the same story without relying heavily on the original source.

This article appeared in *Slate* on March 5, 2008.

SIDEBAR:° COMPARING THE COPY

JACK SHAFER

A short news story printed alongside a longer related article

How different can four news stories generated by the same assignment be? Compare the opening paragraphs of these pieces about the 2005 mad cow disease conference call: the *Bloomberg News* version; the *New York Times* version, which lifts passages from *Bloomberg* without attribution; and the starkly different pieces run by the globeandmail.com and the *Omaha World-Herald*.

> "How different can four news stories generated by the same assignment be?" 1

Opening paragraphs from the July 15, 2005, *Bloomberg News* story by Daniel Goldstein:

The U.S. plans to resume imports of Canadian cattle, after an appellate court 2 cleared the way to end a ban imposed two years ago because of mad-cow disease.° Cattle prices fell and shares of beef producer Tyson Foods Inc. surged.

A brain disease that can be transmitted to humans through consumption of contaminated beef

The first shipments from Canada may arrive at U.S. slaughterhouses in 3 days, U.S. Agriculture Secretary Mike Johanns said today in a conference call. "If things go well, it could very well be next week." USDA and Canadian officials are coordinating how to certify animals for shipment, he said.

A U.S. appellate court° yesterday ruled in favor of the government, which 4 argued Canadian cattle under 30 months of age don't pose a risk of mad-cow disease. Tyson's beef business had a loss of $19 million in the quarter ended April 2, as the lack of available cattle boosted costs and led to plant closings. Canada before the ban supplied about 5 percent of U.S. beef.

A higher court that hears appeals of rulings that were made by a lower court

Opening paragraphs from the July 16, 2005, *New York Times* story by Alexei Barrionuevo:

The United States Agriculture Department said on Friday that it planned to 5 resume imports of Canadian cattle within days, after an appellate court lifted a two-year-old injunction imposed because of mad cow disease.

The first shipments from Canada could arrive at American slaughter- 6
houses as early as next week, Agriculture Secretary Mike Johanns said in a
conference call with reporters. Officials in Canada and the United States are
coordinating how to certify the animals for shipment, he said.

"We want to make sure everything is in place," he said. "If things go well, 7
it could very well be next week."

The news sent shares of the beef producer Tyson Foods and McDonald's 8
restaurants surging. Cattle prices fell. Shares of Tyson rose 7.5 percent in early
trading, and closed at $19.47 a share, a 5 percent increase, while McDonald's
closed at $30.99 a share, up 4.7 percent.

Tyson's beef business recorded a loss of $19 million in the quarter ended 9
April 2. The company was hurt by the ban on cattle from Canada, which
increased costs and led to temporary plant closings. Before the ban, Canada
supplied about 5 percent of the nation's beef.

A United States appeals court ruled on Thursday in favor of the govern- 10
ment, which had argued that Canadian cows under 30 months of age did not
pose a risk of bovine spongiform encephalopathy, or mad cow disease.

**Opening paragraphs from the July 15 globeandmail.com story by
Terry Weber, time stamped 12:28 p.m.:**

The United States is taking immediate steps to reopen the border to Canadian 11
cattle imports, Agriculture Secretary Mike Johanns said Friday.

During a webcast, Mr. Johanns said that Washington has been in touch 12
with Ottawa and that the two sides are now going through the logistical
steps necessary to resume trade of live cattle for the first time since May,
2003.

"Our hope is we're talking about days and not weeks," he said. "If things 13
go well, it could very well be next week, but we have not set a specific date."

Late Thursday, a three-member U.S. appeal court panel in Seattle 14
overturned a temporary injunction issued by Montana Judge Richard
Cebull halting the U.S. Department of Agriculture's March plan to reopen
the border.

Judge Cebull had sided with U.S. ranchers group R-Calf in its argument 15
that reopening the border exposed U.S. ranchers and consumers to unnecessary risks from mad-cow disease. The USDA had been planning to ease
restrictions by allowing cattle younger than 30 months to be imported.

Mr. Johanns noted that Canadian officials had already anticipated the 16
ruling and taken steps to meet U.S. requirements, should Thursday's favor
reopening the border.

"It [the reopening] could be as early as next week, but we want to make 17
sure everything is in place," he said.

Those requirements, he said, including ensuring that animals being 18
imported into the U.S. meet minimal-risk rule criteria, getting documents to
U.S. customs to confirm the shipments are appropriate for entry.

Opening paragraphs from the July 15 *Omaha World-Herald* story by Chris Clayton:

Canadian cattle could start arriving at U.S. feedlots and meatpacking plants as early as next week, U.S. Agriculture Secretary Mike Johanns said Friday. 19

Thursday's unanimous decision by the 9th U.S. Circuit Court of Appeals lifting a lower court's injunction gives U.S. and Canadian officials a nearly two-week window to begin shipping live cattle from Canada before another court hearing, scheduled late this month in Montana. 20

No date has been set, but Johanns said he will move as "expeditiously as possible" to begin importing Canadian cattle once officials work out the ground rules. Canadian and USDA officials anticipated the requirements would be in place at whatever time the legal issues were resolved. 21

"Our hope is we are talking about days, not weeks," Johanns said. "It could be as early as next week, but we want to make sure everything is in place. . . . If things go well, it could very well be next week, but we haven't set a specific date" [*ellipsis in the original*]. 22

Johanns has lamented the closed border since becoming agriculture secretary in late January, saying that it hurts U.S. cattle feeders and meatpackers because the United States continued to import boxed beef from Canada. 23

Higher cattle prices because of tight supplies caused meatpackers to scale back production at U.S. facilities. Industry officials claim to have lost as many as 8,000 meatpacking jobs because of the closed border. 24

"I'm just worried that many of those jobs were impacted in a very permanent way," Johanns said. "My hope is that restructuring now will be abated and this industry can start getting back to a normal flow of commerce here." 25

About 1 million cattle were imported from Canada in the year before the border closed in May 2003 when Canada reported its first case of mad-cow disease, or bovine spongiform encephalopathy. 26

⊘ AT ISSUE: SOURCES FOR UNDERSTANDING PLAGIARISM

1. Identify the passages in the *New York Times* story that you think are too close to the original *Bloomberg News* story.

2. Identify passages in the other two excerpts that convey the same information as the *Times* story (paraphrased or summarized).

3. In his introduction, Shafer says that the passages from the Toronto *Globe and Mail* and the *Omaha World-Herald* are "starkly different" from the *Bloomberg News* story. Do you agree?

4. Can you identify any passages in the *Globe and Mail* or *Omaha World-Herald* excerpts that you believe are too close to the original source?

5. On the basis of what you see here, do you agree with Shafer that the *New York Times* reporter is guilty of plagiarism? Explain your conclusion.

This essay appeared in the *Washington Post* on September 3, 2004.

HOW TO FIGHT COLLEGE CHEATING

LAWRENCE M. HINMAN

Recent studies have shown that a steadily growing number of students cheat or plagiarize in college—and the data from high schools suggest that this number will continue to rise. A study by Don McCabe of Rutgers University showed that 74 percent of high school students admitted to one or more instances of serious cheating on tests. Even more disturbing is the way that many students define cheating and plagiarism. For example, they believe that cutting and pasting a few sentences from various Web sources without attribution is not plagiarism. 1

Before the Web, students certainly plagiarized—but they had to plan ahead to do so. Fraternities and sororities often had files of term papers, and some high-tech term-paper firms could fax papers to students. Overall, however, plagiarism required forethought. 2

Online term-paper sites changed all that. Overnight, students could order a term paper, print it out, and have it ready for class in the morning—and still get a good night's sleep. All they needed was a charge card and an Internet connection. 3

One response to the increase in cheating has been to fight technology with more technology. Plagiarism-checking sites provide a service to screen student papers. They offer a color-coded report on papers and the original sources from which the students might have copied. Colleges qualify for volume discounts, which encourages professors to submit whole classes' worth of papers—the academic equivalent of mandatory urine testing for athletes. 4

The technological battle between term-paper mills and anti-plagiarism services will undoubtedly continue to escalate, with each side constructing more elaborate countermeasures to outwit the other. The cost of both plagiarism and its detection will also undoubtedly continue to spiral. 5

> "The cost of both plagiarism and its detection will also undoubtedly continue to spiral."

But there is another way. Our first and most important line of defense against academic dishonesty is simply good teaching. Cheating and plagiarism often arise in a vacuum created by routine, lack of interest, and overwork. Professors who give the same assignment every semester, fail to guide students in the development of their projects, and have little interest in what the students have to say contribute to the academic environment in which much cheating and plagiarism occurs. 6

Consider, by way of contrast, professors who know their students and who give assignments that require regular, continuing interaction with them about their projects—and who require students to produce work that is a 7 meaningful development of their own interests. These professors create an environment in which cheating and plagiarism are far less likely to occur. In this context, any plagiarism would usually be immediately evident to the professor, who would see it as inconsistent with the rest of the student's work. A strong, meaningful curriculum taught by committed professors is the first and most important defense against academic dishonesty.

The second remedy is to encourage the development of integrity in our stu- 8 dents. A sense of responsibility about one's intellectual development would preclude cheating and plagiarizing as inconsistent with one's identity. It is precisely this sense of individual integrity that schools with honor codes seek to promote.

Third, we must encourage our students to perceive the dishonesty of their 9 classmates as something that causes harm to the many students who play by the rules. The argument that cheaters hurt only themselves is false. Cheaters do hurt other people, and they do so to help themselves. Students cheat because it works. They get better grades and more advantages with less effort. Honest students lose grades, scholarships, recommendations, and admission to advanced programs. Honest students must create enough peer pressure to dissuade potential cheaters. Ultimately, students must be willing to step forward and confront those who engage in academic dishonesty.

Addressing these issues is not a luxury that can be postponed until a more 10 convenient time. It is a short step from dishonesty in schools and colleges to dishonesty in business. It is doubtful that students who fail to develop habits of integrity and honesty while still in an academic setting are likely to do so once they are out in the "real" world. Nor is it likely that adults will stand up against the dishonesty of others, particularly fellow workers and superiors, if they do not develop the habit of doing so while still in school.

⊘ AT ISSUE: SOURCES FOR UNDERSTANDING PLAGIARISM

1. In the first five paragraphs of this essay, Hinman provides background on how plagiarism by students has been changed by the Internet. Summarize the plagiarism situation before and after the development of the Internet.

2. The essay's thesis is stated in paragraph 6. Restate this thesis in your own words.

3. Does Hinman view plagiarism-detection sites as a solution to the problem of college cheating? What are the limitations of such sites?

4. According to Hinman, what steps can "committed professors" (para. 7) take to eliminate academic dishonesty?

5. In paragraphs 8 and 9, Hinman suggests two additional solutions to the problem of plagiarism. What solutions does he propose? Given what you know about college students, do you think Hinman's suggestions are realistic? Explain.

6. Hinman does not address arguments that challenge his recommendations. What opposing arguments might he have presented? How would you refute these opposing arguments?

7. This essay was published more than ten years ago. Do you think Hinman's observations and recommendations are still valid? Why or why not?

This article is from the August 1, 2010, edition of the *New York Times*.

PLAGIARISM LINES BLUR FOR STUDENTS IN DIGITAL AGE

TRIP GABRIEL

At Rhode Island College, a freshman copied and pasted from a Web site's fre- 1
quently asked questions page about homelessness—and did not think he
needed to credit a source in his assignment because the page did not include
author information.

At DePaul University, the tip-off to one student's copying was the purple 2
shade of several paragraphs he had lifted from the Web; when confronted by a
writing tutor his professor had sent him to, he was not defensive—he just
wanted to know how to change purple text to black.

And at the University of Maryland, a student reprimanded for copying 3
from *Wikipedia* in a paper on the Great Depression said he thought its
entries—unsigned and collectively written—did not need to be credited since
they counted, essentially, as common knowledge.

Professors used to deal with plagiarism by admonishing students to give 4
credit to others and to follow the style guide for citations, and pretty much left
it at that.

But these cases—typical ones, according to writing tutors and officials 5
responsible for discipline at the three schools who described the plagiarism—
suggest that many students simply do not grasp that using words they did not
write is a serious misdeed.

It is a disconnect that is growing in the Internet age as concepts of intel- 6
lectual property, copyright, and originality are under assault in the unbridled
exchange of online information, say educators who study plagiarism.

Digital technology makes copying and pasting easy, of course. But that is 7
the least of it. The Internet may also be redefining how students—who came of
age with music file-sharing, *Wikipedia*, and Web-linking—understand the
concept of authorship and the singularity of any text or image.

"Now we have a whole generation of students who've grown up with 8
information that just seems to be hanging out there in cyberspace and doesn't
seem to have an author," said Teresa Fishman, director of the Center for Academic Integrity at Clemson University. "It's possible to believe this information is just out there for anyone to take."

Professors who have studied plagiarism do not try to excuse it—many are 9
champions of academic honesty on their campuses—but rather try to understand why it is so widespread.

In surveys from 2006 to 2010 by Donald L. McCabe, a co-founder of the 10
Center for Academic Integrity and a business professor at Rutgers University,

about 40 percent of 14,000 undergraduates admitted to copying a few sentences in written assignments.

Perhaps more significant, the number who believed that copying from the 11 Web constitutes "serious cheating" is declining—to 29 percent on average in recent surveys from 34 percent earlier in the decade.

Sarah Brookover, a senior at the Rutgers campus in Camden, N.J., said 12 many of her classmates blithely cut and paste without attribution.

"This generation has always existed in a world where media and intellec- 13 tual property don't have the same gravity," said Ms. Brookover, who at 31 is older than most undergraduates. "When you're sitting at your computer, it's the same machine you've downloaded music with, possibly illegally, the same machine you streamed videos for free that showed on HBO last night."

Ms. Brookover, who works at the campus library, has pondered the differ- 14 ences between researching in the stacks and online. "Because you're not walking into a library, you're not physically holding the article, which takes you closer to 'this doesn't belong to me,'" she said. Online, "everything can belong to you really easily."

> "Online, 'everything can belong to you really easily.'"

A University of Notre Dame anthropologist, Susan D. Blum, disturbed by 15 the high rates of reported plagiarism, set out to understand how students view authorship and the written word, or "texts" in Ms. Blum's academic language.

She conducted her ethnographic research among 234 Notre Dame under- 16 graduates. "Today's students stand at the crossroads of a new way of conceiving texts and the people who create them and who quote them," she wrote last year in the book *My Word! Plagiarism and College Culture*, published by Cornell University Press.

Ms. Blum argued that student writing exhibits some of the same qualities 17 of pastiche that drive other creative endeavors today—TV shows that constantly reference other shows or rap music that samples from earlier songs.

In an interview, she said the idea of an author whose singular effort cre- 18 ates an original work is rooted in Enlightenment ideas of the individual. It is buttressed by the Western concept of intellectual property rights as secured by copyright law. But both traditions are being challenged. "Our notion of authorship and originality was born, it flourished, and it may be waning," Ms. Blum said.

She contends that undergraduates are less interested in cultivating a 19 unique and authentic identity—as their 1960s counterparts were—than in trying on many different personas, which the Web enables with social networking.

"If you are not so worried about presenting yourself as absolutely unique, 20 then it's O.K. if you say other people's words, it's O.K. if you say things you don't believe, it's O.K. if you write papers you couldn't care less about because they accomplish the task, which is turning something in and getting a grade," Ms. Blum said, voicing student attitudes. "And it's O.K. if you put words out there without getting any credit."

The notion that there might be a new model young person, who freely 21
borrows from the vortex of information to mash up a new creative work,
fueled a brief brouhaha earlier this year with Helene Hegemann, a German
teenager whose best-selling novel about Berlin club life turned out to include
passages lifted from others.

Instead of offering an abject apology, Ms. Hegemann insisted, "There's no 22
such thing as originality anyway, just authenticity." A few critics rose to her
defense, and the book remained a finalist for a fiction prize (but did not win).

That theory does not wash with Sarah Wilensky, a senior at Indiana Uni- 23
versity, who said that relaxing plagiarism standards "does not foster creativity,
it fosters laziness."

"You're not coming up with new ideas if you're grabbing and mixing and 24
matching," said Ms. Wilensky, who took aim at Ms. Hegemann in a column in
her student newspaper headlined "Generation Plagiarism."

"It may be increasingly accepted, but there are still plenty of creative 25
people—authors and artists and scholars—who are doing original work,"
Ms. Wilensky said in an interview. "It's kind of an insult that that ideal is gone,
and now we're left only to make collages of the work of previous generations."

In the view of Ms. Wilensky, whose writing skills earned her the role of 26
informal editor of other students' papers in her freshman dorm, plagiarism
has nothing to do with trendy academic theories.

The main reason it occurs, she said, is because students leave high school 27
unprepared for the intellectual rigors of college writing.

"If you're taught how to closely read sources and synthesize them into your 28
own original argument in middle and high school, you're not going to be tempted
to plagiarize in college, and you certainly won't do so unknowingly," she said.

At the University of California, Davis, of the 196 plagiarism cases referred 29
to the disciplinary office last year, a majority did not involve students ignorant
of the need to credit the writing of others.

Many times, said Donald J. Dudley, who oversees the discipline office on 30
the campus of 32,000, it was students who intentionally copied—knowing it
was wrong—who were "unwilling to engage the writing process."

"Writing is difficult, and doing it well takes time and practice," he said. 31

And then there was a case that had nothing to do with a younger genera- 32
tion's evolving view of authorship. A student accused of plagiarism came to
Mr. Dudley's office with her parents, and the father admitted that he was the
one responsible for the plagiarism. The wife assured Mr. Dudley that it would
not happen again.

⊘ AT ISSUE: SOURCES FOR UNDERSTANDING PLAGIARISM

1. Gabriel begins inductively, presenting three paragraphs of evidence
   before he states his thesis. Is this the best strategy, or should these
   examples appear later in his discussion? Explain.

2. In paragraph 5, Gabriel notes that "many students simply do not grasp that using words they did not write is a serious misdeed." Is this his thesis statement? Does he take a position, or is he just presenting information?

3. Why, according to Gabriel, is plagiarism so widespread? Do you think the reasons he cites in any way excuse plagiarism—at least accidental plagiarism? Does Gabriel seem to think they do?

4. What is *pastiche* (para. 17)? What is a collage (25)? How does the concept of pastiche or collage apply to plagiarism? Do you see the use of pastiche in TV shows or popular music (17) as different from its use in academic writing? Why or why not?

5. Summarize Sarah Wilensky's views (23–28) on the issue Gabriel discusses. Do you agree with her? Do you agree with Helene Hegemann's statement, "There's no such thing as originality anyway, just authenticity" (22)?

6. Do you think the anecdote in paragraph 32 is a strong ending for this article? Does the paragraph need a more forceful concluding statement? Explain.

This essay appeared on the *New Yorker*'s "Book Bench" blog on August 4, 2010.

TOO HARD *NOT* TO CHEAT IN THE INTERNET AGE?

ELIZABETH MINKEL

A deeply troubling article sat atop the *New York Times'* most-emailed list 1
yesterday (no, not the one about catching horrible diseases at the gym).
"Plagiarism Lines Blur for Students in Digital Age," the headline proclaimed,
pinpointing a problem, weaving a theory, and excusing youthful copycats in
one fell swoop. The story here is that a large number of college students today
are acting as college students always have—baldly lifting whole passages for
their term papers from other sources. But it's the Digital Age now, and between unverifiable, unattributed information sitting around online and the
general ease with which young people obtain, alter, and share creative content
on the Internet, students can't seem to figure out that cheating on a paper is
wrong. In fact, a lot of them can't even tell that they're cheating, and the
Internet is to blame.

Really? When I was in college (I graduated three years ago), I was well 2
aware of the necessity of avoiding minefields of unattributed—and often
incorrect—information on the Web. *Wikipedia* was never an acceptable source,
perhaps because my professors knew they'd get students like the one from the
University of Maryland who, when "reprimanded for copying from *Wikipedia* . . .
said he thought its entries—unsigned and collectively written—did not need to
be credited since they counted, essentially, as common knowledge." There are
probably only two types of people pulling these excuses: the crafty, using the
Digital Age argument to their advantage, and the completely clueless, who, like
plenty in preceding generations, just don't understand the concept of plagiarism. The *Times* asked current students to weigh in (helpfully labelling them
"Generation Plagiarism"), and one wrote:

"I never 'copy and paste' but I will take information from the Internet and 3
change out a few words then put it in my paper. So far, I have not encountered
any problems with this. Thought [*sic*] the
information/words are technically mine because of a few undetectable word swaps, I
still consider the information to be that of
someone else."

The student goes on to say that, "In the
digital age, plagiarism isn't and shouldn't
be as big of a deal as it used to be when people used books for research." The response
leaves me just as confused as I believe he is,

> "I'm pretty
> convinced that he'd
> still be fuzzy on
> plagiarism if he'd   4
> lived back when
> people actually used
> books."

but I'm pretty convinced that he'd still be fuzzy on plagiarism if he'd lived back when people actually used books. But what I've found most frustrating in the ensuing debate is the assertion that these students are a part of some new *Reality Hunger*–type wave of open-source everything—if every song is sampled, why shouldn't writers do the same? The question is interesting, complicated, and divisive, but it has little bearing on a Psych 101 paper.

Excusing plagiarism as some sort of modern-day academic mash-up 5 won't teach students anything more than how to lie and get away with it. We should be teaching students how to produce original work—and that there's plenty of original thinking across the Internet—and leave the plagiarizing to the politicians.

⊃ AT ISSUE: SOURCES FOR UNDERSTANDING PLAGIARISM

1. Minkel's essay is a refutation of Trip Gabriel's article (p. 389), whose headline she accuses of "pinpointing a problem, weaving a theory, and excusing youthful copycats in one fell swoop" (para.1). Do you agree that Gabriel's article excuses plagiarism, or do you think it simply identifies a problem? Explain.

2. In paragraph 1, Minkel summarizes Gabriel's article. Is this a fair and accurate summary?

3. When Minkel quotes the student in paragraphs 3 and 4, is she setting up a **straw man**? Why or why not?

4. How would you characterize Minkel's tone? For example, is she angry? Frustrated? Condescending? Annoyed? Is this tone appropriate for her audience? (Note that this essay first appeared in the *New Yorker*, a magazine likely to be read by educated readers.)

5. In paragraph 2, Minkel identifies herself as a recent college graduate. Why? Is she appealing here to *ethos*, *pathos*, or *logos*?

6. Evaluate Minkel's last paragraph, particularly her concluding statement. Does this paragraph accurately express her reasons for criticizing Gabriel's article? What, if anything, do you think she should add to her conclusion? Why?

This essay appeared in *Newsday* on May 18, 2003.

THE TRUTH ABOUT PLAGIARISM

RICHARD A. POSNER

Plagiarism is considered by most writers, teachers, journalists, scholars, and even members of the general public to be the capital intellectual crime. Being caught out in plagiarism can blast a politician's career, earn a college student expulsion, and destroy a writer's, scholar's, or journalist's reputation. In recent days, for example, the *New York Times* has referred to "widespread fabrication and plagiarism" by reporter Jayson Blair as "a low point in the 152-year history of the newspaper."

In James Hynes' splendid satiric novella of plagiarism, *Casting the Runes*, the plagiarist, having by black magic murdered one of the historians whom he plagiarized and tried to murder a second, is himself killed by the very same black magic, deployed by the widow of his murder victim.

There is a danger of overkill. Plagiarism can be a form of fraud, but it is no accident that, unlike real theft, it is not a crime. If a thief steals your car, you are out the market value of the car, but if a writer copies material from a book you wrote, you don't have to replace the book. At worst, the undetected plagiarist obtains a reputation that he does not deserve (that is the element of fraud in plagiarism). The real victim of his fraud is not the person whose work he copies, but those of his competitors who scruple to enhance their own reputations by such means.

> "There is a danger of overkill."

The most serious plagiarisms are by students and professors, whose undetected plagiarisms disrupt the system of student and scholarly evaluation. The least serious are those that earned the late Stephen Ambrose and Doris Kearns Goodwin such obloquy° last year. Popular historians, they jazzed up their books with vivid passages copied from previous historians without quotation marks, though with footnote attributions that made their "crime" easy to detect.

Abusive language

(One reason that plagiarism, like littering, is punished heavily, even though an individual act of plagiarism usually does little or no harm, is that it is normally very difficult to detect—but not in the case of Ambrose and Goodwin.) Competing popular historians might have been injured, but I'm not aware of anyone actually claiming this.

Confusion of plagiarism with theft is one reason plagiarism engenders indignation; another is a confusion of it with copyright infringement. Wholesale copying of copyrighted material is an infringement of a property right, and legal remedies are available to the copyright holder. But the copying of brief passages, even from copyrighted materials, is permissible under the doctrine of "fair use," while wholesale copying from material that is in the public domain—material that never was copyrighted, or on which the copyright has expired—presents no copyright issue at all.

Plagiarism of work in the public domain is more common than otherwise. 7
Consider a few examples: *West Side Story* is a thinly veiled copy (with music
added) of *Romeo and Juliet*, which in turn plagiarized Arthur Brooke's *The
Tragicall Historye of Romeo and Juliet*, published in 1562, which in turn copied from several earlier Romeo and Juliets, all of which were copies of Ovid's
story of Pyramus and Thisbe.

Paradise Lost plagiarizes the book of Genesis in the Old Testament. Classical 8
musicians plagiarize folk melodies (think only of Dvorak, Bartok, and Copland)
and often "quote" (as musicians say) from earlier classical works. Edouard Manet's
most famous painting, *Déjeuner sur l'herbe*, copies earlier paintings by Raphael,
Titian, and Courbet, and *My Fair Lady* plagiarized Shaw's play *Pygmalion*, while
Woody Allen's movie *Play It Again, Sam* "quotes" a famous scene from *Casablanca*.
Countless movies are based on books, such as *The Thirty-Nine Steps* on John
Buchan's novel of that name or *For Whom the Bell Tolls* on Hemingway's novel.

Many of these "plagiarisms" were authorized, and perhaps none was 9
deceptive; they are what Christopher Ricks in his excellent book *Allusions to
the Poets* helpfully terms *allusion* rather than *plagiarism*. But what they show is
that copying with variations is an important form of creativity, and this should
make us prudent and measured in our condemnations of plagiarism.

Especially when the term is extended from literal copying to the copying 10
of ideas. Another phrase for copying an idea, as distinct from the form in
which it is expressed, is dissemination of ideas. If one needs a license to repeat
another person's idea, or if one risks ostracism by one's professional community
for failing to credit an idea to its originator, who may be forgotten or unknown,
the dissemination of ideas is impeded.

I have heard authors of history textbooks criticized for failing to document 11
their borrowing of ideas from previous historians. This is an absurd criticism.
The author of a textbook makes no claim to originality; rather the contrary—
the most reliable, if not necessarily the most exciting, textbook is one that
confines itself to ideas already well accepted, not at all novel.

It would be better if the term *plagiarism* were confined to literal copying, 12
and moreover literal copying that is not merely unacknowledged but deceptive. Failing to give credit where credit is due should be regarded as a lesser,
indeed usually merely venial, offense.

The concept of plagiarism has expanded, and the sanctions for it, though 13
they remain informal rather than legal, have become more severe, in tandem
with the rise of individualism. Journal articles are no longer published anony-
mously, and ghostwriters demand that their contributions be acknowledged.

Replaceable

Individualism and a cult of originality go hand in hand. Each of us sup- 14
poses that our contribution to society is unique rather than fungible° and so
deserves public recognition, which plagiarism clouds.

This is a modern view. We should be aware that the high value placed on 15
originality is a specific cultural, and even field-specific, phenomenon, rather
than an aspect of the universal moral law.

Judges, who try to conceal rather than to flaunt their originality, far 16
from crediting their predecessors with original thinking like to pretend

that there is no original thinking in law, that judges are just a transmission belt for rules and principles laid down by the framers of statutes or the Constitution.

Resorting to plagiarism to obtain a good grade or a promotion is fraud 17 and should be punished, though it should not be confused with "theft." But I think the zeal to punish plagiarism reflects less a concern with the real injuries that it occasionally inflicts than with a desire on the part of leaders of professional communities, such as journalists and historians, to enhance their profession's reputation.

Journalists (like politicians) have a bad reputation for truthfulness, and 18 historians, in this "postmodernist"° era, are suspected of having embraced an extreme form of relativism and of having lost their regard for facts. Both groups hope by taking a very hard line against plagiarism and fabrication to reassure the public that they are serious diggers after truth whose efforts, a form of "sweat equity," deserve protection against copycats.

Postmodernism is a school of criticism that denies concepts such as scientific certainty and absolute truth.

Their anxieties are understandable; but the rest of us will do well to keep 19 the matter in perspective, realizing that the term *plagiarism* is used loosely and often too broadly; that much plagiarism is harmless and (when the term is defined broadly) that some has social value.

⊃ AT ISSUE: SOURCES FOR UNDERSTANDING PLAGIARISM

1. According to Posner, how do most people define *plagiarism*? How is the definition he proposes different from theirs? Do you think this definition is too broad? Too narrow?

2. Why does Posner believe that the plagiarisms committed by students and professors are the most serious? Can you think of an argument against this position?

3. How do the examples Posner cites in paragraphs 7 and 8 strengthen his argument? Do you agree that the examples he gives here constitute plagiarism? Why or why not?

4. Explain the connection the author makes in paragraph 16 between judges and plagiarism. (Note that Posner himself is a federal judge.)

5. Why, according to Posner, do journalists and historians think plagiarism should be punished severely?

6. According to Posner, "the truth about plagiarism" is that "much plagiarism is harmless and (when the term is defined broadly) that some has social value" (para. 19). Does the evidence he presents in this essay support this conclusion? What connection do you see between this position and his comments about the rise of individualism and the "cult of originality" in paragraphs 13–15?

This article first appeared on July 25, 2014, on Politico.com.

PLAGIARISM AND BUZZFEED'S ACHILLES' HEEL

DYLAN BYERS

In 2013, the satirical website *The Onion* wrote an article titled "BuzzFeed 1 Writer Resigns in Disgrace after Plagiarizing '10 Llamas Who Wish They Were Models.'" It appealed to reporters because it was a clever knock on the state of digital journalism—and because it resonated with a widely held perception about BuzzFeed.

High-profile plagiarism cases are always met with a certain amount of 2 schadenfreude from the media's chattering classes, as well as calls for the defendant's head, but the response to BuzzFeed editor Benny Johnson's serial plagiarism has been especially intense.

There's a reason for that: In the eyes of many journalists, BuzzFeed is con- 3 stantly walking a fine line between aggregation, or "curation," and theft. Go to BuzzFeed.com and click on any one of its lists. In very fine print, buried below each photo, there will be a link to another site—usually Reddit—which is where the photograph came from.

Is this plagiarism? Of course not. Does it feel a little seedy? Yeah, a bit. 4

In 2012, as BuzzFeed was growing into the Internet sensation it is today, 5 *Slate*'s Farhad Manjoo (now with the *New York Times*) wrote a lengthy post explaining "the secret to BuzzFeed's monster online success."

"How does this one site come up with so many simple ideas that people want 6 to spread far and wide? What's their secret?" he wrote. "The answer, in short, is that BuzzFeed's staff finds stuff elsewhere on the Web, most often at Reddit. They polish and repackage what they find. And often—and, from what I can tell, deliberately—their posts are hard to trace back to the original source material."

Because BuzzFeed is so popular, Manjoo wrote, its "pilfered" lists all but 7 eclipse the original sources of content: "Once you understand how central Reddit is to BuzzFeed, it's like spotting the wizard behind the curtain. Whenever you see a popular BuzzFeed post, search Reddit, and all will be revealed."

Jonah Peretti, BuzzFeed's founder, told Manjoo that there was "nothing 8 wrong" with picking up other people's content "because few things on the Web are really original."

Gawker's Adrian Chen (now with the *New Inquiry*) also wrote an exten- 9 sive analysis of BuzzFeed's "plagiarism problem" in 2012.

"BuzzFeed has built a lucrative business on organizing the internet's con- 10 fusing spectacle into listicles easily comprehended by even the most numbed office workers," Chen wrote. "But the site's approach to all content as building blocks for viral lists puts it in an awkward position in relation to internet etiquette and journalistic ethics."

"For example," Chen wrote, "the BuzzFeed listicle '21 Pictures That Will 11
Restore Your Faith in Humanity,' appears to be an almost exact replica of a
couple of posts on an obscure site called Nedhardy . . . BuzzFeed slapped
together many of the same pictures, presented it as an original idea, and it
went Avian-Flu-level-viral, ending up with more than seven million page
views."

Is *this* plagiarism? It's certainly closer to it. Somehow, the Internet came 12
to accept it: The *New York Times* reported, Huffington Post aggregated,
BuzzFeed curated. Maybe "repackaging funny things found on Reddit is just
how the Internet works these days," Chen wrote.

Text, of course, was a different story. You couldn't publish someone else's 13
articles or *Wikipedia* entries and just throw a link to the original source at the
bottom. When BuzzFeed reporters wrote, they were subject to the same rules
as everyone else. Sure you could draw facts from elsewhere—everyone does
—but you had to write it in your own language.

At some point, Johnson probably got lazy and started inserting text into 14
his posts the same way he had been inserting photographs—by pressing
Ctrl+C and Ctrl+V. His mistake was that he forgot to put quote marks around
it and add "according to."

It didn't help reporters' perception of BuzzFeed that, when the first 15
instances of plagiarism were brought to editor-in-chief Ben Smith's attention,
he called them "serious failures" of attribution, rather than "plagiarism," and
simply "corrected" the posts.

"Ben, you can't 'correct' articles that were clearly plagiarized. I know you 16
know this!" Gawker's J. K. Trotter wrote on Twitter.

BuzzFeed is currently conducting an internal review of Johnson's work 17
before deciding on how to proceed. Whatever Johnson's fate, his plagiarism is
one more instance in which the public spotted the
wizard behind BuzzFeed's curtain. And the wizard
seems a little seedy.

Meanwhile, *The Onion*'s satire has become 18
reality.

> "Meanwhile, *The Onion*'s satire has become reality."

"Journalism today," one *Bloomberg News* 19
journalist tweeted: "accused of plagiarism 'for an article it did about former
President George H. W. Bush's socks.'"

Update (July 26) 20

Late Friday evening Smith announced Johnson had been fired after an 21
internal review found 40 instances of plagiarism.

⊙ AT ISSUE: SOURCES FOR UNDERSTANDING PLAGIARISM

1. Do you consider the material typically posted on BuzzFeed to be plagiarized? Explain. (If you are not familiar with BuzzFeed, visit the site
   and read a few posts.)

2. What does "Achilles' heel" mean? In what sense does plagiarism constitute BuzzFeed's Achilles' heel?

3. Why does Byers begin and end his discussion with paragraphs about *The Onion* (para. 1, 18–19)? Is this an effective strategy? Why or why not?

4. In paragraph 3, Byers says that many journalists believe that "BuzzFeed is constantly walking a fine line between aggregation, or 'curation,' and theft." What distinction is he making here? Do you see a difference between BuzzFeed's "aggregation" or "curation" and outright theft? Does Byers?

5. Byers quotes Farhad Manjoo, Adrian Chen, and others. What positions do his sources take on the issue of BuzzFeed and plagiarism?

6. Do you think it matters that Benny Johnson's "repackaging" of material from other sources was done deliberately rather than accidentally? Why or why not?

7. An update to this article notes that Johnson was fired from BuzzFeed "after an internal review found 40 instances of plagiarism." Do you think this punishment was justified? Why or why not?

8. Does Byers take a position on the issue of BuzzFeed and plagiarism? If so, what is that position? Do you see this essay as an argument? Which of the four elements of an argumentative essay are present here? Which are absent?

This summary was posted on July 24, 2014, on the WriteCheck.com blog.

OK OR NOT?

K. BALIBALOS AND J. GOPALAKRISHNAN

OK or not? This is an age-old question on plagiarism that arises during the 1
writing process, whether from researching a topic, incorporating and paraphrasing sources, or supporting arguments within a paper. Students commonly
find themselves in situations in which ethical questions are raised, and, all too
often, students wonder whether the decisions they made were the right ones.

This new poll series brings to light common scenarios—specifically 2
focused on plagiarism and perhaps a few examples on other forms of academic misconduct—and helps students better think critically about situations
in order to make ethical choices. All polls can be found on the WriteCheck
page on Facebook.

POLL QUESTION #1
**"OK or not? You and a partner collaborate on a paper by sharing notes and
paraphrasing the same ideas."**

WriteCheck asked a question.
January 7

OK or not? You and a partner collaborate on a paper,
sharing notes and paraphrasing the same ideas.

Not ok	+28
Depends	+9
OK	+3
+ Add an option...	

Like · Comment · Share   👍 23 💬 2

We started off the series by asking about collaboration because collaborating with 3
peers is a common thing to do among students. Students "collaborate" to
complete schoolwork and to help their friends in need. But collaborating with
peers can sometimes cross ethical boundaries. For example, in this question,
has the student copied-and-pasted the other student's work? The question
doesn't really get into that concern, but we do know that the students shared
the same ideas by "paraphrasing." This is where the question gets tricky. If

done properly, meaning the student wrote the idea in his/her own words and included citations, then paraphrasing is acceptable. Plagiarism is, by definition, the taking of another person's work or ideas.

The Results

The majority of respondents (28) chose "not OK" in response to student collaboration on a paper. However, two viewers who weighed in had a different perspective. 4

English Instructor, Beth Calvano, made the following comment: "If the paper is supposed to be individual, this scenario is not okay. If, according to plagiarism rules, it is not acceptable to use another person's ideas without citing that individual, collaborating in this way is not ethical. Your paper should consist of your own notes and original ideas." 5

Facebook fan Quenna Corchado agreed with Calvano, adding: "I think it's okay if they are citing. It doesn't matter if they are using the same sources as long as they cite it. They are helping each other out, so it makes sense that they are using the same notes and paraphrasing the same thing. What is important is to cite everything accordingly, which doesn't make it plagiarism." 6

Overall, it can be concluded from these responses that it is "OK" to share notes and paraphrase the same idea with proper attribution, unless the assignment is supposed to be done individually. 7

POLL QUESTION #2
"OK or not? You do a Google search of your subject and use *Wikipedia*, blogs, and other social sharing sites as sources because of their easy access."

WriteCheck asked a question.
May 2

Ok or Not? You do a Google search of your subject and use Wikipedia, blogs and other social sharing sites as sources because of their easy access.

Not ok	+20	
Depends	+34	
Ok	+9	

Like · Comment · Share   6   2

This situation resonates with students because of the amount of free, available information due in part to the mass connectivity of the digital age. Nowadays, *Wikipedia* is synonymous with accessibility and reader-friendly information since it provides accurate information on nearly every topic one might be researching. The number of blogs on the internet grows exponentially by the day since anyone has the ability to create a blog and share their thoughts. And, of course, social sites are a normal part of millions of people's lives. However, 8 just because information is available on the web doesn't mean that it's reputable to use as a source in your academic paper.

The Results

Based on 34 respondents, "depends" was the top answer, followed by "not 9 OK" (20 respondents).

To provide some insight, Jason Chu from Plagiarism.org weighed in with 10 the following comment: "It's OK to use Google search, *Wikipedia*, and social sharing sites as the starting point for doing research for a paper. But you should NOT rely on these sources alone. In fact, *Wikipedia* entries typically list references that are great to use in your research in support of your paper. But, by and large, sources that rely heavily on crowd-sourced or shared content — like *Wikipedia* or Yahoo! Answers — do not carry the same authority as a peer-reviewed journal article, for example."

Jessica from WriteCheck argued that it was "not OK," citing educator 11 insight that social sites should never be cited in research papers. Academic writing requires looking at primary or secondary sources, which are typically presented in academic journals, whereas *Wikipedia* is written for the general public.

Overall, it can be concluded that the answer is "depends." Social sites like 12 *Wikipedia* can be used as a starting point for research papers, but adding academic credibility to your sources will result in a more thorough and scholarly research paper.

POLL QUESTION #3
"OK or not? You get 2 assignments with enough overlap to submit the same paper to both."

> **WriteCheck** asked a question.
> June 6
>
> OK or not? You get 2 assignments with enough overlap to submit the same paper to both.
>
> | ☐ Not OK | +26 |
> | ☐ OK | +24 |
> | 3 More... | |
>
> Like · Comment · Share   👍 8 💬 2

The most recent poll was inspired by a recent article on the *Ethicist*, a blog on 13 the *New York Times*, entitled, "Can I Use the Same Paper for Multiple College Courses?" Some readers see it as a stroke of genius, while others view it as the mark of laziness. Some suggest that it is cheating, while others opine that you are only cheating yourself. *International Business Times* writer James DiGioia disagreed with *The Ethicist* in his article, "*The Ethicist* Is Wrong: Self-Plagiarism Is Cheating." Given those different opinions, we wanted to see what our WriteCheck community thought. "Is it OK to submit one paper for two assignments?"

The Results

The results were evenly split among the poll respondents between "not OK" 14 and "OK." *The Ethicist* describes why this situation is tricky, explaining that emotionally, our hearts cry that "this *must* be unethical, somehow," but aside from these emotions, he argued that there were no grounds that inherently make submitting papers to multiple assignments unethical.

Unlike James DiGioia, Jason Chu of Plagiarism.org agreed somewhere in 15 the middle, saying: "OK—if instructor approval is received. Not OK otherwise."

In summary, although debatable, it could be concluded that submitting a 16 paper to multiple assignments is "OK" with approval from both instructors. Otherwise, it may be a violation of university-wide academic integrity codes and generally accepted principles that assignments are unique to a class.

Conclusion

These three scenarios are real-life situations that students may face at one 17 point in their academic journeys. Some scenarios may appear more straightforward than others, however, no plagiarism allegation is simple. Self-plagiarism, for example, may make more sense in a professional or scholarly environment because of copyright issues. Self-plagiarism is a gray area, and a relatively new term within academia, and is still to be explored. *Wikipedia* also is a newly introduced site, becoming popular only within the last decade.

While definitions and rules of plagiarism are debated, learning the defini- 18 tions and how to cite properly, as well as working with instructors when a question arises are all ways to avoid plagiarism and academic misconduct.

Have you encountered situations where you asked yourself "OK or not?" 19

◑ AT ISSUE: SOURCES FOR UNDERSTANDING PLAGIARISM

1. This blog post reports the results of a survey, and it also makes a point. In one sentence, summarize the main point of the post.

2. Which of the writers' three scenarios, if any, do you see as "not OK"? Why? With which majority opinions, if any, do you disagree? Explain.

3. For what purpose did the writers design this poll? Where do they state this purpose?

4. Who is the intended audience for the three poll questions? Is this the same audience as the one the writers expected to read the results of the poll? How can you tell?

5. In poll question #2, what conclusions do the writers draw about the use of *Wikipedia*? What problems does this site, as well as "blogs and other social sharing sites," present for college students?

6. Do you think the writers' conclusion takes a strong enough stand on the issue discussed? Is this post actually an argument? Why or why not?

This essay originally appeared in the *Los Angeles Times* on June 17, 2012.

ESSAY MILLS: A COARSE LESSON IN CHEATING

DAN ARIELY

Sometimes as I decide what kind of papers to assign to my students, I worry about essay mills, companies whose sole purpose is to generate essays for high school and college students (in exchange for a fee, of course). 1

The mills claim that the papers are meant to be used as reference material to help students write their own, original papers. But with names such as echeat.com, it's pretty clear what their real purpose is. 2

Professors in general are concerned about essay mills and their effect on learning, but not knowing exactly what they provide, I wasn't sure how concerned to be. So together with my lab manager Aline Grüneisen, I decided to check the services out. We ordered a typical college term paper from four different essay mills. The topic of the paper? Cheating. 3

Here is the prompt we gave the four essay mills: 4

"When and why do people cheat? Consider the social circumstances involved in dishonesty, and provide a thoughtful response to the topic of cheating. Address various forms of cheating (personal, at work, etc.) and how each of these can be rationalized by a social culture of cheating." 5

We requested a term paper for a university-level social psychology class, 12 pages long, using 15 sources (cited and referenced in a bibliography). The paper was to conform to American Psychological Assn. style guidelines and needed to be completed in the next two weeks. All four of the essay mills agreed to provide such a paper, charging us in advance, between $150 and $216 for the paper. 6

Right on schedule, the essays came, and I have to say that, to some degree, they allayed my fears that students can rely on the services to get good grades. What we got back from the mills can best be described as gibberish. A few of the papers attempted to mimic APA style, but none achieved it without glaring errors. Citations were sloppy. Reference lists contained outdated and unknown sources, including blog posts. Some of the links to reference material were broken. 7

> "What we got back from the mills can best be described as gibberish."

And the writing quality? Awful. The authors of all four papers seemed to have a very tenuous grasp of the English language, not to mention how to format an essay. Paragraphs jumped bluntly from one topic to another, often simply listing various forms of cheating or providing a long stream of examples that were never explained or connected to the "thesis" of the paper. 8

One paper contained this paragraph: "Cheating by healers. Healing is 9 different. There is harmless healing, when healers-cheaters and wizards offer omens, lapels, damage to withdraw, the husband-wife back and stuff. We read in the newspaper and just smile. But these days fewer people believe in wizards."

This comes from another: "If the large allowance of study undertook on 10 scholar betraying is any suggestion of academia and professors' powerful yearn to decrease scholar betraying, it appeared expected these mind-set would component into the creation of their school room guidelines."

And finally, these gems: 11

"By trusting blindfold only in stable love, loyalty, responsibility and hon- 12 esty the partners assimilate with the credulous and naive persons of the past."

"Women have a much greater necessity to feel special." 13

"The future generation must learn for historical mistakes and develop the 14 sense of pride and responsibility for its actions."

It's hard to believe that students purchasing such papers would ever do 15 so again.

And the story does not end there. We submitted the four essays to 16 WriteCheck.com, a website that inspects papers for plagiarism, and found that two of the papers were 35% to 39% copied from existing works. We decided to take action on the two papers with substantial plagiarizing and contacted the essay mills requesting our money back. Despite the solid proof we provided to them, the companies insisted they did not plagiarize. One company even threat-ened to expose us by calling the dean and saying we had purchased the paper.

It's comforting in a way that the technological revolution has not yet 17 solved students' problems. They still have no other option but to actually work on their papers (or maybe cheat in the old-fashioned way and copy from friends). But I do worry about the existence of essay mills and the signal that they send to our students.

As for our refund, we are still waiting. 18

⊘ AT ISSUE: SOURCES FOR UNDERSTANDING PLAGIARISM

1. Consider the title of this essay. What does the word *coarse* mean? What does it suggest in this context?

2. What is an essay mill? Look up the word *mill*. Which of the definitions provided applies to the word as it is used in the phrase *essay mill*?

3. Why does Ariely decide to investigate the services provided by essay mills? What does he want to find out? Is he successful?

4. What does Ariely conclude about the four companies he surveys? Does he provide enough evidence to support his conclusion? If not, what kind of evidence should he add?

5. In paragraph 15, Ariely says, "It's hard to believe that students purchasing such papers would ever do so again." Given the evidence Ariely presents, how do you explain the continued popularity of essay mills?

6. What information does Ariely provide in his conclusion? Do you think he is departing from his essay's central focus here, or do you think the concluding paragraph is an appropriate and effective summary of his ideas? Explain.

TERM PAPERS FOR SALE ADVERTISEMENT (WEB PAGE)

⊘ AT ISSUE: SOURCES FOR UNDERSTANDING PLAGIARISM

1. The Web page above is from a site that offers papers for sale to students. What argument does this Web page make? What counter-argument could you present?

2. Identify appeals to *logos*, *pathos*, and *ethos* on the TermPaperWriter .org page. Which appeal dominates?

3. Study the images of students on the page. What message do these images convey?

4. Unlike the TermPaperWriter.org page, many other sites that offer papers for sale include errors in grammar, spelling, and punctuation. Search the Web for some other sites that offer papers for sale. What errors can you find? Do such errors weaken the message of these ads, or are they irrelevant?

5. One site promises its papers are "100% plagiarism free." Does this promise make sense? Explain.

TEMPLATE FOR WRITING AN ARGUMENT ABOUT PLAGIARISM

Write a one-paragraph argument in which you take a position on where to draw the line with plagiarism. Follow the template below, filling in the blanks to create your argument.

> To many people, plagiarism is theft; to others, however, it is not that simple. For example, some define *plagiarism* as _____
>
> _____ ; others see it as _____
>
> _____. Another thing to consider is
>
> _____
>
> _____. In addition, _____
>
> _____. Despite these differences of opinion,
>
> plagiarism is often dealt with harshly and can ruin careers and reputations. All things considered,
>
> _____
>
> _____

⊜ EXERCISE 11.4

Discuss your feelings about plagiarism with two or three of your class-mates. Consider how you define *plagiarism*, what you believe causes it, whether there are degrees of dishonesty, and so on, but focus on the *effects* of plagiarism—on those who commit it and on those who are its victims. Then, write a paragraph that summarizes the key points of your discussion.

⊜ EXERCISE 11.5

Write an argumentative essay on the topic, "Where Should We Draw the Line with Plagiarism?" Begin by defining what you mean by *plagiarism*, and then narrow your discussion down to a particular group—for example, high school or college students, historians, scientists, or journalists. Cite the sources on pages 383–409, and be sure to document the sources you use and to include a works-cited page. (See Chapter 10 for information on documenting sources.)

⊜ EXERCISE 11.6

Review the four pillars of argument discussed in Chapter 1. Does your essay include all four elements of an effective argument? Add anything that is missing. Then, label the elements of your argument.

⊘ WRITING ASSIGNMENTS: USING SOURCES RESPONSIBLY

1. Write an argument in which you take a position on who (or what) is to blame for plagiarism among college students. Is plagiarism always the student's fault, or are other people (or other factors) at least partly to blame?

2. Write an essay in which you argue that an honor code will (or will not) eliminate (or at least reduce) plagiarism and other kinds of academic dishonesty at your school.

3. Reread the essays by Posner and Balibalos and Gopalakrishnan in this chapter. Then, write an argument in which you argue that only intentional plagiarism should be punished.

4. Do you consider student plagiarism a victimless crime that is best left unpunished? If so, why? If not, how does it affect its victims—for example, the student who plagiarizes, the instructor, the other students in the class, and the school?

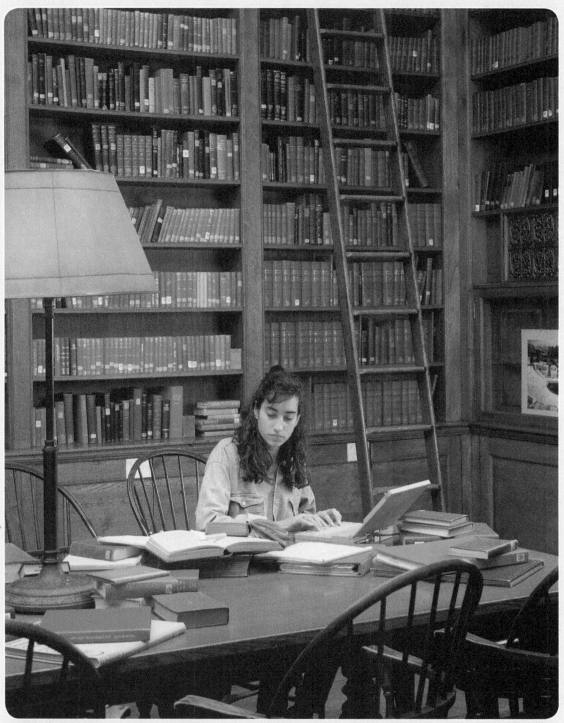

Writing Literary Arguments

When you write an essay about literature, you have a number of options. For example, you can write a **response** (expressing your reactions to a poem, play, or story), or you can write an **explication** (focusing on a work's individual elements, such as a poem's imagery, meter, figurative language, and diction). You can also write an **analysis** of a work's theme, a character in a play or a story, or a work's historical or cultural context. Another option, which is discussed in the pages that follow, is to write a literary argument.

What Is a Literary Argument?

When you write a literary argument, you do more than just respond to, explicate, or analyze a work of literature. When you develop a **literary argument**, you take a position about a literary work (or works), support that position with evidence, and refute possible opposing arguments. You might, for example, take the position that a familiar interpretation of a well-known work is limited in some way, that a work's impact today is different from its impact when it was written, or that two apparently very different works have some significant similarities.

It is important to understand that not every essay about literature is a literary argument. For example, you might use a discussion of Tillie Olsen's short story "I Stand Here Ironing," with its sympathetic portrait of a young mother during the Great Depression, to support an argument in favor of President Franklin D. Roosevelt's expansion of social welfare programs. Alternatively, you might use Martín Espada's poem "Why I Went to College" to support your own decision to continue your education. However, writing a literary argument involves much more than discussing a literary work in order to support a particular position or referring to a character to shed light on your own intellectual development or to explain a choice you made. A literary argument *takes a stand* about a work (or works) of literature.

Stating an Argumentative Thesis

When you develop an argumentative thesis about literature, your goal is to state a thesis that has an edge—one that takes a stand on your topic. Like any effective thesis, the thesis of a literary argument should be clearly worded and specific; it should also be more than a statement of fact.

INEFFECTIVE THESIS (TOO GENERAL)	In "A&P," Sammy faces a difficult decision.
EFFECTIVE THESIS (MORE SPECIFIC)	Sammy's decision to quit his job reveals more about the conformist society in which "A&P" is set than about Sammy himself.
INEFFECTIVE THESIS (STATES A FACT)	The theme of *Hamlet* is often seen as an Oedipal conflict.
EFFECTIVE THESIS (TAKES A STAND)	Although many critics have identified an Oedipal conflict in *Hamlet*, Shakespeare's play is also a story of a young man who is struggling with familiar problems—love, family, and his future.

Here are three possible thesis statements that you could support in a literary argument:

- Charlotte Perkins Gilman's short story "The Yellow Wallpaper," usually seen as a feminist story, is actually a ghost story.

- The two characters in August Strindberg's play *The Stronger* seem to be rivals for the affection of a man, but they are really engaged in a professional rivalry to see who gives the better performance.

- Although many readers might see Wilfred Owen's "Dulce et Decorum Est" as the more powerful poem because of its graphic imagery of war, Carl Sandburg's understated "Grass" is likely to have a greater impact on modern readers, who have been overexposed to violent images.

(For more on developing a thesis statement, see Chapter 7.)

Choosing Evidence

Like any argument, a literary argument relies on evidence. Some of this evidence can be found in the literary work itself. For example, to make a point about a character's antisocial behavior, you would cite specific examples of such behavior from the work. To make a point about a poet's use of biblical allusions, you would present examples of such allusions from the poem.

> **NOTE**
>
> Be careful not to substitute plot summary for evidence. For example, summarizing everything that happens to a character will not convince your readers that the character is motivated by envy. Choose only *relevant* examples—in this case, specific instances of a character's jealous behavior, including relevant quotations from the literary work.

Evidence can also come from **literary criticism**—scholarly articles by experts in the field that analyze and evaluate works of literature. For example, to argue that a particular critical theory is inaccurate, outdated, or oversimplified, you would quote critics who support that theory before you explain why you disagree with their interpretation. (For more on evaluating potential sources for your essay, see Chapter 8.)

Writing a Literary Argument

The structure of a literary argument is similar to the structure of any other argument: it includes a **thesis statement** in the introduction, supporting **evidence**, **refutation** of opposing arguments, and a strong **concluding statement**. However, unlike other arguments, literary arguments follow specific conventions for writing about literature:

- In your essay's first paragraph, include the author's full name and the title of each work you are discussing.

- Use present tense when discussing events in works of literature. For example, if you are discussing "I Stand Here Ironing," you would say, "The mother *worries* [not *worried*] about her ability to provide for her child." There are two exceptions to this rule. Use past tense when referring to historical events: "The Great Depression *made* things difficult for mothers like the narrator." Also use past tense to refer to events that came before the action described in the work: "The mother is particularly vulnerable because her husband *left* her alone to support her children."

- Italicize titles of plays and novels. Put titles of poems and short stories in quotation marks.

- If you quote more than four lines of prose (or more than three lines of poetry), indent the entire quotation one inch from the left-hand margin. Do not include quotation marks, and add the parenthetical documentation after the end punctuation. Introduce the quotation with a colon, and do not add extra line spaces above or below it.

- When mentioning writers and literary critics in the body of your essay, use their full names ("Emily Dickinson") the first time you mention them and their last names only ("Dickinson," not "Miss Dickinson" or "Emily") after that.

- Use **MLA documentation style** in your paper, and include a works-cited list. (See Chapter 10 for information on MLA documentation.)

- In your in-text citations (set in parentheses), cite page numbers for stories, act and scene numbers for plays, and line numbers for poems. Use the word *line* or *lines* for the first in-text citation of lines from each poem. After the first citation, you may omit the word *line* or *lines*.

The following literary argument, "Confessions of a Misunderstood Poem: An Analysis of 'The Road Not Taken,'" takes a stand in favor of a particular way of interpreting poetry.

CONFESSIONS OF A MISUNDERSTOOD POEM: AN ANALYSIS OF "THE ROAD NOT TAKEN"

MEGAN MCGOVERN

Introduction (identifies titles and authors of works to be discussed)

In his poem "Introduction to Poetry," Billy Collins suggests that rather than dissecting a poem to find its meaning, students should use their imaginations to experience poetry. According to Collins, they should "drop a mouse into a poem / and watch him probe his way out" (lines 5–6). However, Collins overstates his case when he implies that analyzing a poem to find out what it might mean is a brutal or deadly process, comparable to tying the poem to a chair and "beating it with a hose" (15). Rather than killing a poem's spirit, a careful and methodical dissection can often help the reader better appreciate its subtler meanings. In fact, with patient coaxing, a poem often has much to "confess." One such poem is Robert Frost's familiar but frequently misunderstood "The Road Not Taken." An examination of Frost's "The Road Not Taken" reveals a complex and somewhat troubling message about the arbitrariness of our life choices and our need to idealize those choices.

The word *lines* is omitted from the in-text citation after the first reference to lines of a poem.

Thesis statement

On the surface, Frost's poem seems to have a fairly simple meaning. The poem's speaker talks about coming to a fork in the road and choosing the "less-traveled" path. Most readers see the fork in the road as a metaphor: the road represents life, and the fork represents an individual's choices in life. By following the less-traveled road, the speaker is choosing the less conventional—and supposedly more emotionally rewarding—route. At the end of the poem, the speaker indicates his satisfaction when he says his choice "made all the difference" (line 20). However, Frost himself, referring to "The Road Not Taken," advised readers "'to be careful of that one; it's a tricky poem—very tricky,'" encouraging readers not to accept the most appealing or obvious interpretation (qtd. in Savoie 7–8). Literary critic Bojana Vujin urges readers to look for "poetic booby traps such as irony or deceit" in this poem and to enjoy the pleasures and rewards of discovering instances of "deliberate deceit on the poet's part" (195). In fact, after the speaker's tone and word choice are carefully examined, the poem's message seems darker and more complicated than it did initially.

2 Refutation of opposing argument

The speaker's tone in the first three stanzas suggests indecision, regret, and, ultimately, lack of power. Rather than bravely facing the choice between one common path and one uncommon path, the speaker spends most of the poem considering two seemingly equal roads, "sorry" not to be able to "travel both" (2). Even after choosing "the other" road in line 6, the speaker continues for two more stanzas to weigh his options. The problem is that the two roads are, in fact, indistinguishable. As several critics have observed, "the difference between the two roads, at least when

3 Evidence: Analysis and explication of Frost poem

Evidence: Literary
criticism

it comes to the amount of treading they have been exposed to, is but
an illusion: "'they both that morning equally lay' and neither is
particularly travelled by" (Vujin 197). The roads are worn "really
about the same" (10). If there is virtually no difference between the
two, then why does Frost draw our attention to this fork in the
road—this seemingly critical moment of choice? If Frost had wanted
to dramatize a meaningful decision, the roads would be different in
some significant way.

Evidence: Literary
criticism

     One critic, Frank Lentricchia, argues that Frost is demonstrating   4
"'that our life-shaping choices are irrational, that we are fundamentally out of control'" (qtd. in Savoie 13). Similarly, another critic
contends that Frost wants his readers "to feel his characters'
inner conflicts and to feel as conflicted as his characters, who are

Evidence: Analysis and
explication of Frost poem

all too often lost in themselves" (Plunkett). These two critical views
help to explain the speaker's indecision in the first three stanzas.
The speaker impulsively chooses "the other" road but cannot accept
the arbitrariness of his choice; therefore, he cannot stop considering
the first road. He exclaims in the third stanza, "Oh, I kept the first
for another day!" (13). In the next two lines, when he finally gives up
the possibility of following that first road, he predicts, "Yet knowing
how way leads on to way, / I doubted if I should ever come back"
(14–15). Here, the speaker further demonstrates a lack of control
over his own decisions. He describes a future guided not by his own
active, meaningful choices but rather by some arbitrary force. In a
world where "way leads on to way," he is a passive traveler, not a
decisive individualist.

Evidence: Analysis and
explication of Frost poem

     Given the indecision that characterizes the previous stanzas, the   5
poem's last two lines are surprisingly decisive: "I took the one less
traveled by / And that has made all the difference" (19–20). Is the
speaker contradicting himself? How has he suddenly become clear
about the rightness of his decision? In fact, the last stanza does not
make sense unless the reader perceives the irony in the speaker's tone.
The speaker is imagining himself in the future, "ages and ages hence,"
telling the story of his moment at the crossroads (17). He imagines
how he will, in hindsight, give his choice meaning and clarity that it
did not have at the time. As Vujin argues, the poem's speaker is

already "mythologizing his self and his life" (198). The narrator, rather than anticipating the satisfaction that will come from having made the right and braver choice, is anticipating rewriting his own life story to make sense of an ultimately arbitrary chain of events. Vujin explains, "This is not a poem about individuality; this is a poem about self-deceit and the rewriting of one's own history" (198). Reading the last stanza ironically allows readers to make sense of the poem as a whole.

Evidence: Literary criticism

There are many possible interpretations of "The Road Not Taken," most of which can be supported with evidence from the poem itself. However, to understand these interpretations, readers need to take the poem apart, look at how its parts fit together, and reach a thoughtful and logical conclusion. To do so, readers must go against some of Billy Collins's well-meaning advice and be willing to tie the poem—and themselves—to a chair: to read it carefully, ask questions, and stay with it until it confesses.

6 Conclusion

Works Cited

Collins, Billy. "Introduction to Poetry." *Sailing Alone around the Room*. Random House, 1998, p. 16.

Frost, Robert. "The Road Not Taken." *Mountain Interval*. Henry Holt, 1920, *Bartleby.com*, www.bartleby.com/119/1.html.

Plunkett, Adam. "Robert Frost Was Neither Light Nor Dark." *New Republic*, 13 Jun. 2014, newrepublic.com/article/118046/art-robert-frost-tim-kendall-reviewed-adam-plunkett.

Savoie, John. "A Poet's Quarrel: Jamesian Pragmatism and Frost's 'The Road Not Taken.'" *New England Quarterly*, vol. 77, no. 1, 2004, pp. 5–24. *Academic Search Premier*, www.ebscohost.com/academic/academic-search-premier.

Vujin, Bojana. "'I Took the Road Less Traveled By': Self-Deception in Frost's and Eliot's Early Poetry." *Annual Review of the Faculty of Philosophy*, vol. 36, no. 1, 2011, pp. 195–203.

⊙ The following literary argument, "Not Just a 'Girl,'" argues against the commonly held position that a key character in the 1925 Ernest Hemingway short story "Hills Like White Elephants" is a stereotype.

NOT JUST A "GIRL"

LOREN MARTINEZ

Introduction

In Ernest Hemingway's famous story "Hills Like White Elephants," 1 a couple, "the American and the girl with him," talk and drink while waiting for a train to Madrid (Hemingway 69). Most readers agree that the subject of their discussion is whether "the girl," called Jig, should have an abortion. Most of the story is told through dialogue, and although the word *abortion* is never mentioned, most readers agree that the pregnancy is the source of the tension between them. However, there are other aspects of the story about which readers do not agree. For example, some critics believe that Hemingway's portrayal of "the girl" is unfair or sexist. More specifically, some see in her the qualities of "the typically submissive Hemingway woman" (Nolan 19). How-

Thesis statement

ever, a close reading of the story reveals the opposite to be true: "the girl" is not a one-dimensional stereotype but a complex, sympathetically drawn character.

Refutation of opposing arguments

Most critics who see Hemingway's portrayal of Jig as sexist base 2 their interpretation on Hemingway's reputation and not on the story itself. For example, feminist critic Katherine M. Rogers points out that because Hemingway himself "openly expressed fear of and hostility to women" (263), it "seems fair" to see his male characters "as representative of Hemingway himself" (248). However, although "the American" in this story may see Jig as just "a pleasant pastime," it would be an oversimplification to confuse the character's opinion of her with the writer's as Rogers would encourage us to do (251). For example, one could argue (as many critics have done) that because the name "Jig" has sexual connotations, it reveals the author's sexism (Renner 38). However, as critic Howard Hannum points out, she is referred to by this name only twice in the story, both times by the male character himself, not by the narrator (qtd. in Renner 38). Critic Stanley Renner agrees with Hannum, rejecting the idea that Hemingway's choice to refer to the character as "the girl" is equally "belittling" (38).

Renner argues that this use of the word *girl* is necessary to show how the character changes and matures in this story. In fact, he sees "her achievement of mature self-knowledge and assertion [as] the main line of development in the story" (39). All in all, the evidence suggests that "the girl," not "the American," is actually the story's protagonist. Given this central focus on "the girl" and the complexity of her character, the accusations that Hemingway's sexism has led him to create a stereotype do not seem justified.

When students who are not familiar with Hemingway's reputation as a misogynist read "Hills Like White Elephants," they tend to sympathize more often with "the girl" than with "the American" (Bauer 126) and to see the female character's thoughtfulness and depth. Although "the American" refers to the abortion as "'really an awfully simple operation'" (Hemingway 72), downplaying its seriousness, "the girl" has a "more mature understanding" of what her decision might mean (Bauer 130). She recognizes that it is not so "simple," and she is not naive enough to think that having the baby will save the relationship. In fact, she responds to his own naive comments with sarcasm. He claims that they will be "'all right and happy'" if she goes through with the operation; he says he's "'known lots of people who have done it.' 'So have I,' said the girl. 'And afterward they were all so happy'" (Hemingway 73). Despite her sarcasm and her resistance to his suggestions, the man continues to insist that this problem will be easy to fix. Finally, the girl becomes irritated with him and, as readers can see by the dashes that end his lines midsentence, cuts him off, finishing his lines for him as he tries to tell her again how "perfectly simple" the operation is (Hemingway 76). Readers understand her pain and frustration when she finally says, "'Would you please please please please please please please stop talking?'" (Hemingway 76).

The argument that "the girl" is a flat, stereotypical character portrayed in sexist terms is hard to support. In fact, a stronger argument could be made that it is the man, "the American," who is the stereotype. As critic Charles J. Nolan Jr. points out, "Hemingway highlights Jig's maturity and superiority as he excoriates the selfishness and insensitivity of her companion" (19). Moreover, "the girl" is certainly the central character in this story—the one in conflict, the one who must

3   Evidence: First point in support of thesis

4   Evidence: Second point in support of thesis

make the final decision, and the one who grows over the course of the story. At times, she seems willing to listen to the man, even going so far as to say, "'Then I'll do it. Because I don't care about me'" (Hemingway 74). However, soon after, she responds defiantly to his comment, "'You mustn't feel that way'" with "'I don't feel any way'" (Hemingway 75). Thus, as Renner notes, Hemingway's dialogue reveals "the self-centered motives of his male character" while at the same time dramatizing the female character's complex inner struggle (38). By the end of the story, the shallow "American" still expects things to be all right between them. But when the man asks, "'Do you feel better?'" Hemingway shows the girl's quiet power—and her transformation—by giving her the final understated words of the story: "'I feel fine. . . . There's nothing wrong with me. I feel fine'" (Hemingway 77). Although we do not learn what her decision is, we can see that she is now in control: she has decided to shut down the conversation, and what the man has to say no longer matters.

Conclusion

In "Hills Like White Elephants," "the girl" proves herself to be neither "'weak *in* character'" nor "'weak *as* character'" as some have described Hemingway's female characters (Bauer 126). Far from being weak *in* character, she constantly questions and pushes against the male character's suggestions. And far from being weak *as* a character, she acts as the protagonist in this story, winning the reader's sympathies. A stereotypically drawn female character would not be able to

Concluding statement

carry off either of these feats. Although Hemingway may demonstrate sexism in his other stories—and demonstrate it in his own life—readers who evaluate *this* story will discover a complex, conflicted, sympathetic female character.

5

Works Cited

Bauer, Margaret D. "Forget the Legend and Read the Work: Teaching Two Stories by Ernest Hemingway." *College Literature*, vol. 30, no. 3, 2003, pp. 124–37. *Academic Search Premier*, www.ebscohost .com/academic/academic-search-premier.

Hemingway, Ernest. "Hills Like White Elephants." *Men without Women*. Charles Scribner's, 1927, pp. 69–77.

Nolan, Charles J., Jr. "Hemingway's Women's Movement." *Hemingway Review*, vol. 4, no. 1, 1984, pp. 14–22. *Academic Search Premier*, www.ebscohost.com/academic/academic-search-premier.

Renner, Stanley. "Moving to the Girl's Side of 'Hills Like White Elephants.'" *Hemingway Review*, vol. 15, no. 1, 1995, pp. 27–41. *Academic Search Premier*, www.ebscohost.com/academic/academic-search-premier.

Rogers, Katherine M. *The Troublesome Helpmate: A History of Misogyny in Literature*. U of Washington P, 1996.

B

Documenting Sources: APA

American Psychological Association (APA) documentation style is commonly used in the social sciences. In APA style, parenthetical references refer readers to sources in the list of references at the end of the paper.* Parenthetical citations must be provided for all sources that are not common knowledge, whether you are summarizing, paraphrasing, or quoting.

Using Parenthetical References

In APA style, parenthetical references refer readers to sources in the list of references at the end of the paper. A typical parenthetical reference includes the author's last name (followed by a comma) and the year of publication: (Vang, 2015). Here are some guidelines for specific situations.

- If the author's last name appears in the text, follow it with the year of publication, in parentheses: According to Vang (2015), recent studies suggest . . .

- When quoting from a source, include a page number, if available: (Vang, 2015, p. 33). Once you have cited a source, you can refer to the author a second time without the publication date so long as it is clear you are referring to the same source: Vang also found . . .

- If no author is identified, use a shortened version of the title: ("Mind," 2015).

- If you are citing multiple works by the same author or authors published in the same year, include a lowercase letter with the year: (Peters, 2014a), (Peters, 2014b), and so on.

---

*American Psychological Association, *Publication Manual of the American Psychological Association*, Sixth Edition (2010).

- When a work has two authors, cite both names, separated by an ampersand, and the year: (Tabor & Garza, 2006). For three to five authors, in the first reference, cite all authors, along with the year; for subsequent references, cite just the first author, followed by et al. When a work has six or more authors, cite just the first author, followed by et al. and the year: (McCarthy et al., 2010).

- Omit page numbers or dates if the source does not include them. (Try to find a .pdf version of an online source; it will usually include page numbers.)

- If you quote a source found in another source, cite the original author and the source in which you found it: Psychologist Gary Wells asserted . . . (as cited in Doyle, 2005, p. 122).

- Include in-text references to personal communications and interviews by providing the person's name, the phrase "personal communication," and the date: (J. Smith, personal communication, February 12, 2015). Do not include these sources in your reference list.

If a direct quotation is forty words or less, include it within quotation marks without separating it from the rest of the text. When quoting a passage of more than forty words, indent the entire block of quoted text one-half inch from the left margin, and do not enclose it in quotation marks. It should be double-spaced, like the rest of the paper. Place parenthetical documentation one space after the final punctuation.

Preparing a Reference List

Start your list of references on a separate page at the end of your paper. Center the title References at the top of the page, and follow these guidelines:

- Begin each reference flush with the left margin, and indent subsequent lines one-half inch. Double-space the reference list within and between entries.

- List your references alphabetically by the author's last name (or by the first major word of the title if no author is identified).

- If the list includes references for two sources by the same author, alphabetize them by title.

- Italicize titles of books and periodicals. Do not italicize article titles or enclose them in quotation marks.

- For titles of books and articles, capitalize the first word of the title and subtitle as well as any proper nouns. Capitalize words in a periodical title as they appear in the original.

When you have completed your reference list, go through your paper and make sure that every reference cited is included in the list in the correct order.

Examples of APA Citations

The following are examples of APA citations.

Periodicals

Article in a journal paginated by volume

> Shah, N. A. (2006). Women's human rights in the Koran: An interpretive approach. *Human Rights Quarterly, 28*, 868–902.

Article in a journal paginated by issue

> Lamb, B., & Keller, H. (2007). Understanding cultural models of parenting: The role of intracultural variation and response style. *Journal of Cross-Cultural Psychology, 38*(1), 50–57.

Magazine article

> Von Drehle, D. (2015, April 20). Line of fire. *Time, 185*(14), 24–28.

Newspaper article

> DeParle, J. (2009, April 19). Struggling to rise in suburbs where failing means fitting in. *The New York Times,* pp. A1, A20–A21.

Books

Books by one author

> Jordan, Jennifer A. (2015). *Edible memory: The lure of heirloom tomatoes and other forgotten foods*. Chicago, IL: University of Chicago Press.

Books by two to seven authors

> McFadden, J., & Al-Khalili, J. (2014). *Life on the edge: The coming of age of quantum biology*. New York, NY: Crown.

Books by eight or more authors

> Barrett, J. M., Smith, V., Wilson, R. T., Haley, V. A., Clarke, P., Palmer, N. B., . . . Fraser, D. (2012). *How to cite references in APA style*. New York: Cambridge University Press.

Edited book

Brummett, B. (Ed.). (2008). *Uncovering hidden rhetorics: Social issues in disguise*. Los Angeles, CA: Sage.

Essay in an edited book

Alberts, H. C. (2006). The multiple transformations of Miami. In H. Smith & O. J. Furuseth (Eds.), *Latinos in the new south: Transformations of place* (pp. 135–151). Burlington, VT: Ashgate.

Translation

Piketty, T. (2015). *The Economics of inequality* (A. Goldhammer, Trans.). Cambridge, MA: Harvard University Press.

Revised edition

Johnson, B., & Christensen, L. B. (2008). *Educational research: Quantitative, qualitative, and mixed approaches* (3rd ed.). Los Angeles, CA: Sage.

Internet Sources

Entire website

Secretariat of the Convention on Biological Diversity. (2015). *Convention on biological diversity*. Retrieved from https://www.cbd.int/

Web page within a website

The great divide: How Westerners and Muslims view each other. (2006, July 6). In *Pew global attitudes project*. Retrieved from http://pewglobal.org/reports/display.php?ReportID=253

University program website

National security archive. (2009). Retrieved from George Washington University website: http://www.gwu.edu/~nsarchiv/

Journal article found on the Web with a DOI

Because websites change and disappear without warning, many publishers have started adding a **Digital Object Identifier (DOI)** to their articles. A DOI is a unique number that can be retrieved no matter where the article ends up on the Web.

To locate an article with a known DOI, go to the DOI system website at http://dx.doi.org/ and type in the DOI number. When citing an article that has a DOI (usually found on the first page of the article), you do not need to include a URL in your reference or the name of the database in which you may have found the article.

> Geers, A. L., Wellman, J. A., & Lassiter, G. D. (2009). Dispositional optimism and engagement: The moderating influence of goal prioritization. *Journal of Personality and Social Psychology, 94,* 913–932. doi:10.1037/a0014746

Journal article found on the Web without a DOI

> Bendetto, M. M. (2008). Crisis on the immigration bench: An ethical perspective. *Brooklyn Law Review, 73,* 467–523. Retrieved from http://brooklaw.edu/students/journals/blr.php/

Journal article from an electronic database

The name and URL of the database are not required for citations if a DOI is available. If no DOI is available, provide the home page URL of the journal or of the book or report publisher.

> Staub, E., & Pearlman, L. A. (2009). Reducing intergroup prejudice and conflict: A commentary. *Journal of Personality and Social Psychology, 11,* 3–23. Retrieved from http://www.apa.org/journals /psp/

Electronic book

> Katz, R. N. (Ed.). (2008). *The tower and the cloud: Higher education in an era of cloud computing.* Retrieved from http://net .educause.edu/ir/library/pdf/PUB7202.pdf

Video blog post

> Green, J. (2015, July 7). Understanding the financial crisis in Greece [Video file]. Retrieved from https://www.youtube.com /watch?v=tigaryz-1y4

Presentation slides

> Hall, M. E. (2009) *Who moved my job!? A psychology of job-loss "trauma"* [Presentation slides]. Retrieved from http://www.cew .wisc.edu/docs/WMMJ%20PwrPt-Summry2.ppt

Student Essay

The following research paper, "The High Cost of Cheap Counterfeit Goods," follows APA format as outlined in the preceding pages.

APA PAPER GUIDELINES

- An APA paper should have a one-inch margin all around and be double-spaced throughout.

- The first line of every paragraph should be indented, and all pages of the paper, including the first, should be numbered consecutively.

- Every page should have a page header (an abbreviated title in all upper-case letters) typed one-half inch from the top of the page.

- An APA paper has four sections: the *title page*, the *abstract*, the *body of the paper*, and the *reference list*:

  1. The **title page** (page 1) should include a running head (in all upper-case letters) at the top:

     Running Head: COUNTERFEIT GOODS

  2. The title page should also include the title of the paper (upper- and lower-case letters), your name (first name, middle initial, last name), and your school.

  3. The **abstract** (page 2) should be a 150- to 250-word summary of the paper. Type the word **Abstract** (centered); skip one line; and do not indent. After the abstract, skip one line and type *Keywords* (italicized and indented), followed by keywords that will help researchers find your essay in a database.

  4. The **body of the paper** should begin on page 3. After the title page, each page of the paper should include the running head (in all upper-case letters), typed flush left, one-half inch from the top of the page:

     COUNTERFEIT GOODS

  5. The **reference list** should begin on a new page, after the body of the paper. (See pages A-14–A-15 for a discussion of how to format the reference list.)

- Citations should follow APA documentation style.

The High Cost of Cheap Counterfeit Goods

Deniz A. Bilgutay

Humanities 101, Section 1

Professor Fitzgerald

March 4, 2015

Abstract

The global trade in counterfeit products costs manufacturers of luxury goods millions of dollars each year. Although this illegal trade threatens the free market, employs underage labor, and may even fund terrorism, many people consider it a victimless crime. Studies show that some consumers even take pride in buying knock-off products. But a closer look at this illicit trade in counterfeit goods shows that consumers in the United States—and around the world—do not understand the ethical implications of the choices they make. Consumers should stop supporting this illegal business, and law enforcement officials should prosecute it more vigorously than they currently do. In the final analysis, this illegal practice hurts legitimate businesses and in some cases endangers the health and safety of consumers.

Keywords: counterfeiting, terrorism, ethics, crime

The High Cost of Cheap Counterfeit Goods

For those who do not want to pay for genuine designer *Introduction*
products, a fake Louis Vuitton bag or knock-off Rolex watch
might seem too good to pass up. Such purchases may even be
a source of pride. According to one study, two-thirds of British
consumers said they would be "proud to tell family and
friends" that they bought inexpensive knock-offs (Thomas,
2007). The trade in counterfeit goods, however, is a crime—and
not a victimless crime. A growing body of evidence suggests
that the makers and distributers of counterfeit goods have
ties to child labor, organized crime, and even terrorism. In
addition, the global economic cost of counterfeiting is estimated at $600 billion a year, according to recent data from the
International Chamber of Commerce (Melik, 2011). For these *Thesis*
reasons, consumers should stop buying these products and *statement*
funding the illegal activities that this activity supports.

Much of the responsibility for the trade in counterfeit
goods can be placed on the manufacturers and the countries
that permit the production and export of such goods. For example, China, which dominates the world counterfeit trade, is
doing very little to stop this activity. According to a recent article in *USA Today* by Calum MacLeod (2011), "a major obstacle
is China's *shanzhai* culture, whereby some Chinese delight in
making cheap imitations, sometimes in parody, of expensive,
famous brands." Chinese counterfeiters have gone so far as to
create entire fake stores: fake Starbucks stores, fake Abercrom-
bie & Fitch stores, and even fake Apple stores. Although some
of these copycats have been prosecuted, there is a high level
of tolerance, even admiration, for counterfeiting in China.
This attitude towards *shanzhai* is reflected in the country's
lax intellectual property protection laws. As one Chinese
intellectual property lawyer observed, "The penalties don't

outweigh the benefits" (as cited in MacLeod, 2011). Given this situation, the production of counterfeit goods in China is not likely to slow down any time soon.

Despite such cultural justifications for counterfeiting, there is still an ethical problem associated with the purchase of knock-offs. As Dana Thomas (2007) has written in *The New York Times*, many of these counterfeit products are made by children who are "sold or sent off by their families to work in clandestine factories." To American consumers, the problem of children laboring in Chinese factories may be remote, but it is serious. If it is reasonable to place blame for this flourishing market on the countries that allow it, it is also reasonable to blame the people who buy most of the counterfeit goods—namely, consumers in the United States and Europe. According to a report by U.S. Customs and Border Patrol, 62% of fake goods seized in the United States in 2011 were produced in China (as cited in Coleman, 2012). In Europe, the numbers are even higher. According to *The Wall Street Journal*, 85% of goods seized in the European Union come from China (Nairn, 2011). Consequently, the simple act of buying a counterfeit Coach handbag implicates the consumer in the practice of forced child labor.

Immoral labor practices are not the only reason why the counterfeit market needs to be stopped. Organized crime is behind much of the counterfeit trade, so "every dollar spent on a knockoff Gap polo shirt or a fake Kate Spade handbag may be supporting drug trafficking, . . . and worse" ("Editorial: The True Cost," 2007). Consumer dollars may also be supporting narcotics, weapons, and child prostitution (Thomas, 2007).

This illicit international system also helps to finance groups even more sinister than crime syndicates. American consumers of counterfeit goods should understand that profits from

Evidence:
Point 1

Evidence:
Point 2

counterfeit goods support terrorist and extremist groups, including Hezbollah, paramilitary organizations in Northern Ireland, and FARC, a revolutionary armed faction in Colombia (Thomas, 2007). According to the International Anti-Counterfeiting Coalition, the sale of knock-off T-shirts may even have funded the 1993 attack on the World Trade Center. Some observers speculate that terrorists annually receive about 2% of the roughly $500 billion trade in counterfeit goods ("Editorial: The True Cost," 2007). According to Ronald K. Noble, secretary-general of the international law enforcement agency Interpol, crime involving counterfeit merchandise "is becoming the preferred method of funding for a number of terrorist groups" (as cited in Langan, 2003).

Evidence: Point 3

Beyond the moral and ethical implications of its links to child labor, crime, and terrorism, counterfeit merchandise also undermines the mainstay of Western business—respect for intellectual property. In the context of a vast international market of counterfeit luxury goods, the issue of intellectual property can seem insignificant. But the creation of new products requires time, energy, and money, and "unrestrained copying robs creators of the means to profit from their works" (Sprigman, 2006). Copyright law exists to make sure that inventors and producers will be motivated to create original work and be fairly compensated for it. This principle applies to the designers of luxury goods and fashion items as well. Christopher Sprigman (2006) disagrees, however, noting that although intellectual property law does little to protect fashion designs, this is as it should be. "Trend-driven consumption," says Sprigman, is good for the fashion industry because the industry's ability to create trends "is based on designers' relative freedom to copy." But even this argument—which addresses the influences of legitimate fashion designers and manufacturers—cannot be used to justify allowing counterfeiters to copy Prada handbags or Hugo

Evidence: Point 4

Opposing argument

Refutation

Boss suits and pass them off as genuine branded articles. Such illicit activity creates no trends—other than perhaps increasing the market for counterfeit products, which siphons off more profits from original designers.

Evidence:
Point 5

The knock-off market is not limited to fashion and luxury goods. For example, fake products such as shoddy brake pads have directly injured many consumers. In addition, each year millions of people in the United States and abroad buy counterfeit drugs that do not work and in many cases are dangerous. Some sources estimate that the majority of drugs used to treat life-threatening diseases in Africa are counterfeit. Not coincidentally, many of the same people who are making and distributing counterfeit luxury goods are also manufacturing these drugs ("Editorial: The True Cost," 2007).

Conclusion

It is time for people to realize the harm that is done by counterfeit merchandise and stop buying it. One way to combat this problem is to educate consumers about the effects of their purchases. As James Melik (2011) of the BBC explains, "People try to save money without realising that the purchase of counterfeit goods can actually harm themselves, the economy and ultimately, their own pockets." Melik urges consumers to "think twice" before buying "products which promote and fund crime." Another way to confront the problem is for law enforcement to address this issue aggressively. Not only should local authorities do more to stop this illegal trade, but national governments should also impose sanctions on countries that refuse to honor international treaties concerning intellectual property. Only by taking this issue seriously can we ensure that this "victimless" crime does not continue to spread and claim more victims.

COUNTERFEIT GOODS   7

References

Coleman, S. (2012, January 20). China still accounts for majority
    of US counterfeit goods. *Canadian Manufacturers and
    Exporters*. Retrieved from http://www.cme-mec.ca/?lid
    =JCKNC-E742G-1W6JA&comaction=show&cid=DVU6K
    -CVBRZ-C6TZQ

Editorial: The true cost: Illegal knockoffs of name-brand products
    do widespread harm [Editorial]. (2007, December 2). *The
    Columbus* [OH] *Dispatch*, p. 4G.

Langan, M. (2003, July 24). Counterfeit goods make real
    terrorism. *Pittsburgh Post-Gazette*, p. A17.

MacLeod, C. (2011, August 2). China takes knock-offs to a
    new level, copying entire stores. *USA Today*. Retrieved
    from http://www.usatoday.com/money/industries
    /technology/2011-07-31-China-counterfeiting-fake-Western
    -goods-stores_n.htm

Melik, J. (2011, December 18). Fake goods save money but at
    what cost? *BBC News*. Retrieved from http://www.bbc
    .co.uk/news/business-16087793

Nairn, G. (2011, October 18). Countering the counterfeiters. *The
    Wall Street Journal*. Retrieved from http://online.wsj.com
    /article/SB10001424052970204226204576600462442044764
    .html

Sprigman, C. (2006, August 22). The fashion industry's piracy
    paradox [Online forum comment]. Retrieved from http://
    www.publicknowledge.org/node/597

Thomas, D. (2007, August 30). Terror's purse strings. *The New
    York Times*, p. A23.

Accurate evidence: Evidence from reliable sources that is quoted carefully and in context.

Ad hominem fallacy: The logical fallacy of undermining an argument by attacking the person who is making the argument instead of addressing the argument itself.

Allusion: A reference within a work to a person, literary or biblical text, or historical event. This shorthand device reminds the reader of something that enlarges the context of the situation being written about.

Analogy: An extended comparison that explains an unfamiliar item, concept, or situation by comparing it to a more familiar one.

Annotating: Making notes of your questions, reactions, and ideas on the document itself.

Antithesis: An opposing statement that tests whether an argumentative **thesis** is debatable.

Appeal to doubtful authority: The use of nonexperts to support an argument.

Applied ethics: The field of philosophy that applies **ethical principles** to real-life issues (such as abortion, the death penalty, animal rights, or doctor-assisted suicide).

Argument: A logical and persuasive presentation of **evidence** that attempts to convince people to accept (or at least to consider) the writer's position.

Argument by analogy: An argument that claims that its position is valid because it is similar in some ways to a position on another issue that readers are likely to accept.

Backing: In a **Toulmin argument**, the evidence that supports the warrant.

Bandwagon appeal: An attempt to convince people that something is true because it is widely held to be true.

Begging-the-question fallacy: An illogical assumption that a statement is self-evident (or true) when it actually requires proof.

Bias: Preconceived ideas or prejudices, which are often used in an argument instead of factual **evidence**.

Brainstorming: Making quick notes on a topic to generate ideas.

Causal chain: A sequence of events in which one event causes the next, which in turn causes the next, and so on.

Cause-and-effect argument: An argument that explains an event or a situation by considering its likely causes or outcomes.

Circular reasoning: An attempt to support a statement by simply repeating the statement in different terms.

Claim: In a **Toulmin argument**, the main point, usually stated as a **thesis**.

Clustering: Creating a diagram to map out your thoughts.

Common ground: Points of agreement that are shared by those on opposing sides of an argument.

Common knowledge: Factual information (such as a writer's date of birth, a scientific fact, or the location of a famous battle) that can be found in several credible sources. Common knowledge does not require documentation.

Conclusion: The last part of a **syllogism**.

Confirmation bias: The tendency that people have to accept information that supports their own beliefs and to ignore information that does not.

Confrontational argument: A kind of argument that is characterized by conflict and opposition.

Contributory causes: The less important causes in a **causal argument**.

Credibility: Trustworthiness. A credible source is believable.

Criteria for evaluation: Standards by which a subject (or source) is evaluated.

Critical response: A passage in which a writer examines the ideas that are presented in an argument and evaluates them.

Current source: A source containing up-to-date information. Current sources are especially important in discussions of scientific subjects and may be less important in other subjects.

Debatable thesis: A thesis statement that presents a position with which people might disagree.

Deductive reasoning: A form of reasoning that moves from general statements (or **premises**) to specific conclusions. See **inductive reasoning**.

Definition argument: An argument that is based on the idea that something fits or does not fit a particular definition of a key term.

Dictionary definition: A structure for definition that consists of the term to be defined, the general class to which the term belongs, and the qualities that differentiate the term from other items in the same class.

Dilemma: A choice between two or more unfavorable alternatives.

Distortion: An unfair tactic of argument in which the writer misrepresents evidence—for example, by presenting an opponent's view inaccurately or by exaggerating his or her position.

Documentation: Information that identifies the sources used in an argument.

Editing and proofreading: The final steps in the writing process, which check that an essay is well organized, convincing, and clearly written and has no distracting grammatical, spelling, and mechanical errors.

Either/or fallacy: Faulty reasoning that presents only two choices when there are actually three or more choices.

Enthymeme: A **syllogism** with one or two parts of its argument (usually the major premise) missing.

Equivocation: The use of two different meanings for the same key term in an argument.

Ethical argument: An argument that focuses on whether something should be done because it is good or right.

Ethical dilemma: A conflict between two or more possible actions, each of which will potentially have negative outcomes.

Ethical principles: A set of ideas or standards that guides someone to an ethically correct conclusion.

Ethics: The field of philosophy that studies the standards by which an act can be judged right or wrong or good or bad.

Ethos: An appeal to the trustworthiness or credibility of a speaker or writer.

Evaluate: To express an opinion about the quality of something.

Evaluation argument: An argument that presents a positive or negative judgment, asserts that someone else's positive or negative judgment is not accurate or justified, or demonstrates that one thing is or is not superior to another.

Evidence: The facts, observations, expert opinion, examples, and statistics that support a thesis statement. In a **Toulmin argument**, the evidence is called the **grounds**.

Fact: A statement that can be verified (proven to be true).

Fallacy: An error in reasoning that undermines the logic of an argument.

False dilemma: See **either/or fallacy**.

Formal argument: An argument developed according to set rhetorical principles in academic discussion and writing. See **informal argument**.

Formal outline: A presentation of an essay's main and subordinate points that uses a number/letter system to designate the order in which the points will be discussed.

Freewriting: Writing continuously for a set time to generate ideas without worrying about spelling or grammar.

Grounds: In a **Toulmin argument**, the evidence that is used to support the claim.

Hasty generalization: An error in reasoning that occurs when a conclusion is based on too little evidence or when the gap between the evidence and conclusion is too wide.

Highlighting: Using underlining and symbols to identify an essay's most important points.

Identifying tag: A phrase that identifies the source of a **quotation**, **paraphrase**, or **summary**.

Immediate cause: In a **causal argument**, the cause that occurs right before an event.

Inductive leap: In **inductive reasoning**, a stretch of the imagination that enables a writer to draw a reasonable conclusion from the existing information.

Inductive reasoning: A form of reasoning that begins with specific observations (or evidence) and moves to a general conclusion. See **deductive reasoning**.

Inference: A statement that uses what is known to draw a conclusion about what is unknown.

Informal argument: An **argument** that occurs in daily life about politics, sports, social issues, and personal relationships. See **formal argument**.

Informal outline: A list of the ideas that will be discussed in an essay. See **formal outline**.

Jumping to a conclusion: See **hasty generalization**.

Logic: The principles of correct reasoning that enable someone to tell whether a conclusion correctly follows from a set of statements or assumptions.

Logical fallacy: A flawed argument.

Logos: An appeal to logic.

Main cause: In a **causal argument**, the most important cause.

Major premise: See **syllogism**.

Means of persuasion: The appeals—*logos*, *pathos*, and *ethos*—that writers use to persuade their audience.

Metaphor: A comparison in which two dissimilar things are compared without the word *like* or *as*.

Middle term: The term in a **syllogism** that appears in both the major and minor premises but not in the conclusion.

Minor premise: See **syllogism**.

Misuse of statistics fallacy: When data are misrepresented.

Non sequitur fallacy: Illogical reasoning that occurs when a conclusion does not follow from the premises or is supported by weak or irrelevant evidence or by no evidence at all.

Objective source: A source that is not unduly influenced by personal opinions or feelings.

Operational definition: A definition of how something acts or works that transforms an abstract concept into something concrete, observable, and possibly measurable.

Opinion: A personal judgment; therefore, an idea that is open to debate.

Parallelism: The use of the same or a similar structure in the repetition of words, phrases, or clauses.

Paraphrase: A passage that presents a source's ideas in detail, including its main idea and key supporting points and perhaps key examples.

Parenthetical references: In MLA and APA **documentation**, citations that identify the source of a paraphrase, quotation, or summary.

Pathos: An appeal to the emotions.

Peer review: The process of having colleagues examine and critique written work. Informally, school work is read by friends or classmates; formally, scholarly work is read by experts in the field to confirm its accuracy.

Persuasion: The act of influencing an audience to adopt a particular belief or to follow a specific course of action.

Plagiarism: The use of the words or ideas of another person without attributing them to their rightful author.

Popular magazine: A periodical that is aimed at general readers. It generally is not an acceptable source for research.

Post hoc fallacy: Faulty reasoning that asserts that because two events occur closely in time, one event must have caused the other.

Premises: Statements or assumptions on which an **argument** is based or from which a conclusion is drawn.

Previewing: During active reading, forming a general impression of a writer's position on an issue, the argument's key supporting points, and the context for the writer's remarks.

Propaganda: Biased or misleading information that is spread about a particular viewpoint, person, or cause.

Proposal argument: An argument that attempts to convince people that a problem exists and that a particular solution is both practical and desirable.

Qualifiers: In a **Toulmin argument**, statements that limit the **claim**.

Quotation: Words or sentences taken directly from a source.

Quoting out of context: Removing a quotation from its original setting for the purpose of distorting its meaning.

Reading critically: Questioning or challenging material instead of simply accepting it as true. This often involves assessing the accuracy of facts in sources and considering the evidence that supports them.

Reason: In a **Toulmin argument**, a statement that supports the **claim**.

Rebuttals: In a **Toulmin argument**, refutations of opposing arguments.

Red herring fallacy: An irrelevant side issue that diverts attention from the real issue.

Refutation: The section of an argumentative essay that identifies opposing arguments and presents arguments against them.

Refute: To disprove or call into question.

Relevant evidence: **Evidence** that applies specifically (not just tangentially) to the topic under discussion.

Remote causes: In a **causal argument**, incidents that occurred in the past but may have had a greater impact than more recent events.

Representative evidence: **Evidence** that is drawn from a fair range of sources, not just from sources that support a particular position.

Revision: The careful and critical review of a draft.

Rhetoric: The effect of various elements working together to form a convincing and persuasive **argument**.

Rhetorical analysis: A systematic examination of the strategies that a writer employs to achieve his or her purpose.

Rhetorical question: A question that encourages readers to reflect on an issue but does not call for a reply.

Rhetorical situation: The combination of the writer, the writer's purpose, the writer's audience, the topic, and the context.

Rhetorical strategies: The ways in which argument writers present ideas and opinions, including but not limited to thesis, organization, evidence, and stylistic techniques (**simile**, **metaphor**, **allusion**, **parallelism**, repetition, and **rhetorical questions**).

Rhetorical triangle: A graphic representation of the three kinds of appeals in an argument—*logos* (reason), *ethos* (credibility), and *pathos* (values and beliefs).

Rogerian argument: A model of argument that assumes that people of good will can avoid conflict by identifying **common ground** and points of agreement. It is based on the work of Carl Rogers, a twentieth-century psychologist who felt that traditional confrontational arguments could be counterproductive.

Scholarly journal: A periodical that is usually written by experts, documented, and peer reviewed.

Scientific method: A way of using induction to find answers to questions. It involves proposing a hypothesis, making a series of observations to test the hypothesis, and arriving at a conclusion that confirms, modifies, or disproves the hypothesis.

Self-evident: A proposition that requires no proof or explanation.

Simile: A figure of speech that compares two unlike things by using *like* or *as*.

Skeptical: Having an open mind but still needing to be convinced.

Slanting: An unfair tactic that makes an argument appear stronger by presenting only evidence that supports a particular position and ignoring evidence that challenges it.

Slippery-slope fallacy: An illogical argument that holds that one thing will cause a series of events that ends in an inevitable, unpleasant conclusion, usually with no evidence that such a sequence will actually occur.

Straw man fallacy: An intentional oversimplification of an opposing argument to make it easier to refute.

Sufficient evidence: Evidence that includes enough facts, statistics, and expert opinion to support the essay's thesis.

Summary: A concise restatement of the main idea of a passage (or article or book) without the examples, explanations, and stylistic devices of the source.

Sweeping generalization: See **hasty generalization**.

Syllogism: A model for **deductive reasoning** that includes a **major premise**, a **minor premise**, and a **conclusion**. Some types of syllogisms are:

Sound syllogism: A syllogism that is both true and valid.

True syllogism: A syllogism in which the **premises** are consistent with the **facts**.

Valid syllogism: A system in which a conclusion follows logically from its premises.

Synthesis: A combination of **summary**, **paraphrase**, **quotation**, and a writer's own ideas that supports an original conclusion.

Taking a stand: Expressing a position in the form of a **thesis statement**.

Thesis: The position that an argument supports.

Thesis statement: A single sentence in an argumentative essay that states a position on an issue.

Thinking critically: Questioning rather than accepting ideas at face value.

Toulmin argument: An argument that includes the **claim** (the main point), the grounds (the **evidence** a writer uses to support the claim), and the **warrant** (the inference—either stated or implied—that connects the claims to their grounds).

Unfair appeal: An appeal to an audience's fears or prejudices.

Visual: An image—such as a chart, graph, table, photo, drawing, or diagram.

Visual argument: An advertisement, chart, graph, table, diagram, Web page, photograph, painting, or other representation that communicates a position through images.

Warrant: In a **Toulmin argument**, the inference or assumption, either stated or implied, that connects a claim to its grounds.

Works-cited list: An alphabetical list of sources that appears at the end of an essay that follows MLA style.

Writing process: The process of planning, drafting, revising, and editing an argument.

You-also fallacy (*tu quoque*): An illogical assertion that a statement is false because the speaker has said or done the opposite. It attacks a person for doing the thing that he or she is arguing against.

Text Credits